D1715957

A FORM OF SOUND WORDS

A FORM OF
SOUND WORDS

The Religious Poetry of Christopher Smart

HARRIET GUEST

CLARENDON PRESS · OXFORD
1989

Oxford University Press, Walton Street, Oxford OX2 6DP
Oxford New York Toronto
Delhi Bombay Calcutta Madras Karachi
Petaling Jaya Singapore Hong Kong Tokyo
Nairobi Dar es Salaam Cape Town
Melbourne Auckland
and associated companies in
Berlin Ibadan

Oxford is a trade mark of Oxford University Press

Published in the United States
by Oxford University Press, New York

British Library Cataloguing in Publication Data
Guest, Harriet
A form of sound words: the religious poetry of
Christopher Smart
1. Poetry in English. Smart, Christopher, 1722–1771
I. Title
821'.6
ISBN 0–19–811744–2

Library of Congress Cataloging in Publication Data
Guest, Harriet.
A form of sound words: the religious poetry of
Christopher Smart.
1. Smart, Christopher, 1722–1771—Criticism and interpretation.
2. Religious poetry, English—History and Criticism.
I. Title.
PR3687.S7Z69 1989   821'.6—dc19   88–36834
ISBN 0–19–811744–2

Set by Hope Services, Abingdon
Printed and bound in Great Britain
by Courier International Ltd.,
Tiptree, Essex

To my parents

Preface

In 1958 Donald Davie suggested that, when the full range of Smart's work comes to be judged, he might be 'thought of as the greatest English poet between Pope and Wordsworth'. Davie's claim poses a considerable challenge to orthodox accounts of the literature of the mid-eighteenth century, for, though he has unfortunately not elaborated on it, it is, I think, clear that the reappraisal of Smart that he urges implies the need for a reassessment of those accounts—a reconsideration of both the nature and the relative importance of the issues we understand the writing of the period as addressing. For Smart's work is not usually accorded the status Davie claims for it. It is more frequently represented as marginal, the work of a minor poet whose madness or mysticism allows him to be treated as the eccentric exception who proves the rule—the explanatory power—of whatever model of the period is in question. But Smart's work as a whole, and in particular his religious poetry, is of major importance to a perception of the mid century which does not seek to impose on the writing of that time the secular concerns of our own. For in order to understand Smart's achievement, it is necessary to examine the extent to which, for writers of the mid century, areas of concern which we now perceive as incongruous or disparate—kinds of writing that range from the devotional to the natural philosophical, from sermons to linguistic theory—were constructed in interrelated terms which were not apparent to visionary Bedlamites and isolated mystics alone. The reappraisal of Smart's work that Davie recommends involves the reconsideration of arguments, and of kinds of writing, that are perhaps too often and too readily excluded from the picture scholars construct of the period, and the attempt to take those into account reveals some of the ways in which we need to reassess the period as a whole.[1]

[1] Donald Davie, *The Late Augustans: Longer Poems of the Later Eighteenth Century* (London, 1958), Introduction xxvii–xxviii. Davie repeats his claim in the Introduction to his anthology *Augustan Lyric* (London, 1974), where he comments: 'So far as I am concerned, my fifteen-year-old claim for Smart still stands; it awaits either vindication or rebuttal' (p. 18). Smart spent most of the years from 1757 to 1763 confined in various madhouses, apparently as a result of his belief in the need for public prayer, as well as his financial insolvency. For accounts of his life, see his nephew Christopher Hunter's introduction to *The Poems of the Late Christopher Smart* (Reading, 1791), and Arthur Sherbo, *Christopher Smart: Scholar of the University* (East Lansing, Mich. 1967).

This book is an attempt to take up the challenge that Davie's claim for Smart has thrown down. Though the Clarendon edition of Smart's *Poetical Works*, now in progress, will enormously increase the ability of scholars to reconsider, as Davie recommends, the whole of Smart's output, I have not attempted, in this study, to engage with this considerable task, but have chosen to focus on Smart's major religious poetry, because it is this substantial area of his work which presents the most considerable obstacles, and offers the most fruitful rewards, to those whose critical interests lie in the mid-eighteenth century. It is, I think, peculiarly and remarkably difficult for modern readers to find a method of approaching eighteenth-century religious poetry. It seems either to embarrass us with its claims to sincerity, to the affective devotion of the heart, or to repel us with the methodical coldness of its praise for an unknowable deity. But it rarely excites the kind of attention and interest which the accounts of contemporary reviewers and readers indicate that it received in the eighteenth century. In Smart's case, it can be perceived as difficult, as both abstruse and eclectic, to a degree that encourages us to take the easy way out, and to dismiss it as insane. But these difficulties are at least in part the result of the failure of modern criticism to examine the function of religious poetry, the place of religious writers in relation to their audiences, whether human or divine, and in relation to contemporary debates about the social role of religion itself; and they reflect our difficulty in coming to terms with the way in which themes and concerns that we recognize as religious are involved in almost every area of eighteenth-century thought, and yet display complications and possibilities apparently peculiar to themselves—religion seems at once too omnipresent and too specialized an area of concern to be examined or engaged with by the literary critic.

In my introductory chapter, I therefore discuss a selection of kinds of writing—some neglected, and some frequently the subject of critical enquiry—which raise issues important to the treatment of religious ideas in eighteenth-century literature. I suggest that the ways in which these texts can be read, the kinds of attention they seem to invite or require, provide us with a means of understanding what is at stake in poetry concerned with religious questions. The chapter is not intended to provide a survey of religious literature, but to indicate, through the discussion of the 'place' of the poet, the context in which I think Smart's poetry can most fruitfully be read, the problems it can be seen as addressing. I go on, in later chapters, to discuss Smart's major religious poetry—the Seatonian Prize poems, *Jubilate Agno*, the *Song to David*, and the *Hymns and Spiritual Songs*. In my discussion of each of these I am concerned to show the relation—often, but not always, the similarities—between the ideas informing Smart's poetry, and the arguments of a range of other contemporary writers, in order to establish that Smart's poetry should not be dismissed as idiosyncratically marginal, and to indicate the extent to which the implications of that dismissal distort and impoverish our understanding of the period. For I believe that it is only if we attempt to understand the historically precise nature of the issues with which Smart's poetry is engaged that we can perceive the ambition and significance of his achievement. I do not, in the course of these chapters, directly address Davie's implication that we might trace a line of chronological descent from Pope, through Smart, to Wordsworth. But the nature of the context I discern for Smart's poetry, in the philosophies of nature, religion, and language, represents, I hope, a contribution to the reassessment of the mid-eighteenth century, through the consideration of issues which have, like Smart's poetry itself, been too often treated as marginal.

Acknowledgements

IN the course of my writing this book, many people have helped me both directly and indirectly. I would like to thank the electors of King's College, Cambridge, for awarding me a research fellowship, which gave me the time to broaden and extend the scope of my interest in the eighteenth century. I am grateful to Donald Davie, Howard Erskine-Hill, Geoffrey Hill, and Lisa Jardine, who read and commented on parts of this manuscript at different stages. David Simpson and Tony Tanner helped me with their encouragement, criticism, and company. My greatest debt is to John Barrell, for his patient advice during some of the most difficult stages of working on this book.

H.G.

University College London

Contents

List of Abbreviations and Short Titles

Smart IV	*The Poetical Works of Christopher Smart*, iv. *Miscellaneous Poems English and Latin*, ed. Karina Williamson (Oxford, 1987)
Stead	Christopher Smart, *Rejoice in the Lamb: A Song from Bedlam*, ed. William Force Stead (London, 1939)
Thayer	*Newton's Philosophy of Nature: Selections from his Writings*, ed. H. S. Thayer (London, 1953)
Young	Robert Young, *Analytical Concordance to the Holy Bible* (1879; this 8th edn. Guildford, 1977)

Introduction

Some Themes and Problems in the Religious Poetry of Eighteenth-Century Britain

I

In this introduction, I want to set out a context for the discussion of Smart's religious poetry, to describe the tradition to which he responds and contributes. But this attempt is immediately confronted by a difficulty which may have encouraged some scholars to see Smart as an exceptional case, that of a determinedly religious poet in an age of largely secular verse. For at least in the first half of the eighteenth century, there appears to be no body of poetry that we can confidently identify as religious, in the sense that we might perhaps recognize a georgic genre, or a mode of pastoral poetry. This is not at all to say, however, that religious themes are conspicuous by their absence in the period, at least from the poems that now seem to us the most important. It is rather that religious poetry cannot be seen as a coherent *kind* of writing, either as it might share a common subject-matter, a common set of themes and ideas, or as it might be defined by common strategies and discourses. Johnson commented, in his life of Milton, that the truths of religion were, in the eighteenth century, 'habitually interwoven with the whole texture of life', and the observation seems to be as true of poetry as of any other sphere of life, where reference to the concerns we might define as religious may be occasionally, and remarkably, absent, but is more usually 'habitually interwoven' with every genre, theme, or discourse.[1]

By the time Smart is producing his Seatonian Prize poems, or his hymns and psalms, a more recognizable 'kind' of religious poetry may be beginning to emerge, but some degree of anachronism must be involved in the attempt to apply this recognition to the poetry of the first half of the century. This is not to say, of course, that all of the poetry of the earlier period is religious—John Dennis had argued, in

---

[1] Samuel Johnson, 'Milton', *Lives of the English Poets* (1779, 1781; this edn. 2 vols., Oxford, 1906), i. 130–1.

his *Grounds of Criticism* of 1704, that religion was not sufficiently often the principal concern of poetry, though its use 'in Poetry was absolutely necessary to raise it to the greatest exaltation, of which so Noble an Art is capable'—but while religious themes are not usually the defining characteristic of the poetry of the following decades, religious language and ideas continually occur or are alluded to in all sorts of different poetic contexts—even Belinda, in *The Rape of the Lock*, keeps Bibles among her 'Puffs, Powders, Patches', and billets-doux. Writing seventy-five years after Dennis, however, Johnson argues that 'poetical devotion cannot often please', and concludes: 'all that pious verse can do is to help the memory, and delight the ear . . . but it supplies nothing to the mind.'[2] The discrepancy between the views of these two critics may indicate that a considerable revolution has taken place in the perceived relation beween religion and poetry in the years that separate their judgements: where Dennis sees religion as a source of exaltation for poetry as a whole, Johnson writes of a particular kind of poetry, which he sees as defined by a set of themes so limited and so familiar that they can neither entertain nor instruct.

Smart's career as a religious poet, his progress from Seatonian poet to 'scribe-evangelist' to Anglican psalmist, occupies an important place in the revolution that separates Dennis from Johnson, but it is not a place that can best be understood by anticipating the conclusions Johnson or his contemporaries might have felt able to draw in 1779, or by regarding Smart as exceptional in his sophisticated treatment of sacred and devotional themes; for to do so would be to ignore, or to conceal, the significance of such themes in much of the poetry of his immediate predecessors.[3] A more capacious idea of the relation between religion and poetry, on the other hand, would include a range of poetry—from hymns to patriotic verses—well beyond the scope of this chapter. I will therefore look at a selection of poems employing religious sentiments or language which raise issues that recur in the contexts of religion and poetry throughout the century, and produce or involve tensions which lie at the heart of the difficulty of defining a religious poetry.

[2] John Dennis, *The Grounds of Criticism in Poetry* (London, 1704), Preface; *The Rape of the Lock* (1714), canto I, l. 138, *The Poems of Alexander Pope: A One-Volume Edition of the Twickenham Text with Selected Annotations*, ed. John Butt (London, 1963; I use this edition throughout); Johnson, 'Waller', *Lives*, i. 211–12.

[3] Christopher Smart, *Jubilate Agno*, ed. W. H. Bond (Harvard, Mass., 1954; hereafter *JA*), B2. 327. Smart's Seatonian poems were first published in 1750–5, and his translation of the Psalms was first published in 1765.

It is my interest in these issues that informs my selection when, for example, I discuss the relation beween natural philosophy and religion in the poetry of Thomson and Aaron Hill, rather than in the perhaps more obviously 'religious' verse-paraphrases of the Book of Job that were commonly produced almost as a form of poetic apprenticeship in the period. Both these kinds of 'religious' poetry look at the relation between creation and creator, at the kind of response or interpretation proper to that relation, but in Thomson and Hill the issues of how the poet conveys that understanding to his audience, of the kind of didactic tone appropriate to this mediated natural revelation, are also called into question, whereas in biblical paraphrases they are avoided in deference to the authority of the original text. It is exactly these kinds of issue, of the terms on which the audience is addressed, the position of the poet, and the nature of his authority, that I suggest are the key terms in understanding both the treatment of religious or moral themes in certain kinds of poetry and their exclusion from others. I therefore examine some of the different didactic postures available to poets who, in employing a Christian discourse, at least implicitly moralize both their song and their audience, either by example or, more directly, by precept. The poets I look at can all be seen as concerned, more or less self-consciously, to *negotiate* the authority with which they speak, the terms in which it is appropriate for them to address their diverse, but usually well-defined, audiences.

II

I shall explore these issues, of poetic authority, audience, and didactic manner, by looking at a range of early eighteenth-century poems that are all, to different extents, concerned with ethical, devotional, and theological ideas which are explicitly religious in their contexts and implications. But the differences between these poems are more striking than their similarities. Their themes involve a considerable variety of concerns, and they do not describe a regular chronological progression: the poems do not represent a survey of a tradition in these terms. But though they do not have an overall generic similarity, the questions, the kinds of self-consciousness they display in response to the attempt to employ religious language or themes, do I think indicate a common sense both of the nature of the problems involved in this attempt and of the areas in which it is appropriate to look for solutions to them. Because of the absence of a specifically and identifiably 'religious' poetry in the period, I begin my discussion of these shared concerns with a brief analysis of critical attitudes towards Milton's *Paradise Lost* in the first half of the century. These changing attitudes supply a loose historical framework for the comparisons that follow, and indicate the extent to which the concerns I trace in those comparisons are reflected in the critical vocabulary seen as appropriate to religious poetry. The first comparison I then offer turns on the different kinds of poetic authority expressed in Pope's *Essay on Man* (1733–4) and Thomson's *Seasons* (1730–46). Whereas the *Essay* is written from a stance of privileged authority, apparently legitimated by its address to, and endorsement by, Pope's aristocratic friend, Henry St John, Viscount Bolingbroke, the poet of *The Seasons* seems to claim a more ambivalent authority. He speaks sometimes with a confidence derived from his intimacy with a group of retired and benevolent patriots, and sometimes with a more private assurance appropriate to the poem's patriotic but more obscure narrator. I argue that in these poems the presence of religious discourses gives the issue of the poet's authority and of the terms on which it is claimed a particular importance, for those discourses can pose implicit questions about poetic authority which sit uneasily with the poet's didactic assurance.

The presence of biblical discourses—constituted by, among other things, the use of biblical phrasing and imagery—also frequently raises the question of the relation between the authority of the poet and natural revelation. Natural philosophy makes available to the poet a kind of authority of knowledge, a power of explanation, which may be presented as supporting arguments for the persuasive force of natural revelation; but sophisticated negotiation is nevertheless required in poetry if the authority of the philosopher is to be combined with the reverent admiration of creation which revelation at least implicitly demands. This is not, of course, an area that preoccupies poetry alone, and I hope in my later chapters to give some idea of the arguments it elicited from philosophers and churchmen. But whereas, broadly speaking, prose arguments could negotiate this difficulty by presenting explanatory insight and reverent praise as successive responses to nature, this tension in poetry tends to be reflected in an inverse proportion between the authority of the poet and the natural variety accommodated by the poem. Pope's commanding authority, for example, is expressed in an omniscient view which can accommodate diversity only in abstract terms which facilitate its description as order.

The *Essay* refers to Nature and Chance only as general and synthetic terms that will reveal them as Art and Direction.[4] Pope's use of natural philosophy provides a justification and clarification of the degree of abstraction necessary to the aristocratic overview he decribes, for its discourses claim to guarantee an empirical and systematic relation between the comprehensive and the particular, a relation founded not in hypotheses but in experiential evidence. The disinterested accumulation of facts by the philosopher underpins, through the analogy implied by Pope's language, the disinterested and comprehensively systematic view of the aristocrat. But when Pope does descend to the 'evidence' of particular cases, in his *Moral Epistles* (1731–5), the philosophical analogy becomes unworkable and inappropriate, and is discarded. Religion ceases to be the context which legitimates arguments from analogy, and becomes the ironized source of authority for the poet's satirical partiality.

The more flexible authority of *The Seasons*, or of Cowper's *Task* (1785), on the other hand, is expressed in a discursive and digressive description of variety which cannot always be comprehended as a unified plan. Johnson argues that Thomson is able to describe both a 'wide expanse of general views' and the 'enumeration of circumstantial varieties' because of his use of blank verse, but he also argues that the verse encourages in Thomson a 'florid and luxuriant diction', which invests his 'images and thoughts' with a 'splendour through which perhaps they are not always easily discerned'. Thomson's diction is not the plain speech of natural philosophy, which promotes clarity and system, although his reception of the new science was a good deal more enthusiastic than was Pope's.[5] I argue, in my discussion of *The Seasons*, that Thomson's splendid fluency enables him to describe the explanations available to small groups of natural philosophers in juxtaposition to the more biblical discourses of natural description and revelation which he employs to portray the very different natures apprehended by the swain or by the wandering eye of the poet. *The Seasons* accommodates but does not assimilate these discourses, for it employs a digressive structure and fluid verse that denies, to either the presentation of nature as the object of philosophical enquiry or its

---

[4] See Pope, *Essay on Man*, epistle I, ll. 289–90.
[5] Johnson, 'Thomson', *Lives*, ii. 376–7. On attitudes to natural philosophy and the new science in the poetry of Pope and Thomson, see Ralph Cohen, *The Unfolding of 'The Seasons'* (London, 1970), 88, and Marjorie Hope Nicolson, *Newton Demands the Muse* (Princeton, NJ, 1946).

celebration as revelation, the absolute authority and power of explanation that they might in other contexts command.

By no means all the poets I will discuss in this introduction share the status either contemporaneously or retrospectively accorded to *The Seasons* and the *Essay on Man*: not many of them enjoyed the kinds of recorded reception these poems received, or have excited the degree of critical interest that has continued to attach itself to those poems. The majority of the poems I will be looking at have indeed been retrospectively obscured by the religious ideas that might have been seen as exalting them, by their perceived conformity with Johnson's view of devotional and pious poetry. But the themes that inspired some of the greatest poetry of the seventeenth century did not fade into insignificance overnight with the Glorious Revolution and the changed relations of Church and State that followed it. Johnson's judgement, and the indifference of modern critical opinion, reflect, I want to suggest, the extent to which the development of a distinctively religious poetry in the eighteenth century charts for that poetry a course which diverges radically from the main stream of more 'secular' poetry—a divergence that seems bridgeable in the poetry of Cowper, and may reconverge in the early poetry of Wordsworth and Coleridge. For the poets of religion in the eighteenth century, if I may summarize rather baldly, become more concerned with clarity, with the perceived need to address a general and heterogeneous audience, at the same time as poets less directly concerned with religious issues acknowledge that their poetry has become 'vocal' only to a small and select group. In the poetry of the first half of the century we can trace the tensions— between silent adoration and sermonic exhortation, authority and pious humility—that inform both of those developments.

These tensions, reflected in the relation between natural philosophy and revelation, are explored in the comparison of Sir Richard Blackmore's *Creation* (1712) and a poem by Aaron Hill. Blackmore's *Creation* was highly praised for its successful popularization of the theories of Newtonian natural philosophy, but I argue that the authoritative discourses appropriate to his account of the hidden particularities of nature introduced difficulties into his ambition to be recognized as a poet of Christianity, because their explanatory authority demanded a foundation in experiential, empirical evidence which the ideas of religion could not supply. In Hill, I look at some of the implications of the description of natural variety for the kinds of authoritative and didactic power available to the poet. Hill celebrates a creative diversity that eludes systematization, but in order to do so he disclaims the authority that might seem necessary to the instructive power of his poetry. I continue the discussion of these issues in a comparison between the *Devout Exercises* of Elizabeth Rowe and an early poem by Bishop Robert Lowth, where I examine how the negotiation of the relation between poet and audience can produce a kind of didactic authority which focuses on the exemplary nature of the poetry rather than on the power of exposition it may demonstrate.

The relation between poetic authority and religion raises the issue of the nature of the audience addressed by the poet, not only in terms of its status—its politeness or ignorance—but in terms also of what I may call the 'situation' of the poet and, especially, of the audience. The 'Knowing *Few*', for example, to whom *The Seasons* is addressed, are precisely defined: they are neither fully and actively engaged in the exercise of power, nor wholly withdrawn and retired from the concern to shape the world they observe. Pope's aristocratic audience, though it may be above the consideration of the 'Forms of Government', the means of wielding power, acquires that disinterestedness as a result of the security of the public position in which its members are addressed.[6] Edward Young, in contrast, appeals to his more various auditors in their private capacity, removed from the distinctions of social position that characterize them as diverse. An exemplary poetry may, similarly, express pious musings or devotions appropriate to the Christian's private prayers, or may, as in the congregational hymn, invite a more public and social participation. Each of these kinds of poetry, like most of the poetry I shall be discussing in this book, is concerned with the situation of its readers, whether public or private, social or solitary, and while this may also be an important concern in poetry which is less directly engaged with religious themes, it is an issue that the religious context of these poems throws into particular prominence. It is to some extent a function of the ministerial role that many of these poets explicitly adopt: Joseph Trapp, for example, discriminates between the different sections of his audience or congregation, to whom different aspects or parts of his poem are directed; and within Young's attempt to address a more comprehensive readership, similar, if more subtly achieved, distinctions are apparent. The last poems I discuss, by

[6] David Malloch, 'To Mr Thomson, On his publishing the Second Edition of his Poem, call'd Winter', l. 11, in James Thomson, *The Seasons*, ed. James Sambrook (Oxford, 1981), app. B. Pope, *Essay on Man*, epistle III, l. 303. See John Barrell, *English Literature in History, 1730–80: An Equal, Wide Survey* (London, 1983), ch. 1.

Joseph Trapp and Edward Young, provide the opportunity to explore the implications of this issue, not only in the terms in which they identify their audiences, but in the definitions of the poet's own role that they offer partly in response to that identification.

These issues of authority, of the diversity of nature, of didactic method, of audience and situation, may all be understood as issues of diction—of whether a poem employs a magisterial or humble manner, an elevated or a more 'common' diction—and I shall sometimes find it convenient to consider them principally in that light. But the terms 'high' and 'low' diction are not always flexible enough to describe the range of positions these poets may adopt. They may, for example, seek to teach a humble or mixed audience by magisterial precept, or address an exemplary poetry of humility to an elevated and exclusive audience. We could, for example, describe Pope's *Essay on Man* as employing a systematic language of abstraction whose rationale lies in its explanatory power, its power to make explicit the plan informing the mighty maze of experience, and contrast this to Thomson's *Seasons*, characterized by a diction which, as I have already quoted Johnson as pointing out, may obscure rather than clarify the poet's ideas. But an account of these poems in terms of Pope's philosophical lucidity and Thomson's splendid opacity remains inadequate unless it also calls into play questions about how those dictions are situated in relation to their audiences. Pope's *Essay*, as Johnson points out, addresses a language of magisterial reasonableness to readers unaccustomed to philosophical poetry. Its aristocratic readership might share Bolingbroke's grasp of its overall scheme, but to many it appeared as an instructive 'manual of piety' whose 'ultimate purpose' was obscured by its occasional brilliance. The very clarity of its 'sparkling sentences' concealed from them its overall philosophical design. Thomson, on the other hand, rarely offers anything resembling explanation or philosophical argument to lend an appearance of overall unity to the shifting scenes his poem describes. But while the descriptive splendour of his diction may seem to detract from the poem's explanatory philosophy, its didactic power, it is exactly the flexibility this affords, both to the poet and to the reader, that allows the poem to 'take . . . possession of the mind', and gives it a persuasive power that extends beyond the knowing few it ostensibly addresses.[7]

The final sections of this chapter examine the treatment of all these

---

[7] Johnson, 'Pope', *Lives*, ii. 287, 'Thomson', ii. 376.

various areas of concern in Edward Young's *Night-Thoughts* (1742–4). Young's *Night-Thoughts*, Thomson's *Seasons*, and Pope's *Essay* were perhaps the three most widely read and influential long poems of the century, and yet of these *Night-Thoughts* now receives comparatively little critical attention. For most modern readers, Young's digressive meditations on death, immortality, and the Christian aim of detachment from wordly preoccupations can seem indigestible and repetitive, but the difficulty of understanding the poem's contemporary reputation arises, I think, because of a concentration on the poem's matter at the expense of its manner. Contemporary critics praised the poem for its sublimity and pathetic power. They admired in the poem qualities which, I suggest, mark Young's achievement in manœuvring his way through the difficulties involved in writing poetry addressing religious questions, and his ability to employ both an authoritatively preceptive and an exemplary manner. For Young's *Night-Thoughts*, like most of the poetry I discuss in this book, can best be understood in the context of a field of endeavour defined not by particular dicourses, themes, or manners of poetic expression, but by the conflict between various opposed and contrasting discourses, manners of authority, and address. Within the implicit context defined by this field of opposition and conflict, a poem, or any particular passage within it, may be read and understood in the light as much of the strategies it does not adopt as of those it does.

   The strategies of religious poetry, I argue, can be understood not in isolation, but in terms of a matter of poetic choices which determined the manner a poet adopted—choices among alternatives which were sufficiently well defined, and sufficiently familiar, to be understood as the common ground of poetry concerned with matters of religion. The flexible address and companionable authority of the poet of the *Night-Thoughts*, therefore, may be defined by their opposition to a rigorous and exclusive didacticism, or an inadequately persuasive humility and toleration, rather than through the dogmatic aphorisms on the inevitability of death that they afford him the means of expressing. This is not to say, of course, that only in poetry primarily concerned with religious ideas does the manner of the poet become important, or that these considerations of manner can somehow be divorced from the matter of the poem; but that in this poetry, to a greater extent than in poetry less concerned with these ideas, the manner of the poet becomes itself the matter of the poem. Religious truths are a part of the fabric of eighteenth-century life; they do not, in themselves, surprise, delight, or instruct, and their treatment in poetry therefore gives an exceptional prominence to their presentation and interpretation, the manner of their delivery. The field of endeavour in which this poetry is involved, as I have suggested, is not an area in which we can chart a chronological progress towards an ultimately successful religious poetry, for it is one in which what is at stake is the question of the nature and aims of the relation forged between religion and poetry. The different manners of address and authority available in that field clearly imply different conceptions of that nature and those aims. Each of the poems I discuss sets up the terms in which we can understand these implications and in which we can negotiate a way through this field of different attitudes towards the place of religion in poetry. The discussion of the poems will, I hope, help us to recognize the achievement of Smart's poetry, both in positive terms, and in relation to the choices that it rejects and the manners it does not adopt, but which describe the context in which the implications of his poetry can best be understood.

III

First, however, I shall offer a brief examination of the critical reception of Milton's *Paradise Lost* during this period. Milton's epic, of course, exerted a dominant influence over the treatment of religion in poetry: an examination of the sphere of its influence, indeed, provides one of the least distorting means of defining a religious poetry in this period, though it is a means that would still, I think, produce some odd exclusions. I will therefore look at the changing ways in which criticism comes to terms with it as at once paradigmatic and inimitable—ways that, I suggest, reveal much about what was expected of a religious poetry, and how it was read.

It will help to provide some indication of the continuing importance both of Milton's poem itself and of the problems it was seen as posing if I first look briefly at a poem by Abel Evans, which attempts an imitation of Milton's subject-matter as well as of his manner. Imitations of this kind were unusual in the eighteenth century, but it will be useful to see some of the difficulties they could encounter, both as the nature of eighteenth-century religious poetry is to some extent defined by its attempts to avoid these, and as they illuminate criticisms of Milton's epic itself. Evans's *Pre-Existence: A Poem, in Imitation of*

Milton (1714) offers a striking account of heavenly pre-history, which is Miltonic in its ambitiousness, but not in its adherence to scriptural sources. The poem opens with the return of the victorious army who have successfully confined the fallen rebel angels to hell. God emerges to greet them from the gates of heaven, and delivers a long speech, in which he praises their success, and decribes the fate awaiting those angels who were led astray, but were 'less involv'd / In crime and ruin', angels who cannot re-enter heaven, but do not deserve the ultimate punishment of hell.[8] God describes his intention to imprison these angels in bodies, and force them to live out miserable lives as men on the hostile earth that he will create for the purpose, and the bulk of the poem is devoted to God's account of the dreadful fate that life represents.

The poem, as this account of it may be sufficient to suggest, describes an unrelentingly pessimistic vision: God sees as equally worthless and doomed the different lives available to heroes, philosophers, and primitive peoples, and derides the value of both rural solitude and urban sociability; and it was perhaps because of this extreme pessimism, as well as because of the unusual nature of the religious beliefs the poem expresses, that Thomas Gray wrote of it, in a letter to Walpole: 'Dr Evans is a furious madman; and Pre-existence is nonsense in all her altitudes.' But it is difficult to see that the poem is either mad or nonsensical, for though it clearly mocks or attacks various beliefs important in eighteenth-century British poetry, it does so in the context of a series of allusions to those features of *Paradise Lost* that had been the subject of critical controversy, and its relation to *Paradise Lost* suggests that its more nonsensical features may be the consequence of imitation, rather than of madness. Thus, for example, the poem opens with the victorious angels, 'Hot with pursuit', and 'reeking with the blood / Of guilty cherubs smear'd in sulphurous dust'—a description which, in its anthropomorphism, closely resembles those which critics found difficult to excuse in Milton. God is then introduced speaking, and though Evans emphasizes that his 'enlarged speech' is 'majestically long, repugnant all / To princes customs here', he does not qualify or explain his own ability to reproduce this divine speech in poetry. God goes on to describe the imprisonment of the soul in the body as 'The dreadful monument of just revenge', although, as critics of *Paradise Lost* repeatedly pointed out, an

---

[8] [Abel Evans], *Pre-Existence*, ll. 17–18, in Dodsley's *Collection of Poems in Three Volumes. By Several Hands* (2nd edn., London, 1748), vol. i.

omnipotent God cannot be described as experiencing dread at his own works, for this reaction can only be appropriate to the poet or to the reader. These allusions to Milton's epic are delivered in the poem with an imperturbable authority—even a Miltonic aloof majesty—which does not allow us to determine their role: are they straightforwardly, if unorthodoxly, didactic, or do they alert the reader to the possibility that the poem is an elaborate parody of *Paradise Lost*, with no Christ, no mercy, and no mitigating explanations of the poet's ability to perceive and represent things beyond mortal ken?[9]

In his judgemental speech, God stresses that one of the more refined tortures the humanized lapsed angels must endure is that their reason and judgement can produce only 'A Chaos of wild science'. Any attempt by man to conceive of God, fate, or 'th'eternal round' can only demonstrate human inadequacy, because 'the turning maze' of life 'Eludes his art': man's reason and judgement serve to embroil him further in the miserable complexity of his existence. This emphasis on human helplessness might call into question the poet's ability to offer an account of God, fate, and the nature of the eternal round, but the sub-Miltonic 'exotic language' and 'formal style' of the poem obscure and preclude any possible indication of the manner in which these problems are advanced, and deflect responsibility for its unorthodox history, and for the difficulties it poses the reader, onto the poem's insistently imitative nature, and thus onto its epic model. The poem appears accessible to three interpretative strategies: it may present an unusual religious vision, or an indirect and implicit criticism of aspects of the vision described in *Paradise Lost*, or it may be 'nonsense in all her altitudes', inviting our dismissal; but its authoritative and didactic

---

[9] *Correspondence of Thomas Gray*, ed. Paget Toynbee and Leonard Whibley, with corrections and additions by H. W. Starr (rev. edn., Oxford, 1971), i. 296. For a similarly unorthodox doctrine see William Law, *A Practical Treatise upon Christian Perfection* (1726), ch. 2. See e.g. *Pre-Existence*, ll. 281–318, on the heroic tyrant's use of the concept of the chain of being:

> earth, water, fire,
> Are made (dire elements of cruelty!)
> Subservient to his lust, and power to kill;
> Yet shall the herd endure, and dare not break
> United their imaginary chain . . .   (ll. 295–9).

On Milton's account of angelic pain see e.g. John Clarke, *An Essay upon Study* (London, 1731), 207. *Pre-Existence*, ll. 94, 91–2, 201; see Dennis, *Grounds*, pp. 60–1: 'nothing is more impossible than that God should either Fear or Admire His own Creatures'; and see Joseph Addison, *The Spectator*, 315 (1 Mar. 1712). All references to *The Spectator* are to the edition by Donald F. Bond (Oxford, 1965).

manner makes each of these readings unsatisfactory, and prevents us from choosing among them. It returns us to God's description of man, engaged in the uneasy struggle the poem itself describes:

> Now, he tries
> With all his might to raise some weighty thought,
> Of Me, of fate, or of th'eternal round,
> Which but recoils to crush the labouring mind.[10]

The difficulty of assessing the tone of Evans's *Pre-Existence* results from its character as a didactic religious narrative: the problematic status of the poem's theme seems compounded by its expression in a Miltonic style that here arrogates authority to itself without displaying the grounds of that authority through an apostrophe to the poet's muse, or supportive allusions to the authority of scripture. The narrator makes neither the appropriate claim to authority, nor the appropriate disclaimer, and his impersonal invisibility gives the reader no opportunity to confirm or to dismiss his powerful vision.

This problem of the assumption of didactic authority in a narrative whose authority is not beyond dispute underlies the unease some eighteenth-century critics expressed about Milton's treatment of his subject-matter in his heroic poem, for his subject, 'the history of a miracle, the Creation and Redemption', demands almost exclusively the description of superhuman figures—pre-lapsarian man, Satan, God, and Christ—'characters' who are by their natures beyond description and knowledge. Milton's choice of the epic mode makes it necessary for him to represent eternal truths in terms of actions taking place within time, and the nature of his theme therefore immediately establishes a tension between two parallel aspects of the epic, for while the epic involves the representation of action, it is also a preceptive and didactic form. As Charles Leslie puts it, the purpose of poetry is 'to Express *Truth* in an *Exalted* and *Manly* Improvement of Thought', and for him it can only be in contradiction to this that

Poets . . . have dress'd *Angels* in *Armor*, and put *Swords* and *Guns* into their Hands, to Form *Romantick Battles* in the *Planes of Heaven*, a *Scene* of Licentious *Fancy*; but the *Truth* has been Greatly *Hurt* thereby, and Degraded at last, even into a *Play*, which was Design'd to have been *Acted* upon the *Stage*: And tho'

---

[10] *Pre-Existence*, ll. 249, 254, 258, 259. Pope on *Paradise Lost*, in Joseph Spence, *Anecdotes, Observations and Characters of Books and Men*, ed. Samuel Weller Singer, intro. Bonamy Dobrée (1st pub. 1820; this edn. London, 1964), 117–18. *Pre-Existence*, ll. 252–5.

once Happily Prevented, yet has Pass'd the *Press*, and become the Entertainment of *Prophane Raillery*.

For Leslie, as for other readers, the extent to which Milton is successful in translating his theme into terms representable in epic, into terms of action and visual immediacy or accessibility, and of a plot structure capable of closure, and indeed of representation on the stage, is exactly the extent to which the poem is an 'Effeminat *Romance*', and involves a culpable abuse of its didactic function. Leslie is horrified that Milton's description of Satan as believing himself to be self-begotten 'has Deluded some foolish *Men*, into that *Blasphemous* and *vain* opinion'. The criticisms of John Clarke, the classical scholar and schoolmaster, involve a similar understanding of the poem's didactic function as incompatible with its dramatic coherence, for he too is alarmed by the presentation of the blasphemies of the fallen angels 'without any Interruption or Correction' from the poem's aloof and authoritative narrator.[11]

Those aspects of *Paradise Lost* that troubled Charles Leslie and John Clarke did not, however, deter other critics. Joseph Addison's series of essays on the poem in the *Spectator* of 1712 established and celebrated its sublimity, but involved a rather different understanding and interpretation of the didactic nature of the epic to that which had informed the reservations of Clarke and Leslie. Addison asserts his significantly different understanding of the function of epic poetry at the beginning of the first of his papers on the poem when he writes:

It will be sufficient to its Perfection, if it has in it all the Beauties of the highest kind of poetry; and as for those who alledge it is not an Heroick Poem, they advance no more to the Diminution of it, than if they should say *Adam* is not Æneas, nor *Eve Helen*.

Addison dismisses the distinction between heroic and divine poetry, which had assumed a crucial importance in the criticism of John Dennis, as 'irksom', and represents the poem as directly comparable with the *Iliad* and the *Aeneid*. This dispensation enables him to argue that when Milton writes of Satan that 'God and his Son except, / Created things nought valued he nor shunned', Milton is not committing the serious heresy of describing God and Christ as

---

[11] Johnson, 'Milton', *Lives*, i. 124. Charles Leslie, *The History of Sin and Heresie attempted* (London, 1698), Preface; the play Leslie refers to is probably Dryden's *The Fall of Angels and Man in Innocence*. Clarke, *Study* 205.

'created Beings', but is merely making 'a little Slip. . . in the Grammar or Syntax' which 'a good-natured Reader . . . overlooks'. Addison is not, of course, dismissing the didactic function of the epic—he describes the poem as 'more useful, and instructive, than any other poem in the language'—but he is assuming that the reader of the epic is not reading it primarily for instruction in the basic truths of the Christian religion: Addison's 'good-natured Reader' is already sufficiently educated and discriminating to recognize that Milton has made a slip, and that that slip is minor, whereas Clarke is thinking primarily of the schoolboy reader, and Leslie does not exclude 'foolish Men' from the audience.[12]

But it is not only age and wisdom that Addison assumes as preconditions of the ability to read and appreciate (or perhaps qualifications requisite for entry into the audience of) *Paradise Lost*, for, as a correspondence begun in the *Gentleman's Magazine* in 1738 shows, the Addisonian reader must be prepared to distinguish between Milton as a poet and as a religious authority: he must discriminate between theological and literary criticisms of the poem in a manner that may be commonplace by the time of Johnson's *Lives of the Poets*, but is extremely rare in criticism throughout the first half of the century. 'Theophilus', writing to the *Gentleman's Magazine* in 1739, is aware of the distinction between theological and literary criticism implicit in Addison's discussion, but though he understood the nature of this distinction, he was, more predictably, less confident of its propriety. He remarks of Addison's judgement:

I don't think it ought to be intirely decisive, and the rather, because he was himself a Poet, and, at the time he wrote those excellent Criticisms, might be so heated with the Beauties of the Poem as to overlook Faults in it, that did not belong to its Character *as such*.

Theophilus discriminates between Milton 'as a Poet' and 'in his Religious Character', as he does between *Paradise Lost* as a poem ('*as such*') and as an instructive expression of Christian belief, and it is the confusion or conflict between these two roles, in both poet and poem, that concerns him. He is perhaps less confident than Addison had been, or than his respondent 'Philospec' appears to be, that the audience for the poem is limited to, precisely, those who will be able to admire its authoritative and didactic manner with the very critical

---

[12] Joseph Addison, *Spectator*, 267 (5 Jan. 1712). *Paradise Lost*, ed. Alastair Fowler (London, 1971), bk. II, ll. 678–9. *Spectator*, 285 (26 Jan. 1712).

detachment which it seeks to disarm, and which does not respond to command, to instruction. In response to Theophilus's argument that Milton may be admired as a poet though not as a Christian, Philospec reiterates the Addisonian argument, seeking to defend Milton from theological criticism on the grounds of poetic necessity, and Theophilus's reply illustrates both the extent to which Addison had attempted to reform criticism of religious poetry in the first half of the eighteenth century, and the doubts that were more widely entertained about *Paradise Lost* as religious poetry. For Theophilus regards what might be described as the patriotic literary formalism of Addisonian criticism as inappropriate to religious poetry:

'The Character of *Mammon*, and the description of *Pandaemonium* may have their Beauties,' as Mr *Addison* observes, so far as they are considered as Pieces of mere Fancy and Invention, to which a Latitude may be allow'd where Religion is not concerned; (and this was the Light in which that ingenious Critic considered them): But to make religious Truths give Way to these, rather than spoil a Scene in a Poem, is what I am not yet convinc'd can be consistent with the Regard that is due to Religion.

Theophilus goes on to argue that the poem should more properly be styled a 'Romance', for he clearly does not regard his criticisms of the poem as criticisms of its *literary* merit: his major objection to *Paradise Lost* is based on its claim to an authoritative religious vision, and if it were to describe itself as a 'romance', a fiction, and thus to disclaim that didactic authority, he would feel able to acknowledge its sublimity.[13]

Philospec, however, did not perceive or recognize the distinctions on which Theophilus's argument depended, and it seems probable that other readers similarly failed to perceive them, for the distinction between Milton as a poet and as a religious authority is not clearly reiterated as a solution to the problem of his sublimity and heresy until as late as 1757. The debate is then taken up by William Wilkie, in his discussion of epic poetry in the Preface to his *Epigoniad*. Wilkie argues that the themes of the true religion provide unsuitable subject-matter

---

[13] *Gentleman's Magazine*, 9 (Jan. 1739), 5; 8 (Mar. 1738), 125; see ibid. (8 Apr. 1738), 201–2; (9 Jan. 1739), 5–6. the importance of claiming a literary, as distinct from religious, merit for *Paradise Lost* can be understood in terms of the perceived need for a national epic, and the difficulties, both political and doctrinal, of according the poem this status. But these difficulties cannot be isolated from consideration of the changing position of religious poetry in this period, as the criticisms I have been discussing, and in particular Johnson's life of Milton, clearly indicate.

for epic poetry because it is primarily a didactic genre: epic sets 'before us images of whatever is great and noble in the human character', but divine persons provide unsuitable images as they are not human, and 'imperfect characters interest us more than perfect ones'. Milton has presented an anthropomorphized idea of the deity, and therefore he 'has offended notoriously . . . and tho' no encomiums are too great for him as a poet, he is justly chargeable with impiety, for presuming to represent the Divine Nature, and the mysteries of religion, according to the narrowness of human prejudice'. Wilkie argues that Milton has particularized or characterized God, and this judgement leads him to a conclusion which seems directly opposed to that of John Dennis: epic poetry, he argues, should employ the gods of Greek mythology, not the God of the Christian religion.[14]

IV

These changing attitudes to *Paradise Lost* do not, of course, indicate that eighteenth-century critics were insensitive to the poem's sublimity, but they do reveal that the acknowledgement of that sublimity involved a series of distinctions within the idea of a fit readership, the role of the critic, and the terms in which the poem itself is described. These distinctions frequently involve discriminations between the provinces appropriate to poetry and religion, literary and theological criticism, and the reader who looks for instruction as opposed to the reader who looks for pleasure, and these discriminations reflect the increasingly problematic status of didactic authority in religious poetry. *Paradise Lost* itself, for Johnson writing in 1779, has become a poem no Englishman can like to see criticized, but, he comments, 'We read Milton for instruction, retire harassed and overburdened, and look elsewhere for recreation; we desert our master, and seek for companions.'[15] By 1750 the Miltonic style of masterful and sublime instruction is almost entirely absent from religious poetry, and is succeeded, as Johnson suggests, by more companionable discussions and meditations which are either accessible to emulation, or involve an authority based in the recognizable or companionably mortal position of the poet. I shall now look at some of the strengths and problems of the kind of authority

[14] William Wilkie, *The Epigoniad, a Poem* (Edinburgh, 1757), Preface, pp. xvi, xxix, xxviii.

[15] Johnson, 'Milton', *Lives*, i. 132; cf. Addison, *Spectator*, 369 (3 May 1712).

available to religious poetry in the first half of the century in the poetry of Thomson, Aaron Hill, and Pope, and examine the implications of that authority for the ability of this poetry to accommodate the variety of creation and experience.

In Thomson's *Seasons*, as I suggested at the beginning of this introduction, we encounter shifting and occasionally incongruous descriptive perspectives which contrast with the superhuman authority of the poet of *Paradise Lost*, and might seem to indicate a loss of impersonality and detachment that might jeopardize the authority of the wandering and companionable poet. The heterogeneity of *The Seasons* seems to depend for its acceptability on the ability of the narrator to elude identification with any particular stance he adopts, while he nevertheless infuses each stance with an apparently unquestionable and acceptable authority: the poet's ambivalent impersonality eludes commitment to any one exclusively defining position, and allows him to adopt a range of positions without appearing to contradict himself. The claim implicit in his shifting positions is that they do not express convictions inconsistent with his omniscient overview, but an apprehension of variety which substantiates it. In 'Summer', for example, the poet describes the appearance of a comet:

> The rushing Comet to the Sun descends;
> And as he sinks below the shading Earth,
> With awful Train projected o'er the Heavens,
> The guilty Nations tremble. But, above
> Those superstitious Horrors that enslave
> The fond sequacious Herd, to mystic Faith
> And blind Amazement prone, th'enlighten'd Few,
> Whose Godlike Minds Philosophy exalts,
> The glorious Stranger hail. They feel a Joy
> Divinely great; they in their Powers exult,
> That wondrous Force of Thought, which mounting spurns
> This dusky Spot, and measures all the Sky;

Here the narrator is, typically, ambivalent about the extent to which he can claim to share the perspective of the philosophical eye—clearly, he shares it to an extent that enables him to describe both its perceptions and its pleasures, but he disclaims a thorough knowledge or possession of it, in much the same way as he distances himself from the superstitious awe of the crowd. He notes, apparently without question or reservation, that 'The guilty Nations tremble', and then goes on to qualify this vision by attributing it to (and incidentally identifying the

Nation with) the fond sequacious herd. But the wise philosophers nevertheless remain 'they', rather than 'we', though Thomson goes on to describe, with detail and precision, their conception of the comet's role in a theistic natural-philosophical system.[16]

The implications of Thomson's narrative strategy for an understanding of *The Seasons* as a religious poem can perhaps be seen most clearly in the passage from 'Summer' which describes the death of one of a pair of lovers struck by lightning. The poet sets the incident in a religious context: before it occurs, Celadon watches the fated Amelia 'as Angels look / On dying Saints', and his later grief is compared to that of a mourner on a marble tomb. Celadon comforts Amelia, in her fear of the storm, through a description of the morality of natural events which resembles the superstitious beliefs attributed to the fond herd observing the comet; but in his depiction of the incident itself, the poet restrains himself from offering any comment, any moral explanation:

> But who can paint the Lover, as he stood,
> Pierc'd by severe Amazement, hating Life,
> Speechless, and fix'd in all the Death of Woe!

Ralph Cohen argues that, in this scene, Thomson mocks the naïvety of Celadon's belief in a moral universe, but though Celadon's words to Amelia are obviously fraught with irony, Thomson's revisions of the passage suggest rather a scrupulous restraint, a concern to preserve the integrity of the scene, and to maintain the poet's ability to describe it with conviction, without becoming identified with Celadon's simple beliefs, and without the implications of its abrupt and arbitrary conclusion imposing the need for the sort of philosophical justification which, it seems, it is beyond the scope of the poem to offer.[17]

In the 1727 edition of the poem, the paragraph which immediately followed the close of the incident went on to describe the dispersal of the storm in terms which might lend some substance to Cohen's interpretation: the poet hailed the blue sky that followed the storm:

> That constant Joy to every finer Eye,
> That Rapture! swells into the general Arch,

[16] 'Summer', ll. 1708–19; see Harriet Guest and John Barrell, 'On the Use of Contradiction: Economics and Morality in the Eighteenth-Century Long Poem', in *The New Eighteenth Century: Theory, Politics, English Literature*, ed. Felicity Nussbaum and Laura Brown (New York and London, 1987).

[17] Thomson, 'Summer', ll. 1202–3 (ll. 1220–2, on Celadon's resemblance to the 'well-dissembled Mourner' in marble, suggest a classical as well as religious context for the incident); ll. 1217–19; Cohen, *Unfolding*, pp. 157–8.

> Which copes the Nations.—On the lilly'd Bank,
> Where a Brook quivers, often, careless, thrown,
> Up the wide Scene I've gaz'd whole Hours away,
> With growing Wonder . . .

This earlier version might indeed suggest that Celadon's romantic morality indicates his lack of refinement, and it certainly distances the careless figure of the pastoral poet from his monumental despair. But in the final version of the lines, while the incident is contrasted with, or perhaps contained by, the sublimity of the blue 'interminable Sky' that succeeds the storm, there is no suggestion of an alternative perspective which might invalidate or disclaim the significance of the previous scene.

> As from the Face of Heaven the shatter'd Clouds
> Tumultuous rove, th'interminable Sky
> Sublimer swells, and o'er the World expands
> A purer Azure. Nature, from the Storm,
> Shines out afresh; and thro' the lighten'd Air
> A higher Luster and a clearer Calm,
> Diffusive, tremble; while, as if in Sign
> Of Danger past, a glittering Robe of Joy,
> Set off abundant by the yellow Ray,
> Invests the Fields, yet dropping from Distress.

The lines offer no direct comment on the sentimental tragedy of the lovers: we might detect a naturalizing allusion to their fate in the distress of the fields, the 'shatter'd Clouds', but we are not, I think, encouraged to do so, for this seems at most a residual allusion which envelops their story in a generalized natural continuum where pastoral morality and romantic sentiment have no place.

The biblical sublime of the 'Face of Heaven' and the 'Robe of Joy' indicates the use of a discourse of bold imagery and sudden transitions—a descriptive and figurative, as opposed to explanatory mode, inhospitable to the syntax which might make explicit relations of cause and effect. In these lines, the syntactical relations between the clauses are precise but indeterminate: 'as', 'while', and 'yet' introduce clauses which describe apparently simultaneous events, unconnected by any causal or explanatory logic. The poet's silence on the moral implications of the lovers' tale does not indicate his disillusion, or fatalism, but a detachment from the 'circumstantial varieties' he portrays which is here implicitly compared to the stance of the inspired biblical historian or prophet: he produces for our inspection successive events which it is not necessarily his role to interpret or comment on. The 'moral' of the tale of Celadon and Amelia lies in the impassive, prophetic silence of the poet, and the ease with which the discourse of the biblical sublime assimilates the incident to its 'clearer Calm'.[18]

I have already alluded to Johnson's judgement on *The Seasons*, that the poet had:

a mind that at once comprehends the vast and attends to the minute. . . . His is one of the works in which blank verse seems properly used. Thomson's wide expansion of general views, and his enumeration of circumstantial varieties, would have been obstructed and embarrassed by the frequent intersections of the sense which are the necessary effects of rhyme.

Thomson's blank verse, as Johnson also points out, is his own rather than Milton's, and is a paragraphic and forward-moving style which displays the luxuriance of its diction rather than the complexity of its syntax. This fluid verse facilitates the description of the vast and the minute, the general and the circumstantial, through enabling the poet to adopt the apparently seamless series of perspectives necessary to their description, and to maintain an elusive narrative identity that, as it gives continuity to the various voices of the poem, implies that it may also comprehend them as harmonious and non-contradictory. The poet invests each perspective with instructive assurance, while remaining free to withdraw, and to take up, perhaps, an opposing perspective, and this strategy represents the elusiveness of the comprehensive or absolute authority that may inform the whole poem as a necessary effect of the immense variety of the social and natural landscape.[19]

The landscape of the poem is, on the one hand, appropriately described as 'this dark State, / In wayward Passions lost and vain Pursuits', and, on the other, a labyrinth presided over by the '*ever-making Eye*' of providence: a labyrinthine landscape which resists explanation because it depends on an order it cannot make visible except as a 'dark State', and which therefore expresses an authority

---

[18] 'Summer' (1727), ll. 890–5; (1746), ll. 1224, 1223–32. (For a discussion of the various revised editions of the *Seasons*, see the Introduction to James Sambrook's Oxford edition of the poem.) On the biblical sublime see e.g. Aaron Hill, 'Preface to Mr. Pope, concerning the Sublimity of the Ancient Hebrew Poetry, and a material and obvious Defect in the English', in *The Creation* (London, 1720), and John Husbands, 'The Preface Containing some Remarks on the Beauties of the Holy Scriptures, More especially of the Old Testament, where they are consider'd in a Classical View', in *A Miscellany of Poems By several Hands* (Oxford, 1731). Johnson, 'Thomson', *Lives*, ii. 376.

[19] Johnson, 'Thomson', *Lives*, ii. 376; see 376–7.

that cannot be seen as residing absolutely in any one of its parts—its order, its authority, is continually deferred to a source beyond itself. In Thomson's poem, this religious idea of an ultimate external source of coherence takes a peculiarly elusive form which, I think, we may best understand by unpacking a little more the idea of the poet's authority. The striking characteristic of this authority, as I have suggested, is that it expresses a power distinct from explanation. Unlike Pope, or Milton, the poet does not validate his position through the claim that he can justify or vindicate, that he can make reasons, causes and effects, explicit. The conventional connection between poetic authority and interpretative or explanatory power may still be strong enough to suggest that the variety of the poem describes an implicit unity that could be made explicit, but while the poetic authority of *The Seasons* may lead us to trust the poet's ability to explain, and perhaps even invite us to expect interpretation, it also allows him to imply that if an explanation cannot be given, it is because the poet writes only in response to a world he never claimed to vindicate, with an authority never vested in the power of explanation.[20]

The poet attributes to his aristocratic friends a view of the world as sometimes entirely good, sometimes on the brink of collapse—as, therefore, in a paradoxical state they, in retirement, have not been responsible for creating—and he suggests that he like them possesses in potential the power to reconcile any contradictions this view may describe. Thomson's poem seems to manifest or describe the transition between the authoritatively religious poetry of *Paradise Lost*—or of the *Essay on Man*—and the poetry of private devotion which Johnson saw as ultimately silent, in so far as the poem maintains a tension between the labyrinthine digressiveness it presents and the hermeneutic act of comprehension it seems to promise: its implicit explanatory power and explicit lack of coherence. It offers, as possible sources of explanatory coherence, the active government dispensed by patriots, Industry, the 'kind Source of every gentle Art, / And all the soft Civility of Life', and natural philosophy, without which man is a savage, 'devoid of every finer Art / And Elegance of Life'; and its religious context accommodates these diverse discourses, rather than offering a further possible choice, for it is specifically the religious nature of the poet's authority (as we saw in the Celadon and Amelia incident from 'Summer') that legitimates the divorce of authority from

[20] 'Summer', ll. 1800–1; 'Winter', l. 1020. See *Essay on Man*, epistle I, l. 16; *Paradise Lost*, bk. I, l. 26.

explanation. Religious discourses therefore function in the *Seasons*, rather as they do in Young's *Night-Thoughts*, to offer a context in which sudden transitions are not a threat to coherence, but evidence of the sublime, and of immanent power. They function as a prophetic guarantee of explanation so comprehensive that local and explicit explanation appears redundant, or even a possible threat to the final act of exegesis performed by providence. In this context, the poet's ability to describe takes precedence over any power of explanation, and his wandering lack of direction becomes the guarantee of his impartiality, and of the inevitability with which providential history will make explicit and present his potential power.[21]

V

Pope's *Essay on Man*, in contrast, employs an abstract and apparently explanatory discourse in which moral judgements frequently depend on the authority with which they are expressed for their persuasive power. Pope explicity invites comparison between his authority and that of Milton through the direct allusion expressed in his intention to 'vindicate the ways of God to Man', though in the following paragraph he qualifies that intention and places it in implicit contrast to Milton's:

> Say first, of God above, or Man below,
> What can we reason, but from what we know?
> Of Man what see we, but his station here,
> From which to reason, or to which refer?
> Thro' worlds unnumber'd tho' the God be known,
> 'Tis ours to trace him only in our own.

The poet here turns away from the attempt to imitate the adventurousness of Milton's song: his own essay does not represent God, and is not epic poetry, but a '*short* yet not *imperfect* system of Ethics', which, he states in the 'Design',

is only to be considered as a *general Map* of MAN, marking out no more than the greater parts, their *extent*, their *limits*, and their *connection*, but leaving the particular to be more fully delineated in the charts which are to follow. . . . I am here only opening the *fountains*, and clearing the passage.

---

[21] See Barrell, *Survey*, pp. 54 ff. Johnson, 'Waller', *Lives*, i. 211–12. See e.g. 'Autumn', ll. 910–28; 'Winter', ll. 17–40; 'Autumn', ll. 45–6; 'Summer', ll. 1761–2.

The *Essay* is a general map of argumentative theory whose detailed application is charted in the more personal and ironic epistles of the *Moral Essays*.[22]

This shift from Heaven to man, from epic to argument, does not, however, result in any comparative diminution of the authority with which the poet feels able to speak. In much of the *Essay*, the poet advances his argument through series of questions and assertions addressed to 'Presumptuous Man', which follow closely the sublime questioning of the last few chapters of the Book of Job, where the Lord answers Job 'out of the whirlwind', demanding, 'Where wast thou when I laid the foundations of the earth? declare, if thou hast understanding'. Pope, in a similar vein, demands: 'Is the great chain, that draws all to agree, / And drawn supports, upheld by God, or thee?' The concise authority of the couplet, and the weight it places on the final question, make it difficult for the reader to question the validity of the great chain without also questioning the superiority of divine power. Pope argues that man, as an imperfect part, cannot know the perfect whole of the providential plan, and cannot question its existence, and he assures the reader:

> All Nature is but Art, unknown to thee;
> All Chance, Direction, which thou canst not see;
> All Discord, Harmony not understood;
> All partial Evil, universal Good.[23]

Like Thomson's *Seasons*, the *Essay* employs religious arguments for a deferred explanatory coherence, but, as the comparison with Job may suggest, the *Essay* involves the further assumption that the poet is privy to that comprehensive coherence, that he can ask questions only God could put to Job, and can assert the existence of an art and direction he has described imperfect man as unable to apprehend. The poet addresses man, first as the 'fool' and later as his 'friend', from an elevation that makes it difficult to distinguish his voice from that of nature, and, finally, from that of God—for 'The state of Nature was the reign of God'. Responsibility for this authority is, to some extent, deferred to Lord Bolingbroke, in the references to him at the beginning and end of the poem, which call into play the theory that it is the privilege of a disinterested aristocracy to be elevated to a

---

[22] *Essay on Man*, epistle I, ll. 16, 17–22; 'The Design', p. 502.
[23] Epistle I, l. 35; Job 38: 1, 4 (I use the Authorized Version throughout); epistle I, ll. 33–4, 289–94.

perspective from which they can see over, and oversee, the complex though harmonious whole of society; but finally the poet seems to claim for himself an equal privilege, though it may still be a position which depends on that of his patron. He writes, in the conclusion to the poem:

> Shall then this verse to future age pretend
> Thou wert my guide, philosopher, and friend?
> That urg'd by thee, I turn'd the tuneful art
> From sounds to things, from fancy to the heart;
> For Wit's false mirror held up Nature's light;
> Show'd erring pride, WHATEVER IS, IS RIGHT.

Though Bolingbroke may guide and urge the poet, it is he who holds up 'Nature's light', and who asserts, with ironic justice, that 'Heav'n and I are of a mind'.[24]

It is therefore important to examine the precise nature of the claims Pope makes for his authority as a poet, for while he does appear to claim an absolute authority, it is an authority which he presents as persuasive and forceful rather than rational or virtuous. The philosophical basis of his argument obliges him to accommodate evil as well as good, and to argue that a Borgia contributes as much to what is right as a saint; and this philosophy produces a defence, a presentation, vested in the necessity of the irrational, of sin and evil, and in the powerless irresponsibility of reason. The force of his poetry is thus not that of reasoned coherence, but of the authority of apparent power, of persuasive force, and it is an authority that can only come to terms with the details of the design, can only descend from abstraction to the delineation of particulars, by taking on the equivocal irony of the satirist—an irony that may indicate that in order to preserve the authority of power the poet must suspend any claim to rational argument in favour of the pointed antithesis, the effective but not necessarily logical or morally unambiguous attack. In order to retain the power to rearrange the map and direct the fountains, he must set aside the privilege of viewing it in the comprehensive and consistent

---

[24] When Zophar the Naamathite asks Job: 'Canst thou by searching find out God? canst thou find out the Almighty unto perfection?' Job responds in terms which might also seem appropriate to the questions posed by Pope's *Essay*: 'I have understanding as well as you; I *am* not inferior to you: yea, who knoweth not such things as these?' (Job 11: 7; 12:3; translators' italic). Epistle III, l. 27; epistle IV, l. 200; epistle III, l. 148. See Barrell, *Survey*, pp. 35–6; epistle IV, ll. 389–94; Moral Essays, *Epistle III. To Allen Lord Bathurst*, l. 8.

terms that reveal its order, and thus he must undermine his previous claims to systematic coherence.[25]

Pope seems to acknowledge that his argument involves an emphasis on nature at the expense of the rational in the second Epistle of the *Essay*, where he writes:

> As Man, perhaps, the moment of his breath,
> Receives the lurking principle of death;
> The young disease, that must subdue at length,
> Grows with his growth, and strengthens with his strength:
> So, cast and mingled with his very frame,
> The Mind's disease, its ruling Passion came;
> Each vital humour which should feed the whole,
> Soon flows to this, in body and in soul.
> Whatever warms the heart, or fills the head,
> As the mind opens, and its functions spread,
> Imagination plies her dang'rous art,
> And pours it all upon the peccant part.
>   Nature its mother, Habit is its nurse;
> Wit, Spirit, Faculties, but make it worse;
> Reason itself but gives it edge and pow'r;
> As Heav'n's blest beam turns vinegar more sowr.

Here the extended metaphor of the long disease of life works to enclose the 'peccant part' within the discourse of medical pathology, but the religious connotations of peccancy, in the context of this allegory of original sin, seem irrepressible, and may be reaffirmed by the last line of the quotation, where the place of heaven in a natural philosophical rather than religious discourse is insecure. The poet's account of the genesis of the ruling passion needs to be insulated from the religious implications of its language, from the pervasive insistence of a religious discourse which threatens the coherence of his philosophy by introducing fixed moral values—of peccancy, good and evil—despite the understanding, central to the poem's argument, of these terms as flexible, even interchangeable. In this passage, 'peccancy' serves to confirm the presence of a religious discourse inconsistent with the philosophy of the poem, which the belief, expressed a few lines later, that 'Nature's road must ever be preferred'

---

[25] See epistle I, ll. 141–64. It might be argued that the contrasts between the *Essay* and the Moral Essays can best be understood in terms of genre, but if this is the case, then the relation between the different genres of epistolary satire and ethic epistle, the necessity of moving from one to the other, nevertheless requires further examination and discussion.

cannot sufficiently exclude or reclaim. The intrusive presence of the religious implications of the peccancy of nature suggests that it may not 'Suffice that Reason keep to Nature's road', and it may be partly in response to this difficulty that 'Eternal Art' is introduced at the conclusion of this argument to graft virtue onto natural passion.[26]

These difficulties threaten the persuasive power of Pope's argument here, and are formally expressed in the problematic relation between the *Essay* and the Epistles that follow it. They expose the tensions that inform the resounding ambiguity of the poet's conclusion that 'WHATEVER IS, IS RIGHT': the problems of a rational argument advocating the government of natural passion, in an explicitly religious poem which divinizes Nature as the mother of peccancy; a poem which implies the identity of the views of the poet and God, but allows the poet to castigate the errors he also praises as necessary to the general good. The poem portrays man (and therefore the poet) as a jest, a riddling paradox, and maintains its judgemental authority by deferring the ironic laugh on to the ambivalently personal satire of the Moral Essays. Where Milton's justification of the ways of God had perhaps been flawed by its anthropomorphic description of those ways, Pope's vindication cuts the ground from under its own feet by destabilizing the terms of reason, right, and argument on which its success depends. The force of his arguments, then, depends less on their philosophical plausibility than on the apparent infallibility of their expression, on the polished use of the 'closed' (rather than open-ended) couplet form which lends an assured surface to the precepts it contains; but this was an authority it was difficult, and perhaps not even desirable, for later poets to attempt.[27]

VI

It was not, for example, appropriate to the poetry of Aaron Hill, who argues in 'Free Thoughts upon Faith: Or the Religion of Reason' that man is not in a position to celebrate a unified whole visible only from heaven, and should celebrate rather the variety that he does experience:

[26] Epistle II, ll. 133–48, 161, 115, 175.
[27] Epistle IV, l. 394.

>   *—Can* it *be*,
> That he, who fill'd each crowded element,
> With unresembling sons of endless change—
>
> .   .   .   .
>
> —Can it be possible—that HE,—pleas'd power!
> Who o'er Creation's glebe, sow'd *seeds of change*,
> Shou'd, but from *Unity's bald harvest*, reap!
> And burn,—for *tares*—those beauteous growths, he rais'd,
> To smile such *lov'd variety*!

Hill argues that we can only believe that God is kind, and that we should take pleasure from '*Every* view' rather than from a single perspective:

> To *me*:—nor let the rev'rence of my *pause*
> Offend the power that caus'd it!—it shou'd seem
> More impious, to DECIDE, of God, than *doubt*.

Clearly, for Hill, Pope's voice could represent no more than one 'view' among many available for 'Unprejudic'd' consideration; its exclusive authority is denied as inappropriate, impossible.[28]

The contrast between the approaches of the two poets can be seen in the different verse forms they employ: where Pope, as I have said, offers a highly finished verse form, in which the antithetical heroic couplet can become an aphoristic unit of sense that apparently retains its universal significance and truth almost regardless of context—many of Pope's couplets have acquired a proverbial authority as isolated quotations—Hill employs a version of Miltonic blank verse that is choppy and ejaculatory, broken up with dashes, exclamations, and digressions in sense. A brief isolated quotation from Hill's poem does not acquire the superpersonal conciseness of a proverb or saw, and, as the following example suggests, is often more likely to refuse any particular application than to display a general relevance. He describes 'Survey's charm'd outlet' extending:

>   —O'er this *upper* sea,
> Where meditation *founders*, —flights immense

---

[28] 'Free Thoughts', in *The Works of the Late Aaron Hill, Esq: In Four Volumes* (London, 1753), iii. 240, 242, 221, and 242, where Hill writes: 'PEACEFULLY patient, let me travel out / Life's unoffending journey. Mark, well-pleas'd, / New prospects, manners, tastes, beliefs, chang'd modes, / New systems—*Every* view, that *sides* my way, / Unprejudic'd to *any*'.

Cross-cut the winnow'd *Æther*. Black, white, grey,
Red, blue, brown, golden, verdant, motley-stain'd—
Distant in *size*, as *colours*!

Hill approaches the problem of the 'great view', the Popean prospect, from, as it were, the other end of the telescope. Where Pope celebrates a unity, a plan, which can only be perceived from the vantage-point of aristocratic eminence, Hill strives to represent the unassimilable profusion of distinction experienced within the view Pope oversees, and, indeed, in the 'Preface' to *Creation* he contrasts Pope's superiority with 'the poor Figure I am making, in the bottom of the Prospect'.[29]

This description of the 'wing-divided *air*' is typical of his technique, which attempts to create an almost Coleridgean sublimity through piling up the details, the particulars, into an overwhelming confusion in which the distinction necessary to variety is at once celebrated and lost in an all-embracing plenitude. We cannot here distinguish between the air and the wings that by dividing define and describe it, though we are apparently invited to do so; the description of the air as the '*upper* sea' (rather deliberately) distinguishes the air from the sea as it confuses it with it, and, again, the air is 'winnow'd *Æther*', and thus both the effect and the cause of the winnowing process, and this series of descriptive possibilities serves to emphasize the indescribable omnipresence of the element the poet surveys. The effect the poem attempts to achieve is perhaps most apparent in the catalogue of colours: the colours themselves are presented as potentially either nouns or adjectives until we arrive at 'motley-stain'd', which can be more confidently identified as adjectival, but the birds that the colours qualify or describe, though they are referred to in the phrases 'wing-divided *air*' and, perhaps, 'flights immense', are not recognizable as the potential subject until almost the end of this verse-paragraph. The colours might therefore at first seem to refer to the flights of meditation, or to the air as perceived by 'Survey's charm'd outlet', and indeed it becomes apparent that their confusing status results from and expresses the sublimity of the view from the 'jutting CLIFF' at which 'meditation *founders*'.[30]

The poet reflects almost immediately on the confusion this passage involves, reassuring the reader that the confusion is not theirs alone:

[29] Hill, 'Free Thoughts', p. 239. Pope, *Essay*, epistle II, l. 238. 'Preface to Mr. Pope', *The Creation*, p. 3; for a further example of Hill's use of this emblematic topography see 'The Statesman', *Works*, iii. 234.
[30] Hill, 'Free Thoughts', p. 239.

'STOP thy endanger'd *foot*. Recal the range / Of thy recovering *eye*'—
though of course what the poet may halt here is the process by which
the eye recovers, or orders and thus denies, the sublimity it has
experienced; for the poem then plunges again into the diversity it has
just withdrawn from:

> Ponder the DEEP's dumb legions—Infinite
> Their numbers! still *more* infinite, their shapes,
> Bulks, movements!—Swift, slow, timid, fierce, horn'd, barb'd,
> Coatless, finn'd, scaly, shell'd, wing'd, motionless:
> All *diff'ring*—till immensity grows *tir'd*.

Hill's descriptive method resembles some comprehensive but unsys-
tematized catalogue of a natural philosopher's observations, but here it
is exactly that systematization and appropriation that Hill's language
works to deny. The poet only speaks with confidence, clarity, and
fluidity when he describes his own lack of ambition: 'Let me', he
concludes: 'Thro the dusk / Thought fails to penetrate, *revere* what
is— / Undaring to *describe* it'.[31]

Hill's self-consciously qualified and personal manner is in extreme
contrast to the comprehensive generality and confident authority of
Pope's *Essay on Man*. The provisional and interrupted language of his
poetry almost denies itself the means, the fluency, to address its
audience, and was, as he knew, unlikely to meet with great acclaim in
an age which welcomed the articulation of minute particularity in the
instructive and systematic discourse of the poetry of natural philosophy.
The reverent precision and sublimity of his language is equally alien to
the abstractions of Pope's couplets, and to, for example, Sir Richard
Blackmore's detailed description of the fate of his audience's dinner:

> Two adverse rows of teeth the meat prepare,
> On which the glands fermenting juice confer;
> Nature has various tender muscles placed,
> By which the artful gullet is embraced;
> Some of the long funnel's curious mouth extend,
> Through which ingested meats with ease descend;
> Other confederate pairs for Nature's use
> Contract the fibres, and the twitch produce.

The contrast between Blackmore's systematic description and Hill's
more vagrant epistemology adds some further terms to the contrast I

---

[31] Hill, 'Free Thoughts', pp. 239, 240, 241.

traced in discussing *The Seasons* and the *Essay on Man*. That contrast suggested that, where Thomson's ambivalent authority allowed him continually to withhold explanation while suggesting that its absence strengthened rather than threatened the potential coherence and plausibility of his arguments, Pope's more authoritative manner, which claimed for itself an explanatory power his arguments could not demonstrate, could not evade or retreat from the evident incompatibility between its religious discourses and its social philosophy, which could be yoked in harness only by the forceful irrationality of their presentation. The contrast between Hill and Blackmore, to some extent, supports this interpretation, for in Hill's poetry religious awe as a response to variety displaces the need for systematization and explanation, whereas the authority of Blackmore's philosophical discourse led him into explanatory descriptions of religious concepts that the *Plain Dealer*, the periodical edited by Aaron Hill and W. Bond, found 'almost blasphemous'. But Blackmore's *Creation* might also be seen as the natural descendant of Dennis's arguments for the interrelation of religion and poetry: in his poem, religion exalts scientific precept, while the arguments of natural philosophy lend force to those of religion. Johnson, considering it as a philosophical rather than religious poem, wrote that 'In his descriptions, both of life and nature, the poet and the philosopher happily co-operate; truth is recommended by elegance, and elegance sustained by truth.'[32]

Hill and Blackmore share a common interest in detail, a common attention to the particularity of creation. Hill's descriptive catalogues are no less precise than Blackmore's anatomical analyses, but their different understandings of the relation between natural philosophy and religion, and thus of the didactic role of the religious poet, place them in contrast. Johnson commented on Blackmore, with some asperity, that he 'cannot keep his poetry unmingled with trade', and the authority of his exposition proceeds, not from an aristocratic and disinterested eminence capable of grasping variety only in abstract terms, but from a professional vantage secured by experimental knowledge. Blackmore argues, in the Preface to *Creation*, that the wisdom of God can be most persuasively exemplified in the systems of astronomy or anatomy which his professional interests have placed him in a position to make accessible to the 'general Apprehension and

---

[32] Sir Richard Blackmore, *Creation. A Philosophical Poem. In Seven Books* (London, 1712), vi. 489–96. *The Plain Dealer*, ed. A. Hill and W. Bond (1724; this edn. 2 vols., London, 1730), i. 459. Johnson, 'Blackmore', *Lives*, ii. 51.

Capacity of Mankind', and he therefore attempts to popularize his knowledge, to 'bring Philosophy out of the secret Recesses of the Schools, and to strip it of its uncouth and mysterious Dress, that it may become agreeable, and admitted to a general Conversation'. But his 'conversational' discourse of natural philosophy, of physical cause and effect, does not always wed happily with the task of 'Christian Poets, as well as Christian Preachers', which is 'to instruct the People' and 'endeavour to confirm and spread their own true Religion'. He writes, for example, of the 'divine imagin'd plan' of creation:

> Thy glance survey'd the solitary plains,
> Where shapeless shade inert and silent reigns;
> Then in the dark and undistinguish'd space,
> Unfruitful, uninclos'd and wild of face,
> Thy compass for the world mark'd out the destin'd place.
> Then didst thou thro' the fields of barren night
> Go forth, collected in creating might.
> Where thou almighty vigour didst exert,
> Which emicant did this and that way dart
> Thro' the black bosom of the empty space:
> The gulphs confess th'omnipotent embrace,
> And pregnant grown with elemental seed,
> Unfinish'd orbs, and worlds in embryo breed.

Here the poet seems to assume an unproblematic relation between the description of creation in the natural-philosophical discourse familiar to the surgeon and the instructive but theologically precise discourse of the preacher-poet. He is careful to exclude from the 'Philosophical and Argumentative parts of this Poem' any 'Metaphor and Description' that might 'darken and enfeeble' the propriety of his words, but that very accuracy, in combination with the dogmatic pedagogy he sees as appropriate to the Christian poet, produces in these lines a factual description which seems to recognize no distinction between God and his works as the objects of the scrutiny of the natural philosopher.[33]

Blackmore's *Creation* suggests, then, that the poetry of natural philosophy demands, through the abolition of metaphor and other 'Ornaments of Poetical Eloquence', an unmediated gaze defined by the absence of that self-consciousness which dominates the poetry of Aaron Hill. He sees natural philosophy as demystifying nature, identifying in it the handwriting of divine wisdom, and translating its cryptic utterances into the currency of 'general Conversation'. This

---

[33] Johnson, 'Blackmore', *Lives*, ii. 40. Blackmore, *Creation*, Preface, pp. xxxiii, xxxv, xxxvii; *Creation*, vii. 701, 703–15. Preface, pp. xxxv, xxxvi.

process appears to involve a kind of iconoclastic radicalism, which turns the secret goddess of the schools into a common prostitute, but it also, of course, reinforces the authority of the poet who is both preacher and philosopher, and who looks through nature up to nature's God and tells us what he sees. His role as instructor demands that he assumes an authority—based on the power to make explicit the relations of cause and effect, the secrets of generation, that he detects in creation—which becomes problematic when it is applied to religious subjects in the same terms as to natural subjects of philosophy; and it is, I want to suggest, for this reason that, although Blackmore describes himself as a Christian poet, primarily concerned to establish the existence and wisdom of the deity through his exposition of natural philosophy, *Creation* is discussed by Johnson as a philosophical and not as a religious poem. The didactic authority with which he produces his explanations of natural phenomena is at odds with the reverent uncertainty which Hill describes as mediating his apprehension of natural variety.[34]

This is not to say, of course, that either didacticism or explanatory power are incompatible with a properly religious poetry. In Hill's poetry, the variety of nature and the poet's acceptance of that variety are explicitly tied to his advocacy of religious freedom: the dissenting churches, for example, have 'Hedg'd in th' eternal's COMMON', they have delimited the natural diversity available to common ownership which Hill describes as the exemplary lesson of nature. His poetry teaches by enjoining its readers to share in the exemplary position of the poet, who recognizes the authority of nature. The explanatory power of a religious natural philosophy, however, tends to work, as we shall see, either by emphasizing its analogical relation to science, and thus identifying itself as a different though comparable kind of philosophy, or by stressing the extent to which its reading of nature is mediated by religious belief, and is thus detached from the directly explicit conversation claimed by natural philosophy.[35]

VII

The distinction between, on the one hand, pedagogically preceptive poetry and, on the other, poetry which is instructive through the

[34] Blackmore, *Creation*, Preface pp. xxxvi, xxxv. See Samuel Johnson, *A Dictionary of the English Language* (1755), 'To Converse', v. n. 5.
[35] Hill, 'Free Thoughts', p. 200.

examples it presents, provides a means of understanding the didactic function of much of the devotional poetry of the century. John Gay's 'A Thought on Eternity', for example, describes an exemplary posture of devotion, an exemplary meditation, which makes itself available to its readers as a model for the way in which this 'boundless theme extends our thought', though the apparently occasional inconsequence of the poem's title, which does not claim any exceptional authority or distinction for the poet's thought, may obscure from the modern reader the poem's public and exemplary seriousness. Exemplary poetry can, as my discussion of Aaron Hill may suggest, imply in both the poet and their readers a passive acceptance of powerlessness, a sort of shared helplessness and detachment in the face of 'New prospects, manners, tastes, beliefs, chang'd modes, / New systems', that would identify its lack of authority as a failure of control, and the first example I want to look at, the *Devout Exercises* of Elizabeth Rowe, both raises this issue and suggests that these may not be the most appropriate terms to bring to an understanding of this kind of writing.[36]

The mixture of poetry and poetical prose which make up the *Devout Exercises* was first published after Rowe's death in an edition (of 1737) supervised by Isaac Watts. Watts, in his Preface, described the response he regarded as appropriate to it: he recommended that those who read her work should:

> try how far they can speak this Language, and assume these Sentiments as their own: And by aspiring to follow them, may they find the same Satisfaction and Delight, or at least learn the profitable Lessons of Self Abasement and holy Shame: And may a noble and glorious Ambition excite in their Breasts a sacred Zeal to emulate so illustrious an Example.

This process of emulation through appropriation of the language of devotion does not depend on an understanding of their author as a representative Christian. Her piety, Watts cautions, is not the 'Test and Standard' for that of every Christian, and her devout achievements exceed even his own. Her 'secret and intense Breathings' are private, exceptional, and almost mystical, and their public function, in rendering the lives of her readers 'more holy and heavenly' through the inspiring example they offer, seems to depend, for Watts, on the perception of her language and sentiments as expressing an uncommon attainment of the common aspiration. Her devotions, and the piety

---

[36] John Gay, 'A Thought', l. 31, in *The Poetical Works of John Gay*, ed. G. C. Faber (Oxford, 1926). 'Free Thougths', p. 242.

they express, have an exemplary didactic power both as they *are* an imitable model, and as their exceptional nature, vested in the particular nature of their author's piety, places them beyond common achievement, and teaches the 'Lessons of Self Abasement and holy Shame'.[37]

Rowe's *Exercises*, then, have more in common with the representation of devotion in Thomson, the poet of retired but nevertheless potential power, and in Hill, in so far as his exemplary reverence is based in his refusal of classificatory enclosures and exclusions, than with the controlling comprehensive systems of Pope or Blackmore. Rowe's writing, as Watts is careful to emphasize, represents an extreme instance of the avoidance of authorial explanation, interpretation, or systematization that I traced in Thomson and Hill. He writes of the poetical nature of her writing:

As her Virtues were sublime, so her Genius was bright and sparkling, and the Vivacity of her Imagination had a Tincture of the Muse almost from her Childhood. This made it natural to her to express the inward Sentiments of her Soul in more exalted Language, and to paint her own Ideas in Metaphor and Rapture near a-kin to the Diction of Poesy.

Watts sees Rowe, the retired contemplative woman, not as exercising a rational, systematic power over her ideas and sentiments, but as naturally or involuntarily expressing these 'Dictates of her Heart' in the 'Language of Holy Passion': he speaks of her as *constrained* to employ 'pathetick and tender Expressions'. As a woman, and as a devotional writer who asserts with conviction: 'I dread nothing more than the Guidance of my own blind Desires; I tremble at the Thoughts of such a fatal Liberty: Avert, gracious God, that miserable Freedom', she writes a religious language of powerlessness, of acceptance, which is nevertheless not a language of passivity, for its very powerlessness becomes the sign of its purity, and the means by which it excites 'glorious Ambition' in its readers. In Rowe, lack of systematization, the absence of authority, become the guarantee of her exemplary didactic power over her readers—a power that, for Watts, reconciles the opposition between 'Self Abasement' and 'glorious Ambition'.[38]

It may sound, from this account of her writing, as though what I am describing as Rowe's exemplary power may have more to do with self-abasement than ambition, and may manifest the kind of poetic refusal of

---

[37] Isaac Watts, Preface to Elizabeth Rowe's *Devout Exercises of the Heart in Meditation and Soliloquy, Prayer and Praise* (London, 1737; this 2nd edn. 1739), pp. xxiv, xxv, x, xxv, xxiv.

[38] Watts, Preface, pp. xi–xii, xi, xiv; Rowe, *Exercises*, p. 120.

explanatory command, and the celebration of a plenitude that eludes system, that I discussed in relation to the poetry of Thomson and Hill, as uncontrolled effusion. But this judgement would, I think, underestimate the significance of Rowe's expressed desire for publication, and the importance she attaches to 'reading the Experiences of others' in strengthening her 'unbounded Desires'. Rowe's religious experiences are certainly private—they are, as Watts stresses, suitable for reading in retirement, and their exemplary power supports his own emphasis on the importance of the private conscience of the individual Christian. But it is through their privacy, in the absence of any exceptional status that Rowe feels able to claim for her experiences, that they express a tension central to much of the religious poetry of the century. Though many religious poets continue to employ the position Blackmore describes, in which the Christian poet speaks as a sort of occasional preacher, instructing and usually reprimanding his congregation, the didactic authority of this position is inappropriate either to the attempt to express the devout meditations produced by faith, or to 'kindle the Flame of Devout Love in the Heart of the lowest and most despised Christian'. Poets concerned with these issues require a kind of poetry that can express their experience of faith, both because they regard it as their duty to offer praise and thanksgiving, and because they are more concerned to spread than to correct belief, believing that the 'experimental Part of Religion has generally a greater Influence than its Theory'.[39]

Exemplary poetry attempts, then, to describe the experience of religion in terms accessible to the 'lowest and most despised Christian', to describe private experiences which are also universal, and to express an idea of God as both dwelling 'in Heights of Glory, to which no human Thought can soar, and yet . . . more near and intimate to my Soul than any of the Objects of Sense'. This attempt raises the problem for the poet of finding a voice, a language, which does not rise 'above our Ideas', but is not rooted in those 'Objects of Sense' that might define their experience as exclusively personal, rather than universally accessible: Rowe writes: 'But oh! in what Language shall I speak? with what Circumstance shall I begin? . . . Shall I speak in general of all the Nations of the Redeemed? or, to

[39] I refer to, and quote from, Rowe's letter 'To the Reverend Dr. Watts, at Newington', in *Exercises*, pp. xxvii, xxviii. Rowe is, of course, addressing primarily a polite audience, and it is the terms on which she addresses that audience, the distinctions she does or does not make within it, that concern me here.

excite my own Gratitude, shall I consider myself, my worthless self.' It is not, of course, a question she can return a direct answer to, beyond the assertion that it would be still more reprehensible to fail to speak at all, and not to share her experience of faith; but there are two implications of this repeated questioning which I want to point out here. The first is that this questioning serves to give the language of the exemplary poets a peculiarly problematic status: where Blackmore, like other proponents of the new science, could argue that by stripping his language of poetical eloquence he reveals its philosophical accuracy, its basis in the unmediated evidence of experiment, which admits no ambiguity, no interpretative uncertainty, the language of these devout exercises parades, in its 'Metaphor and Rapture', the ambivalence of its relation to general or personal experience and circumstances. It points out, as it were, that the extent to which language is controlled by the 'Guidance of my own blind Desires' may be a 'miserable Freedom' from the intentions, the meanings of God.[40]

The second implication I want to point out is that Rowe regards the expression of faith as a duty: she concludes that it is 'unutterable', that 'narrow Thoughts, and narrower Words' are defective, but she asserts that 'should Man be silent, the mute Creation would find a Voice to upbraid him'. Her language thus appears as a further form of voluntary confinement, a form of self-abasement that is the only means to further her glorious ambition. The publication of her *Devout Exercises* translates the inadequacy of 'my worthless self' into the assurance that 'Whatsoever Ardours of divine Love have been kindled in a Soul united to Flesh and Blood, may also be kindled by the same Influence of Grace in other Spirits, labouring under the same Clogs and Impediments', and gives her writing an exemplary function her 'worthless self' was powerless to assume, but could assume precisely because of its powerlessness, its lack of any defining or discriminating *worth*.[41]

This tension between worth and worthlessness, expressed in the need to redefine both the language of religious poetry and the 'self' of the religious poet, is, I want to suggest, a major preoccupation of the religious poetry of the period. It represents a move away from the causal syntax exemplified in Blackmore, where potent creativity must have a source, a cause, in primal 'vigour', and it defines its explicitness,

---

[40] Rowe, *Exercises*, p. 34. Watts, Preface, p. xiv. *Exercises*, pp. 123–4. Preface, p. xii. *Exercises*, p. 120.

[41] Rowe, *Exercises*, pp. 124, 123. Watts, Preface, pp. xxiv–xxv.

its ability to kindle the souls of a general audience, not in the authority capable of harnessing disparate discourses, but in a redefinition of the 'self' of the poet to express personal experience whose worth is identified in its readability, its ambitious capacity to speak for universal 'unbounded Desires'. Watts's claims for the *Devout Exercises* of Rowe focus, I have suggested, on her language, the manner of her expression; what she has to say is, for him, almost unimportant beside the metaphor and rapture of the exercise, the speech. Her language is not explicitly didactic in its ability to describe the hidden wonders of creation, but it is instructive in its ability to make explicit the hidden and personal ardours of the devout.[42]

VIII

Exemplary devotion does not always, of course, involve the effacement of the poet's circumstances, for these may be understood, instead, as a metaphor for the rapture of the poet. In Robert Lowth's early poem on *The Genealogy of Christ; As it is represented in the East-Window in the College Chappel at Winchester* (1729), for example, the rapturous figures are, primarily, those depicted in the stained glass of the window, while the poet acts as mediator and guide, displaying them to the audience, and it is difficult to determine whether the devotion we are invited to emulate is that of the poet, the artist, or the heroes the window portrays. The poem directs the public reverence, rather than the retired meditations, of its readers, apparently addressing them as they stand before the window it describes, and its language is therefore more appropriate to ministerial guidance than to devout breathings. Though Lowth, who went on to become Bishop of London, wrote the poem while still a schoolboy, it continued to be published in anthologies throughout his life, and it is of particular interest here not only because of the positions it describes as available to the religious poet, but because it appeared in William Dodd's *Christian's Magazine*, which also published some of Smart's poetry, in 1761, at a time at which Smart may have been particularly interested both in the general contents of that magazine and in the bishop's works, as my later chapters on *Jubilate Agno* will make clear.[43]

[42] Blackmore, *Creation*, vii. 710. Rowe, letter to Watts, *Exercises*, p. xxviii.

[43] Lowth's poem also appeared in e.g. Pearch's *Collection of Poems in Four Volumes. By Several Hands* (London, 1770); and in *Sacred and Moral Poems on Deity: Creation—*

In the opening lines of the poem, Lowth offers an account of the process by which exemplary art or poetry excites the reader to emulation:

> At once to raise our Rev'rence and Delight,
> To elevate the Mind and please the Sight;
> To pour in Virtue at th'attentive Eye,
> And waft the Soul on Wings of Ecstasie;
> For this the Painter's Art with Nature vies,
> And bids the visionary Saint arise.
> Who views the sacred Forms, in Thought aspires,
> Catches pure Zeal, and as he gazes, fires,
> Feels the same Ardor to his Breast convey'd,
> Is what he sees, and emulates the Shade.

The poet sees the viewer of the window as identified, through zeal, with 'what he sees', and poetry, which is described as 'Some emanation of her sister Muse' of painting, is similarly effective. This process does not involve the qualifications, the degrees of attainable ardour, and difference among the particular forms available to piety, that Watts entertained, but the direct transmission of the 'same Ardor', shared by the viewer and the viewed. But this process, in Lowth's poem, is made complex by the presence of the two intermediary figures of the 'visionary Saint' and the painter himself. For it is not clear in these lines whether he 'who views the sacred Forms' is the viewer of the window or the visionary saint of the preceding line. It might be the saint—perhaps the dreaming figure of Jesse—who has the vision of the sacred forms, or the saint might be the medium who makes these forms available to the viewer through his devotion. Or, of course, it might be the artist himself who, having conjured up the saint, goes on to emulate the shade of the sacred forms in his painting, and who, by pouring in 'Virtue at th'attentive Eye', excites a visionary ardour in his public.[44]

Life:—Death:—and Immortality. By the Late and Present Ld. Bishops of London And Others (3rd edn., London, 1789), the editor of which asserts that 'The productions of a MILTON, a POPE, a JOHNSON, a GRAY, a LOWTH, a PORTEOUS, and a HAWKESWORTH, can never be neglected, while Poetry is felt, or Religion reverenced' (Preface, p. vii). For an account of Lowth's career, see Brian Hepworth, *Robert Lowth* (Boston, Mass., 1978). See pp. 123–96 below.

[44] Robert Lowth, *The Genealogy of Christ* (London, 1729), 7–8. The window depicted the Tree of Jesse. The original glass was destroyed in the course of restoration work in the 19th c., but some idea of its composition can be gained from the version that replaced it.

It is worth going through these different possibilities, because the complexity they reveal, in the apparently simple act of identification the last lines describe, qualifies the nature both of the act of ministry the poet undertakes and of the emulation he advocates. The poet goes on to depict David, the most celebrated of Christ's matrilineal ancestors, and to portray in him the heroic role of the religious poet, and the relation between the poet and the inspired psalmist—the question of whether the poet here is 'what he sees', and of the terms in which he emulates David's achievement, provides a focus for the issue of Lowth's understanding of the role of the religious poet. He writes:

> And lo! the Glories of th'illustrious Line
> At their first Dawn with ripen'd Splendour shine,
> In DAVID all exprest, the Good, the Great,
> The King, the Hero, and the Man compleat.
> Serene he sits, and sweeps the golden Lyre,
> And blends the Prophet's with the Poet's Fire.
> See! with what Art he strikes the vocal Strings,
> The God, his Theme, inspiring what he sings!
> Hark—or our Ears delude us—from his Tongue
> Sweet flows, or seems to flow, some Heav'nly Song.
> O! could thine Art arrest the fleeting Sound,
> And paint the Voice in magick Numbers bound;
> Could the warm Sun, as erst when *Memnon* play'd,
> Wake with his rising Beam the vocal Shade;
> Then might *He* draw th'attentive Angels down,
> Bending to hear the Lay, so sweet, so like their own.

Here the poet's description of the artist's inability to paint the voice seems to schematize and emphasize his own distance from David. The painting is unable to translate the static virtues of the 'Man compleat' into action or music, and though the poet's own 'magick Numbers' can produce in him the possible delusion that he hears the psalmist's 'Heav'nly Song', it is not a performance his poetry can emulate.[45]

David's ideal completeness, the integrity of his character as poet, prophet, king, and hero, makes him the expression of every virtue, of all the glories of his line. He is the paradigmatic performer of devout exercises, but neither music nor poetry is here described as able to imitate his active performance, rather than his static demonstration of virtuous worship, and it is the reverence and delight of the poet, as he shares the saint's vision of David's angelic posture of adoration, that

[45] Lowth, *Genealogy*, pp. 9–10.

the reader is encouraged to emulate. It is as though, in this poem, the poet is obliged to choose between exemplary devotion which takes God as its theme and inspiration, and praise which directs our attention rather to the superior virtues of the psalmist, not his song, and he elects to make the ministerial or mediatory postures of reverence of the artist, the saint, and the psalmist the subjects of our emulation, rather than the inspired language the devout poet sings. This is a choice which illuminates a further implication of Watts's praise for the exemplary devotions of Elizabeth Rowe. For Lowth suggests that it is because David has an ideal integrity, as the 'Man compleat', that he is able to produce his 'Heav'nly Song', and be the subject of the emulation of every Christian. In Rowe, conversely, Watts perceives not a plenum of virtue but an absence. Her lack of worldly power and concerns is taken as an ideal selflessness, which makes her exercises accessible to every devout reader, and 'congenial to . . . Angels and unbodied Minds'.[46]

IX

It may be helpful if, at this stage of my argument, I attempt to summarize the different positions that I have discussed. In the first place, I have suggested that in the poetry of Pope and Blackmore, the systematization which represents variety as order attributes to the poet a degree of control that may be incompatible with the expression of religious reverence. The authority of exposition that they demonstrate in describing creation is in conflict with the need to describe God as incomprehensible, unknowable. The very discourses by which that authority is manifested—the use of the languages of the Bible or of the liturgy—also introduce into their poetry ideas which undermine their claim to authority, ideas of the imperfection of man, the mystery of God's ways and works, which imply a demand for reverence in the treatment of religious issues.

The power of exposition which poets like Pope and Blackmore assert may not be acknowledged as problematic within their own poetry, but it certainly comes to seem so when we compare their treatment of religious themes with the practice of other poets of the

[46] Watts, Preface, p. xii. See Smart, *A Song to David* (1763), stt. iv–xvi, in *The Poetical Works of Christopher Smart*, ii. *Religious Poetry 1763–1771*, ed. Marcus Walsh and Karina Williamson (Oxford, 1983; hereafter *Smart II*), and below, p. 283.

period. Thomson, I suggested, may have been able to sidestep the problem by claiming no more than a potential power, and by employing the digressive structure of Georgic, which distracts attention from the coherence or inconsistency of the explanations he offers. In Aaron Hill's poems, however, the problematic relation beween poetic authority or power and the treatment of religious issues seems to produce a poetry in which reverence entails a positive abjuration of system and control. Hill implies that a properly religious poetry must attempt to embrace variety at the expense even of syntactical control. This can look like an equation of devotion with powerlessness, with an obligation to tolerance which reveals all disagreement or inconsistency as no more than diversity of opinion, and which defines conviction or commitment as an act of appropriation, of enclosure.

This is not, however, the only path available to exemplary religious poetry, and the *Devout Exercises* of Elizabeth Rowe indicate how powerlessness can itself become a form of power, in the context of a characteristically dissenting emphasis on the value of personal experience and the expression of the self. Rowe, I suggested, achieves this resolution of power and powerlessness, and struggles, successfully in Watts's account, with the tension between the duties of silence and of expression, because as a reclusive woman she is able to achieve a sort of emptying of the self, or an expression of the self as a vacuum in which the personal and the universal can meet. The particular and exceptional nature of her self is its very selflessness, and this for Watts is the condition of its being universally accessible. But that idea of the empty self is, I think, the product of a peculiar configuration of dissent and femininity which unites 'breathings' and poetic eloquence in terms only appropriate to the retired worshipper in the closet; and Lowth's poem of exemplary devotion works, in the context of my discussion, to translate some of those terms into a more public and Anglican context.

In Lowth's poem, I suggest, the ideal emptiness of the self that Watts sees in Rowe is replaced by the ideal of the 'Man compleat', of the plenitude represented by the inaccessible example of the divinely inspired psalmist. Lowth claims for the artist and the poet, in their capacity as mediators or ministers, some of the powers of the psalmist, by claiming for them the ability to represent a rapture with which the viewer, the audience, can achieve absolute identity, as they become what they see. But Lowth is ambiguous about the extent to which he, as a poet, can enact or exemplify, rather than preceptively describe, this process, and he may defer the power to enact it to the inspired figures of the saint and the psalmist. This ambiguity is, I think, important to the reconciliation of powerful authority and exemplary devotion that the poem effects.

Now clearly this account of the poetry I have been discussing involves a range of ideas of power and authority, which are necessarily simplified in a brief summary. But the important point, for my purposes, is that the idea of power which is manifested in the ability to describe variety as order excludes, or is apparently incompatible with, that power which is characterized in terms of potency of expression, of the effects it produces in the poet's audience, and which can express an exemplary powerlessness, a humble lack of authority, and even of control. It is this issue, of the audiences addressed by poets concerned with religion, and in particular the manner in which they are addressed, which I now want to examine.

X

The exemplary writing of Lowth and Rowe is characterized by the terms in which it addresses, and invites the participation of, its audience. Clearly, there are considerable differences between the two examples I have discussed: Watts assumes that the reader will engage in the *Devout Exercises* 'when they have shut out the World, and are reading in their Retirements', whereas Lowth's audience are invited to join in contemplating the window in Winchester College Chapel. But both involve an audience of Christians whose distinctive qualities emerge as a result of their reading, and are not a precondition to it. Their virtues as Christians are reinforced by their reading, but neither text attempts to discriminate among those who read it, to suggest that some are addressed on different terms, or in different parts of the argument, and neither defines their audience by excluding sections of the Christian community (though Watts defends Rowe from the scrutiny of profane readers). This capacity of religious poetry to address a general rather than a limited audience is not confined to exemplary poetry alone, and it is common for religious poets of this period to see their subject-matter as, in some respects at least, liberating them from some of the problems of audience addressed by other genres: religious poetry, they claim, need not be dependent on patronage, on pleasing the likes and dislikes of a specific patron, for in so far as some religious poetry does possess a self-definition, it is that it is a virtuous activity in itself, appealing to a virtue in the reader which it is difficult for them to disown.[47]

The prize for religious poetry set up in the will of Thomas Seaton, which I will be discussing in my next chapter, was understood by the entrants to recognize and support this independence. John Lettice, for example, argues in his prize-winning poem of 1764 that Seaton's ghost 'Breathes nought save peace, religion, and the love / Of sacred verse', because, in promoting religious poetry, it recovers 'The chaster honours of poetic lore' and 'the dignity of ancient song'. Earlier poets had felt able to claim a similar freedom of address, though not necessarily to maintain the independence it suggested. Edward Young, in his early poem on the *Last Day* (1713), celebrates the 'deeper scene' its theme makes available to him, and writes, in the introductory paragraph of the second book:

> The Muse is wont in Narrow Bounds to sing,
> To *Teach the Swain*, or *Celebrate the King*:
> I grasp the Whole, no more to Parts confin'd,
> I lift my Voice, and sing to *Humankind*:
> I sing to Men and Angels . . .

The opportunity to address a wider audience with a freedom and (as Young suggests) universal charity which escapes the constraints of interested patronage, and the mocking condescension of Georgic, can, as I have already indicated, be understood as one of the most important considerations shaping poetry which takes religious themes as its subject-matter, and I shall look now at the work of two poets—Joseph Trapp and Edward Young—which clearly demonstrates some of the implications of this consideration.[48]

Joseph Trapp was a prominent churchman, most notable for his Lectures on Poetry, and his attacks on the danger of being 'Righteous over-much', which engaged him in often bitter controversy with the dissenters and, most notably, William Law. His poetical *Thoughts upon the Four Last Things* (1734) are addressed from the pulpit, and take up

[47] Watts, Preface, p. xxiv; Watts further distinguishes between reading as the 'Labour of the *Head*', and as the '*Exercises of the Heart*', p. xxiii. On the exclusion of unsuitable readers see pp. xiv, xviii.

[48] John Lettice, *The Conversion of St. Paul*, ll. 3–4, 7, 8, in *Cambridge Prize Poems. A Complete Collection of such English Poems as have obtained the annual premium instituted in the University of Cambridge by the Rev. T. Seaton, M.A. From the Year 1750 to the Year 1806*, 2 vols. (Cambridge, 1817), vol. i. Edward Young, *A Poem on the Last Day* (Oxford, 1713), bk. II, p. 24. See also the concluding paragraph of the Preface to Husbands's *Miscellany*.

or reflect many of the arguments—for the compatibility of religion with natural philosophy, and with the ethics of the market-place—that he had pursued with success elsewhere. His poem, he writes in the 'Advertisement to the Reader', is 'intended for the Use of All, from the Greatest to the Least', and aims to combat the 'Infidelity, and Atheism' of the age; but though Trapp suggests that these failings are common to the age, and therefore to his audience, he attempts to address this differently according to the 'Capacitys' or 'Class' of his readers. Trapp makes little or no attempt to find a language or voice appropriate to both the greatest and the least, and indeed it becomes increasingly unclear that the former are in need of reformation at all. Trapp explains that in order to avoid appearing 'intolerably flat and insipid' he has attempted 'to *entertain* the *Upper* Class of Readers', while his attitude towards 'the *Lower*' is more straightforwardly didactic: he means 'by Notes to *explain* such Passages . . . as might be *difficult*' to them. The use of notes to discriminate between different classes of readers, different audiences, was a common strategy of grammars, though, as Murray Cohen points out in his discussion of these in *Sensible Words*, there it was usual for the notes to explain to the more privileged readers the rules directed at their inferiors in the text; whereas in Trapp's poem, the '*Upper* Class' enjoy the uninterrupted entertainment offered by the text, while 'the *Lower*' receive instruction from the notes in points of 'Divinity, Philosophy, History' which the more pleasurable fluidity of the verse might have obscured from them.[49]

These different terms of address are also clearly indicated by Trapp in the arguments the poem advances. His stance, as I have said, is that of the preacher, and 'the Least', with an eye to the notes, will recognize that their pastor 'has all along quoted Chapter and Verse, as if his four *Poems* were so many *Sermons*', but in different parts of his argument he turns to address different sections of the congregation. At first, he addresses 'the Best', and assures them that the pomp of a grand funeral is no guarantee of virtue; but even here there is some

---

[49] I quote from the title of Joseph Trapp's well-known treatise on *The Nature, Folly, Sin, and Danger of being Righteous over-much* (1739; this 4th edn. London, 1739), which attacks in particular Law's *Christian Perfection*. For Law's response, see his *An Earnest and Serious Answer to Dr. Trapps's Discourse of the folly, sin and danger of being righteous over-much* (1740). Trapp, *Thoughts upon the Four Last Things: Death; Judgment; Heaven; Hell. A Poem In Four Parts* (London, 1734), Advertisement. Murray Cohen, *Sensible Words: Linguistic Practice in England 1640–1785* (Baltimore, Md., and London, 1977), 53–6.

consolation for them, as he flatters their exclusive knowledge of 'The Herald's Art! much gaz'd at, understood / By few!' He goes on to describe the Just Man, who 'Thro' the whole Moral Scheme his piercing Sight / Directs', and to illustrate his moral justice in his correct knowledge of the causes and effects described by natural philosophy, which allows him to understand the natural and the moral world 'in its native Light'. Trapp's poem was distributed free to all of his parishioners, but it cannot have been a consolation to all of them to discover that the just man 'Knows ev'n HIMSELF, knows what he *Was* and *Is*' because he has a solid grounding in the principles of the new science.[50]

Trapp later assures his readers that death is the 'Great Leveller' of the inequalities of worldly fortune:

> The Wealthy may be wretched, blest the Poor,
> Yet let not *These* presume, or be secure:
> Let not by Them, thro' Poverty's vain Pride,
> The sacred Parable be misapply'd:
> Millions of Beggars may be doom'd to Hell,
> And many Rich in *Abraham's* Bosom dwell.

This argument provided the basis for Trapp's attacks on Law and religious enthusiasm, and will be familiar to the reader of early eighteenth-century sermons; its significance for my argument lies in the way Trapp combines a confident knowledge of the commercial interests of the '*Upper* Class' of his audience in the City of London and Westminster with his interest in natural philosophy, and his pastoral position, to produce an authoritative manner which accommodates the agreement or participation of his polite audience, while it demands the acquiescence of those it instructs. Trapp's poetry seems most confident and direct, and is perhaps most successful, in those passages which are explicitly didactic, and explicitly aimed at particular sections of his audience (like the lines I have just quoted), or those where he conjures up and apostrophizes the figure of an erring auditor who is neither so specifically personified that the general audience are excluded, nor so lacking in identity that the poet seems to berate the general audience before him, rather than this intermediate figure:

---

[50] Trapp, *Last Things*, Advertisement. 'Death', ll. 64–5, 150–1, 151, 152; cf. Pope's *Essay on Man*, epistle IV, ll. 327–40, and *Windsor-Forest* (1913), ll. 235–56; but the natural philosophy seen as necessary to happiness or virtue in these passages is a more general knowledge of nature.

'Rejoice, O Young Man, in thy Youth; Rejoice, / But still with Innocence: Hear Nature's Voice, / But Nature uncorrupt . . .'. Here his manner is assured, and his language, as the notes painstakingly point out, directly biblical, and this use of the language of the Bible appears to allow the poet to ignore and thus erase the distinctions within his audience that his use of the parable of Dives and Lazarus, or his praise of heraldry, for example, had depended on.[51]

The juxtaposition of these two different kinds of address, implying a unified or a divided audience, however, raises tensions or difficulties which, I think, reveal the limitations and inflexibility of the authority the preacher-poet claims. He describes himself as an exemplary figure, capable of physical and emotional as well as financial self-restraint, and, through his use of a biblical language that is exemplary and instructive, he attributes to himself the capacity to speak for his general audience. In, for example, his thoughts on 'Heaven', he writes:

> Alas! how vain is This Poetick Paint,
> Fancy's fond Imag'ry! how weak, how faint!
> What is with Innocence delightful Here
> We raise to Heav'n, and dream it must be There.
> Perhaps it may—But whether So, or Not;
> 'Tis That, or Better—What no human Thought
> Can figure, or conceive . . .

Here he claims to participate in what the general audience dream, and his inability to conceive of heaven is described as a common human failing. But it is, I want to suggest, as much because of the shared and general nature of the experience he describes as because of the nature of this subject-matter that he here loses the confident authority that usually characterizes his thoughts. He does, after all, devote a whole book to the subject of heaven, but in these lines, confronted with a problem which he acknowledges to be universal, he seems unable to accomplish the transition to a poetry of exemplary humility and reverence, and to abandon the authority that defines his position as the preacher-poet.

The biblical language of the poem raises the issue of human fallibility, but while Trapp acknowledges this as human or common when he addresses his audience as a whole, the terms in which he does so reproduce and reinforce the division within his audience, indicated

---

[51] Trapp, 'Death', ll. 437–42. See e.g. the arguments against spiritual pride in *Righteous over-much*, pp. 31–2. *Last Things*, Advertisement. 'Death', ll. 562–4.

by the physical arrangement of the text and notes of his poem: all humanity may be fallible, but there is not much that is common in the manifestations of that fallibility. Thus, for example, he tells his congregation that the unforgivable sins include 'The Poor's Profuseness, th'Unprovok'd man's Rage, / The Avarice of Youth, the Lust of Age.' Rage, avarice, and lust appear to be general sins, common to the audience as a whole, but there is no suggestion of inconsistency in the rebuke to the poor for a profuseness or excessive hospitality which (in their youth) might be thought to conflict with their tendency towards avarice, for in his poem the generous biblical categories—of Young Men, or of Age—turn out not to apply to a united and homogeneous congregation but to distinguish further categories within its divided composition.[52]

Trapp's *Thoughts* attempt to combine the manners appropriate to didactic and to exemplary poetry, to offer a systematic account of creation, and to claim an exemplary humility and reverence for the poet, by distinguishing between the audiences appropriate to these different kinds of poetry. But the biblical language which is common to these, and which serves to indicate the position from which the poet might achieve this feat, confuses the clear distinctions between different passages of the poem—in implying for example that the poor might also be young men—and this produces in the poet an uncertainty of manner which undermines his authority while denying him the possibility of exemplary reverence. While in his treatment of, for example, the parable of Lazarus and Dives, Trapp does seem to achieve at once the reassurance of his polite audience, and a rebuke to those of lesser capacities, he cannot succeed in erasing the traditional moral of the parable, and nor can he abandon the authoritative position that makes that moral unacceptable to him.

The inflexible authority of Trapp's manner provides a strong contrast to Young's use of the freedoms afforded by the diverse audience he claims for his *Last Day*, and it is, I think, in terms of this contrast that we can best understand the extraordinary success of Young's poetry in the eighteenth century, as well as, perhaps, its lack of readers today. For in Young's poetry the range and diversity of his audience is matched by the flexibility of the poet's approach, the mobility of the positions he defines for himself. Young's *The Complaint, or Night-Thoughts* is of course his most important and influential poem,

---

[52] Trapp, 'Judgement', l. 436. 'Heaven', ll. 98–104. 'Judgement', ll. 497–8. See Johnson, *Dictionary*, 'Profuseness', *n. s.*

but before I go on to discuss it, I want to look at his earlier *Poem on the Last Day*, which introduces, in a less diffuse form, some of the characteristic features of his poetry. I have suggested that Trapp's *Thoughts* fail to find a mode of address, a manner, suited to all rather than a part of their audience, and perhaps the most significant achievement of Young's poetry is its success in finding a manner capable of expressing both authoritative and privileged statement, and retired and provisional meditation, the 'thoughts' both of the pulpit and of solitude.

Young's *Last Day*, as I have pointed out, claims all of '*Humankind*' as its audience, and, in the following passage, in which the poet distinguishes his own ambitions from those of his muse, he defines the meaning of this designation in terms that also illuminate the manner he sees as appropriate to its address:

> Since Adam's Family, from First to Last,
> Now into One distinct Survey is cast,
> Look round Vainglorious Muse, and You whoe'er
> Devote your selves to Fame, and think her Fair,
> Look round, and View the Lights of human Race,
> Whose shining Acts Time's brightest Annals grace;
> Who founded Sects; Crowns conquer'd, or resign'd;
> Gave names to Nations; or fam'd Empires joyn'd;
> Who rais'd the Vale, and laid the Mountain low;
> And taught obedient Rivers where to flow;
> Who with vast Fleets, as with a mighty Chain,
> Cou'd bind the Madness of the roaring Main:
> All Lost? all undistinguisht? no where Found?
> How will this Truth in *Bourbon's* Palace Sound?

A distinct survey is not, I take it, one survey as distinct from any other, but a survey which is 'capable of making clear distinctions', of representing the human race as one body made up of many differentiated members. The muse is invited to particularize and divide that body, as the first example, 'Who founded Sects', suggests, but finds that, though the individual members are distinct, they are not distinguished by their particular achievements: they are united in a religious apprehension which is common, universal, and though it is particular to each one of them it does not particularize them. The address appropriate to this distinct but undistinguished race is, paradoxically, personal, with 'but few touches of personal character'. In this context the poet's humility, his personal confessions of inadequacy, license the authority with which he speaks as available to 'Man', who can 'View the whole Earth's vast Landskip Unconfin'd, / Or view in *Britain* all her Glories joyn'd'. His authority and humility are based in the exemplary perceptions of piety, in his use of personal confession as the intimate but common response to God. The poet assumes that the 'hidden Treasures' of the heart are distinct but undistinguished, hidden and personal, but universal, and it is this claim that validates the didactic authority of his concluding injunction: 'Think deeply then, O Man, how Great Thou art, / Pay thyself Homage with a trembling Heart.' The paradox, the opposition of greatness and subservience the poet invites man to recognize in himself, is also the basis of the poet's claim to 'sing to *Humankind*'.[53]

This paradox is, of course, similar to the opposition I described Trapp as unable to resolve or to maintain in his *Thoughts*, but in Young's poem, the problems that Trapp had attributed to the composition of his audience are firmly appropriated to the first person of the poet-narrator, and barely disturb the assured movement of his verse. He exclaims, for example, with an almost Milton-like confidence:

> I behold (but mortal Sight
> Sustains not such a rushing Sea of Light!)
> I see on an Empyreal flying Throne
> Awfully rais'd Heaven's Everlasting Son;
> Crown'd with that Majesty, which form'd the World,
> And the Grand Rebel flaming downward hurl'd.

Here, the hesitation suggested in the 'but' of the first of the lines, the possibility that he would behold these things *except* that mortal sight cannot, does not prevent the poet from going on to give a fairly lengthy description of Christ, which reveals the meaning of that 'but' as a more guarded but unrestrictive 'unless'. The poet moves easily, and with the 'equability and propriety' that Johnson praised in the poem, between a position of impossible authority, and an apparently vindicating humility.

Young defines for the poet a narrative manner that can claim with authority, 'I grasp the Whole, no more to Parts confin'd', and can represent his successive humility as a part of that whole, and as a

---

[53] Young, *Last Day*, bk. III, p. 55. *OED*, 'Distinct', *ppl. a. (sb.)*, 3e. Revd John Mitford, 'The Life of Edward Young', in *The Poetical Works of Edward Young*, 2 vols. (London, 1906), vol. i, p. xxxvii. *Last Day*, bk. I, pp. 3, 4; bk. III, p. 73; bk. II, p. 24.

necessary underpinning to that confident power. He writes, following his description of the day of judgement:

> Such is the Scene, and one short Moment's space
> Concludes the Hopes, and Fears of human Race.
> Proceed who dares, I tremble, as I write;
> The Whole Creation swims before my Sight:
> I see, I see the judges frowning Brow,
> Say not 'tis distant, I behold it *Now*;
> I Faint, my tardy Blood forgets to flow,
> My Soul recoils at the Stupendous Woe;
> That Woe, those Pangs which from the guilty breast
> In these, or Words like these shall be Exprest.

Here the apparently personal and private confession of weakness, 'I tremble, as I write', serves both to stress the poet's humanity—his stance is not judgemental, not superhuman—and to license the assertion of the prophetic present that follows: 'I behold it *Now*'. The transition from fear to authority, from hesitation to certainty, appears sudden, and it thus bears the hallmark of biblical sublimity, but it does not appear awkward or disruptive, as it might have done in Trapp's hands, for the urgency of the poet's apparent emotion, his apparently irresistible and spontaneous urge to share the vision his meditations produce, remains insistently constant.[54]

The *Last Day* was described by Johnson as Young's 'first great performance', and despite his distrust of devotional poetry, he awarded it qualified praise. Herbert Croft, the friend who contributed the bulk of the 'Life of Young', noted that it won the approval of the ministry, perhaps largely for political reasons, but it certainly seems to have marked the beginning of Young's career as a successful poet.[55] I think that we can best understand the poem's success in terms of the manner in which it presents the poet, for it is Young's ability, developed as we shall see in the *Night-Thoughts*, to present the first person of his poetry as distinct but undistinguished, as representative and even publicly authoritative as a result of his privacy, that, I suggest, won him a large audience in the eighteenth century, and marks his contribution to the development of a religious poetry in the period.

---

[54] Young, *Last Day*, bk. II, p. 37. Johnson, 'Young', *Lives*, ii. 457. *Last Day*, bk. II, p. 24; bk. III, p. 61.

[55] Johnson, 'Young', *Lives*, ii. 457. Croft comments that the poem 'is not without a glance to politicks, notwithstanding the subject. The cry that the church was in danger, had not yet subsided. The *Last Day*, written by a layman, was much approved by the ministry, and their friends' (p. 421).

XI

Young's *Night-Thoughts* was extremely well received in the eighteenth century—Boswell's admiring judgement that it is 'a mass of the grandest and richest poetry that human genius has ever produced' is typical of the order of praise it received—and its example dominated religious poetry throughout the second half of the century. We can, I think, best understand this success in the context of the issues I have discussed in this chapter: in terms of its exemplary or preceptive strategies, its unsystematic but authoritative power, and its representation of the mutually defining relations of poet and reader; but the two qualities of the poem which distinguish it most markedly from the *Last Day*, and which I should mention first, are its lack of any continuous theme, and its use of blank verse rather than the heroic couplet— qualities that are, as Johnson acknowledged, interrelated. Johnson compares the poem to a Chinese plantation, which similarly possesses 'the magnificence of vast extent and endless diversity', and argues that 'diffusion of sentiments, and . . . digressive sallies of imagination, would have been compressed and restrained by confinement to rhyme'. He finds that, apparently as a result of the combination of diversity and blank verse, 'particular lines are not to be regarded; the power is in the whole'. Johnson allows the poem an extraordinary liberty in terms of its theme, and his disregard for 'particular lines' seems also to involve a disregard for the qualities which made the 'power . . . in the whole' praiseworthy and, indeed, powerful, and the 'detail' contributed by Herbert Croft offers us rather more critical edge on the poem than Johnson's description of its 'magnificence'. Croft refers to 'Young's art, which displayed itself so wonderfully . . . in the *Night-Thoughts*, of making the publick a party in his private sorrow', and it is this 'art', capable of resolving the tension between the modes of address suited to the public audience and private occasion, that gives the poem its power—a power that can be accurately described as residing 'in the whole', in that it is expressed in the whole narrative strategy of the poem.[56]

[56] James Boswell, *Life of Johnson*, 3 vols. (Dublin, 1792), iii. 226. Johnson, 'Young', *Lives*, ii. 458, 418, 458. On the reception and influence of the *Night-Thoughts* see R. D. Havens, *The Influence of Milton on English Poetry* (Cambridge, Mass., 1922), and Croft's aside: 'none who has read the *Night Thoughts*, and who has not read them? . . .' ('Young', *Lives*, ii. 435). See also David B. Morris, *The Religious Sublime: Christian Poetry and Critical Tradition in Eighteenth-Century England* (Lexington, Ky., 1972), 149 ff.

The primary characteristic of the poet of the *Night-Thoughts* is that he belongs to the night. The poet is represented as sleepless for nine consecutive nights—the 'nights' or books of the poem—and the inspiration afforded by darkness (described in the *Last Day* as the 'Gloom of solemn Night' which 'To sacred thought may forcibly invite') is frequently invoked. Young also announced in the Preface to Night 1 that 'As the Occasion of this Poem was *real*, not *fictitious*, so the method pursued in it, was rather *imposed*, by what spontaneously arose in the author's mind, on that occasion, than *meditated*, or *designed* . . . the facts mentioned did naturally pour these moral reflections on the thought of the writer.' These two features, that the poem is understood as a spontaneous and almost involuntary reaction to a real historical event, and that it seeks the inspiration of 'Silence and Darkness' when the poet is apparently troubled by a bout of insomnia as a result of his bereavement, seem initially to place the poem firmly in a private sphere.[57]

The audience are invited to become 'a party' in a particular and identifiable situation, the private status of which is confirmed by the colloquial tone of our introduction to the first-person narrator: 'From short (as usual) and disturb'd Repose, / I wake.' At first we seem invited almost to overhear the poem as we may overhear, or gain an ostensibly illicit access to, the soliloquies of Shakespeare's tragedies, and indeed the poet seems to draw our attention to the potential relevance of this comparison from the outset:

> I wake: How happy they, who wake no more!
> Yet that were vain, if Dreams infest the Grave.
> I wake, emerging from a Sea of Dreams
> Tumultuous . . .

The language of these opening passages seems closer to that of Hamlet's most famous soliloquy than to that of Milton's *Paradise Lost*. The poet is alone, and speaks to darkness, but this 'soliloquy' does not resemble that of the poet of Gray's *Elegy*, who speaks 'to darkness, and to me'; for the speaker in the *Night-Thoughts* almost immediately abandons any air of quiet intimacy: he invokes silence and darkness, but also, and in more ambitious language, the God of creation, and his '*moral reflections*' almost immediately acknowledge the presence of his

---

[57] Young, *Last Day*, bk. II, p. 45. Young, *The Complaint: or, Night-Thoughts on Life, Death and Immortality. A New Edition, Corrected by the Author* (1742–6; this corrected edn. 1755, hereafter *N-T*), Preface, p. iii; Night 1, p. 2.

audience in their preceptive tone, and, more ambiguously, in the use of the first-person plural:

> The Bell strikes *One*. We take no Note of Time,
> But from its Loss. To give it then a Tongue,
> Is wise in Man.[58]

This apparently private and particular tone of address is sufficiently pervasive to have caused some problems for the poem's readers. Croft, like other eighteenth-century commentators, devotes a considerable proportion of his discussion of the poem to the question of the particular identity of Lorenzo, the sinner the narrator attempts to reform, and to the problem of the relation of the three bereavements mentioned in the poem to the details of Young's life. But the poet's nocturnal and retired stance draws on a tradition which identifies the private with more than the particular, local, and partial. Such a stance can, for example, license an abnegation of the potential authority of the poet—it allows Cowper to employ his poetic skill on the lowly, and apparently trivial theme of the sofa: it can also afford the poet a detachment, a privileged disinterestedness, which can claim to transcend any particular distractions or partisan interests and elevate the poet to a perspective from which he might view the whole. It affords Cowper the authority that can assert 'God made the country, and man made the town', and it is comparable to the retirement that allows the poet of the *Seasons* to make a comprehensive survey while continually deferring the question of the explanatory source of that comprehension. We can trace the development of this potential of the retired narrator in both Thomson and Cowper—in, specifically, the tradition which exploits the potential ambiguity or ambivalence of the Miltonic style to express apparently inconsistent or incongruous views in the context of a digressive and discursive poetic structure; and though the use of this form is clearly related to the georgic tradition, in Young's *Night-Thoughts* the relation between this discursive tradition and the poetical religious meditation assumes greater prominence. The poem displays the influence of Pope, and, more markedly, of the lessons of pulpit oratory, but the debt to Milton that it also demonstrates owes as much to 'Il Penseroso' as to the impersonal authority of *Paradise Lost*.[59]

[58] *N-T*, Night 1, p. 1. Gray, 'Elegy Written in a Country Churchyard', l. 4, in *The Poems of Gray, Collins and Goldsmith*, ed. Roger Lonsdale (London, 1969). *N-T*, Preface, p. iii; Night 1, p. 3.
[59] William Cowper, *The Task* (1785), bk. I, l. 749, in *Poetical Works*, ed. H. S. Milford,

The apparently private position of the poet of the *Night-Thoughts* affords him a 'mental Liberty' which is comparable to the freedom of fancy Cowper enjoys in his retired 'Winter Evening'. It allows him the licence implied in his description of the pleasures of contemplation:

> Dazl'd, o'erpow'r'd, with the delicious Draught
> Of miscellaneous Splendors, how I reel
> From Thought to Thought, inebriate, without End!

And it also affords him access to those 'visionary Vales' and 'prophetic Glooms' where the poet of *The Seasons* hoped to see 'Angel-Forms athwart the solemn Dusk'. His retirement allows him the philosophical detachment necessary to the investigation of the miscellaneous, the independence that can 'Tour thro' *Nature's* universal Orb' in the night sky, and thus perceive that

> *Nature* delineates her whole Chart at large,
> On soaring Souls, that sail among the Spheres;
> And *Man* how purblind, if unknown the Whole!

This ability to know 'the Whole' of, at least, the *natural* system from a position of privacy rather than of social eminence, may support Joseph Warton's report that 'Young wrote his Night Thoughts in direct opposition to Pope's view of life in his Essay on Man', for though their descriptions of the comprehensive gaze are often similar, in Young this forms part of a religious discourse which values solitude rather than society on the basis of the assurance, created by the exemplary and pathetic power of retired devotion, that the social world fosters accidental and distracting accretions which obscure the underlying unity and common purpose described by the 'whole Chart'. Thus in Young, the blindness to the whole that appeared as the *felix culpa* of Pope's scheme becomes the sign of a reprehensible failure to take advantage of retired detachment. Where in Pope's *Essay* the comprehensive view had charted the economic and social relations of man, and supported the privileged position of a powerful aristocracy, in Young it produces a poetry whose 'miscellaneous Splendors', and lack of system, or structure, reflect the sense in which the 'whole Chart' the poet surveys depends for its wholeness and its unity on the exclusion or marginalization of social and economic factors. Those factors might

rev. Norma Russell (London, 1971). See e.g. *Seasons*, 'Winter', ll. 572–616. See also John Sitter, *Literary Loneliness in Mid-Eighteenth-Century England* (Ithaca, NY, 1982), ch. 5.

disrupt, or serve to question the privileged status of the nocturnal solitude on which the poet's capacity to perceive the whole depends, and they might also reveal the system informing his apparently spontaneous digressions. They might, in other words, demand that the consistency of the poet's ability to evade system while grasping unity be made explicit in social as opposed to personal, retired, and implicit terms.[60]

The privacy of the narrator of the *Night-Thoughts* does not, however, exclude the public world from his poetry entirely. As Croft noted, 'Of the *Night-Thoughts*, notwithstanding their author's professed retirement, all are inscribed to great or to growing names.' These addresses employ a kind of social command, an urgency of interruption into public affairs, that is authorized by the universality of the poet's private concerns: he writes, for example:

> A Much-indebted Muse, O YORKE, intrudes.
> Amid the Smiles of Fortune, and of Youth
> Thine Ear is patient of a serious Song.
> How deep-implanted in the Breast of Man
> The Dread of Death? I sing its sov'reign Cure.

Here, the poet adopts an almost sermonizing manner, but he does not immediately proceed with the contemplation of death that he seems to promise. He goes on, instead, to talk about his own ambitions and his exemplary resignation and acceptance of his failure to find a remunerative and appreciative patron. This passage of the poem, movingly describing the poet's lack of worldly ambition, and his happiness with the shed, plank, or hut that his humble aspirations have secured, makes his address to Yorke, even if it is only addressed to the common 'Breast of Man' in him, slightly puzzling and incongruous. The juxtaposition, certainly, provoked the mockery of those familiar with Young's 'frequent complaints of being neglected', and this uneasiness reflects the difficulty for the poet of representing the social world as included within his 'whole Chart': a difficulty that seems almost the mirror image of the problems raised by the intrusive presence of religious discourses in the *Essay on Man*.[61]

The poet of the *Night-Thoughts* is, however, able unhesitatingly to

---

[60] *N-T*, Night 5, p. 83. See *Task*, bk. IV, ll. 36–310. Night 9, p. 256. *Seasons*, 'Autumn', ll. 1031, 1032, 1033. Night 9, p. 243. Warton quoted in Mitford, 'Life of Young', in *Poetical Works*, vol. i, p. xxxvii n.

[61] Johnson, 'Young', *Lives*, ii. 442. *N-T*, Night 4, p. 52. Croft, in Johnson, 'Young', *Lives*, ii. 454.

assume the pastoral and preceptive function of the preacher: a role which he describes as justifying his persuasive use of a form that might be seen as lacking in gravity, as well as the passionate didacticism of his arguments:

> Ye sons of Earth! (nor *willing* to be more!)
> Since *Verse* you think from Priestcraft somewhat free,
> Thus, in an Age so gay, the Muse plain Truths
> (Truths, which, at Church, you *might* have heard in Prose)
> Has ventur'd into Light; well-pleas'd the Verse
> Should be forgot, if you the Truths retain;
> And crown her with your Welfare, not your Praise.

In this address to the general congregation of mankind—for the poet explains to Lorenzo that all men are subject to the folly of worldliness—the discriminating factors of fortune and age that had made the appeal to Yorke intrusive seem no longer to pose any difficulty, perhaps because the poet does now address an audience he understands as too general to be defined in terms of these distinctions, but also—he suggests more directly—because of the nature of the plain truths he has to relate. The poet suggests here that he speaks an almost transparent language, and that the truths he has to deliver will be memorable at the expense of, or as he suggests elsewhere in spite of, the manner of their expression: the same truths, he observes, could have been heard in the public oratory of the sermon.[62]

The poet describes the truths he impresses on the elusively particular but representative figure of Lorenzo, to whom most of the poem is addressed, in similarly self-effacing terms. He writes:

> . . . in his Ear, and level'd at his Heart,
> I've half read o'er the Volume of the Skies.
> For think not Thou hast heard all This from *me*;
> My Song but echoes what Great *Nature* speaks.

He claims that his presence, his powers of exposition, interpretation or systematization barely intervene between his audience and the language of plain truth and nature: he claims, in effect, that his poetry includes and transcends all discourses—of patriotism, or of Newtonian science, for example—in its ability to express the truths accessible to nocturnal solitude. His poetry emulates the universal and asocial language of nature, which he describes in the ninth Night:

[62] *N-T*, Night 8, p. 233.

                                    'Tis Unconfin'd
         To *Christian* Land, *or Jewry*; fairly writ,
         In Language universal, to MANKIND:
         A Language, Lofty to the Learn'd; yet Plain
         To Those that feed the Flock, or guide the Plough
         Or, from its Husk, strike out the bounding Grain.
         A Language, worthy the GREAT MIND, that speaks!
         Preface, and *Comment*, to the *Sacred Page!*

This 'Stupendous Book' is legible to all: 'who *runs*, may *read* : / Who
reads, can *understand*'; but the insomniac poet has been able to study it
with more care because it is 'open'd, NIGHT! by Thee'. The task of the
poet, in the *Night-Thoughts*, is not so much to explain how the
miscellaneous splendours he describes can be perceived as a whole
chart, but to direct the attention of the audience, either through the
exemplary power of the pathetic, or through the authoritative
didacticism of the poetic pulpit, to the self-explanatory language of
nature, and the apparently self-effacing posture in which that language
can best be read. It is to this end that the poet employs the
intermediary figure of Lorenzo, and explains to him the terms on
which he can become a fit audience for the poem, and can, like the
poet, perceive the chart it reveals.[63]
   The poet writes that despite the accessibility of the divine language
of nature to mankind, Lorenzo is 'Unskill'd, or dis-inclin'd, to read it',
and he recommends that Lorenzo acquire the necessary skill in this
way:

         Such Proof insists on an attentive Ear;
         'Twill not make One amid a Mob of Thoughts,
         And, for thy Notice, struggle with the World.
         Retire;—The *World* shut out;—Thy Thoughts call Home:—
         Imagination's airy Wing repress;—
         Lock up thy *Senses*:—Let no *Passion* stir;—
         Wake all to *Reason*:—Let *her* reign alone;
         Then, in thy *Soul*'s deep Silence, and the Depth
         Of *Nature*'s Silence, Midnight, thus inquire,
         As *I* have done; . . .
            'What am I? and from *Whence?*—I nothing know,
         But that I *am* . . .

---

[63] *N-T*, Night 9, p. 283; cf. S. T. Coleridge, 'Frost at Midnight' (1798). ll, 59–64.
Night 9, p. 273.

Whatever seems to specify Lorenzo, to identify him as a particular man—the clues in the poem whereby some eighteenth-century readers tried to identify him—are, for the poet, the accidental accretions of worldliness, which make Lorenzo a 'Figure', not a member of mankind, and which the retirement he recommends would strip away:

> Deny'd the public Eye, the public Voice,
> As if he liv'd on others Breath, he dies.
> Fain would he make the World his Pedestal;
> Mankind the Gazers, the sole Figure, He.

Lorenzo here 'dreams himself ascending in his Fall', much as Young's readers apparently mistakenly dreamed him the 'sole Figure', the identifiable anti-hero, of the poem, and the poet attempts to invert the scale of these heroic qualities, in imitation of Christ the paradigm, 'Who sees the Creation's Summit in a Vale'. He admonishes Lorenzo:

> Dost grasp at Greatness? First, know what it is:
> Think'st thou thy Greatness in Distinction lies?
> Not in the Feather, wave it e'er so high,
> By *Fortune* stuck, to mark us from the Throng,
> Is Glory lodg'd: 'Tis lodg'd in the Reverse;
> In that which joins, in that which equals, All,
> The Monarch, and his Slave;—'A Deathless Soul,
> Unbounded Prospect, and Immortal Kin,
> A Father God, and Brothers in the Skies:'

This inversion of heroic distinction, this finding of identity in its abandonment, is, of course, particularly appropriate to the religious poem, and we can perhaps trace an allusion in this passage to Christ's abjuration of his earthly family as they represent a limiting definition of his significance.[64]

It is, however, also apparent that the good man, as he is depicted in this account of glory and greatness, is not himself a monarch or a slave: he is capable of giving bounty, though he conceals its source, and of enjoying a privacy which can exclude the world. Like the gentlemen and patriots of *The Seasons*, he possesses 'An Eye impartial, and an even Scale', and he must have a breadth of vision that suggests social as well as spiritual greatness:

> The Mind that would be *happy*, must be *great*:
> Great, in its *Wishes*; Great, in its *Surveys*.

[64] *N-T*, Night 9, pp. 266–7. Night 8, pp. 197, 198. Night 9, p. 278. Night 8, pp. 195–6.

> Extended Views a narrow Mind extend;
> Push out its corrugate, expansive Make,
> Which, ere-long, *more* than Planets shall embrace.
> A Man of *Compass* makes a Man of *Worth*;
> *Divine* contemplate, and become *Divine*.

If Lorenzo is to emulate the good man, and to share the vision of wholeness perceived by the poet, he must retreat from the world into a solitude and nocturnal invisibility that is represented as asocial, but which, in so far as it depends on '*Compass*', is also defined in terms of a recognizable social position.[65]

In so far as the poet succeeds in addressing the retired Lorenzo, he suggests that he succeeds in addressing every man, in a manner which recognizes no distinctions, but 'which joins, in that which equals, All'. Young attempts to address that shared 'deep Silence' of soul and nature with the voice of reason, which exclaims '*Believe* a GOD', and '*Reason* heard, is the sole Mark of Man'; he speaks to a common identity of which he partakes. His success in this attempt is illustrated by an anecdote from the diary of Frances Burney:

> Young, he (Mr. Fairly) said, was an author not to read on regularly, but to dip into, and reflect upon, in times of solitude and sadness. Nevertheless he opened and read.
> What a nobleness of expression, when noble, has this poet! what exquisite feeling! what forcible ideas!—I forgot, while I listened, all my own little troubles and disturbances.

Mr Fairly's response indicates that Young's copiousness is not necessarily seen as disadvantageous, and that he has succeeded in prescribing the conditions on which the poem should be read: he regards the poem as suitable to solitude, rather than to sociable appreciation; and Fanny Burney's appreciation of the poem's 'forcible ideas' recognizes its sublimity, and its power to address something in the reader beyond their own particular circumstances.[66]

Mr Fairly suggests that the poem is not suitable for reading in society, and is particularly adapted to 'times of . . . sadness', and it is in spite of these qualities that he and Fanny Burney are able to share the experience of appreciating it. For Young argues that in order to find

---

[65] *N-T*, Night 8, p. 217. Night 9, p. 265.
[66] *N-T*, Night 9, p. 268. *Diaries and Letters of Madame D'Arblay*, ed. Charlotte Barrett (7 vols., 1842–6; this edn. 4 vols., London, 1981; hereafter Burney, *Diaries*), iii. 165.

'Real Greatness', that portion of man which we may judge, and on which we may 'impose their Name', or identity, we must:

> Of Fortune's *Fucus* strip them, yet alive;
> Strip them of Body, too; nay, closer still,
> Away with all, but *Moral*, in their Minds . . .

What remains is obviously hard to define, but God, Young asserts, delights in 'An Humble Heart', and he implies, recognizes true nobility in 'The private Path, the secret Acts of Men'. The community of souls which houses greatness and glory for Young seems only achievable by the desocialization of man, for each man must '*Retire*:— The *World* shut out', in order to find the portion of himself that partakes of that community.

It is difficult to translate this conception of a retired spiritual communion into the terms of a socialized public virtue, as Young's representation of 'the *Man Immortal*' shows:

> With Aspect mild, and elevated Eye,
> Behold him seated on a Mount serene,
> Above the Fogs of *Sense*, and *Passion*'s Storm;
>
> . . . .
>
> *Earth*'s genuine Sons, the Sceptred, and the Slave
> A mingl'd Mob! a wand'ring Herd! he sees,
> Bewilder'd in the Vale; in All unlike!
> His full Reverse in All! What higher Praise?
> What stronger Demonstration of the Right?

If the virtue of the 'Man on Earth devoted to the skies' is demonstrated by his opposition to all '*Earth*'s genuine Sons', then the possibility of communion is perhaps held out by the example of the shared appreciation of Mr Fairly and Fanny Burney: each reader in retirement (or at least in metaphorically retired detachment) might partake of the communal vision the poem offers.[67]

This possibility would, however, involve, I think, recognizing the poem's narrator as its 'hero'. For his language does not have the impersonality of Milton's; it attempts to address the readers' ears and hearts as well as their souls, and to address a specific occasion as well as to fulfil a more general function. The conclusion of the poem,

---

[67] *N-T*, Night 8, pp. 196, 197. See Young, *Conjectures on Original Composition* (London, 1759), where the private path is seen as that of the 'Original' and Young argues that 'All Eminence, and Distinction, lies out of the beaten road; Excursion and Deviation, are necessary to find it; and the more remote your Path from the Highway, the more reputable . . .' (pp. 22–3; see also pp. 37, 55). Night 8, p. 214.

indeed, is saved from the embarrassing implications of the precept that 'Man is responsible for *Ills* receiv'd' by its insistence on the particular and personal nature of its theme:

> My Change of *Heart* a Change of Style demands;
> The CONSOLATION cancels the COMPLAINT,
> And makes a Convert of my guilty Song.

Here Young returns to the theme of bereavement that had informed the first four 'nights' of the poem, and, in doing so, limits its appeal to those 'times of . . . sadness' that had further qualified Mr Fairly's solitary and irregular 'dips' into the poem.[68]

XII

This personal and occasional aspect of the poet's theme and manner might make him the 'hero' of the poem in the sense in which the poet can be understood as the 'hero', the protagonist, of *The Task*, where the eye of the retired poet lends a unity to what might otherwise seem an aimless series of digressions from an absent central theme. But the *Night-Thoughts* is not as personal, and occasionally intimate, as Cowper's *Task*: the poet may assure us of the spontaneity and genuine passion of his verse, but he does not introduce us to his pet hare, or invite us to admire his cucumbers. The poet of the *Night-Thoughts* exploits the liberty offered by a retired stance, which licenses the mind that 'riots thro' the Luxuries of Thought', while attempting to preserve an authoritative tone and privileged perspective that are magisterial rather than riotous. The difficulty of maintaining these two positions is reflected in the tension between the poem's digressive structure and thematic coherence: the poem strives to be both unconstrained *Night-Thoughts*, and a narrative that advances towards resolution and closure—*The Complaint and the Consolation*.[69]

This tension can be described in terms of the two incompatible positions which the *Night-Thoughts* attempts to maintain, and which dominate Anglican religious poetry. The poem attempts to maintain the liberty of private conscience, but it also represents a didactic attempt to regulate and govern the consciences of those it addresses: it

---

[68] *N-T*, Night 9, pp. 239, 240.

[69] Young justifies the passion of his poem in terms that emphasize the universal and public, rather than intimate and exclusive, nature of his poetic emotion: 'Oh ye cold-hearted, frozen, Formalists! / On such a Theme, 'tis impious to be calm; / Passion is reason, Transport, Temper, *here*' (*N-T*, Night 4, p. 71). *N-T*, Night 9, p. 255.

attributes a magisterial authority to the poet, which depends on, but is incompatible with, the private and retired nature of his meditations. This paradox, in so far as it is successfully contained, describes the achievement of the *Night-Thoughts*, but, in so far as its opposing elements are not reconciled, it may also describe its failure. The terms in which Young attempts this reconciliation, which I have indicated in the characterization of Lorenzo, are further illuminated by the contrast between the *Night-Thoughts* and Cowper's *Task*.

The poetic styles of Young's *Night-Thoughts* and Cowper's *Task* are strikingly different, and yet both poems are written in versions of Miltonic blank verse. It has often been said that the verse of the *Night-Thoughts* is hardly Miltonic, and, for some critics, perhaps hardly verse at all: it is choppy and aphoristic, and often falls into something like unrhymed couplets. The poet himself, in some of the passages I have quoted, seems to suggest that his verse is little more than prose made more palatable, sugared with metre; but he is not always so self-deprecating:

> Think'st thou, LORENZO! to find Pastimes here?
> No guilty Passion blown into a Flame,
> No Foible flatter'd, Dignity disgrac'd,
> No Fairy Field of Fiction, all on Flow'r,
> No Rainbow Colours, *here*, or silken Tale:
> But solemn *Counsels*, Images of Awe,
> *Truths*, which Eternity lets fall on Man
> With double Weight, thro' these revolving Spheres,
> This Death-deep Silence, and incumbent Shade.

Young strives for a 'double-Weight' that is far removed from Cowper's 'pleasure in poetic pains': Cooper's verse has an appearance of ease, a remarkable fluency, that stems in part from his command of syntactical complexity. Here, his brief announcement of the poet's pleasure is followed by a sentence seventeen and a half lines long, and even if this were syntactically simple, it would represent an achievement, and a notion of poetic language, quite foreign to the author of the *Night-Thoughts*. The structure of Young's verse is repetitious, and is based on sequences of very short sentences, suitable to the ejaculations of passion, didactic aphorisms, and, traditionally, the religious sublime: it is, above all, emphatic.[70]

[70] On Young's verse, see Havens, *The Influence*, pp. 151, 158, and Donald Davie, *The Late Augustans: Longer Poems of the Later Eighteenth Century* (London, 1958), Introduction, pp. xix–xx. *N-T*, Night 5, p. 79. Cowper, *Task*, bk. II, ll. 285.

Cowper describes the poet's skills as:

> . . . occupations of the poet's mind
> So pleasing, and that steal away the thought
> With such address from themes of sad import,
> That, lost in his own musings, happy man!
> He feels th' anxieties of life, denied
> Their wonted entertainment, all retire.

He goes on to say that 'the hearers of his song' are 'Aware of nothing arduous', and that he does not wish to trifle; but his readers may be unaware not only of the poet's labours, for they too may become lost in the pleasing fluency of his verse, and may forget the arduous anxieties of their lives in the syntactical sophistication of his musings. Young's readers, on the other hand, must, like Fanny Burney, forget their particular troubles as they succumb to the forcible double weight of the poem's aphoristic pronouncements. Cowper attempts to 'arrest the fleeting images that fill / The mirror of the mind, and hold them fast', and perhaps the 'faithful likeness' his good-natured fluency conveys is that of transitory images or thoughts, rather than of the cohesive mental power that might hold them fast. Young, in comparison, attempts to present 'Pastimes' as 'solemn *Counsels*, Images of Awe, / *Truths*', and the magisterial weight with which he pronounces these images may preclude the possibility of a syntax that could express their coherence. It may be the result of Young's 'exquisite feeling' and 'forcible ideas', his ability to move the hearts and impress the minds of his contemporary readers, that he is unable to make explicit the relation between his miscellaneous thoughts and the 'whole Chart' he describes them as expressing; his readers, like the poet himself, retire into solitude to find their hearts, and the 'dippings' into the poem they find it appropriate to make there confirm the poem's character as a miscellany which speaks to their dislocated isolation.[71]

In so far as the *Night-Thoughts* does succeed in translating the poet's private 'omnipotence of Thought' into a controlled expression of magisterial power, it defers the problematic authority the poem expresses onto the figure of the poet himself, and it is significant in this respect that the youthful and ideal poet has a prominent role in Blake's illustrations to the poem, and that his night-gowned figure occupies a central position in the frontispiece George Vertue engraved for it. The

---

[71] Cowper, *Task*, bk. II, ll. 298–303, 305, 307, 290–1, 293. *N-T*, Night 5, p. 79. Burney, *Diaries*, iii. 165.

figure of the poet, confident that the private and public, various and comprehensive aspects of his poem describe a harmonious unity, appears in the final Night of the poem as the model reader, grateful for 'sacred Silence whisp'ring truths divine': he writes:

> This final Effort of the moral Muse,
> How justly Titled? Nor for me alone;
> For all that read; what Spirit of Support,
> What heights of CONSOLATION, crown my Song!

The poet's reception of 'The Consolation' promised in the title of the last Night demonstrates the compatibility of the exemplary and preceptive strains of religious poetry by locating both in the person of the poet.[72]

In the poem as a whole, as I have shown, this also involved an extensive redefinition of the reader, who becomes isolated, desocialized, insulated from their own 'little troubles' in recognition of the poet's nobility, his superior powers. Young's poetry, as I have said, enjoyed considerable public success and influence, but it was not a success which, in this poem, succeeded in identifying its miscellaneous readers as confirmed members of a whole congregation, except, perhaps, in their capacity as sinners or failed readers, 'Sons of Earth'. The example set by the poem is widely apparent in the poetry of the second half of the century, in its digressiveness, its didacticism, or its personal and occasional nature, and, as we shall see, its influence is clearly detectable in the language of Smart's early religious poetry. But for Smart, the isolation of the reader that Young's poetry imposes is inappropriate to his understanding of the ecclesiastical function of religious poetry, not as a means of delivering the weighty truths of the pulpit, but of emphasizing the congregational nature even of private praise.

XIII

At the beginning of this chapter, I referred to Johnson's 'Life of Waller', and suggested that the lack of enthusiasm for religious poetry

---

[72] N-T, Night 6, p. 125. I refer, in particular, to Blake's illustrations of pp. 1 and 10 of N-T, in Night Thoughts: or The Complaint and the Consolation, ed. Robert Essick and Jenijoy LaBelle (New York, 1975). In contrast, see Blake's engravings for Robert Blair's The Grave (1743). Vertue's frontispiece to N-T appears in the 8th edn. of 1749. N-T, Night 9, p. 239.

which he expressed there might arise from the problem of defining it. Johnson discussed six possible 'kinds' of 'poetical devotion': the didactic, the celebration of nature, 'Contemplative piety', the 'topics of devotion', the 'employments of pious meditation', and 'sentiments purely religious', or the 'ideas of Christian theology'. These 'kinds' are not, of course, always easy to distinguish, but Johnson's discussion of them is revealing both in relation to his understanding of the function of religious poetry, and as it illuminates the aspirations and achievements that Smart's poetry describes.[73]

Johnson dismisses didactic poetry as depending on 'the happy power of arguing in verse', to which the nature of the subject-matter is secondary; he rejects the poetry of natural description as a celebration of God's works rather than of God himself. But his criticism of the remaining 'kinds', which significantly do not include epic or dramatic poetry of the kind exemplified by *Paradise Lost*, is based on two assumptions. Johnson assumes that the language of poetry cannot be sufficiently elevated to do justice to, or to enhance, the reader's understanding of the divine attributes as comprising 'Whatever is great, desirable, or tremendous'—an understanding which, he implies, is either unproblematic and accessible, or which it is beyond the province of poetry to nurture; and he assumes further that devotion is essentially a private act: thanksgiving, for example, 'is to be felt rather than expressed'. While the deeply private nature of Johnson's own faith is generally recognized, it should also be remembered that these lives date from the last quarter of the eighteenth century, by which time religious poetry (with the exception of the hymn) has largely moved into the more private and solitary sphere inhabited by Cowper. In 1750, at the outset of Smart's career as a religious poet, this private road, apparently advancing towards the silence Johnson advocates, does not appear as the only path available to the religious poet. Smart's poetry shows that religion as the major concern of poetry could promote an ambitious adventurousness which defines the poet neither as meditative recluse nor as preacher, but as the psalmist capable of expressing the universal integrity of Christian concern.[74]

I have argued in this essay that poetry concerned with religious ideas can most fruitfully be described not in terms of its matter, its explicit arguments and preoccupations, but through an examination of its

[73] Johnson, 'Waller', *Lives*, i. 211–12.
[74] Ibid. 211, 212. See Charles E. Pierce, jun., *The Religious Life of Samuel Johnson* (London, 1983), 68–9.

manner, of the kind of authority claimed by the poet, in relation to the audience addressed by the poem. I suggested that this idea of manner became, in some of this poetry, the matter of central concern, and if we look at this poetry in these terms we can broadly discriminate between, on the one hand, poetry which addresses its audience with the authority of exclusive knowledge, and, on the other, an exemplary poetry which attempts to excite its audience to emulation rather than acceptance of the precepts it offers. The success of Young's poetry in particular, I argued, could be understood in term of his ability to address a diverse and potentially general audience both in preceptive and exemplary terms that confirm his retired and solitary readers in their membership in a common, but asocial, body, united in participation in his pathetic and moral sentiments, and in acquiescence to his lessons. But while Young's poetry unites its readership as a party in his private sorrow, it is able to do so only through an emphasis on the privacy of that sorrow that allows him to demand the solitary attention of his readers. The basis of a religious sense of congregational community for Young must lie in the dispersal of his readers, in a desocialization that discriminates them from 'Earth's genuine Sons', and is reflected in the diffuse digressiveness of his *Thoughts*. This tension in Young's poetry fosters, on the one hand, a poetry of private devotion, in which Cowper, for example, enjoys an Eden available only to solitude and transient thought, and which Johnson sees as ultimately silent, and, on the other hand, the idea of a poetry which addresses a readership of Christians whose faith is so comprehensive that, as their idea of 'perfection cannot be improved', religious poetry is redundant. It addresses itself with privileged authority to an exclusive readership defined precisely by their previous knowledge of the lessons it has to offer.[75]

It is this tension which, I want to suggest, Smart's poetry addresses, in employing both the language of retired devotion and of congregational praise. Smart defines the role of the religious poet as the reviver of adoration in England, as the prophetic psalmist of a sense of national community that collapses the distinctions between high and low, polite and vulgar. But the ambitious attempt his poetry represents, to unify and address a mixed congregation of the faithful, demands that it create a new audience for itself, rather than attempting to address one already available, and his poetry comes to demand of its readers that

---

[75] Johnson, 'Waller', *Lives*, i. 212.

they should learn new methods of reading, and develop a quite new concept—or a concept new to them—of how it is that poems mean. There is no evidence that his readers were up to the task, and a religious poetry whose *raison d'être* was its communal accessibility, suffered instead the fate, either of remaining unpublished, or of becoming a byword, in Smart's own lifetime, for its inaccessibility.

1 'The human tongue new-tun'd'

Smart's Seatonian Poems and the 'pure' Poetry of Praise

I

MOST of Smart's earlier religious poetry was written in competition for the Seatonian Prize. This prize was instituted in the will of Thomas Seaton and involved a fairly generous reward of about £30 for a 'Poem, or Ode, or Copy of Verses', on, initially, some attribute of the Supreme Being specified by the judges. The prize was first awarded in 1750 and Smart won it for each of the five poems he submitted in the years 1750–5 (he did not enter in 1754). Seaton's will stipulated that the poem should be 'conducive to the honour of the Supreme Being and recommendation of Virtue', but his only positive direction about the handling of the subject was that the poem must 'be always in English'. The prize was prestigious as well as remunerative: the winning entry was printed, and, at least at first, widely reviewed. Smart's success in gaining this prize seems to have been a major factor in the decision to keep his name on the books of Pembroke College, Cambridge, despite his marriage and departure for London.[1]

Smart chose to compose his five entries in Miltonic blank verse, and to offer a discursive treatment of his subject-matter; decisions which, as the variety of material discussed in my introduction shows, were not as straightforward or inevitable as recent criticism has tended to suggest. The *Monthly Review* saw his early entries as confirming the very promising reputation his earlier publications had claimed for him, and Christopher Hunter, who produced an edition of Smart's poems in 1791, described them as 'written with the sublimest energies of religion, and the true enthusiasm of poetry; and had the pen of their author stopped with these compositions, they alone would have given him a very distinguished rank among the writers of verse'. The example set by Smart's poems dominated later entries for the prize for several decades; but more recent criticism has failed to appreciate the

---

[1] I quote from 'A Clause of Mr *Seaton*'s Will', which prefaces Smart, *On the Eternity of the Supreme Being. A Poetical Essay* (Cambridge, 1750). See Arthur Sherbo, *Smart: Scholar of the University* (East Lansing, Mich., 1967), 63.

significance of Smart's engagement, in these poems, with the issues informing the treatment of religious ideas in the poetry of this period, and has emphasized, instead, the contrast between his earlier work and the radical innovations of his later religious poetry. The audience of the Seatonian poems was, at least initially, limited to the judges: the Cambridge Greek Professor, the Vice-Chancellor, and the Master of Clare Hall—an academic audience which, Hunter notes, might have influenced the 'accuracy' the poems display. But the terms in which they address these judges, as well as the wider audience the successful entry could expect, are directly related to the issue of the style of address appropriate to the treatment of religion in poetry in general.[2]

I want to begin my discussion by looking at Smart's first Seatonian poem, *On the Eternity of the Supreme Being* (1750), in which he explores and defines positions that have significant implications for his later poetry, and that offer him a resolution to some of the difficulties encountered by religious poetry in the first half of the eighteenth century. *On the Eternity* is described, in its title, as a *Poetical Essay*, and a close reading of the poem reveals the tentative and provisional nature of its essays, its unfinished attempts, to address this extremely demanding theme. The first twelve lines of the poem set out the two basic positions which inform these various attempts, and which can also be understood as setting the poem in the context of two rather different 'kinds' or traditions of religious poetry.

The poem opens with a confident and authoritative address to the

---

[2] *Monthly Review*, 4 (May 1751), 508–10; see also vol. 7 (Aug. 1752), 131–43. Christopher Hunter, 'The Life of Christopher Smart', in *Poems of the Late Christopher Smart*, 2 vols. (Reading and London, 1791), vol. i, p. xxxiv. For more recent critical assessments of Smart's Seatonian poems see Sophia B. Blaydes, *Christopher Smart as a Poet of his Time: A Re-Appraisal* (The Hague and Paris, 1966), ch. 4; *Poems by Christopher Smart*, ed. Robert Brittain, (Princeton, 1950), 269–72; Moira Dearnley, *The Poetry of Christopher Smart* (London, 1969), ch. 5; Christopher Devlin, *Poor Kit Smart* (London, 1961), 50–1; Hoxie Neale Fairchild, *Religious Trends in English Poetry: ii. 1740–1780: Religious Sentimentalism in the Age of Johnson* (New York, 1942), 168; Geoffrey Grigson, *Christopher Smart* (London, 1961), 13; R. D. Havens, *The Influence of Milton on English Poetry* (Cambridge, Mass., 1922), 365; David B. Morris, *The Religious Sublime: Christian Poetry and Critical Tradition in Eighteenth-Century England* (Lexington, Ky., 1972), 127–9; Sherbo, *Scholar*, pp. 62–7; Marcus Walsh, *The Religious Poetry of Christopher Smart* (Oxford, 1972), Introduction, 11; and *Christopher Smart: Selected Poems* (Manchester, 1979), Introduction, 10–11; *The Poetical Works of Christopher Smart*, iv. *Miscellaneous Poems English and Latin*, ed. Karina Williamson (Oxford, 1987; hereafter *Smart IV*), Introduction, pp. xxv–xxxi.

Supreme Being, which is, however, immediately checked and qualified by the humble statement of the poet's inadequacy:

> Hail, wond'rous Being, who in pow'r supreme
> Exists from everlasting, whose great Name
> Deep in the human heart, and every atom
> The Air, the Earth or azure Main contains
> In undecypher'd characters is wrote—
> INCOMPREHENSIBLE!—O what can words
> The weak interpreters of mortal thoughts,
> Or what can thoughts (tho' wild of wing they rove
> Thro' the vast concave of th'aetherial round)
> If to the Heav'n of Heavens they'd win their way
> Advent'rous, like the birds of night they're lost,
> And delug'd in the flood of dazling day.

In these lines, Smart sets up an opposition between, on the one hand, the authoritative discourse of religious poetry, which can claim for the poet the problematic ability to explain the system of Creation and the nature of God from a perspective denied to the audience, and thus to assume a power to demystify whose basis is itself mysterious; and, on the other hand, the tentative and self-critical discourse of an apparently more personal devotion whch may, in its reluctance to claim any exceptional authority or perspective for the poet, leave him only the possibility of a stuttering or silent reverence. These two positions are clearly related to those I traced in the *Night-Thoughts*, for example, and Smart's treatment of them allows him to achieve by the end of the poem a position which enables him to reject the choice they represent.[3]

Smart's achievement in redefining the role of the religious poet is considerable, and it involves a sophisticated use of poetry as a means of exploration rather than argument, which makes difficult and sometimes unfamiliar demands on the modern reader. In the first place, we must be able to appreciate the terms in which the poem is, in Hunter's description, 'accurate', or in which it treats its sacred themes with an appropriate caution and precision—a task which, it seems likely, was not as unfamiliar or testing for an eighteenth-century audience as it is for most twentieth-century readers. The poem adopts a series of positions which it expects its readers to recognize and to be critically aware of, and which it treats, if not as problematic, still as evidently tentative and temporary statements. To read the poem closely, we

---

[3] *On the Eternity*, ll. 1–12, in *Smart IV*; all further quotations from Smart's Seatonian poems, in the text, are from this edition.

must also read it sequentially: for it is important to the poem's meaning that we should examine each paragraph in the light of what seems to be its meaning as we first encounter it—allowing the problems it raises to emerge from the provisional strategies it adopts—rather than in the light of the resolution the poem finally offers.[4]

The opening verse-paragraph of *On the Eternity* juxtaposes two different kinds of religious poetry: kinds that, as I have suggested, may be identified in terms of the issues I traced in the range of poetry discussed in my Introduction. Neither is, in itself, unfamiliar, but what is strikingly unusual here is to find them co-existing in the exordium to the poem, in the place where, commonly, the kind of poetry we are being offered is established. In the opening lines, the poem speaks with confident authority of the universal signature, the presence of which usually indicates that the poet will go on to trace the evidence of divine omnipresence in the abstract but precise terms of natural philosophical argument. It usually serves to herald the idea of the book of nature as a testament whose study offers rewards, insights into the divine nature, which parallel those afforded by the study of the Bible. Blackmore, for example, writes in the opening lines of *Creation*:

> See thro' this vast extended Theater
> Of Skill Divine what shining Marks appear:
> Creating Pow'r is all around exprest,
> The God discover'd, and his Care confest.

His philosophical exposition of these marks is, simultaneously, an exposition of the 'Power Divine', and he thus feels able to unveil the ways of God with the same authority that he brings to bear on the secrets of nature. The poet of the *Night-Thoughts* similarly sees, legible in the night sky, a 'Fair Heiroglyphic' of God's power, which he reads as a divine mandate for his paternal didacticism. Blackmore employs the divine inscription to underwrite his argument for a natural philosophical understanding of nature which reveals its imperfections as incentives to the industry of man, whereas for Young it guarantees a moral universe in which the commentaries of British mathematicians take second place to the lessons of the pulpit. But for both it is important that it should be a legible signature which supports the authority of their arguments.[5]

---

[4] Hunter, 'Smart', *Poems*, vol. i, p. xxxiv.

[5] Sir Richard Blackmore, *Creation. A Philosophical Poem. In Seven Books* (London, 1712), i. 34–7, 47. *N-T*, Night 9, p. 258. See *Creation*, iii. ll. 385–92.

The almost liturgical confidence of the opening lines of *On the Eternity* might seem, in all but the indecipherability of the signature, to herald the sort of masterful and instructive discourses Blackmore and Young employ. It is, however, almost immediately countered by the failure of confidence expressed in the second half of the verse-paragraph, where the poet reflects, with exemplary modesty, on the inadequacy of his ability to do justice to his theme, in language reminiscent of the private devotional meditations of Elizabeth Rowe. Rowe writes:

O narrow Thoughts, and narrower Words! here confess your Defects; these are Heights not to be reach'd by you. Adorable Measures of infinite Clemency! unsearchable Riches of Grace! with what Astonishment do I survey you! I am swallowed and lost in the glorious Immensity. All hail, ye divine Mysteries, ye glorious Paths of the unsearchable Deity! let me adore tho' I can never express you.

This kind of exclamation does, of course, attempt to indicate the power of the idea of God through the humility it excites, but, as I showed in the Introduction, its main achievement is to demonstrate the exemplary posture of the worshipper, and to emphasize manner at the expense of matter. Where the opening lines had seemed to promise the explanatory exposition of the matter of the universal 'undecypher'd characters' (l. 5), in these lines the reader is offered not argument but rapturous example.[6]

The juxtaposition of these very different kinds of poetry does not announce the replacement of an explanatory mode, defeated by the scale of the task it confronts, with a retired, exemplary mode, which demonstrates the impossibility of explanation. It defines, rather, the terms of the debate between these modes in which the poem is engaged. These opening lines establish a poetic space that makes this debate, this questioning of the nature of religious poetry, possible; they create a context in which the poet can explore the relation between what are, as we have seen, more often mutually exclusive modes of poetry. But the close resemblance of the structure of the paragraph— and indeed of much of the first third of the poem—to Milton's invocation to light in Book III of *Paradise Lost* (which I will return to later in this chapter), may encourage us to read it with a speed that

---

[6] Elizabeth Rowe, *Devout Exercises of the Heart in Meditation and Soliloquy, Prayer and Praise* (London, 1737; this 2nd edn. 1739), 124. See also Isaac Watts, *Hymns and Spiritual Songs. In Three Books*, ed. Selma L. Bishop (1707; this edn. London, 1962), bk. II, hymn lxxxvii.

obscures the complexity and precision of its language. It may obscure, for example, the importance of the oddness of tense in the first two lines of the poem: 'Hail, wond'rous Being, who in pow'r supreme / Exists from everlasting', or the implications of the exclamation or apostrophe 'INCOMPREHENSIBLE', which bridges the shift from authority to humility. In his use of this term, in the senses both of inconceivable to thought, and boundless, immense (the Latin *immensus* was controversially translated as 'incomprehensible' in the Athanasian Creed), the poet demonstrates an accuracy appropriate to his academic audience and accessible to those who read 'academic' religious poetry for instruction. He uses the term both to confirm his own inadequacy—'what can thoughts' (l. 8)—and as an achievement, a deciphering of the 'great Name' (l. 2) as a precise attribute. His use of tense, similarly, signals a scrupulous accuracy of a kind familiar to eighteenth-century audiences, who would recognize the allusion to one of Isaiah's most frequently cited prophecies, where he exclaims: 'thou, O LORD, *art* our father, our redeemer; thy name *is* from everlasting'. Watts seems to expect his followers to show a similarly sophisticated understanding of the appropriateness of the present tense to the idea of everlasting eternity, perhaps again in reference to Isaiah, when he writes in his famous psalm:

> Before the Hills in order stood,
> Or Earth receiv'd her Frame
> From Everlasting Thou art God,
> To endless Years the same.

This kind of academic accuracy, this demonstration of the demands theological precision makes on normal syntax, calls on a knowledge of the language of the Bible and the Prayer Book that would not strain the capacity of the devout eighteenth-century reader, but would nevertheless, I think, serve to indicate that this essay involves debates and explorative arguments and thus a kind of critical awareness which the authoritative precepts of Blackmore or Pope tend rather to discourage.[7]

---

[7] See St John's description of Christ in the Revelation: 'he had a name written, that no man knew, but he himself' (19:12). John Wesley comments that this 'naming' of Christ signifies that 'As God, he is incomprehensible to every creature' (*Explanatory Notes upon the New Testament*, 1754; this edn. London, 1817). For a discussion of the problem of representing the incomprehensible deity see Jonathan Richardson, *An Essay on the Theory of Painting* (London, 1725), 178–9. See also Aaron Hill, *The Works of the Late Aaron Hill, Esq., In Four Volumes* (London, 1753), iv. 10, 88. Isa. 63:16. On the use of 'everlasting' see George Campbell, *The Philosophy of Rhetoric*, 2 vols. (London, 1776), i. 463–4. Isaac Watts, *The Psalms of David, Imitated in the Language of the New Testament*,

On the Eternity creates a poetic space in which ideas can be tentatively offered for the reader's inspection, or in which the poet can almost stage as a dialogue the tensions between two different kinds of religious poetry, not only through demonstrating a challenging but accessible academic precision, but through displaying, in these lines and the following invocation, an exemplary uncertainty that demands a highly critical attention from the reader. The poem does not conjure the reader, as Young does Lorenzo, to listen and comply, but invites us to explore the paradoxical language in which it approaches its theme, to examine its descriptive strategies, and learn from their exemplary caution and accuracy. It is, of course, central to this idea of religious poetry as the site of a conflict which does not develop into explicitly preceptive argument that its manœuvres are only possible in poetry, as the terms of Smart's plea for divine assistance make clear:

> May then the youthful, uninspired Bard
> Presume to hymn th'Eternal; may he soar
> Where Seraph, and where Cherubin on high
> Resound th'unceasing plaudits, and with them
> In the grand Chorus mix his feeble voice?
> He may—if Thou, who from the witless babe
> Ordainest honor, glory, strength and praise,
> Uplift th'unpinion'd Muse, and deign t'assist,
> GREAT POET OF THE UNIVERSE, his song.   (ll. 13–21)

The poet's activity is potentially Godlike, authorized by the example of divine creativity, but while this example makes it possible for him to continue, to meditate on that creativity, he remains silent about whether or not divine assistance is granted. He does not claim for himself the kind of privileged insight that Blackmore, and many of the later Seatonian poets, use to support their authority, but emphasizes his own fallibility, and thus requires his readers to remain alert to the possibility that they may learn from his mistakes as well as from his achievements.[8]

and applied to the Christian State and Worship (London, 1718), Ps. 90, p. 183; Watts's psalm closely follows the language of the AV: 'Before the mountains were brought forth, or ever thou hadst formed the earth and the world, even from everlasting to everlasting thou *art* God' (Ps. 90: 2).

[8] Blackmore writes: 'While I this unexampled Task essay, / . . . / Celestial Dove, Divine Assistance bring.' He appeals to the dove to 'Sustain me on Thy strong extended Wing', and confidence in man's ability to share its flight, and to receive divine assistance, so that he may also see 'the full Extent of Nature', provides the support necessary to the scope and authority of the poem's arguments (*Creation*, i. 14, 16, 17, 20). See also

From this position of acknowledged weakness, however, the poet is able to go on to write in praise of divine creativity with a confidence that may seem surprising. He writes:

> Before this earthly Planet wound her course
> Round Light's perennial fountain, before Light
> Herself 'gan shine, and at th'inspiring word
> Shot to existence in a blaze of day,
> Before 'the Morning-Stars together sang'
> And hail'd Thee Architect of countless worlds—
> Thou art—all-glorious, all-beneficent,
> All Wisdom and Omnipotence thou art.   (ll. 22–9)

This authority seems to be achieved as a consequence of the loss of confidence expressed in the previous lines: it does not necessarily indicate that the poet assumes that the assistance he requested has been granted, but nor does it involve a complete reversal of the hesitance with which he made his request. The lines suggest rather that, as a result of recognizing his human and shared weakness, the poet is able to return with confidence to the forms that are available to that weakness, for these praises combine the familiar structure of Milton's invocation with a precise use of tense that is liturgical in its scrupulosity. The lines express the kind of liturgical authority that is available to the exemplary and selfless poet, rather than a confidence based in any commanding insights they might produce.[9]

The contrast between these kinds of authority, and the way Smart employs the familiar phraseology of these lines, both to provide a guarantee of his orthodoxy, and as a contrast with the more exploratory and tentative essays that surround them, can be seen by comparing them with John Gay's short poem, 'A Thought on Eternity', which begins:

> E'ER the foundations of the world were laid,
> E'er kindling light th'Almighty word obey'd,

George Bally, *On the Wisdom of the Supreme Being* (1756), 54; John Hey, *The Redemption* (1763), 149–50; Charles Jenner, *The Gift of Tongues* (1767), 200–1, in *Cambridge Prize Poems. A Complete Collection of such English Poems as have obtained the annual premium instituted in the University of Cambridge by the Rev. T. Seaton, MA. From the Year 1750 to the Year 1806*, 2 vols. (Cambridge, 1817), vol. i.

[9] Dearnley, however, argues that the poet of *On the Eternity* does assume that assistance has been granted him (see *Christopher Smart*, p. 38), in an argument that is supported by the apparent ease with which assistance is gained or assumed in e.g. Samuel Boyse's *Deity* (1741).

Thou wert; and when the subterraneous flame
Shall burst its prison, and devour this frame,
From angry heav'n when the keen lightning flies,
When fervent heat dissolves the melting skies,
Thou still shalt be; still as thou wert before,
And know no change, when time shall be no more.
O endless thought! divine eternity!

Gay's lines are an exercise on the tenses appropriate to the divine eternity, almost a reincantation of the *Gloria Patri*, illustrating the accuracy demanded by theological meditations; and their liturgical propriety allows the poet to go on to assume an authority of manner that has more in common with the proverbial wisdom of gravestones than the didactic pastoralism of Young or of Trapp. The poet addresses his audience directly, but he seems to rebuke rather than threaten their errors: 'Is mouldy treasure in thy chest confin'd? / Think all that treasure thou must leave behind.' The authority of his 'Thought' stems from the common wisdom of 'our life'—as the slight ambiguity of 'this frame' in the lines I quoted may confirm—rather than from the professional vantage, and paternal insight that Young and Blackmore claim.[10]

In *On the Eternity* the consideration of God's previous existence works, similarly, to underwrite the poem's exemplary status, to anchor it in the dependable structures of the liturgy. But unlike Gay, Smart goes on to make, not statements of proverbial wisdom, but conjectures whose problematic nature is emphasized by their juxtaposition with these lines. He asks:

But is the aera of Creation fix'd
At when these Worlds began? Cou'd ought retard
Goodness, that knows no bounds, from blessing ever,
Or keep th'immense Artificer in sloth?
Avaunt the dust-directed crawling thought,
That Puissance immeasurably vast,
And Bounty inconceivable cou'd rest

---

[10] Gay, 'A Thought', in *The Poetical Works of John Gay*, ed. G. C. Faber (Oxford, 1926), ll. 1–9, 17–18. Gay writes that 'thou wert present when our life began, / When the warm dust shot up in breathing man' (ll. 11–12), and this idea of a common life of humanity, originating in Adam, rather than of a life distinguished or individuated by professional or social qualifications, or by the particular moment of birth, echoes the possibility that 'this frame' refers both to the frame of the world and, more specifically, to the frame of the poet, stripped of its distinctive qualities. See the contrasting confidence of Blackmore's invocation in *Creation*, vii. 682–93.

> Content, exhausted with one week of action—
> No—in th'exertion of thy righteous pow'r,
> Ten thousand times more active than the Sun,
> Thou reign'd, and with a mighty hand compos'd
> Systems innumerable, matchless all,
> All stampt with thine uncounterfeited seal.

(ll. 30–42)

These questions are unusual, in that they are not posed by an apostrophized sceptic or atheist, a Lorenzo, or an Epicurean philosopher —a device that commonly serves, as I have said, to introduce an interlocutor distinct from the audience and the poet, and therefore to admit a kind of deflected didacticism into the poem. Here the questions introduce a conjectural mode into the poem that influences the responses as well as the speculative inquiries, and dramatizes the tension between the fallible and authoritative manners the poem has contrasted.

The complex implications of this strategy describe a strong contrast to the almost prosaic simplicity sought by the later Seatonian poets, who are careful to describe their own positions, and the manner in which they address their audience, in terms which will, they hope, remove all ambiguity from their statements, and render their language transparent. They caution, with different degrees of explicitness, against the freedom of speculation that might question their authority, or obscure the directness of their precepts. John Hey, for example, who won the prize in 1763 for his poem on *The Redemption*, wishes his verse to 'flow, transparent, uncongeal'd / By th'icy breeze of Infidelity'. He presents his poem as an exposition of the Bible, which we should 'read with cautious fear; lest falsehood sly / Cloath'd in conjecture's captivating guise, / Win us unwary to her foul embrace', and the prosaic language of his poetry works to deny the uncertainty which he sees as a consequence of the fall.[11]

Smart's poetry, in contrast, exploits the problematic status which, I suggested in my discussion of Rowe's *Exercises*, language can acquire in exemplary devotion. In these lines the conjectural mode he adopts allows him to expose the implications of his earlier acknowledgement

---

[11] Hey, *Redemption*, pp. 150, 153. The Seatonian poems of the later 1750s and 1760s are characterized by their emphasis on the persuasive power of sincerity, conviction, and inelaborate diction—see e.g. Thomas Zouch, *The Crucifixion* (1765), 183–4; Jenner, *Tongues*, 202–3; John Lettice, *The Conversion of St. Paul* (1764), 177–8; James Scott, *Purity of Heart* (1761), 129–30, in *Cambridge Prize Poems*, vol. i.

that thoughts and words are deluged and lose their direction if they attempt to adventure into 'the Heav'n of Heavens' (l. 10). The questions the poet poses culminate in the possibility that, the creation completed, the 'immense Artificer' is kept in sloth (l. 33), an idea which is contradicted by the previous assertion of his omnipotence, his uninterrupted and active power, and which, through its reference to one of the traditional deadly sins, brings into play a theological discourse which cannot admit the possibility of a slothful and therefore sinful God. The questions thus reveal themselves to be invalid, and the refutation that follows them is confident; but the weight of the denial the poet then makes of their validity rests on terms which are negatively descriptive, and which reveal the basis of his certainty to be the knowledge that God is incomprehensible—inconceivable, 'immeasurably vast' (l. 35)—and the creator of other systems, innumerable, matchless, and mysterious.

This conjectural mode, which exposes the difficulty of writing a religious poetry that attempts to do more than assert the existence of God with exemplary humility, is continued in the next verse-paragraph of the poem:

> But yet (if still to more stupendous heights
> The Muse unblam'd her aching sense may strain)
> Perhaps wrapt up in contemplation deep,
> The best of Beings on the noblest theme
> Might ruminate at leisure, Scope immense
> Th'eternal Pow'r and Godhead to explore,
> And with itself th'omniscient mind replete.
> This were enough to fill the boundless All,
> This were a Sabbath worthy the Supreme!   (ll. 43–1)

The prefatory 'But' and 'Perhaps' emphasize the speculative and provisional status of the passage, and the parenthetical reference to the muse's 'aching sense' draws our attention to the peculiarly poetic nature of the passage's rhetoric, both in the kinds of presentation of divine activity that it offers, and in its ability to encourage us to accept its statements while proffering the difficulties and inconsistencies that may prevent us from doing so. For the passage reveals itself as peculiarly the product of 'th'unpinion'd', the uninspired muse in its attempt to translate abstract divine attributes into the terms of action, of the heroic, which represents the 'best of Beings' as the 'noblest theme' (ll. 20, 46). It applies to God the anthropomorphizing descriptive terms which alarmed scholarly critics of *Paradise Lost*, without the disclaimer Raphael had offered there and which had barely served to mitigate their disapproval. The muse may draw the reader's attention to the impropriety of this kind of description of the 'INCOMPREHENSIBLE' in terms that are slightly more direct that those of the previous passage, for there is perhaps a small check to our acceptance of this description in the sequence of 'ruminate', 'replete', 'enough to fill'—a sequence more obviously appropriate to the animal creation than to the creator. This check may be sufficient, in the context of an academic prize poem, to alert the reader to the incompatibility of the ideas of omniscience and exploration, or the inappropriateness of filling the 'boundless ALL'.[12]

The challenge this part of the poem presents may be clarified by comparison with a later Seatonian Prize poem, part of which alludes to this passage. George Bally's prize-winning poem of 1758, on *The Providence of the Supreme Being*, clearly owes a considerable debt to the precedent set by Smart, and employs very similar images to those I have been discussing to describe the 'Conceit absurd' which grows in 'Epicurus' garden rank with weeds / That kill Religion's root'. He writes:

> In Heav'n, some say
> Blaspheming, sits in majesty supine
> Th'eternal King, and slumb'ring on his throne,
> From Earth, and all its cares alike remov'd,
> A listless dull beatitude enjoys.

He directs our attention to the anthropomorphism of the idea that God's 'Bliss would be impair'd' if 'Nature's vast moliminous concerns / Shou'd violate the Sabbath of his rest', and instructs us that the order visible in Creation proclaims a God.

> Who sits not idle in th'empyreal sphere,
> Wrapt up in contemplation of Himself
> Thro' endless ages, but who all surveys
> In Space, his boundless sensory . . .

There is no reason to believe that Bally is correcting an error in Smart's poem that had escaped the notice of his judges, critical reviewers, and wider audience. His borrowings from Smart are copious, and the allusion seems rather to indicate the speed with which the Seatonian Prize established a self-referential sub-genre of its own.

---

[12] See *Paradise Lost*, bk. v, ll. 564–76.

This allusion does indicate, however, that later Seatonian poets were either unable or unwilling to handle the didactic function of their prize poems with the subtlety and sophistication Smart brought to the task. Bally's *Providence* describes itself as 'A Poem', rather than a poetical essay, and it spells out and condemns the folly of heterodox notions with inflexibly pedagogic insistence. Smart represents those notions as internally incoherent, and invites his readers to examine the errors of an over-curious faith, where Bally extracts the portrait of a 'Philosophising fool', and invites his readers to share in deriding follies whose origins and persuasive power remain mysterious.[13]

Smart goes on to present a third possible account of divine activity, again prefaced with that conjectural and precautionary 'Perhaps':

> Perhaps enthron'd amidst a choicer few,
> Of Spirits inferior, he might greatly plan
> The two prime Pillars of the Universe,
> Creation and Redemption—and a while
> Pause—with the grand presentiments of glory.   (ll. 52–6)

This third possibility does at least acknowledge that God may continue to be interested in the fate of his creation, but it nevertheless betrays again the muse's inability to conceive of the divine except in terms of her own 'aching sense'. For the muse again represents God in the epic context of time and space that was perceived as the flaw in Milton's power to 'see and tell / Of things invisible to mortal sight'. Smart's poetical essay, as I have already mentioned, continually alludes to Milton's invocation to Book III of *Paradise Lost*:

> Hail, holy Light, offspring of heaven first-born,
> Or of the eternal co-eternal beam
> May I express thee unblamed? since God is light,
> And never but in unapproached light
> Dwelt from eternity, dwelt then in thee,
> Bright effluence of bright essence increate.
> Or hear'st thou rather pure ethereal stream,
> Whose fountain who shall tell? Before the sun,

[13] George Bally, *The Providence of the Supreme Being. A Poem* (Cambridge, 1758), ll. 54, 55–6, 49–53, 61, 62–3, 93–6, 64. Bally does not invite his readers to examine the implications of the problematic and heterodox Newtonian idea of space as God's sensorium, though this had provoked a considerable amount of discussion and criticism. See Richard S. Westfall, *Never at Rest: A Biography of Isaac Newton* (Cambridge, 1980), 772–3.

Before the heavens thou wert, and at the voice
Of God, as with a mantle didst invest
The rising world of waters dark and deep,
Won from the void and formless infinite.

The structures of the opening lines of *On the Eternity*, and of the verse-paragraph in which the poet asserts the existence of God prior to the creation of physical light—the two most authoritative passages of the first section of the poem—clearly derive from those of Milton's invocation, which also displays a similarly alternating pattern of humility and assurance.

This allusion to *Paradise Lost* is unsurprising in the light of the dominating influence of Milton on the treatment of religious themes in eighteenth-century poetry, but Smart's poetical essay throws an intriguing light on the difficulty of accommodating that influence in a religious poetry concerned to 'essay' with accuracy and exemplary propriety. For though the language of the poetical essay is closest to Milton's where it is assured and authoritative, the essay's representation of God is most reminiscent of *Paradise Lost* in those passages in which the poet invites us to subject his descriptive and conjectural strategies to critical examination. Here it is the poem's provisional character as an essay that allows him to consider the eternal deity as pausing, the 'all-glorious' as entertaining 'grand presentiments of glory' (ll. 28, 56). Where Milton's presentation of God depended upon the impersonal authority of the epic poet, that of *On the Eternity* depends upon the recognition of the poet as neither wholly authoritative nor feeble, but able to produce out of the tension between these possibilities a self-consciousness that places the manner in which poetry may essay the divine subject in question.[14]

I have argued that the three representations of God offered in these two verse-paragraphs demonstrate their own inadequacy, and I have suggested that they act as exemplary models which expose the impossibility of fathoming or representing the incomprehensible. But the encouragement to critical reading of the poem has been almost entirely implicit, and it may seem that I have been admiring as a sophisticated mode of poetic exploration and debate—inviting analysis

---

[14] *Paradise Lost*, bk. III, ll. 54–5, 1–12. On Milton's authority and 'Majesty' see e.g. John Dennis, *The Grounds of Criticism in Poetry* (London, 1704), 25, 37. It is, of course, significant that it should be this apparently more personal invocation, rather than a passage from the main body of the poem, that *On the Eternity* alludes to, for the invocation was seen by some 18th-c. critics as an 'excrescence', a digression from the epic mode. See e.g. Addison, *Spectator*, 315 (1 Mar. 1712).

and objection—what should more properly be dismissed for its failure
to identify the contradictions that undermine it. At this stage of the
poem, however, the check to the poet's didactic authority which I saw
in the exemplary reverence of the first verse-paragraph, and in the
doubts about the strained sense of the muse, becomes explicit, and the
reservations that I have argued that the poem invites are voiced:

> Perhaps—but all's conjecture here below,
> All ignorance, and self-plum'd vanity—
> O Thou, whose ways to wonder at's distrust,
> Whom to describe's presumption (all we can,—
> And all we may—) be glorified, be prais'd.   (ll. 57–61)

The lines stress the conjectural nature of all attempts at representation,
and reject any authority those attempts may have claimed in the poem.
The poet suggests that his muse, far from being divinely assisted, is
'self-plum'd', and dismisses any possible vindication or justification of
the ways of God as founded on 'distrust' and 'presumption'. He
concludes at this point that all he can offer, within the strict
requirements of scrupulous accuracy, must be the exemplary poetry of
praise.[15]

II

I have discussed this section of the poem as, first, setting up a debate
or dialogue between two different kinds of religious poetry placed in an
unusual juxtaposition, and then creating through this debate, this
tension, a poetic space which allows the poet to make provisional, even
questionable statements. This space is marked by the contrast between,
on the one hand, the liturgical assurance of the poet's assertion of
God's pre-temporal existence, and, on the other, the conjectural and
uncertain status of his attempts to understand and represent that pre-
existence. The contrast between these two approaches to the problem
of pre-existence, I have suggested, is not explicitly resolved, but is
deferred to the judgement of the reader, until the poet finally concedes
that curious wonder, and representation through description, are

---

[15] See Hill's similar acknowledgement of man's inadequacy in 'Free Thoughts':
'Whence had man's insect arrogance of guess / Such impotent outstarting—to presume,
/ His momentary *nothingness* of grasp / Cou'd know, task, limit, and describe—his GOD!'
(*Works*, iv. 219). Hill, however, seems ultimately to advocate a silent reverence.

inappropriate to the Christian duty of praise. The next, middle section of the poem is devoted to a description of the awful wonders of the Last Day, and involves a kind of poetry that is most closely paralleled in the confident affirmation of God's existence before light was created. I shall not discuss this section of the poem with the detailed attention that has, so far, been appropriate, but I do need to consider the implications of the poet's return to this mode of poetry at this stage of his poem.

The description of the Last Day is directly comparable with the assertion of God's previous and unchanged existence. It uses similarly regular and repetitive syntactical constructions, and it too follows immediately after lines which express a contrasting uncertainty in the poet's ability to offer acceptable praise. He writes,

> A Day shall come, when all this Earth shall perish,
> Nor leave behind ev'n Chaos; it shall come
> When all the armies of the elements
> Shall war against themselves, and mutual rage
> To make Perdition triumph; it shall come,
> When the capacious atmosphere above
> Shall in sulphureous thunders groan, and die,
> And vanish into void; the earth beneath
> Shall sever to the center, and devour
> Th'enormous blaze of the destructive flames.   (ll. 62–71)

He piles up the adverbial clauses, which, like those of the earlier verse-paragraph, give prominence to the poet's use of tense, his reincantation of the *Gloria Patri*, rather than to the events he imagines to take place. These clauses express a prophetic authority which is based in the acknowledgement of a common fallibility. In both passages, this shared sense of mortal incapacity causes the poet to turn to a manner of praise in which the acceptable structures of the liturgy anchor or guarantee his conjectures, and provide a context which restrains them from diverging into the expression of presumption or distrust. In the earlier passage, this reassuring common ground seemed to encourage a freedom of enquiry, but confirmed the inability of the poet's muse to adventure beyond it; but in this passage, following the resolution of that debate, the poet gains not an individual freedom of imaginative speculation, but a prophetic authority more closely related to the confident moral stance of Gay's 'Thought'. For the first time in the poem, the poet speaks in the first person, claiming an insight that is authoritative, not because it is exclusive, but because it emerges from the sacred certainties of liturgical praise:

> Nor shall the verdant vallies then remain
> Safe in their meek submission; they the debt
> Of nature and of justice too must pay.
> Yet I must weep for you, ye rival fair,
> Arno and Andalusia; but for thee
> More largely and with filial tears must weep,
> O Albion, O my Country; Thou must join,
> In vain dissever'd from the rest, must join
> The terrors of th'inevitable ruin.   (ll. 85–93)

It is the strength of this passage on the Last Day, after the difficult tensions and demands of the first section of the poem, that the poet is able to speak with an unproblematic assurance that is both exemplary and didactic.

In his description of the Last Day, then, the poet adapts the phraseology of the liturgy to express the devout awe that informs 'all *we* can,— / And all *we* may' offer (ll. 60–1, my italics). He ceases to challenge his audience, to demand that they test his every statement, and attempts to speak for them as a distinct but undistinguished member of the congregation of the faithful; and the resemblance of this manner of praise to that offered by Young, in the *Last Day*, and in parts of the *Night-Thoughts*, is emphasized by the use of the prophetic present:

> He comes! He comes! the awful trump I hear;
> The flaming sword's intolerable blaze
> I see; He comes! th'Archangel from above.
> 'Arise, ye tenants of the silent grave,
> Awake incorruptible and arise: . . .'   (ll. 111–15)

The lines allude to the visionary language of the *Night-Thoughts*, where Young writes of the same event:

> I think of nothing else; I see! I feel it!
> All *Nature*, like an Earthquake, trembling round!
> All *Deities*, like Summer's Swarms, on Wing!
> All basking in the full Meridian Blaze!
> I see the JUDGE inthron'd! the flaming Guard!

For the poet of the *Night-Thoughts*, and perhaps also for Smart, the intense importance of the event is reflected in the immediacy with which it is described. In Young's words: 'I find my Inspiration in my

Theme; / The Grandeur of my Subject is my Muse', but where for Young this prophetic vision is a privilege gained through retired absorption in private meditation, and signals a wisdom unavailable to the more worldly Lorenzo, in *On the Eternity* its immediacy and conviction stand in contrast to the presumptuous representations of heaven afforded by speculation, and it therefore seems to indicate the power of a liturgical or psalmic religious poetry, in contrast to the strained heroic descriptions offered by the muse.[16]

The concluding paragraphs of the poem, which contemplate the 'everlasting calm' that succeeds the end of time, again allude to the *Night-Thoughts* in conjunction with the liturgical language of the Psalms, in terms that allow us to understand more fully the differences between the role and manner seen as appropriate to the religious poet in this poem, and in Young. The poet compares the mind to the ark, which finds secure dry land only in heaven, and writes:

> 'Tis then, nor sooner, that the deathless soul
> Shall justly know its nature and its rise:
> 'Tis then the human tongue new-tun'd shall give
> Praises more worthy the eternal ear.
> Yet what we can, we ought;—and therefore, Thou,
> Purge thou my heart, Omnipotent and Good!
> Purge thou my heart with hyssop, lest like Cain
> I offer fruitless sacrifice, and with gifts
> Offend and not propitiate the Ador'd.   (ll. 127–35)

This sense of praise as a compelling duty is, as I have already noted, a feature of exemplary poetry, but the poet's acknowledgement of this obligation here takes a form which alludes to one of the most celebrated passages of the *Night-Thoughts*. Young writes of the task of describing the death-bed of his friend Philander:

> O had he let fall
> One Feather as he flew; I, then, had wrote,
> What Friends might flatter; prudent Foes forbear;
> Rivals scarce damn; and ZOILUS reprieve.
> Yet what I can, I must: It were profane
> To quench a Glory lighted at the Skies,
> And cast in Shadows his illustrious Close.

For Young here, his theme again has an urgent virtue which, in his terms, spontaneously 'compels' his poetry. The death of Philander

---

[16] *N-T*, Night 9, pp. 233, 231.

emerges as a scene of 'resistless Demonstration': it has a pathetic power which both the poet and his audience are helpless to resist, and both find themselves subject to its religious sublimity as together they enter into 'the Temple of my Theme'. Thus, though the dead Philander cannot inspire his poetry with an angelic 'Feather'—his muse is, like Smart's, 'unpinion'd' (l. 20)—his death does produce a theme of such compelling power that the poet seems barely responsible for the verse he produces—'the Theme intoxicates my Song!' To some extent, as we shall see, Smart's reference to the duty of praise has similar implications, but in his lines, the suggestion of an obligation that excuses any feebleness in the poet's voice is countered by the lines from David's penitential psalm praying for the cleansing of the poet's soul and acknowledging the possibility that his failings may make his praise offensive.[17]

David prays to be cleansed with hyssop after he has confessed his sins in Psalm 51, familiar to eighteenth-century readers from its place in the Commination service for Ash Wednesday. But Smart's reference to the psalm serves both to emphasize that his fallibility may be dangerously offensive, rather than excusable, and to confirm that the role the poet's essays have secured for him is not that of private meditation on occasional themes, but public or ministerial. David's psalm, repenting the seduction of Bathsheba, was understood by seventeenth- and eighteenth-century commentators not as making the public of Israel a party in his private sorrow but as an 'unparalleled piece of heroic virtue', which made his private sins the occasion to instruct the people in virtue 'Both by precept and example', for it made his repentance and self-abasement 'a part of the public worship of his kingdom'. *On the Eternity*, in its use of the distinctive language of David's mortification, indicates that the poet perceives his obligation to offer sacrifice in similar terms. The tension between the modes of humility, of conjecture, and of authority, which can be seen as a debate between the distinct figures of the 'youthful, uninspired bard' (l. 13), and the speculative, unpinioned muse, is here resolved by the poet's determination to express his uncertainty in the form of public prayer exemplified by David's psalm, rather than by confirming himself and the members of his audience in their isolated privacy. He therefore adopts the first-person identity of the Psalmist in his expressions of congregational and national religious sentiment: an identity that is

[17] *N-T*, Night 2, pp. 32–3, 33.

impersonal, but nevertheless allows the poet to express his duty of praise in terms of a devotion that is provisional and exemplary rather than authoritatively didactic.[18]

The implications of this resolution are demonstrated in the concluding lines of the poem:

> Tho' gratitude were bless'd with all the pow'rs
> Her bursting heart cou'd long for, tho' the swift,
> The firey-wing'd imagination soar'd
> Beyond ambition's wish—yet all were vain
> To speak Him as he is, who is INEFFABLE.
> Yet still let reason thro' the eye of faith
> View Him with fearful love; let truth pronounce,
> And adoration on her bended knee
> With Heav'n-directed hands confess His reign.
> And let th'Angelic, Archangelic band
> With all the Hosts of Heav'n, Cherubic forms,
> And forms Seraphic, with their silver trumps
> And golden lyres attend:—'For Thou art holy,
> For thou art One, th'Eternal, who alone
> Exerts all goodness, and transcends all praise.'   (ll. 136–50)

Here the emblematic tableau of human attributes forms a counterpart to the question of the youthful bard, who wished to soar 'Where Seraph, and where Cherubin on high / Resound th'unceasing plaudits' (ll. 14–15). In the course of the poem, its language has defined itself as possessing the liturgical but abstract precision which allows it to express the devotion of reason, faith, love, truth, and adoration, rather than the 'feeble voice' of the humble and individuated poet, and thus to join the 'grand Chorus' of praise (l. 17). The poet's sense of the duty of sacrifice allows the urgent devotion of these abstract qualities to speak through him, and to produce a praise which (as the presentation of the final lines here as quotation, not as direct speech, indicates) is not the responsibility of the ambitious imagination of the poet, but a congregational confession of faith. The self-consciousness which, I suggested, was necessary to the poet's explorations of the propriety of conjecture, becomes, in these final lines, a selflessness which allows the poet to speak the common and public language of praise. This does not depend only on the sense of worthlessness, of the value of inarticulate breathings, that Watts saw in Rowe, but on the abstraction and idealization, through duty, of the self of the poet into an exemplary complete voice, capable of expressing the virtuous praise of the unified congregation.

III

The development I have traced in *On the Eternity*, from the debate between the authoritative and humble modes of religious poetry at the beginning of the poem to the confident collective praise of the final lines, involves a redefinition of the terms of the poem's address which is illuminated by comparison with Watts's hymn on 'The Divine Perfections:

> How shall I praise th'eternal god,
> That infinite Unknown?
> Who can ascend his high abode,
> Or venture near his throne?
>
> The great Invisible! he dwells
> Conceal'd in dazzling light;
> But his all-searching eye reveals
> The secrets of the night.
>
> Those watchful eyes that never sleep
> Survey the world around;
> His wisdom is a boundless deep
> Where all our thoughts are drown'd.
>
> Speak we of strength? his arm is strong
> To save or to destroy;
> Infinite years his life prolong,
> And endless is his joy.
>
> He knows no shadow of a change
> Nor alters his decrees;
> Firm as a rock his truth remains
> To guard his promises.

Watts employs a series of paradoxes to describe the incomprehensibility of God, the difficulty of praising him adequately, but for him, in a manner which to some extent parallels Smart's poetical essay, the recognition that God is inaccessible to thought seems to license a freedom that raises what is almost a conversational and colloquial kind of language—'Speak we of strength?'—into a general and congregational form of praise. In the last of the stanzas I have quoted, the worshipper in this semi-biblical narrative engages in a liturgical recitation of statements of faith whose confident certainty develops from the assurance that the weakness of the 'I' of the first stanza is common to the congregation, to 'our thoughts'. The first person of the hymn thus becomes, by the fifth stanza, representative of the confidence of the congregation, whose internal debates serve to confirm their congregational identity, as their dialogue produces and itself becomes their creed and common statement. Thus when, in the final stanza of the hymn, the first person is reassumed, it is able to express a prayer which is understood, in the manner of the biblical Psalms, as common to the congregation as a whole:

> Now to my soul, immortal King!
> Speak some forgiving word;
> Then 'twill be double joy to sing
> The glories of my Lord.[19]

Watts's hymn, of course, speaks 'for' a well-defined congregation, and there are important differences between the sort of common affirmation of faith that performance of the hymn involves, and the provisional statement and qualification available in poetical essay. But the parallel between its strategies, and the development, in *On the Eternity*, of a voice capable of producing, and of participating in a general chorus of praise, may nevertheless serve to indicate the importance of some of the features they share. It suggests the importance, to religious poetry of the period, of the achievement of forms of expression which are accessible to congregational, rather than individual, devotion, and gives prominence to the features, to be found in the poetical essay as well as in the hymn, which contribute to this achievement. The most significant of these, at least in the context of a discussion of Smart's poetry, are that both poems use a structure of debate or dialogue to advance their 'arguments', and to confirm a kind of congregational identity in their readers or participators, and that both employ the language of liturgy and of the Psalms, to express the

---

[19] Isaac Watts, *Hymns and Spiritual Songs*, bk. II, hymn clxvi, stt. 1–5, 8. Johnson writes of Watts that 'happy will be that reader whose mind is disposed by his verses or his prose, to imitate him in all but his nonconformity, to copy his benevolence to man, and his reverence to God' Samuel Johnson, 'Watts', in *Lives of the English Poets* (1st pub. 1779, 1781; this edn. 2 vols., Oxford, 1906), ii. 385.

identity of the forms of worship appropriate to public devotion or to the private meditations of the individual.[20]

The Psalms are the model or primary source of inspiration for Smart's later Seatonian Prize poems: with the exception of his poetical essay *On the Omniscience of the Supreme Being* (1752), each of them acknowledges its debt to the poetry of David in its opening lines. I have suggested that allusion to David, in the conclusion to the first Seatonian poem, indicates the poet's ambition to create a poetry which is, like the Psalms, 'agreeable to all degrees and conditions of men', and which can be understood as 'the address of the whole Church to Almighty God'. The Psalms are the paradigm of exemplary religious poetry because they are sublime and inspired, and because, as Charles Wheatly explains in his influential *Rational Illustration of the Book of Common Prayer*, 'a devout man may . . . as well use these Psalms in his closet, as in the Church; if so be he consider himself, notwithstanding his retirement, as one of that large and vast body, who serve and worship God, according to these forms, night and day': they are suitable to private devotion in so far as they confirm the congregational identity of the retired worshipper. I shall now consider some of the further implications of Smart's allusions to the Psalms in his later poetical essays. I do not intend to discuss Smart's later Seatonian poems in as much detail as the first, and it will be more appropriate to discuss his conceptions of the Davidic role of the religious poet at length in relation to the poetry he published after his release from confinement, but I do want here to discuss some of the features which are, I think, most significant for the understanding of these poems. First, I shall look at the implications of the relation between the compulsion or duty to praise and the exemplary status of the poet, and secondly I shall consider the implications of Smart's biblical model for the treatment of the attributes proposed by the judges of the Seatonian competition.[21]

Smart's Seatonian poem of 1751, *On the Immensity of the Supreme Being*, takes up in its opening lines the positions arrived at in the conclusion to *On the Eternity*. He writes:

[20] See Madeleine Forell Marshall and Janet Todd, *English Congregational Hymns in the Eighteenth Century* (Lexington, Ky., 1982), ch. 2, and Donald Davie, *A Gathered Church: The Literature of the English Dissenting Interest, 1700–1930* (London, 1978), 28–30.

[21] Charles Wheatly, *The Church of England Man's Companion, or a Rational Illustration of the Harmony and Usefulness of the Book of Common Prayer* (1710; this 7th edn. London, 1752), ch. 2, sect. 9, pp. 132, 133.

> Once more I dare to rouse the sounding string
> *The Poet of my God*—Awake my glory,
> Awake my lute and harp—my self shall wake,
> Soon as the stately night-exploding bird
> In lively lay sings welcome to the dawn.
>   List ye! how nature with ten thousand tongues
> Begins the grand thanksgiving, Hail, all hail,
> Ye tenants of the forest and the field!
> My fellow subjects of th'eternal King,
> I gladly join your Mattins, and with you
> Confess his presence, and report his praise.   (ll. 1–11)

The poet, or perhaps the 'sounding string', is here identified as '*The Poet of my God*' with a confidence that clearly contrasts with the uncertainty of the 'youthful, uninspired bard', but which emerges in the following lines as the product of a sense of the duty of praise, which, I argued, informed the closing lines of *On the Eternity*. The poet claims this title because his words are the re-expression of the Psalm used in the church service for Ascension Day, and David, the Psalmist of God, thus speaks through him, and because the praise the poem offers is represented as produced by the 'grand thanksgiving' of nature, which the poet confesses and reports. The awakening of the poet's self, the lines suggest, depends on the cock crow, which, in its welcome, alerts him to the declaration of God's presence everywhere in nature—in the course of the poem, the poet describes a series of natural scenes, and asserts of each of them that 'God himself is there' (l. 82). The 'self' of the poet is defined as the passive agent for the transmission of the natural declaration of divine immensity: he reproduces, or confesses and reports, the divinely inspired poetry of the Psalms and of creation, and it is in this sense that he is '*The Poet of my God*'.[22]

In the opening lines of *On the Power of the Supreme Being* (1753) the poet describes his muse responding with transport to the representation of nature in the Psalms: she traces the power of God in creation in terms of the sublime conception of its forces that David's example authorizes. Finally, in *On the Goodness* (1755), the poet requests David's inspiration to 'lift me from myself' (l. 13), and to support the

---

[22] Ps. 108; see also Ps. 57. Gray considered using these words of the Psalmist as an epigraph to his 'The Progress of Poesy' (1757), but rejected the biblical verse in favour of a classical allusion emphasizing the inaccessibility of poetry; see *The Poems of Gray, Collins and Goldsmith*, ed. Roger Lonsdale (London, 1969), 'The Progress of Poesy. A Pindaric Ode', ll. 1–2 and n.

aspirations of the muse. He thus repeatedly represents his poetry as subject to a pressure of inspiration, an urgency of praise, comparable to that of the Psalmist himself, and this characteristic establishes an important distinction between Smart's Seatonian poems and those of later prize winners. Smart's poetical essays do not, on the whole, offer arguments, they do not attempt to prove or even to define the precise nature of the divine attributes of immensity, omniscience, power, and goodness; rather, they represent the natural world in terms that provide evidence of the presence of these qualities, and support the poet's exhortations to praise. I have suggested that this poetry of assertion rather than argument defines the poet as an exemplary figure rather than as a didactic authority, and argued that this distinction turns on the nature of the authority with which the poet addresses his audience. I have discussed this primarily in terms of an aesthetic choice between two modes of poetry—a choice that involves the consideration of the kinds of authority available to the poet through patronage, and professional or ecclesiastical position, but may not be entirely determined by these issues: Young and Trapp, for example, both take advantage of the authority of the pulpit, but their manners of address remain clearly distinct.[23]

In Smart's Seatonian poetry, however, we can see some of the further implications of this choice for the particular kinds of religious belief the poet advocates: for the expression of views that may be ecumenical, or may be identified with a particular sect or denomination. It is considerations of this order which, I think, inform the contrast between Smart's successful entries, and the poem which gained the prize in the year he did not enter: George Bally's *On the Justice of the Supreme Being*. Bally's poem begins:

> O Thou, whose Justice awes the moral world,
> Dread Judge, and Governor supreme! Thine eye
> Thro' the vast amplitude of space diffus'd,
> No action 'scapes, no thought that bubbling springs
> In the heart's troubled deep. In vain the wretch,
> Specious in borrow'd vizor, lifts his front
> Triumphant: Thee no artificial gloss
> Deceives: the monster walks beneath Thy ken
> Foul with unnumber'd spots. His deeds are noted
> In Thy eternal volumes . . .

[23] See e.g. Robert Glynn, *The Day of Judgement* (1757), in *Cambridge Prize Poems*, pp. 72–3.

Although Bally won the prize twice in the 1750s, his poetical powers are not striking, and the judges were perhaps commending, rather, the kind of explicit theological orthodoxy which I suggested earlier that his poem *On the Providence* displayed. But the contrast between his poetry and Smart's is not only a matter of the ability to handle poetic simile. Bally immediately announces that he will treat the attribute of justice in the context of the 'moral world', the world in which the duties of the Christian are practised. God's judgement is exercised in discerning and recording all the deeds, actions and thoughts that make up the moral world, and this emphasis on conduct, on salvation through works rather than through faith, confirms that he writes from a position of orthodox Anglican belief, and establishes his distance from the dissenting sectarians and churchmen who saw faith as the one thing needful. On the basis of this statement of his position, Bally can proceed to discriminate between vice and virtue, and advocate the obedience he believes is necessary to salvation, with authoritative command.[24]

Smart's exemplary poetry, on the other hand, is not concerned to offer instruction in Christian conduct, and it is difficult to detect in it a statement comparable to Bally's. Clearly, it would be rash to make the lack of such a statement, or the absence of discussion of the 'moral world', the basis on which the nature of Smart's beliefs could be identified with any confidence, but nevertheless I think we can recognize in Smart's poetry the recurrent presence of a set of themes and ideas that constitute a discourse significant in both the natural philosophy and the religion of the period. But in order to understand fully the implications of the contrast between the kinds of faith expressed in the Seatonian poems of Smart and Bally, it will be necessary to look briefly at the position of the Anglican Church on these issues of faith and works in the mid century.

IV

In the first half of the century, the Church had been concerned to consolidate its established position through emphasizing the inclusive nature of its beliefs, and the compatibility of religion with Newtonian science and with the ethics of a market economy. These goals were

---

[24] George Bally, *Justice* (1754), ll. 1–10, in *Cambridge Prize Poems*, p. 29.

best served by promoting the importance of natural religion rather than revelation. The Bible, as I have mentioned, was of course still perceived to express the basic tenets of belief, but the obscurity and ambiguity of the terms in which it did this produced, as the upheavals of the previous century testified, not uniformity or all-inclusivity, but differences of opinion that were upheld by the Protestant tradition that authorized the private interpretation of scripture, but weakened the authoritative position of the Church. The Protestant Bible did not lend itself to the support of any one incontrovertible, public and 'officially' sanctioned religion—an idea that smacked of the absolutism of Catholic doctrines—but to the proliferation of incompatible dissenting interpretations. The accessibility of the Bible to private interpretation was undermined by the arguments of, for example, Locke, which described its text as corrupt, and as primarily informed by its historical context, rather than by transcendent truths, and therefore as susceptible to the authoritative researches of scholars rather than to the inquiries of the private individual unmediated by professional or ecclesiastical interference. But these arguments, in the early century, tended to demote the authority of the Bible by casting its statements in doubt, rather than to encourage the production of the geographical and historical research which flourished in the second half of the century.[25]

[25] John Locke, *A Paraphrase and Notes on the Epistles of St. Paul to the Galatians, Corinthians, Romans, Ephesians. To which is prefixed, An Essay for the Understanding of St. Paul's Epistles, by consulting St. Paul himself* (1705, 1706, 1707), in *The Works of John Locke. A New Edition*, 10 vols. (London, 1823), viii. 4–5, 16, 20–1. See also e.g. A. Blackwall, *The Sacred Classics Defended and Illustrated: or, an Essay Humbly offer'd towards proving the Purity, Propriety, and True Eloquence of the Writers of the New Testament* (1725; this 3rd edn. 2 vols., London, 1737), i. 287; vol. ii, *The Nature, Folly, Sin, and Danger of being*) Preface. Joseph Trapp, *Righteous over-much* (1739; this 4th edn. London, 1739), 10, 12, 40. Nicholas Brady, 'Sermon V. The Usefulness and Authority of an Established Ministry', in *Select Sermons on Practical Subjects, Preach'd before the Queen, and on other occasions* (London, 1713). George Bull, 'Sermon VI. A Visitation Sermon concerning the great Difficulty and Danger of the Priestly Office', in *Some Important Points of Primitive Christianity Maintained and Defended; in several Sermons and other Discourses* (London, 1713). Charles Leslie, *Of Private Judgement and Authority in Matters of Faith* (1726). It would clearly be inappropriate to attempt any detailed documentation of the broad trends I am describing in these notes, though the works I refer to may help to indicate their nature. For further discussion of these issues see Margaret C. Jacob, *The Newtonians and the English Revolution, 1689–1720* (Hassocks, Sussex, 1976); Norman Sykes, *From Sheldon to Secker: Aspects of English Church History, 1660–1768* (Cambridge, 1959); John Redwood, *Reason, Ridicule and Religion: The Age of Enlightenment in England, 1660–1750* (London, 1976); G. V. Bennett, *The Tory Crisis in Church and State, 1688–1730: The Career of Francis Atterbury, Bishop of Rochester* (Oxford, 1975); J. C. D. Clark, *English Society, 1688–1832: Ideology, Social Structure and Political Practice during the Ancien Regime* (Cambridge, 1985).

In the earlier decades of the century, natural religion was seen to offer a religion verifiable by experience, and free from the mystery and ambiguity produced by the Bible. Natural religion, as we have seen, promoted the theory, central to the emergent ideology of the market economy, that the imperfections of creation provided an incentive to the rectifying power of industry; and, while it described a set of beliefs founded in the experience of nature accessible to everyman, it privileged the systematizing skills of aristocratic, or, increasingly, professional, overseers. It lent itself to an understanding of religion as compatible with and accessible to common reason, while at the same time stressing the authoritative power of those best situated for the cultivation of exceptional rational insight. It described the system of divine government as analogous to the constitution of nature, and finally, to the constitution of the British government. Natural religion also, of course, emphasized the importance of works, as opposed to faith. Joseph Butler, in his famous *Analogy*, writes:

Christianity is a republication of natural religion. It instructs mankind in the moral system of the world: That it is the work of an infinitely perfect Being, and under his government; that virtue is his law; and that he will finally judge mankind in righteousness, and render to all according to their works, in a future state. And, which is very material, it teaches natural religion in its genuine simplicity, free from those superstitions with which it was totally corrupted, and under which it was in a manner lost.

Revelation is, farther, an authoritative publication of natural religion, and so supports the evidence of testimony for the truth of it.

In the arguments of the first half of the century, then, natural religion is represented as speaking directly to the rational faculties of everyman, whereas the Bible is seen as obscured by the historically remote customs that inform it. Natural religion speaks the rational language of the heart, whereas the Bible describes a faith that is obscurely miraculous in its operations, that demands an unquestioning obedience to mysterious decrees, and that (in what is only an apparent contrast) promotes a divisive and sectarian proliferation of private dissenting opinions.[26]

[26] See e.g. the influential arguments of William Wollaston, in *The Religion of Nature Delineated* (1722); Robert Lowth, sermons I, III and IV, in *Sermons, and Other Remains, of Robert Lowth, D.D. some time Lord Bishop of London: Now first collected and arranged, partly from original manuscripts* (London, 1834); J. T. Desaguliers, *The Newtonian System of the World, the best Model of Government. An Allegorical Poem* (London, 1728). For a discussion of the political implications of natural religion, see Margaret C. Jacob, *The Radical Enlightenment: Pantheists, Freemasons and Republicans* (London, 1981); Joseph Butler, *The*

By the second half of the century, however, the terms of this debate have altered radically. Anglican orthodoxy is expressed in the enormous volume of sermons devoted to the didactic exposition of the New Testament as the guide to practical piety. While arguments from design—from the correspondence of natural religion and natural philosophy—reinforce the precepts of Christ, the simplicity and sublimity of his demotic language, and the customary authority of his moral lessons, take precedence. Arguments purely from natural religion, stressing the historical nature of the Bible, become the province of advocates of enlightened social change, and are commonly perceived to conclude in atheism. These positions are, of course, complex: though Bishop Lowth's translation of *Isaiah* (1778), for example, took full advantage of European researches into the geography, natural history, archaeology and anthropology of the Hebrews, it is not a politically radical document, but a defence of the insuperable barriers of national identity addressed to a scholarly audience.[27]

The texts most often employed in sermons on practical devotion and morality were the parables and sayings of Christ, which could be understood as offering, through the mediation of ministerial guidance, the bases of universal morality, but the Old Testament was rarely perceived to transcend national and historical boundaries unless through a sublimity that encouraged awe and not interpretation and conjecture, or through the cautious researches of scholars and virtuosi who found in it abstruse knowledge rather than practical instruction. In this later period the role of faith as the basis of practical obedience and praiseworthy conduct becomes more prominent: in, for example,

Analogy of Religion, Natural and Revealed, to the Constitution and Course of Nature (1736; this edn. Edinburgh, 1813), pt. II, 'Of Revealed Religion'; ch. 1, 'Of the Importance of Christianity', pp. 180–1.

[27] See e.g. William Enfield, *Sermons for the Use of Families* (1771); William Dodd, *Sermons to Young Men* (1771); James Fordyce, *Sermons to Young Women* (1766). The direction of these volumes of sermons to specific social groups indicates their concern with practical advice applicable to particular and identifiable circumstances. For attitudes to the Bible as a historical document see e.g. John Wilkes's review of Bishop Lowth's *De Sacra Poesi Hebraeorum*, in *Gazette littéraire de l'Europe*, iii/37 (30 Sept. 1764); [?Peter Annet], *The Life of David: or, The History of the Man after God's Own Heart* (1761, 1772); Thomas Paine, *The Age of Reason* (1794). In contrast, see the more exclusively scholarly approach exemplified in Benjamin Kennicott, *The State of the Printed Hebrew Text of the Old Testament Considered* (1753); George Campbell, *The Four Gospels, Translated from the Greek: with Preliminary Dissertations, and notes critical and explanatory* (1788).

Bellamy's revised and edited collection of sermons, *The Family-Preacher*, 'the Salvation purchased by Jesus Christ' through faith,

> will carry . . . such irresistible obligations, such strong motives to induce all of us . . . to turn from our wicked ways, and lead holy and religious lives (which is the only available belief in *Jesus Christ*) that where it is considered with due attention, it can hardly fail, I conceive, of producing that great and good effect.

Revealed religion demands, through its ministers, obedience to the practical dictates of the faithful heart. Its precepts are ratified by custom rather than by any appeal to reason, and faith is understood as translating directly into conduct, without the significant mediation of rational assent. The Church in this later period is less directly concerned with the religious morality of an economy perceived as too complex to be understood. The faithful must attempt to preserve their individual righteousness, and their own religiously-inspired goals of profit through fair-dealing, but they are not usually seen as able to influence the moral integrity of the system as a whole. Increasingly therefore the Church concentrates on the duties expected of the commercial citizen on Sundays, or in his hours of privacy or domestic responsibility, or in his plans for future retirement and repentance—as does, conversely, the language of private devotion, which stresses the universality of the language of the heart, of faith, prior to action or social practice.[28]

The mid-century period of Smart's Seatonian poems is more difficult to sketch. It is characterized by the transitional instability of the terms I have been looking at, and its major texts both produce and are informed by that instability. It is, for example, difficult to distinguish in Wesley's early sermons between the meanings that, a decade after their composition, they seem almost incontrovertibly to express, and those that they might have offered their first audiences. The mixed responses of his contemporaries, ranging from sympathy or

---

[28] For discussion of the importance of the parables, see e.g. William Dodd's Preface to his *Discourses on the Miracles and Parables of our Blessed Lord and Saviour Jesus Christ* (1757); Walter Harte's Preface to *The Amaranth: or, Religious Poems; consisting of Fables, Visions, Emblems, &c.* (London, 1767), pp. vii–viii. On the biblical sublime see e.g. Courtney Melmoth [Samuel Jackson Pratt], *The Sublime and Beautiful of Scripture: being Essays on Select Passages of Sacred Composition*, 2 vols. (London, 1777), esp. essay 1, 'Chaos and Creation', and i. 17–18. D. Bellamy, 'Sunday VI. Of the Salvation purchased by Jesus Christ', in *The Family-Preacher: Consisting of Practical Discourses for Every Sunday throughout the Year. As Also, for Christmas-Day, Good-Friday, and other particular occasions*, 2 vols. (London, 1754), i. 62; these sermons are compilations and original compositions, of which Bellamy is not necessarily the author.

even admiration, to horror and condemnation, seem to indicate that instability of meaning may have been their original achievement. His sermons seem to have embodied both sectarian enthusiasm and a reanimating defence of Anglican orthodoxy, in a combination, or perhaps identity, of terms that would be too complex to attempt to distinguish here, and which it is not clear to me that we best understand by defining with a distinct clarity that must ignore the unstable dialectic they describe.[29]

I shall not therefore look at the religion of the mid century in terms of an antagonism between Wesleyan 'dissent' and established religion, but shall trace in it a few of the main arguments that span the transition between the periods I have described, and which respond to the difficulties becoming apparent in the supremacy of natural religion. For natural religion was seen to belong to the complex of ideas (expressed in the new science, in the Bangorian controversy, in ideologies of republicanism) that described institutions—of natural law, of the Church, of government—as able to perpetuate themselves in isolation from, on the one hand, the absolute powers of God and king, necessary to their original foundation, and, on the other, the application to everyday practical circumstances—of physical evidence, moral or social conduct—that had been the product and the condition of their power. In their retreat from this conception of absolute moral law, produced by natural religion, churchmen increasingly emphasized the authority of revelation, which evidenced God's miraculous ability to suspend the laws of nature, and demanded faith in his ability to intervene in history again. This strain of argument, in, most notably, the sermons of Thomas Sherlock, the Bishop of London, laid stress on the necessary but difficult alliance of faith and reason, of the influence of custom, and the free determinations of the individual will.

Sherlock argues against the sufficiency of natural religion in isolation from revelation: he argues that those who think 'Nature is sufficient to direct you' must imagine that they are not in need of the

---

[29] For further discussion of Wesley and Methodism in this period see Davie, *A Gathered Church*, lects. 2 and 3, and Donald Davie, *Dissentient Voice: The Ward-Phillips Lectures of 1980 with some Related Pieces* (Notre Dame, Ind., 1982), lect. 2, 'Enlightenment and Dissent'; Rupert E. Davies, *Methodism* (London, 1963), chs. 3–6; A. D. Gilbert, *Religion and Society in Industrial England: Church, Chapel and Social Change 1740–1914* (London, 1976), pt. i; David Hempton, *Methodism and Politics in British Society 1750–1850* (London, 1984), ch. 1; Bernard Semmel, *The Methodist Revolution* (London, 1973), chs. 1–3; E. P. Thompson, *The Making of the English Working Class* (London, 1963, 1968), esp. chs. 2–3.

redemption from guilt and sin only revelation can offer, 'and what else is this but to distinguish yourself from all the World, as if you were only privileged against the common Failings and Corruption of Mankind?' Natural and purely rational religions, he argues, can only be sufficient for a privileged few, who think that 'in Natural Religion there can be no Cheat, because in that every Man judges for himself, and is bound to nothing but what is agreeable to the Dictates of Reason and his own Mind'. But this is either to assume that all men can possess the privileges of the leisure and capacity necessary if they are to reason for themselves, or to claim an exceptional, and, he thinks, unjustifiable authority to understand and overrule the divine but not necessarily rational laws of creation.[30]

It is a measure of the difficulty of charting the religion of the period along the axes of orthodoxy and dissent that these arguments are strongly supported by the extreme Calvinist Robert Sandeman, who writes, in a rare moment of approval for the Wesleyan James Hervey's descriptions of creation:

How different is your strain of reasoning here, from that of most of our religious philosophers? While they awaken our admiration at the number, magnitudes, and distances of the stars, and call up our attention to the wise and beneficial order of the universe, they employ all their eloquence to persuade us, that the grandest view of the divine Majesty, that the brightest display of his perfections, is to be found there. They would regulate our devotion, and animate our hopes, according to the character of him which they are pleased to read us from thence. And all of this with a supercilious neglect of, and as it were, in a contemptuous contrast to that discovery of the divine perfections, which was shown to men when God was made manifest in the flesh.

Sandeman's anger, like Sherlock's disapproval, is directed at the natural religion of the philosophers because its apparent accessibility to common sense is a cheat, not because it is a cheat in itself. For all its appeal to reason, he perceives that it tells us only what the philosophers 'are pleased to read us from thence'. Sherlock's arguments for the importance of faith, of course, have little in common with those Sandemanian beliefs that were subversive to the authority of the national Church and the king, and drove the Scottish sect Sandeman led to emigrate to New England. But they do depend upon a very similar distrust of arguments from natural religion, which do not

[30] Thomas Sherlock, *Several Discourses preached at the Temple Church* (1754; this 3rd edn. 4 vols., London, 1755), vol. i, discourse I, pt. i, p. 12; pt. ii, p. 29.

recognize that, though reason may establish a 'Rule of Life', the limits of comprehension, and fear of divine judgement, the difficulty of understanding the ways of heaven or of earth, impose the need for faith in the apparent mysteries of the revelation—apparent only because 'there is no such Thing as a Mystery . . . when we say this Thing is a Mystery, of the Thing we say nothing, but of ourselves we say, that we do not comprehend this Thing'.[31]

Sherlock argues that faith underwrites the power of reason: faith is the grace given by the spirit, but it does not command assent: 'The first Work of Faith upon the Minds of Men . . . is to dispose them to listen after and obey the Will of God.' Faith does not provide the assurance that Wesley, at times in his career, argued it did, but 'leaves a man free to examine the Proofs of Religion, and does not influence his Mind one Way or other in judging the Truth'. His assent to the truths of religion therefore remains as purely voluntary an 'Act of Reason' as it has been for latitudinarian orthodoxy: Sherlock is not prepared to sacrifice the reasonableness of religion argued for by his predecessors, but attempts to inoculate that rationality against the infection of deism by demonstrating its compatibility with, and dependence on, God-given faith. In this strain of his argument, then, the Bishop attempts to combine the rational appeal seen as necessary to religion in an age of experimental philosophy and competitive commercial expansion—faith does still forward the ends of fair and gainful trade, and derive strength from the persuasive analyses of natural philosophy—with the appeal of faith as the ground of religious conviction—an appeal that is closely related to Wesleyan arguments for regenerative justification through faith, and for a common 'disposition of the heart' which is the mysterious gift of grace. Sherlock does not go so far as Wesley, in asserting that merely rational assent to religious truths is 'the faith of a devil', but he does argue that the rational knowledge of nature on which natural religion is founded is restricted to the examination of secondary effects, and that only revelation can give any apprehension of the first cause. To this extent he proposes a doctrine of faith in the truths apparent to everyman's conscience that might come to seem radical in the 1780s, but in the mid century confirms the constitutional position of the established Church.[32]

---

[31] Robert Sandeman, *Letters on Theron and Aspasio. Addressed to the Author* (1757; this 3rd edn. 2 vols., Edinburgh, 1762), vol. i, letter I, p. 20. Sherlock, *Discourses*, vol. i, discourse I, pt. iii, pp. 49, 43.

[32] Sherlock, *Discourses*, vol. ii, discourse III, pp. 55, 56, 57. John Wesley, 'Sermon I,

Sherlock's arguments for the importance of custom and education in sustaining belief may seem difficult to reconcile with the stress he places on its reasonableness. He argues that not all men could be expected to engage in a philosophical understanding of the grounds of belief, but that the faith of a 'plain Countryman' is 'as beneficial to the Man' as that of a philosopher. He explains that 'Religion is not made for Scholars only: The Use of it is to govern and direct the World, and to influence the practice of Mankind', and the countryman, whose faith is the result of custom and education, and 'the Reverence which Men naturally have for what they esteem to be Religion', may be in these practical terms a better Christian than the scholar. The distinction he makes, between those (philosophers) able to give a rational assent to religion, and those (countrymen) who accept apparently without thought or investigation the religion they are born into, serves to limit the power of rational argument and privilege custom in terms that resemble those of Mandeville or of Pope's *Essay on Man*, but which here defend the Church against the deism Pope's arguments could foster. He writes:

There are but few Workmen, perhaps, who know the Reason, and can demonstrate in the mechanic Powers of the Instruments they use; but, being perfect in the Use and Application of these Powers, they are able Workmen and Master-builders; which is all that is required of them. In like manner, if true Religion is so introduced into the Mind, as to work in the Heart of Man, and make him upright and honest, the End and Purpose of Religion is answered.

The workman here is not pursuing private vices or selfish interests, but gains a moral and religious rectitude because he is ignorant of the common ends he contributes towards. His practical goodness may ultimately serve a social end, but the end of religion is satisfied by its purely local virtue.

This argument is the mainstay of the sermons of the second half of the century, in their emphasis on practical piety and the direct appeal to the heart (as opposed to the mind), but it may seem incompatible with the Bishop's argument that assent to faith is 'the most reasonable Thing a Man can do'. It describes a faith that is the product neither of revelation nor reason, but of habitual 'Use and Application'. But,

Salvation by Faith. Preached at St. Mary's Oxford, Before the University, on June 18, 1738', *Sermons on Several Occasions: First Series* (1771), in *The Works of John Wesley*, 14 vols. (London, 1872), v. 9.

Sherlock argues, the customs and traditions of peoples have foundations so strong that they can be shaken or altered only by miracles or the sword. Those miracles—for he does not describe conquest as the means of imposing Christianity—invite the rational assent of the philosophic few; and that historical combination of revelation and reason is a sufficient basis for the vulgar belief of the modern world. It is, however, clear that this argument for practical religion does not emphasize the idea of reason that had played so significant a role in Sherlock's argument for the rationality of revelation. It does involve a redefinition of the terms of assent, and of what is meant by religion in the 'Heart of Man', which demonstrates the instability of terminology, the process of negotiation, that I suggested characterized the middle years of the century. While Sherlock emphasizes, on the one hand, the limitations of reason, and the mysteries nature presents even to the religion of the philosopher, on the other he stresses the importance of works as well as faith, and of practical rather than 'mystical' religious understanding.[33]

In this context, then, the contrast between Smart and Bally is not best understood in terms of any simple opposition between orthodoxy and dissent. While Bally's emphasis on the conduct appropriate to the Christian places him in a tradition of Anglican orthodoxy exemplified, in my survey, by the arguments of Bishop Butler's *Analogy of Religion*, both Sherlock and Wesley stress the importance of moral action as the result, the evidence, of faith achieved through grace. Smart's poetical essays, on the other hand, describe a concept of faith which, at least in the retrospective context of later decades, appears to have much in common with the beliefs of Methodists and dissenters. We can trace this apparent unorthodoxy in a number of aspects of his poetical essays, not all of which might seem to be directly concerned with matters of doctrine. So, for example, the prominent role he gives to inspiration, in representing his poetry as the report and confession of the thanksgiving of creation, closely parallels the operation of faith in Wesley's teaching. The poet is the chosen vehicle of his 'fellow subjects', he wakes to express their urgent praise through the compelling inspiration of David, and in Wesley's account, similarly, the Christian awakes to the need for faith, which is the gift of the inspiration of the Holy Spirit. This awakening inspiration allows the poet to 'Confess his presence, and report his praise' with nature: it

---

[33] Sherlock, *Discourses*, vol. i, discourse IV, pt. i, pp. 150, 150–1, 144, 142, 153; vol. ii, discourse III, p. 57; vol. i, discourse IV, p. 153, see p. 148.

allows him to express belief and thanksgiving with and for the 'ten thousand tongues' of creation (*Immensity*, ll. 11, 6), which are too varied and universally grand to be described in terms of action, of works, rather than of faithful praise.[34]

It may also be significant in the context of this discussion that in the year Smart failed to submit an entry, despite the considerable difference which, as Professor Sherbo has shown, the prize money made to his circumstances, the subject proposed by the judges should have been the justice of the Supreme Being. For the treatment of this attribute would have made it difficult for the poet to avoid making explicit his conception of the relation between faith and works as the subjects of divine judgement. The subject Smart did essay, which most nearly required the treatment of these issues, was the *Power of the Supreme Being*, the topic for 1753. In the course of his discussion of the evidence of divine power in creation, Smart mentions the recent earth tremors in London, which expressed 'Thy threaten'd indignation' (l. 53); and the kinds of poetic response he sees as appropriate to these are interesting both for what they do explicitly involve, and for what they omit. The responses of Smart's contemporaries to the earthquakes of the 1750s are well known: the disaster of Lisbon, and the tremors felt in London, provoked an upsurge of arguments against the licentiousness of London life, the most influential of which was probably that of Bishop Sherlock, but while Smart does see the London earthquakes as evidence of divine displeasure, he does not see them as occasions for the condemnation of the conduct of London life. He writes:

> O spare us still,
> Nor send more dire conviction: we confess
> That thou art He, th'Almighty: we believe.
> For at thy righteous power whole systems quake,
> For at thy nod tremble ten thousand worlds.   (ll. 56–60)

He does see these displays of power as the work of the 'Incens'd Omnipotent' (l. 54), but he does not emphasize the causes of divine anger, and dwells instead on the conviction and confession of belief that they should produce, and that will avert their recurrence.[35]

---

[34] See e.g. John Wesley, 'Sermon XIX. The Great Privilege of those that are Born of God', esp. p. 226, and Charles Wesley, 'Sermon III. Awake, thou That Sleepest: Preached on Sunday, April 4, 1742, before the University of Oxford', in *First Series*, in *Works of John Wesley*, vol. v.

[35] Sherbo, *Scholar*, pp. 62–3. Sherlock, *A Letter from the Lord Bishop of London to the Clergy and People of London and Westminster, on Occasion of the late earthquakes* (London,

In the second half of the poem, he describes miraculous instances of God's power over the laws of nature, and asserts that the redemption brought about through Christ's sacrifice is the greatest miracle of divine power. He concludes that through this miracle Christ offers salvation to 'those that love him' (l. 135); and he therefore suggests that the believer's love of God is the primary sacrifice that his 'Regenerate, and pure' heart can offer (*Omniscience*, l. 12). The reformation of conduct may well, of course, be implicit in this sacrifice, but the stress Smart's poem places on the efficacy of faith is nevertheless striking. Wesley, in his popular and widely-read pamphlet of *Serious Thoughts occasioned by the late Earthquake at Lisbon* (1755), argues that only conviction can avail against divine wrath, and exhorts his reader: 'Love God then, and you are a true worshipper. Love mankind, and God is your God, your Father and your Friend'; but he also finds it appropriate to comment, on the 'affair of the Whitson Cliffs', that for this display of power, God 'purposely chose such a place, where there is so great a concourse of nobility and gentry every year', in order to reprove them. Smart's restraint, and the predominance he gives to the miracle of salvation, do not, I think, indicate that he attaches less importance to issues of conduct in these poems than Wesley did, or than he later showed in *Jubilate Agno*, but they do reveal a concern with questions of faith and redemption which at this period, I have suggested, characterize the Church's cautious withdrawal from its alliance with the commanding philosophical and moral overviews of the first half of the century.[36]

The didactic poetry of Bally, and Smart's exemplary praises, describe contrasting views of religion, but both can be understood in terms of different aspects of the Church's position in the mid century. Smart's emphasis on faith and inspiration, as I have suggested, is paralleled in the writings of Sherlock and Wesley, though the moral instructions derived by those writers from the earthquakes of the 1750s have more in common with Bally's interest in the 'moral world' than with Smart's 'grand thanksgiving'. Earlier I described Bally's practical piety as belonging to the tradition of Butler's *Analogy of Religion*, but Butler, whose famous defence of the compatibility of natural and revealed religion was first published in 1736, writes in a

---

1750). This letter is said to have sold 100,000 copies in a month, see Clark, *English Society*, p. 171.

[36] Wesley, *Serious Thoughts*, pp. 11, 2, 5, in *Works*, vol. xi.

context in which the claim of public virtue to overlook and guide the moral world can still be maintained, though with qualification. Bally continues to assert that providence does describe and comprehend the 'vast dimensions of th'harmonious whole', but it is no longer a whole he can claim, for himself or for any other mortal man, the ability to overlook: he cannot confidently measure the morality of the individual man he addresses in relation to the whole, and his poem instead adopts the monitoring role of 'Conscience, God's dread official here below'. He advocates trust in the providential coherence of history, and directs his poetry, either to reveal the pathetic power of incidents from scripture history which describe the typical significance of domestic and familial events, or to correct the moral hypocrisy and backsliding men think concealed in their breasts. His poetry belongs to the didactic tradition of Young, and the concern it describes for the deeds of the individual is reflected in the appeal of Seatonian poets later in the century to the hearts of their audience: in Sherlock's terms, they appeal to the countryman rather than the philosopher, and enjoin the personal morality of individual uprightness.[37]

In Smart's poetry, on the other hand, we can trace a development of the contemporary debate about the relation between natural and revealed religion, and though he is not directly concerned, in these poems, with the moral world, this debate emerges as central to his conception of the public place of religious poetry in the world, and to the attempt, both here and in his later poetry, to address both Sherlock's philosopher and countryman. Smart treats each of the attributes of the Supreme Being that he essays as a further occasion to express the grateful praise of creation, and in all of the Seatonian poems except *On the Omniscience*, he alludes to the inspiration and example of David, who similarly, in his Psalms, praises the divine attributes in terms of their revelation in nature, rather than as abstract qualities. I shall now look at the kinds of description of nature that Smart offers, in relation to the contemporary arguments I have outlined, and examine the terms in which the reconciliation of natural and revealed religion he achieves allows him to claim for religious poetry a significance that he explored throughout his career, but that history failed to recognize.

---

[37] Bally, *Justice*, l. 1. See Butler, *Analogy*, pt ii, ch. 6, pp. 276–8. *Justice*, ll. 60, 248.

V

Smart's second Seatonian poem describes a movement, a use of contrast, that is characteristic of his poetic descriptions of nature: the poet's mind measures a 'pathless walk' along the 'spangled Sky', he roves from the ocean bed, through the 'bowels of the earth', to 'Pegu or Ceylon', and into 'man at home, within himself'; he continually moves from expansive views to closely observed details, and finds in each evidence of the *Immensity of the Supreme Being* (ll. 29, 28, 60, 65, 136). At the beginning of a frequently quoted passage, for example, he mounts

> Up to the mountain's summit, there t'indulge
> Th'ambition of the comprehensive eye,
> That dares to call th'Horizon all her own.   (ll. 85–7)

And almost immediately fulfils and denies that comprehensive ambition in the detailed perception that:

> . . . Thou art there, yet God himself is there
> Ev'n on the bush (tho' not as when to Moses
> He shone in burning Majesty reveal'd)
> Nathless conspicuous in the Linnet's throat
> Is his unbounded goodness—Thee her Maker,
> Thee her Preserver chants she in her song.   (ll. 96–101)

He juxtaposes general and particular ideas in a movement that usually, in eighteenth-century poetry, implies some causal or explanatory relation between the two, here that expectation is fulfilled only by the repeated assertion that 'God himself is there'. The relation between the different views and diverse details the poet observes remains mysterious, frustrating the appropriating ambition of the 'comprehensive eye', and providing instead a lesson in 'Obedience to God, the Lord of Nature'. This lesson, which Sherlock argues that both natural and revealed religion teach, is reinforced by the contrast between the miraculous revelation Moses experienced, and the natural revelation of the linnet, though the bird's song is nevertheless sufficient to instruct the 'emulative vocal tribe' in the 'grateful lesson' of praise (ll. 102, 103).[38]

Smart's characteristic use of this movement, to imply a coherence in

---

[38] Sherlock, *Discourses*, vol. i, discourse I, pt. ii, p. 20.

his descriptions substantiated only by the assertion of the mysterious divine presence, imitates or transposes, sometimes through allusion, and sometimes more explicitly, the descriptive language of the Psalms. The relation of his poetry to those inspired odes allows him not only to perceive in nature the 'Seeds and Principles of Religion' that Sherlock had described it as offering to reason, but to cultivate these seeds in the light of revelation, and thus to report their declaration of divine immensity. In the opening lines of *On the Power*, Smart writes:

> 'Tremble, thou earth! th'anointed poet said,
> At God's bright presence, tremble, all ye mountains
> And all ye hillocks on the surface bound.'
> Then once again, ye glorious thunders roll,
> The Muse with transport hears ye, once again
> Convulse the solid continent, and shake,
> Grand musick of omnipotence, the isles.
> 'Tis thy terrific voice, thou God of Power,
> 'Tis thy terrific voice; all Nature hears it
> Awaken'd and alarm'd . . .   (ll. 1–10)

The poet commands or invokes the thunders of omnipotence in the terms of David's address to the sublime landscape of the Psalms, and the phrase connecting the two—'once again'—emphasizes the similarity of address, and suggests that the European continent, whose awakening the poet describes, repeats—and is again—the animated nature of the Psalms.[39]

Smart's poetry attempts to achieve 'Some portion' of the 'genuine spirit' of David (*Goodness*, l. 12), and in his last Seatonian poem, *On the Goodness of the Supreme Being* (1755), he describes the power of the sublime rhetoric he imitates:

> ORPHEUS, for so the Gentiles call'd thy name,
> Israel's sweet Psalmist, who alone couldst wake
> Th'inanimate to motion; who alone
> The joyful hillocks, the applauding rocks,
> And floods with musical persuasion drew;
> Thou who to hail and snow gav'st voice and sound,
> And mad'st the mute melodious!   (ll. 1–7)

In David's poetry, nature is not the object of systematic survey, but a vocal chorus of subjects. Nature, under the pressure of inspiration, becomes not only the ground of rational arguments which make mortal

---

[39] Sherlock, *Discourses*, vol. i, discourse I, pt. i, p. 13.

reason the measure of divine power, but rather a source of revelation which demands the assent of faith. Smart represents nature as the poetry of God, as a mediated revelation which is at least comparable to the miraculous revelation of God in the burning bush at Mount Horeb, and, as I have suggested, this presentation of the contribution of nature to faith can be understood in terms of Sherlock's arguments for the precedence of faith over natural religion. But this is an argument which could have very different implications for religious poetry, as the contrast between the treatments Smart and Bally give of the very similar divine attributes of omniscience and wisdom shows.

Bally wrote on divine wisdom for the prize of 1756, and the argument of his poem covers ground familiar from the debate over natural and revealed religion: he argues that if natural religion is sufficient in itself, then the philosophers of Greece and Rome should have been model Christians, and, like Sherlock, he points out that advocates for natural religion must assume that they possess an unaccountable superiority over their audiences:

> That philosophic tow'r, from whence you boast
> To look all Nature through, and pity man
> Bewilder'd in the mazy vale below,
> Shook with each slight interrogation nods:
> And, when the storm of argument assaults,
> The treach'rous basis sinks, and down it falls.

The references to the *Essay on Man* are clear, and, by this date, the criticism these pose is hardly adventurous: what is perhaps surprising is that they occur in the context of an argument that borrows many of the terms and strategies of Pope's, and which attacks the 'boastful Reason' of Aristotelian philosophy through the contrast it presents, not with revelation, but with the natural philosophy of the new science. Bally upbraids the philosopher:

> Say, sceptic, can thine eye pervade the whole,
> See system on dependent system verge,
> And causes with effects connected all
> In one unbroken chain?

While he may succeed in identifying some of the contradictions in the philosophy of the *Essay on Man*, he does so by reproducing very similar contradictions in his own argument. Bally contrasts the aristocratic grasp of the whole plan of creation with the confident assertion that the whole plan exists despite man's inability to comprehend it. He contrasts the rationalism of Aristotelian philosophy with the rationalism of the new science, but he is reluctant to base the distinction between them on conviction or faith alone, and instead describes new science and natural religion as produced by 'Reason, yet with prejudice unting'd'. He attempts to preserve the rational power of arguments from natural religion and philosophy as well as to deny in them any suggestion that reason might either question the nature of the plan conviction asserts, or question the validity of conviction itself.[40]

The problems of Bally's arguments are not, in themselves, of enormous significance: although I have referred to his work quite frequently, I make no claim for its unrecognized importance; but his poetry does provide a useful contrast with Smart's in its perhaps rather crude reflection of the philosophies of the period. In his poem *On the Wisdom*, for example, Bally exemplifies the sense in which Sherlock, in his criticisms of natural religion, had attempted to negotiate a position in which he could have his cake and eat it, or in which he could curb the threat to religion which he saw implicit in the prominence of reason over faith and custom, while continuing to maintain, in defence of religion, that it is 'the most reasonable Thing a Man can do'. So Bally, for example, opposes the vanity of rational philosophy to the wise perception that the roundness of the earth produces a beneficial climate:

> Had another shape
> Been giv'n, impeding angles had oppos'd
> The breezy currents, and mankind had droop'd
> Sickly and faint from th'intercepted gale.

This argument is one of the favourite observations of natural philosophers, and most notably of John Ray, who saw in it a divine sanction and incentive to Britain's expanding trade empire. In employing it, the poet attempts to confirm 'in the nat'ral as the moral world', the alliance with rational religion, that had, by the mid century, become unstable and potentially disadvantageous to the position of the established Church.[41]

The arguments which Bally sees as appropriate to the praise of divine wisdom emphasize the interdependence of rational religion and

[40] Bally, *Wisdom*, see ll. 162–88; ll. 156–61. See *Essay on Man*, epistle I, ll. 1–16, epistle IV, ll. 309–52, but also *N-T*, Night 8, p. 214. *Wisdom*, ll. 29, 37–40, 116.

[41] Sherlock, *Discourses*, vol. ii, discourse III, p. 57. Bally, *Wisdom*, ll. 356–9. See John Ray, *The Wisdom of God Manifested in the Works of Creation* (1691), pt. i, 'Of terrestrial and inanimate simple bodies'; pt. ii, 'Of the usefulness of the present figure, constitution and consistency of the several parts of this terraqueous globe'. *Wisdom*, l. 399.

natural philosophy, and indicate the support both give to mercantile progress, and it was these kinds of arguments which James Grainger criticized Smart's failure to adopt, in his review of the poet's last Seatonian essay, *On the Goodness of the Supreme Being* (1756). Grainger gives a clear sketch of the possibilities available in the poetical treatment of the divine attributes, which Smart has neglected to explore:

Should he not have praised God for the admirable structure and faculties of man; for the animal creation; for his inspiring us with a love of society, and making our greatest happiness consist in the exertion of benevolence? Should he not have shown the Divine goodness in subjecting us to pain; in creating us imperfect, yet capable of eternal improvement? Should he not have displayed this attribute in the return of the day and night; of the variety of the seasons; and even in the dispensation of plagues, earthquakes, &c.

Smart fails to praise God for placing the sun 'neither too near, nor too remote, from the earth', or to adopt the themes which the example of 'a Milton, a Cowley, or a Thomson' would have suggested. But the religious poetry Grainger wants to see, and which Bally perhaps produces, is no longer appropriate to a period in which the Church experiences an increasing lack of confidence in its ability to under-write the morality of the social machine to which the countryman contributes, rather than the personal uprightness of heart it instructs him in. In the sermons of the Bishop of London, and in Smart's poetry, the fall does not appear as the incentive to 'eternal improvement', the contribution to the general good, that it had been in the philosophies of Pope or Blackmore. In Smart's Seatonian poems it is post-lapsarian man's 'dim eye / That makes the obscurity' (*Immensity*, ll. 25–6) which prevents him from looking through nature up to nature's God. The fall accounts for the focus of the Church on the individual, because it is as a result of it that knowledge advances from the particular instance, the individual case, towards the unattainable general idea, the whole:

> Woful vicissitude! when Man, fall'n Man,
> Who first from Heav'n from gracious God himself
> Learn'd knowledge of the Brutes, must know by Brutes
> Instructed and reproach'd, the scale of being;
> By slow degrees from lowly steps ascend,
> And trace Omniscience upwards to its spring!
> (*Omniscience*, ll. 160–5)[42]

---

[42] *Monthly Review* (June 1756), pp. 557, 556. See the natural-philosophical treatment

It had been possible for Butler to argue that while the 'bulk of men' could only consider the part of society which 'comes under our immediate notice'—the neighbour with whom 'we have to do'—in the 'upper part of the world' there were public-spirited patriots who could comprehend the good of the whole country. But though Sherlock does reproduce this distinction in his descriptions of the philosopher and the countryman, the philosopher's reliance on faith, and his necessary acceptance of mystery or obscurity, indicate that he no longer has the confident grasp of Butler's Bolingbrokean patriot. The assertion of that confident optimism produces and perhaps lends a superficial coherence to the contradictions of Bally's verse, and would seem necessary to the sort of celebration of divine goodness in 'creating man imperfect' that Grainger is nostalgic about. Grainger complains, rather irritably, that he cannot see what Smart's praise of cathedral worship in *On the Goodness* has to do with the divine attribute, but the Davidic relation of the poet to congregational worship, which I discussed earlier, is central to the new kind of religious poetry Smart produces in response to the changing relations of Church and society that I have sketched.[43]

The kind of poetry Smart is writing responds to the complex position of the Anglican Church in the mid century, when churchmen have come to mistrust institutions which may appear self-perpetuating in isolation from the absolute and original power of God, king, or ecclesiastical authority. They distrust instituted systems of thought— of natural religion or natural philosophy—which may facilitate independence of judgement to an extent that threatens to disrupt the fragile balance of private liberty (of interpretation) and established authority on which the Church depends. Natural philosophy and natural religion threaten either to make the minds of all men 'Godlike', or to exalt those whose minds are, the systems whose logic is so

of some of the topics Grainger recommends in William Derham, *Astro-Theology: or, A Demonstration of the Being and Attributes of God, from a Survey of the Heavens* (1715), bk. VII, ch. 2; *Physico-Theology: or, A Demonstration of the Being and Attributes of God, from his Works of Creation* (1713), bk. II, ch. 4; and John Ray, *Works of Creation*, pt. i, 'Of the heavenly bodies'; Blackmore, *Creation*, bk. III, ll. 450–90. See *Essay on Man*, epistle IV, ll. 361–72, where the ability of the mind to 'Take ev'ry creature in, of ev'ry kind' (l. 370) seems an unproblematic and natural progression.

[43] Joseph Butler, 'Sermon XII.—Upon the Love of Our Neighbour', in *The Analogy of Religion Natural and Revealed to the Constitution and Course of Nature. To which are added: Two brief Dissertations: On Personal Identity and on the Nature of Virtue; and Fifteen Sermons* (*Fifteen Sermons* preached at the Rolls Chapel, 1726; this edn. London, 1898), 499. See *Monthly Review* (June 1756), p. 554.

privileged or enlightened, into a position from which the authority of the Church appears irrelevant. Churchmen also, however, distrust questioning of, or attempts to rationalize or comprehend, the historical mysteries of the monarchy and established Church, originated by divine authority and institutionalized by custom. Reason had worked to demystify religion, to free it from the self-perpetuating values of historically instituted morality, and accommodate in their changed context, or in their place, the needs of an empirically based, practical commercial morality. But it could, further, threaten to institute that practical morality as self-justifying, inimical to established authority, and self-perpetuating in its response to the empirical needs of the moment: it threatens to institute commercial morality as independent of customary divine or ecclesiastical authority. Religion, therefore, comes to stress personal morality, personal rational economy, which because it is personal, and applicable only to immediate circumstances, cannot itself become a rational and theoretical institutional system. This devout personal morality undermines the validity or the seriousness of those systems of thought that have become institutionalized, like natural religion or natural philosophy, because it opposes their rationality to its own customary and practical applicability; but, as a result of its personal basis, this morality can be represented as the product not of practical necessity, but of the absolute and mysterious authority of faith. It is the dictates of conscience or the heart, rather than of the moment, which govern this personal morality, and those dictates are the mysterious voice of the divine authority instituted only in the established church.[44]

Smart's poetry responds to these changing positions, I have suggested, in its emphasis on the relation between natural revelation and faith, and in its characteristic movement from particular detail to general statement. His poetry is exemplary in its attempt to speak for the complete and unified congregation, to express a faith which is that of every man 'inside himself' (*Immensity*, l. 136), peering through the common eye of faith to perceive a revelation that is both private and universal, and it is the bridge of faithful assertion which enables this

[44] It is these issues which in part inform the discussions of personal identity that are a major preoccupation for religious writers in this period. See e.g. Wollaston, *Religion of Nature*, sect. VI, pts. i. ii; Joseph Butler, *Two Dissertations on Personal Identity* (1736); Sherlock, *Discourses*, vol. i, discourses VI, XIV; Thomas Morgan, *Physico-Theology: Or, A Philosophico-Moral Disquisition concerning Human Nature, Free Agency, Moral Government, and Divine Providence* (1741), ch. 5, sect. 3. On religion as 'a Rule or Institution', see Sherlock, *Discourses*, vol. i, discourse I; I quote from discourse I, pt. iii, p. 36.

Davidic movement from the personal to the public and general. I want now to look in more detail at the representation of creation in poetry that addresses these problems.

VI

In his poetical essay *On the Omniscience* (1752) Smart stresses the difference between the wisdom of natural philosophy and of faith. In his own childhood, he experiences all knowledge as the gift of God, and not the reward of industry:

> Perception's gradual light, that ever dawns
> Insensibly to day, thou didst vouchsafe,
> And taught me by that reason thou inspir'dst,
> That what of knowledge in my mind was low,
> Imperfect, incorrect—in Thee is wondrous,
> Uncircumscrib'd, unsearchably profound,
> And estimable solely by itself.   (ll. 24–30)

Man's philosophical knowledge, on the other hand, is the product of 'slow experience' (l. 52), and is limited to natural effects. Causes, the 'pow'rs' of nature, are studied 'in vain', and Smart contrasts the 'vast genius' of Newton with the knowledge of primary causes which only God, 'who knew his works, / Before creation form'd them', can possess (ll. 55, 59, 93, 94–5). This contrast, with the praise of the 'prophetic soul' (l. 78) of instinct in animals that accompanies it, is striking in its emphasis on the distance separating the two kinds of knowledge, for earlier poems on this theme tend to emphasize rather the advances that philosophy has made in dispelling ignorance and superstition, and to praise the divine wisdom that Newtonian science has revealed in the wonderful contrivances of nature and the universe.

Smart's praise of divine omniscience, however, does not only contrast man's benighted state with divine wisdom. At the beginning of his discussion of the 'heaven-taught' sagacity of the brute creation, he writes that this 'secret pow'r' is 'thy wisdom, / That glorious shines transparent thro' thy works': like the divine immensity, it is everywhere apparent although it seems secret to man's 'dim eye' (ll. 89, 31, 34–5; *Immensity*, l. 25). The sage granted the 'golden key' which allows him to interpret this transparent secret is King Solomon, who employed it in 'descanting on the brutes . . . To God's own honour, and good will

to man', and the example of Solomon, in conjunction with that of
David is, I think, important to an understanding of Smart's poetic
conception of nature as revelation (ll. 104, 107, 109).

Throughout his poetry, Smart continually stresses the variety of
nature: in this poem, for example, he writes that despite the fall,

> Still with ten thousand beauties blooms the Earth
> With pleasures populous, and with riches crown'd.
> Still is there scope for wonder and for love
> Ev'n to their last exertion—show'rs of blessings
> Far more than human virtue can deserve,
> Or hope expect, or gratitude return.   (ll. 171–6)

Creation seems almost to overburden him with a sheer plenitude that
eludes description and baffles systematization, and this sense, in his
poetry, of a pressure always to celebrate, to give thanks, for more than
language can express, produces an idea of natural diversity which
cannot be adequately comprehended by the descriptive discourses of
the 'comprehensive eye, / That dares to call th'Horizon all her own', or
of the philosophic eye that looks through nature (*Immensity*, ll. 86–7).
Smart looks neither over nor through nature, but 'thro' the eye of
faith', he describes a creation in which the particular instance is
overcharged with emblematic significance (*Eternity*, l. 141). The
movement of his poetry, between general survey and particular detail,
expresses a landscape of animated analogy in which there are
continually too many meanings, too many voices for his poetry to
contain or to exclude.

Smart's use of emblem and analogy is, of course, a development of a
well-established eighteenth-century tradition, which I will need to
return to a number of times in this book. It provides the basis of Bishop
Butler's defence of revealed religion, and the means of charting the
chain of being, which was, Young recognized, essential to the claim for
the reasonableness of religion:

> . . . grant the Soul of man
> Eternal; or in man the Series ends
> Wide yawns the Gap, Connexion is no more;
> Checkt *Reason* halts, her next step wants support;
>   Striving to climb, she stumbles from her Scheme;
> A scheme, *Analogy* pronounc'd so true;
> *Analogy*, man's surest Guide below.

But perhaps its most prominent mid-century exponent was James

Hervey. His two volumes of *Meditations* (1746–7) describe a religious apprehension of nature which contrasts strongly with the natural religion exemplified in Pope and Bally. Though, in his contemplation of the night sky, he sees the 'occult' Newtonian forces of gravity and attraction as a revelation of the divine laws of universal government, he describes the habit of mind in which he offers to educate the devout reader as distinct from, or even opposed to, those of the historian and natural philosopher. Like the poet of the *Night-Thoughts*, from whom he frequently quotes, Hervey addresses his reader in retirement from the business of the world, and though he wishes to lead the liberty of fancy they enjoy into ordered habits of thought, the instruction he offers is presented in a series of '*agreeable Pictures*', which will have more appeal to the polite than '*the laborious Method of long-deduced Arguments, or close-connected Reasonings*'. His *Meditations* are, as their title suggests, written in an occasional, discursive style, which offers pleasant improvement to the leisure hours of the faithful, rather than rational arguments for the conversion of the worldly. Hervey writes that his pictorial style 'turns even the *Sphere of Business* into a *School of Instruction*', but it is perhaps a predictable result of his Wesleyan beliefs that his attitude to the relation between religion and trade remains ambivalent: at some points the world of commerce is well lost for salvation, while at others it is itself a religious pursuit.[45]

This ambivalence is characteristic of Hervey's analogical style, which 'renders the most ordinary Objects a Set of Monitors', but does not attempt to suggest, as I think Smart does, that this rendition reveals their intrinsic religious significance. Though Hervey's rambling excursions encounter landscapes of legible instruction, the process of analogical rendition is continually prominent, reminding the reader that these are 'ordinary Objects'. Hervey's attitude to the ordinary, based on the example of Christ's teaching, is an important precedent both for Smart's poetry, and for the sermons and poetry of the later eighteenth century, but there are significant differences between the use of analogy in Smart's poetry and Hervey's prose. Hervey writes, in his 'Reflections on a Flower-Garden':

Some rear their Heads, with a majestic Mien; and overlook, like *Sovereigns* or *Nobles*, the whole Parterre. Others seem more moderate in their Aims, and

---

[45] *N-T*, Night 6, p. 274. Hervey, *Meditations and Contemplations*, 2 vols. (this 13th edn. London, 1757), vol. ii, Preface, pp. xv, xiv n. See vol. ii, pp. 228–33, 124. For further discussion of 18th-c. uses of analogy see Paul J. Korshin, *Typologies in England, 1650–1820* (Princeton, NJ, 1982), chs. 3–5.

advance only to the middle Stations; a genius turned for Heraldry, might term them, the *Gentry* of the Border. While others, free from all aspiring Views, creep unambitiously on the Ground, and look like the *Commonalty* of the Kind.—Some are intersected with elegant *Stripes*, or studded with radiant *Spots*. . . . In some, the predominant Stain, softens by the gentlest *Diminutions*; till it has even stole away from itself. . . . In others, you would think, the fine Tinges were emulous of Pre-eminence. Disdaining to mingle, they *confront* one another, with the Resolution of Rivals, determined to dispute the Prize of Beauty; while each is improved, by the Opposition, into the highest Vivacity of Complexion.[46]

The passage takes advantage of the leisurely prolixity of the discursive prose structure of the *Meditations*, and I will not quote it in full, but this example illustrates some of the features of Hervey's style that suggest that of Cowper rather than Smart. His agreeable picture of the flowers as an image of society has a light-heartedness appropriate to his perception of the garden as the pleasant, even luxurious, product of a private feminine economy. Like Cowper, in Book III of the *Task*, he understands the setting to license freedom of fancy because it excludes, and is excluded from, the social world it becomes a playful analogy for. Hervey's descriptions are frequently prefaced by a movement of exclusion—night falls, limiting his view, he enters the enclosed graveyard, the walled flower garden, leaving the mundane world behind, and he is then at liberty to select in his description only those features of the scene he observes that are suited to his entertaining analogical picture. Here the description of the flower garden, secluded from the '*Sphere of Business*', provides an image of the social world whose predominant characteristics are its colourful variety and innocent playful charm, and the less pleasant features of its organization are excluded from Hervey's agreeable '*School of Instruction*' apparently by the nature of the analogy he employs, rather than by any inadequate limitation of the religious belief that informs it.[47]

Smart's use of analogy in the Seatonian poems does not necessarily offer a more comprehensive view—as I have said, he refers to this ambition of the appropriating eye only to disappoint it; but, in comparison to the pictures of nature Hervey presents, the scope of his emblematic portrait emerges as more inclusive, and more public than these pleasant meditations of retired devotion. His description of

Solomon descanting on the ant, the 'best œconomist of all the field (*Omniscience*, l. 115), employs the short-focused observation of detail that might seem, like Hervey's flower garden, to exclude all but the private sphere of 'unexampled housewifry' (l. 131), but its scope includes a degree of precision—the ant nipping the grain to prevent its growth—that is appropriate to the researches of the natural philosopher rather than to the fancies of devout leisure, at the same time as this precision is counterbalanced by the emblematic presentation of the beehive, whose scope is contrastingly comprehensive:

> . . . behold,
> Where yon pellucid populous hive presents
> A yet uncopied model to the world!
> There Machiavel in the reflecting glass
> May read himself a fool. The Chemist there
> May with astonishment invidious view
> His toils outdone by each plebeian Bee,
> Who, at the royal mandate, on the wing
> From various herbs, and from discordant flow'rs,
> A perfect harmony of sweets compounds.   (ll. 144–53)

The beehive presents an image of an ideal society, in an extended movement which, I want to suggest, is typical of Smart's use of analogy to express, not the ordered simplicity of the social garden, but rather the over-abundant complexity which lends a continual sense of urgency to his poetry. In the analogical portrait of the ant, as I have mentioned, Smart describes the ant's providential harvest, and goes on to include the ant's care to prevent its grain store from germinating— he explains not only the natural history of the ant, but some of that of the corn it gathers as well. In the beehive, similarly, Smart does not only present the familiar image of the social organization of the hive, but extends it to the 'discordant flow'rs' they harvest from; and this movement, which increases the scope of each analogical portrait, appears as a response to and reflection of the pressure of the 'ten thousand tongues' his poetry strives to report (*Immensity*, l. 6).[48]

Smart's poetry does not, of course, extend beyond the private confines of Hervey's excursions simply because the beehive describes a more complex society than the flower garden; but Smart's use of analogy, in the context of his attempt to write a poetry like that of David or Solomon, serves a rather different purpose to Hervey's

[48] See Derham, *Physico-Theology* (this 5th corrected edn. London, 1720), pp. 212–13, 371–3.

entertaining lessons. The achievement of David was that his poetry spoke to and for a congregation made up of worshippers whose circumstances and capacities were diverse. His poetry united all of creation in thanksgiving. In Smart's poetry, analogy does not serve as the guide to rational religion that Young sought, or as the means of pleasurable instruction that Hervey employed, but as a method of describing the relation between the comprehensive survey and the particular detail, in terms that are, like David's, appropriate both to the 'man at home' and to the cathedral congregation (*Immensity*, l. 136). As we have seen, natural philosophy provided a means of describing these relations from the perspective of the privileged few with 'Godlike Minds'. Analogy, the response of faith to this rationalist argument, described these relations, in Hervey and Young, in terms available to the limited perspectives of solitary retirement. But the perspective Smart adopts attempts to reclaim for the religious poet the ministerial and prophetic role that David and Solomon both patronized and actively exemplified.[49]

This idea of the religious poet is most clearly demonstrated in Smart's last Seatonian poem, *On the Goodness of the Supreme Being*, where, having celebrated David's ability to make mute nature melodious, he praises his power drive 'Satan from the heart of Saul' (l. 10). Smart's poetry aspires to this power of conversion through musical exhortation. In the first half of the poem, he expresses gratitude for the light of the sun, which excites the thanksgiving of nature, and Grainger's comment, that Young would not have given it the epithet of 'thought-kindling light', draws attention to the contrast between Smart's public, bardic praise, and Young's nocturnal privacy. Smart illustrates the natural incentives to praise in flowers, which have a largely implicit and residual emblematic significance acknowledged in the simile of God 'the florist' at the end of the poem, and in the response of the birds to their creator, who 'bade them call for nurture, and receive' (ll. 133, 50). He writes:

> And lo! they call; the blackbird and the thrush,
> The woodlark, and the redbreast jointly call;
> He hears and feeds their feather'd families,
> He feeds his sweet musicians,—nor neglects
> Th'invoking ravens in the greenwood wide;
> And tho' their throats coarse ruttling hurt the ear,

[49] James Thomson, *Seasons*, 'Summer', l. 1715.

> They mean it all for music, thanks and praise
> They mean, and leave ingratitude to man;—   (ll. 51–8)

There are two features of these lines that I want to point out here: first, Smart asserts that the 'coarse ruttling' of the ravens *means* thanks and praise. In this poem, as in several of his earlier Seatonian poems, the 'cherub Gratitude' takes the central place in the analogical structure that describes the relations of correspondence between different aspects of the poem, and gratitude is revealed as the meaning of the birds' song (l. 72). The birds are not here *rendered* a 'Set of Monitors', for their meaning, their essential significance, is expressed in their analogical relation to gratitude, and not in their appearance as 'ordinary Objects' or unmusical birds. Secondly, this analogy informs the significance of the catalogue of different varieties of British birds. The poet asks David, in his invocation, 'each low idea raise, refine, / Enlarge, and sanctify' (ll. 14–15), and here the 'low idea' of specific native birds is raised and enlarged through the analogy of grateful praise, which reveals these birds, not as a catalogue limited by, say, the opportunity for private observation, but as representative of all those 'sweet musicians' who express praise and thanksgiving.[50]

This list of birds, as is so often the case in Smart's poetry, works, through its specificity, as an inclusive rather than exclusive catalogue; but I can perhaps best exemplify the sense in which Smart's poetry overcharges the specific instance with analogical figurative significance through comparison with the second half of the poetical essay. There, Smart calls on the 'quarters of the world' to 'attend, / Attest, and praise' (ll. 86, 85–6), and each is represented by an emblematic poetic tableau of appropriate exotica:

> Stoop, sable Africa, with rev'rence stoop,
> And from thy brow take off the painted plume;
> With golden ingots all thy camels load
> T'adorn his temples, hasten with thy spear
> Reverted and thy trusty bow unstrung,
> While unpursu'd thy lions roam and roar,
> And ruin'd towers, rude rocks and caverns wide
> Remurmur to the glorious, surly sound.   (ll. 98–105)

The pictorial and emblematic quality of these descriptions, culminating in the presentation of Europa clothed in the armour of Christianity, is

[50] The medicinal powers of music were, of course, widely debated in the 18th c. See e.g. Derham, *Physico-Theology*, pp. 132–6. Grainger, *Monthly Review* (June 1756), p. 555 and n.; he refers to *Goodness*, l. 23. Hervey, *Meditations*, vol. ii, Preface, p. xiv.

evident: the specificity with which the 'wealthy maid' of America is described, for example, confirms her representative status and makes explanation, or the laborious introduction of the nature of this synecdoche, redundant. The lists of the first half of the poem express a similar significance, which, as I have suggested, culminates in the figure of the 'cherub Gratitude' presiding over the praises of the cathedral congregation. The task of the poet is to exhort humanity to participate in this 'general chorus of all worlds', and to establish a form of poetic language that expresses both the congregational and the specific or distinct nature of this praise (l. 124).

Smart's Seatonian poems are not a fully liturgical form of poetry, but the relation this religious poetry was understood to have to the service is indicated by the diarist Thomas Turner, who notes that he read them on a Sunday when he did not attend church, and, perhaps as a supplement to the service, on Christmas Day in 1755. This secondary or supplementary role may be reflected in Smart's use of the exemplary poetry of analogy to describe the figurative correspondence between private and universal forms of praise, but we can, as I have suggested, also perceive the role he defines for the religious poet in relation to the issue of the position of the Church in the mid century. In my discussion of this I suggested that the increasing importance of the role of faith as opposed to reason, in the mid century, was accompanied by an emphasis on the significance of the practical duties of the individual; that faith indeed comes to be understood as synonymous with the personal uprightness of heart and practical obedience of Sherlock's countryman. But in the mid century the advantages of this yoking together of faith and works were not so readily apparent as they were to become by the last quarter of the century. In the earlier period, to churchmen like Wesley and Sherlock, the identification of faith with works seemed appropriate to the power of the Church to 'influence the Practice of Mankind', but less compatible with the Church's duty to 'govern and direct the World'. For Sherlock, as we saw, these different spheres of influence seemed to create the need for two not entirely compatible philosophies of religion. Smart's poetry, I have suggested, can be understood in terms of the attempt to address and reconcile the religious interests of the countryman and the philosopher. For, by emphasizing faith, as opposed to works, Smart attempts to reclaim for religious poetry the term central both to the practice and to the theoretical government of religion. He employs the gratitude inspired by faith to express the essential correspondence between all the various different and accidental forms of creation.[51]

This central source of unifying analogy, however, is an idea that he represents religious poetry as expressing almost involuntarily, under the urgent pressure of inspiration. His poetry offers itself as the means of describing the harmony of 'discordant flow'rs' (*Omniscience*, l. 152), the analogical relations that unify creation, but it does not propose the religious poet as the figure capable of taking on the mantle, and comprehensive vision, of, for example, Butler's public-spirited man. In the final lines of *On the Eternity*, poetry does become able to speak for the unified congregation, as a result of the pressure of inspiration which abstracts and idealizes the self of the poet, but the concluding lines, expressing that congregational praise, are represented as a quotation, indicating, I think, that the degree of idealization, of 'completeness', required of the poet is not yet compatible with his direct speech. The prime cause, the source of unity in this analogical view, remains finally sublime and transcendent, in the figure of the cherub Gratitude, presiding over the cathedral.

> Here, as her home, from morn to eve frequents
> The cherub Gratitude;—behold her Eyes!
> With love and gladness weepingly they shed
> Ecstatic smiles; the incense, that her hands
> Uprear, is sweeter than the breath of May
> Caught from the nectarine's blossom, and her voice
> Is more than voice can tell; to him she sings,
> To him who feeds, who clothes, and who adorns,
> Who made and who preserves, whatever dwells
> In air, in stedfast earth, or fickle sea.   (ll. 71–80)

In Smart's later poetry I think we can trace the development of this sublime figure into forms that do speak with mortal voice, but it is in these early poems that Smart first attempts to claim for poetry a central role in the concerns of religion and the Church, and to explore a poetic avenue in the philosophy of religion that the Church itself did not, could not, pursue.

[51] *The Diary of Thomas Turner, 1754–1765*, ed. David Vaisey (Oxford, 1984), 11, 19; see also Turner's comment that 'I also read Bally's poem on the wisdom of the Supreme Being, which I think is a very sublime piece of poetry and almost too much for my mean capacity. But as I find the author's views are good, I do, as I am bound in duty, like it very much' (p. 73). See Hugh Blair, *Sermons*, 5 vols. (this 10th edn. London, 1804), vol. iv, sermon xx. Sherlock, *Discourses*, vol. i, discourse iv, pt. i, p. 144.

2 'The matchless deed's... DARED'
The Form of Pure Praise in *Jubilate Agno*

IN *Jubilate Agno* Smart abandons the traditional and conventional genres he had explored in his earlier poetry, and creates a new and highly ambitious form in an attempt to express the pure poetry of faith. *Jubilate Agno* is so unlike anything else written in the eighteenth century that critics, baffled by the strangeness of the text, have frequently tried to make sense of it by treating it as though it were part of the literature of the seventeenth century, or of the Romantic period, or, more simply, by treating it as an aberration occasioned by Smart's mental ill-health. I believe, however, that the surviving fragments of the poem represent an experiment in the use of a form which is both sufficiently free and sufficiently structured to describe the scope of Smart's religious vision. The 'daring' involved in the use of this innovative form is not, I argue, a result of Smart's illness, as some have suggested, and certainly does not provide grounds for describing the poem as little more than a 'common-place book'; but is, rather, a striking and illuminating instance of the search for a new poetic 'voice' which characterizes much of the poetry of this period.[1]

Karina Williamson's recent edition of the poem, with its informative introduction and annotations, will no doubt contribute enormously to the appreciation of the importance of the poem; but the startling unfamiliarity or strangeness of both the form and content of *Jubilate Agno* may still obscure the recognition of its importance, in terms both of our understanding of Smart's development as a poet, and of its broader literary context. I have therefore chosen to concentrate on those aspects of the poem that seem to me to be the most problematic, and also the most crucial to our understanding of it; though there are certainly other themes and issues which invite discussion, and would also do much to illuminate the nature and implications of Smart's

---

[1] John Bayley, 'A Poet at his Pranks', *TLS* (30 Jan. 1981), 100. See also Moira Dearnley, *The Poetry of Christopher Smart* (London, 1969), 144; A. Sherbo, 'The Probable Time of Composition of Christopher Smart's *Song to David*, Psalms and *Hymns and Spiritual Songs'*, *Journal of English and Germanic Philology*, 55 (1956), 54; *Poems by Christopher Smart*, ed. Robert Brittain (Princeton, NJ, 1950), 275; see also *JA*, 'Introduction', p. 21.

achievement. The primary issue is the structure of the poem, for this structure is informed by the nature of Smart's faith—it is the appropriate 'vehicle' for the expression of that faith. Smart's faith also informs his perception of the created world, his natural philosophy; and the theory informing the language in which that structure is built, and that mode of perception expressed, reveals itself as an essential dimension of Smart's perception of the position of the religious poet, and of his religious vision.[2]

Because of the difficulties of approach presented by the poem—the problem of how we are to read it at all—I have attempted, in the following chapters, to discuss its structure, language and content in some degree of isolation from each other. Such a distinction is obviously artificial, but the form of the poem is so very strange, so unlike anything else in English poetry, that it represents a considerable obstacle to an understanding of what the poem means—its content— and of how it means—the functions of language within it. I have therefore attempted to discuss the form and structure of the poem first, although I do not anticipate being able to avoid commenting from time to time on the content, where to do so may help us to understand the form. In my later chapters on *Jubilate Agno*, on its language, and on its natural philosophy, the interrelation of these aspects of the poem will I hope be made clear.

II

The fragmentary state of the manuscript of *Jubilate Agno*, and the fact that 'there is no evidence that Smart ever actually contemplated the publication' of the poem, have meant that it poses considerable editorial problems. The manuscript consists of three reconstructed double folios and ten single sheets; some of these contain verses beginning with the word 'Let'; the others, verses beginning with the word 'For'. The folios have traditionally been thought of as separate fragments—A, B1, B2, C, and D—of an originally longer, complete poem. Some of these fragments consist of 'Let' or 'For' verses only, and some of both together. Nowhere in the manuscript do 'Let' and 'For' verses occur on the same single or double folio sheet. William Force Stead, who published the first edition of the poem in 1939,

---

[2] *The Poetical Works of Christopher Smart*, i. *Jubilate Agno*, ed. Karina Williamson (Oxford, 1980; hereafter Smart I).

believed that the 'Let' and 'For' verses formed two separate but related poems, and arranged the pages of the manuscript accordingly; but fifteen years later W. H. Bond argued for the presence of a far closer interrelation between the 'Let' and 'For' lines, and, in his edition of the poem, rearranged the pages in order to emphasize the 'line-for-line correspondence between the *Let* and *For* verses'. Bond's edition, on which Karina Williamson's is based, is generally recognized as the first authoritative edition of the poem.[3]

W. H. Bond's rearrangement of the text reveals, as he claims, a 'most remarkable congruence' between the 'Let' and 'For' sections of the poem, but I have some reservations about the 'entirely new reading' of the poem which he sees as established by that congruence. Bond argues that, following the example set by 'portions of the service in the Book of Common Prayer' and the Psalter, 'The poem was intended as a responsive reading; and that is why the *Let* and *For* sections are physically distinct while corresponding verse for verse': he claims that the 'Let' and 'For' verses are antiphonal, and based on the structure of the litany and of Hebrew poetry as it was thought to be exemplified in the Psalms and other poetic books of the Bible, and he sees the poem as 'an attempt to adapt to English verse some of the principles of Hebrew verse as expounded by Bishop Robert Lowth in his pioneering study, *De sacra poesi Hebraeorum*, first published in

---

[3] *JA*, 'Introduction', pp. 17, 18. Christopher Smart, *Rejoice in the Lamb: A Song from Bedlam*, ed. William Force Stead (London, 1939; hereafter Stead). The holograph manuscript of *Jubilate Agno*, in the Houghton Library at Harvard, consists of 32 pp. of text—3 reconstructed double fos. and 10 single leaves. The 'Let' section of the poem is made up of 3 double fos., numbered 1, 10, and 11; and 3 single leaves, one of which is numbered 3. The 'For' section is made up of 7 single leaves, 3 of which are marked 3, 4, and 5. Bond designates 4 pp. 'Fragment A' (113 'Let' verses); 8 pp. 'Fragment B1' (295 'Let' verses and 295 'For' verses); 8 pp. 'Fragment B2' (473 'For' verses); 4 pp. 'Fragment C' (62 'Let' verses, and 162 'For' verses); and 8 pp. 'Fragment D' (237 'Let' verses). *Smart I* does not distinguish between B1 and B2, but refers to them as 'Fragment B', and counts Bond's lines B2. 580–2 as one line, therefore enumerating lines B2. 583–770 (*JA*) as B. 581–768. I quote from Bond's *JA* throughout, and have chosen not to quote from *Smart I* because the presentation of the text there predetermines the issue of the relation between the 'Let' and 'For' verses of the poem, in representing them as alternating down the page despite their absolute physical separation in the MS—in *JA* the 'Let' verses of Fragment B1, for example, are printed on the left-hand page, and the 'corresponding' 'For' verses are printed on the opposing right-hand page, a presentation that allows the reader considerably greater freedom, and respects the evidence of catchwords in the MS, which indicate that one 'Let' verse is followed by another, and not by a 'For' verse (see *JA*, 'Introduction', p. 18). *Smart I* also silently expands contractions in the text, which I discuss as a significant feature (pp. 186–7 below). For a fuller description of the MS see W. H. Bond, 'Christopher Smart's *Jubilate Agno*', *Harvard Library Bulletin*, 4 (1950), 39–52.

1753'. I shall discuss the significance of Lowth's approach in relation to *Jubilate Agno* shortly, but we should first consider in particular the antiphonal verse of the Bible, 'revealed' in Lowth's argument, which Bond sees as having greatly influenced the form of *Jubilate Agno*.[4]

The antiphonal structure is a simple one, consisting of a proposition, and a response, qualification, explanation, or justification. The following verses from Psalm 95 provide a pertinent example:

> 2. Let us come before his presence with thanksgiving,
>   and make a joyful noise unto him with psalms.
> 3. For the LORD *is* a great God,
>   and a great King above all gods.

The Levites were thought to have divided themselves into two choirs when singing such psalms, the choirs singing alternate verses. However, the quotation of this psalm, or of other examples of this form in the Bible, can be a doubtful guide to the nature of Hebrew poetry as it was understood in the eighteenth century. Smart was clearly greatly influenced by the form and rhythms of the poetic books of the Bible, but his persistent use of this particular antiphonal formulation—the opening of almost every line of *Jubilate Agno* with either 'Let' or 'For'—may not derive as directly from the Bible as Bond believed. If we look at a complete psalm, two verses of which have frequently been quoted to illustrate the magnitude of Smart's debt to the Bible, I think we shall see that Smart's use of 'Let' and 'For' could be explained along quite different lines. Psalm 149, for example, illustrates the biblical tradition that influenced Smart's poem, in the sententious rhythms of its exhortations to praise, but the 'Let' / 'For' formulation it contains seems to me to be only tenuously related to the form Bond sees in *Jubilate Agno*:

> 1. O Sing unto the Lord a new song:
>   let the congregation of saints praise him.
> 2. Let Israel rejoice in him that made him:
>   and let the children of Sion be joyful in their King.
> 3. Let them praise his Name in the dance:
>   let them sing praises unto him with tabret and harp.

---

[4] *JA*, 'Introduction', pp. 18, 25, 20. While Lowth's views on Hebrew poetry were enormously influential in the 18th and 19th cc., they are no longer generally accepted as uncontroversial: see 'Literary Observations', *The Universal Visiter* (Jan. 1756); Brian Hepworth, *Robert Lowth* (Boston, Mass., 1978); James L. Kugel, *The Idea of Biblical Poetry: Parallelism and its History* (New Haven, Conn., 1980).

4. For the Lord hath pleasure in his people:
   and helpeth the meek-hearted.
5. Let the saints be joyful with glory:
   let them rejoice in their beds.
6. Let the praises of God be in their mouth:
   And a two-edged sword in their hands;
7. To be avenged of the heathen:
   and to rebuke the people:
8. To bind their kings in chains:
   and their nobles with links of iron.
9. That they may be avenged of them, as it is written:
   Such honour have all his saints.

To quote only a pair of 'Let' and 'For' lines from this psalm may be misleading. The emphasis is, surely, on the continuation from 'Let' to 'Let', rather than on the dependence of a 'Let' verse on a 'For' verse.[5]

A further problem arising in Bond's reading of the poem is that the correspondence between the 'Let' and 'For' verses is not always direct and regular: a given 'For' verse may not relate immediately to the 'Let' verse with which it is juxtaposed, and this raises two questions about Bond's approach. First, Bond argues that the dates mentioned in the course of the poem suggest that the 'Let' and 'For' lines were composed at much the same rate, but it seems to me to be worth questioning, both that the pairs of verses were written concurrently, and that they were composed in pairs. Secondly, Bond's rearrangement of the manuscript suggests that, where no 'Let' or 'For' verses are found to match the verses in the manuscript, those verses must be 'missing'; but this, of course, may not be the case—there may be, for example, no 'For' verses missing from Fragment A. Smart's use of this 'Let'/'For' formulation represents a highly original choice, and the relation between the 'pairs' of verses may be more complex and problematic than W. H. Bond has claimed; but the question of why Smart chose this repetitive, emphatically and rigorously *structured* form, and of how we are to read it, remains.[6]

One indication of a source for this form can, however, be gathered from Lowth's *Lectures on the Sacred Poetry of the Hebrews*, which Smart had praised as 'one of the best performances that has been published

---

[5] Ps. 95: 2, 3. Ps. 149: 1–9; I quote this Psalm from the Book of Common Prayer (BCP). See Dearnley, *Christopher Smart*, p. 140.

[6] *JA*, 'Introduction', p. 23. See also A. Sherbo, 'The Dating and Order of the Fragments of Christopher Smart's *Jubilate Agno*', *Harvard Library Bulletin*, 10 (1956), 201–7.

for a century'. The influence of Lowth's *Lectures*, or at least of the attitude towards primitive poetry as the expression of a remote and foreign culture which they represent, is everywhere apparent in *Jubilate Agno*, and is a subject I will return to, but for the moment I refer to Lowth to make one, specific point. In his lecture on 'The Sublime in general', Lowth asserts that the greatest example of the sacred poetry of the Hebrews is to be found in the book of Job, and especially in Job's first speech. Here, he tells us:

Not only the force, the beauty, the sublimity of the sentiments are unrivalled; but such is the character of the diction in general, so interesting the assemblage of objects, so close and connected the sentences, so animated and passionate the whole arrangement, that the Hebrew literature itself contains nothing more poetical.

Lowth goes on to comment on the 'concise and abrupt form of the . . . verse', and argues that 'if any person should attempt to make it more copious and explanatory, he would render it less expressive of the mind and feelings of the speaker'. This speech, so highly praised by Lowth as a paradigmatic example of sublime poetry, might well, then, have interested Smart, and I shall quote the first few verses:

> 2. And Job spake, and said,
> 3. Let the day perish wherein I was born;
>   and the night *in which* it was said,
>   There is a man child conceived.
> 4. Let that day be darkness;
>   let not God regard it from above,
>   neither let the light shine upon it.
> 5. Let darkness and the shadow of death stain it;
>   let a cloud dwell upon it;
>   let the blackness of the day terrify it.
> 6. *As for* that night, let darkness seize upon it;
>   let it not be joined unto the days of the year,
>   let it not come into the number of the months.
> 7. Lo, let that night be solitary,
>   let no joyful voice come therein.
> 8. Let them curse it that curse the day,
>   who are ready to raise up their mourning.
> 9. Let the stars of the twilight thereof be dark;
>   Let it look for light, but *have* none;
>   neither let it see the dawning of the day.

Here, as in Psalm 149, the sentences which are 'so close and connected' are linked by the initial repetition of the word 'let'.[7]

A further indication of the nature of the parallelism Lowth discusses can be found in Hugh Blair's *Lectures on Rhetoric and Belles Lettres*. Blair acknowledges that his discussion of Hebrew poetry is closely modelled on Lowth's; he is 'following the track of that ingenious Author', and in describing the antiphonal nature of Hebrew poetry he gives the following examples:

When, for instance, one band began the Hymn thus: 'The Lord reigneth, let the earth rejoice'; the chorus, or semi-chorus, took up the corresponding versicle: 'Let the multitudes of the isles be glad thereof'.

It is clear, in Blair's discussion, that the antiphonal structure is based on the correspondence of '*let* the earth rejoice' and '*Let* the multitudes . . . be glad', and thus on the relation of one 'Let' versicle to another, and that he sees the antiphonal development in the verse as occurring after the caesura, rather than in a discrete successive verse-sentence.[8]

A further striking example of the biblical style that may have influenced the style of Smart's poem is provided by the apocryphal book the Wisdom of Solomon, which *Jubilate Agno* also often resembles in content. It is translated as a series of verses which have a repetitive syntactical construction. The passage in which the 'ungodly' reason with themselves, 'but not aright', provides a fine example of a series of exhortations each introduced by the word 'Let', and comparable to Job's speech:

> 6. Come on therefore, let us enjoy the good things that are present:
>   and let us speedily use the creatures like as in youth.
> 7. Let us fill ourselves with costly wine and ointments:
>   and let no flower of the spring pass by us:
> 8. Let us crown ourselves with rosebuds, before they be withered;

---

[7] *Universal Visiter* (Jan. 1756). Robert Lowth, *Lectures on the Sacred Poetry of the Hebrews*, trans. G. Gregory (1787; repr., with Introd. by Victor Freimarck, 2 vols., Hildesheim, 1969), vol. i, Lect. xiv, pp. 313, 314–15. Job 3: 2–9.

[8] Hugh Blair, *Lectures on Rhetoric and Belles Lettres* (1783; this edn. 3 vols., Edinburgh, 1813), iii. 166, 170. This argument is indirectly supported by C. P. MacGregor, 'The Poetry of Christ: Christopher Smart's *Jubilate Agno*, its Structure, Logic, and Place in the Development of his Work' (Ph.D. diss., University of Cambridge, 1975). MacGregor finds a logical linear continuity in the use of biblical allusion in *JA*, but his argument, as he acknowledges, is almost entirely restricted to the 'Let' verses of Fragments A, B1, and C, and may thus implicitly support my argument that the 'Let' verses describe a continuity not necessarily developed through their relation to the 'For' verses.

    9. Let none of us go without his part of our voluptuousness:
       Let us leave tokens of our joyfulness in every place:
       for this is our portion, and our lot is this.
  10. Let us oppress the poor righteous man,
       let us not spare the widow,
       nor reverence the ancient gray hairs of the aged.
  11. Let our strength be the law of justice:
       for that which is feeble is found to be nothing worth.

It is also significant that almost the whole of the first chapter is made up of verses introduced by the word 'For'. Though these verses all proceed from an initial exhortation, they also provide an occasion for more general discussion, similar to that which, I shall argue, we find in the 'For' verses of *Jubilate Agno*. The book begins:

    1. Love righteousness, ye that be judges of the earth:
       think of the Lord with a good (heart,)
       and in simplicity of heart seek him.
    2. For he will be found of them that tempt him not;
       and sheweth himself unto such as do not distrust him.
    3. For froward thoughts separate from God:
       and his power, when it is tried, reproveth the unwise.
    4. For into a malicious soul wisdom shall not enter;
       Nor dwell in the body that is subject unto sin
    5. For the holy spirit of discipline will flee deceit,
       and remove from thoughts that are without understanding,
       and will not abide when unrighteousness cometh in.
    6. For wisdom is a loving spirit;
       and will not acquit a blasphemer of his words:
       for God is witness of his reins,
       and a true beholder of his heart,
       and a hearer of his tongue.
    7. For the Spirit of the Lord filleth the world:
       and that which containeth all things hath knowledge
       of the voice.

Though there is some controversy about whether Wisdom was first written in Hebrew or in Greek, it is clear that the poem is constructed in the forms traditional to Hebrew poetry: as E. G. Clarke writes, 'the Hebrew literary form known as "parallelism" in the poetry is very much in evidence' in the book.[9]

[9] Wisd. 2: 1, 6–11; 1: 1–7; this formulation in ch. 1 is maintained almost without interruption for a further 11 verses. *The Wisdom of Solomon*, commentary by Ernest G. Clarke (The Cambridge Bible Commentary, Cambridge, 1973), 7–8; Lowth comments

These examples establish that, had Smart intended *Jubilate Agno* to be read as two separate but related poems, one a structure of 'Let' verses, the other of 'For' verses, he would have found models in the Bible and Apocrypha for this design more readily than for an antiphonal structure of 'Let' and 'For' verses together. I do, however, agree with Bond's notion that the structure of the poem is based upon antiphonal parallelism, though I would modify that notion considerably. If we look, for example, at the opening verses of Fragment B there are several kinds of parallelism at work.

3. Let Elizur rejoice with the Partridge, who is a prisoner of state and is proud of his keepers.

3. For I am not without authority in my jeopardy, which I derive inevitably from the glory of the name of the Lord.

(B1. 1)

First, there is the parallelism operating between the 'Let' and the 'For' verses: Elizur was 'not without authority', for he was one of 'the renowned of the congregation, princes of the tribes of their fathers, heads of thousands in Israel'; and we read in Ecclesiasticus: 'Like as a partridge taken [and kept] in a cage, so is the heart of the proud', which clearly relates to Smart's pride in 'the glory of the name of the Lord', and to his incarceration, though his 'jeopardy' may relate more closely to David's comparison of his persecutor, Saul, with 'one [who] doth hunt a partridge in the mountains'.[10]

that: 'The construction is occasionally sententious, and tolerably accurate in that respect, so as to discover very plainly that the author had the old Hebrew poetry for his model' (*Lectures*, ii. 179). The apocryphal books were far more widely circulated and read in the 18th c. than they are now, as the quantity of references to them in many forms of literature indicates. The 6th Article of Religion says of them, following Jerome, that 'the Church doth read for example of life and instruction of manners; but yet doth it not apply them to establish any Doctrine' (BCP). See the introductory discussions of the Wisdom of Solomon in *The Holy Bible, According to the Authorized Version; with Notes, Explanatory and Practical; taken principally from the most eminent writers of the United Church of England and Ireland: together with appropriate Introductions, Tables, Indexes, Maps, and Plans*, prepared and arranged by George D'Oyly and Richard Mant (this edn. Oxford, 1817), and *The Family Bible, containing The Sacred Text, of the Old and New Testaments with the Apocrypha. Illustrated by Marginal References, and Notes, Collected from the Bible of Dr. Dodd, and other Eminent Divines*.

[10] Num. 1: 16; Ecclus. 11: 30, translators' parentheses; 1 Sam. 26: 20. Elizur means 'God is my strength, my rock; *or* stone, *or* rock of God'; see Alexander Cruden, 'An Alphabetical Table of the Proper Names in the Old and New Testament; together with the Meaning or Signification of the Words in their Original Languages', in *A Complete Concordance to the Old and New Testament or a Dictionary and Alphabetical Index to the Bible* (1737; this edn. Youngman's unabridged text; hereafter Cruden).

Such parallelism between the pairs of verses, however, is not, as I have said, always apparent; but almost all of the 'Let' lines of Fragment A (which contains no 'For' verses), and Bond's Fragment B1 (which contains both 'For' and 'Let' verses), demonstrate their own internal parallelism. In the 'Let' verse under discussion this parallelism is evident in the description of the significance of the partridge in the second half, or responsive rejoinder, of the verse; and it may be significant in the light of the absence of the 'For' verses of Fragment A that this internal parallelism is more fully developed in that Fragment. The self-reflexive parallelism in each of these two lines, for example, is unmistakable:

Let Nebuchadnezzar bless with the Grashopper—the pomp and vanities of the world are as the herb of the field, but the glory of the Lord increaseth for ever.
Let Naboth bless with the Canker-worm—envy is cruel and killeth & preyeth upon that which God has given to aspire and bear fruit.

(A.69–70)

In Lowth's examples of antiphonal parallelism (as in Blair's), this structure is almost always shown within a single sentence, in the relation of clause to clause, rather than in the relation of distinct sentences.

I have argued that the 'Let' lines, at least in the earlier stages of the poem, contain their own internal parallelism, and form a body of poetry which may not be directly related to the 'For' verses with which they are juxtaposed, though that does not mean that we cannot sometimes *relate* the 'For' verses to the 'Let' verses which Bond's edition pairs them with; and in the pages that follow I shall often quote and discuss 'Let' and 'For' verses as pairs. But before I go on to discuss the relation between the two kinds of verses, it will be helpful to glance briefly at an aspect of the content that informs the structure, and at the implications of the use of the biblical paradigm.

III

The reservation Smart expresses about the interpretative methods of the new science when applied to the work of the divine 'GREAT POET'—'. . . if a man consult not the WORD how should he understand the WORK?' (B1. 220)—seems equally applicable to the relation of his own poetic creation to its biblical paradigm. In this verse he is asserting that 'Newton is ignorant', and that 'the philosophy of the times evn now is vain deceit' (B1. 219), because it is not based on the principles of revelation: it builds up general notions or theories from analyses of particular instances, rather than attempting to understand each instance through perceiving its relation to the whole revealed to faith. Smart writes that 'the Scotchman seeks for truth at the bottom of a well, the Englishman in the Heavn of Heavens' (B2. 378): the Scotchman's truth is sought through the accumulated distinctions and classifications of memory, the Englishman's through imagination and inspiration, through breadth rather than particularity of vision. For Smart, as for Coleridge: 'Not only is the Whole greater than a Part; but where it is a Whole, and not a mere All or Aggregate, it makes each part that which it is'; and in *Jubilate Agno*, that whole is the Word of revelation. Smart's criticisms of Newton, I suggest, closely resemble those which a correspondent of the *Christian's Magazine* metes out to those who disagree with his interpretation of scripture:

To those, indeed, who see things partially, attending only to the remote indefinite view of single objects, detached *from*, and uncomposed *with*, the whole horizon of the New Testament; to those I mean, who reason from *particulars* to generals, and not from generals to particulars, as they should do, in all cases relative to the Christian faith, it may, and I know it does, appear otherwise.[11]

This informing 'Whole' for Smart is 'the WORD', which has several specific but interrelated meanings: Christ is the 'Word' (λόγος) in the Gospel of St John; the Bible itself, and especially the Gospels, are also the 'Word'; and 'word' or *logos* describes the active principle in the created universe. These aspects of the Word are so closely interrelated that reference to any one aspect usually involves reference to the others; for the Word in each case represents the whole that is greater than the sum of its parts. The 'Word' that Newton should have consulted, and which we must now consult, is described more specifically in Smart's other, very similar, comment on Newton:

[11] See *Smart I*, B. 378 n. I quote Coleridge's annotation of a passage in Lessing's *Ernst und Falk*, quoted in S. T. Coleridge, *On the Constitution of the Church and State*, ed. J. Colmer (Princeton, NJ, 1976), 65 n. See also p. 20: 'In the idea of principle, Life, . . . the vital *functions* are the result of the organization; but this organization supposes and pre-supposes the vital *principle*. The bearings of the planets on the sun are determined by the ponderable matter of which they consist; but the *principle* of gravity, the *law* in the material creation, the *idea* of the Creator, is presupposed in order to the existence, yea, to the very conception of the existence, of matter itself.' *Christian's Magazine*, 2 (1761), 667–8.

Let Candace rejoice with the Craw-fish—How hath the Christian minister renowed the Queen.
Let The Eunuch rejoice with the Thorn-Back—It is good to be dis-covered reading the BIBLE.

For CHASTITY is the key of knowledge as in Esdras, Sr Isaac Newton & now, God be praised, in me.
For Newton nevertheless is more of error than of the truth, but I am of the WORD of GOD.

(B1.194–5)

For reasons concerning the biblical significance of the eunuch, I interpret these lines as meaning that Newton's error, in Smart's eyes, resulted from a quality of his attitude to the Bible, rather than the quality of his chastity. Smart is not necessarily saying that all science must be based (in a fundamentalist manner) on specific statements about natural science made in the Bible, but is referring to the Bible as the 'Word'—as the paradigmatic entity that is greater than the sum of its parts; as the informing 'Whole' that renders its contents significant through their relation to it; and as the paradigm of divinely inspired and authoritative revelation.[12]

This understanding of the Bible as an authoritative and comprehensive text was, of course, not above controversy, but its significance, and its importance to the way the Bible was read, is clearly evident in discussions of the nature of scripture prophecy. Bishop Lowth, whose *Lectures* are often seen as describing a newly scientific and even irreligious attitude to the poetry of the Old Testament, nevertheless assumes that prophecy is the fruit of divine inspiration and involves an apparent obscurity only dispersed when the predicted event is accomplished and recognized: prophecy is a sketch, whose implicit detail is substantiated or recognized by the future. The types of the Old Testament, similarly, are fulfilled, completed, by the appearance in the New of that which is typified. Anthony Blackwall, in his *Sacred Classics Defended*, describes the Old and New Testaments as the complementary volumes of a single book: the second not only gives substance to the shadows of the first, but 'clears all the obscurities and

---

[12] In Acts 8: 26–39 Philip's conversion of the eunuch occasions the mention or 'renown' of Queen Candace, but the term 'eunuch' in the Bible can be used to signify anyone holding a position of authority—e.g. a minister. Perhaps the most important statement on the subject is Jesus' saying: 'For there are some eunuchs, which were so born from *their* mother's womb: and there are some eunuchs, which were made eunuchs of men: and there be eunuchs, which have made themselves eunuchs for the kingdom of heaven's sake. He that is able to receive *it*, let him receive *it*' (Matt. 19: 12; see also 1 Cor. 9). The term here is usually taken to refer, not to emasculation, but to those who have chosen to dedicate their lives to worship.

difficulties of the prophecies; and lets us know the reason why they were express'd in obscure terms'. The 'wonderful harmony and agreement' he perceives as uniting the two volumes assumes the integrity of the books that make up those volumes, and also describes the Bible as possessing a coherent unity of structure, a fully satisfactory capacity for closure, for containing and answering every obscurity and ambiguity, every potential loose end that might lead elsewhere, that does at least suggest an understanding of its all-embracing and almost super-temporal scope similar to that expressed by Charles Leslie, to whose *Short and Easy Method with The Jews* Blackwall refers us.[13]

Leslie describes the extension of this structure of prophecy and accomplishment to the structure of post-biblical human history, anticipating the conversion of his audience:

Be not afraid to lose your law or your prophets, you will hear them read every day in our churches; and their true and full import explained and fulfilled in the gospel: for the gospel is the best commentary upon the law, and the law is the best expositor of the gospel: they are like a pair of indentures, they answer in every part; their harmony is wonderful; and is of itself a conviction: no human contrivance could have reached it; there is a divine majesty and foresight in the answer of every ceremony and type to its completion: and there is one yet to be completed. O the glorious day when that shall come!

For Leslie, the correspondence between prophecy and event reveals the Bible as an absolutely binding contract, controlling and authenticating future events through their agreement to its exposition, its checklist. Bishop Thomas Newton, in his *Dissertations on the Prophecies*, describes prophecy as

history anticipated and contracted; history is prophecy accomplished and dilated: and the prophecies of scripture contain, as you see, the fate of the most considerable nations, and the substance of the most memorable transactions in the world from the earliest to the latest times.

The prophecies of Daniel and St John, he argues, 'may really be said to be a summary of the history of the world, and the history of the world is the best commentary upon their prophecies'. Newton describes the relation between history and prophecy in the terms

---

[13] See Hepworth, *Lowth*, p. 36; and Peter Hall, 'Introductory Memoir', in Lowth, *Sermons and Other Remains, of Robert Lowth, D.D.* (London, 1834). Lowth, *Lectures*, vol. i, lect. xi, pp. 246–9. A. Blackwall, *The Sacred Classics Defended and Illustrated: or, an Essay Humbly offer'd towards proving the Purity, Propriety, and True Eloquence of the Writers of the New Testament* (1725; this 3rd edn. 2 vols., London, 1737), i. 309 and n.

Leslie applied to the relation of the law and gospel: he represents all human history as internal to the book, which, as the expression of God's word, participates in or figures forth the synchronic nature of the divine eternity.[14]

Jubilate Agno implies a similar sense of the power of the word of God in the lines:

Let Shamgar rejoice with Otis, who looks about him for the glory of God, & sees the horizon compleat at once. For the word of God is a sword on my side—no matter what other weapon a stick or a straw.

(B1. 20)

Here the Otis, which 'sees the horizon compleat at once', might be seen as analogous to the Bible; the 'Word of God', for while it occupies a single and determinate position as a finite entity, the Bible also represents, or figures forth the immanence of, that synchronic eternity which 'sees the horizon' both physical (or temporal) and spiritual, 'compleat at once'. Shamgar is also relevant to the confidence Smart expresses in the 'For' verse, for he was one of the judges or deliverers of Israel, and slew six hundred Philistines with an ox goad. The Hebrew letter ל (lamed) means 'ox goad', but through its relation to the letter 'l' Smart also writes that it is 'the letter ל which signifies GOD by himself' (B2. 477), and Shamgar's weapon is thus 'the word of God'. That 'word', then, which is Smart's 'sword', is the eternal word of God as represented in the Bible, which is interpreted as a synchronic text.[15]

This view of the Bible, as the arguments I have quoted from a range of ecclesiastical authorities indicate, is not in itself remarkable, but Smart's use of it again reveals the distrust of rational religion and natural philosophy which I discussed in my last chapter. It involves a conception of the authority of the biblical text that became increasingly unusual as the century progressed—in Johnson's sermons, for example, the sufficiency of the scriptures as the guide to salvation is repeatedly affirmed, but it is almost invariably the New Testament that

[14] *A Short and Easy Method with The Jews* (1709), in *The Theological Works of the Rev. Charles Leslie*, 7 vols. (Oxford, 1832), i. 168–9. Thomas Newton, *Dissertations on The Prophecies, which have remarkably been fulfilled and at This Time are Fulfilling in the World* (1754–8; this 13th edn. London, 1823), 736.

[15] See Judg. 3: 31; 5: 6. Smart equates the letter 'l' with the Hebrew word *el*, which signifies God. I discuss this play on sounds below (p. 172). Smart's 'sword' may involve a play on the combination of 'word' with the letter 's', which 'is soul' (B2. 530, C. 11), to emphasize that it is the spiritual sword that is on his side. See the image of the 'whole horizon' of the NT in *Christian's Magazine*, quoted above.

is cited in this context. By the end of the century, the view of the Bible described by Beilby Porteus, the then Bishop of London, is probably representative of the main stream of ecclesiastical thought: Porteus stresses the coherence of the Bible as a continuous historical narrative, rather than as a synchronic text, and though he advises his audience to read the whole book, he tells them 'to begin with the New Testament first, and read it over most frequently'. The conception of the Bible which, I think, we need to bear in mind while we read *Jubilate Agno*, is most closely echoed in the writings of controversial figures like John Newton, the Calvinist rector of Olney, rather than in the main body of Anglican orthodoxy; but this is not to say, of course, that the view of the Bible as a synchronic 'landscape' rather than a sequential history had dissenting implications in the mid century, when its connection with the miraculous power of prophetic revelation made it, rather, a sword on the side of the defence of faith against the encroachments of natural religion.[16]

IV

Having consulted 'the WORD', we are now perhaps in a position to 'understand the WORK', *Jubilate Agno* itself; and to understand that its debt to the Bible in form and content is greater, and of a rather different nature, than critics have supposed. In my earlier discussion of the structure of the poem I suggested that the relation between the 'Let' and 'For' verses paired by W. H. Bond is highly complex and problematic, and that though I would not disagree with Bond's reorganization of the poem, I would question the way in which the poem, thus rearranged, should be read. Smart himself gives us some clues: he refers at a fairly early stage of the poem to 'my MAGNIFICAT' (B1. 43), and he may at this stage still have been considering the poem as a publishable work. This reference can only be taken to refer to *Jubilate Agno* as we know of nothing else written by him that could have been referred to in this way. The import of the Magnificat may be

---

[16] See Samuel Johnson, sermons 3, 22, *Sermons*, ed. Jean Hagstrum and James Gray, in *The Yale Edition of the Works of Samuel Johnson*, xiv (New Haven, Conn., 1978), esp. 29–30, 235. Beilby Porteus, lect. i, *Lectures on the Gospel of St. Matthew: delivered in the Parish Church of St. James, Westminster, in the years 1798, 1799, 1800, and 1801*, 2 vols. (1801; this 11th edn. London, 1810), i. 25. On John Newton, see sermons V, VI, 'On Searching the Scriptures', in *Discourses, or Sermons, as intended for the pulpit* (1760), and pp. 222–5 below.

summarized: 'My soul doth magnify the Lord . . . For he that is mighty hath magnified me: and holy is his Name.' The notion of the poem as a magnificat has interesting implications in relation to its content, and it is significant in the context of Smart's known desire to reform and reorganize the church service. Smart continued to treasure this ambition after his release from confinement, as his translation of the *Psalms* (1765) and version of the *Hymns and Spiritual Songs for the Feasts and Festivals of the Church of England* (1765) illustrate; and he refers to his plan several times in *Jubilate Agno*, for example in the lines:

For it would be better if the LITURGY were musically performed.

For it were better for the SERVICE, if only select psalms were read.

For the Lamentations of Jeremiah, Songs from other scriptures, and parts of Esdras might be taken to supply the quantity.

(B1. 252; B2.511–12)

—and with slightly different implications, in the lines:

Let Nicanor rejoice with the Skeat—Blessed be the name of the Lord Jesus in fish and in the Shewbread, which ought to be continually on the altar, now more than ever, and the want of it is the Abomination of Desolation spoken of by Daniel.

Let Junia rejoice with the Faber-Fish—Broild fish & honeycomb may be taken for the sacrament.

For NEW BREAD is the most wholesome especially if it be leaven'd with honey.

For a NEW SONG also is best, if it be to the glory of God; & taken with the food like the psalms.

(B1. 206, 243; B2. 389–90)

Bread, fish, and honeycomb were the food of Christ resurrected, and the lines suggest that the sacrament of the resurrection should replace the sacrament of the crucifixion and death of Christ, and also, that the Old Testament should be reinterpreted in the light of the New.[17]

In *Jubilate Agno* Smart carries out the second of these ideas, as the first few verses of the poem imply:

---

[17] I quote from the Magnificat in the BCP. See Luke 24: 30, 42–3. On the movement for reform of the liturgy, see G. J. Cumming, *A History of Anglican Liturgy* (1969; this 2nd edn. London, 1982). ch. 8. See also Marcus Walsh, 'Smart's *Psalms* and Worship and Belief in the English Church', in the Introd. to his edn., *The Poetical Works of Christopher Smart*, iii. *A Translation of the Psalms of David* (Oxford, 1987; hereafter *Smart III*).

Let Noah and his company approach the throne of Grace, and do homage to
the Ark of their Salvation.
Let the Levites of the Lord take the Beavers of y^c brook alive into the Ark of
the Testimony.

(A. 4, 16)

Stead notes of the second of these two lines that the use of the Ark
represents a confusion of ideas, and Bond adds that beavers are non-
biblical creatures. But Smart is here telescoping three apparently
distinct ideas of the ark into one atemporal type: the ark of Noah's
salvation is at once the historical ark that saved him from the flood, and
Christ, the 'ark' or vessel of God on earth, and the ark of the covenant.
The Ark of the Levites, taken in conjunction with this line, is Noah's
ark, which the beavers entered alive, and is simultaneously the 'Ark of
the Testimony'. The testimony is the word of God, as it was received
by Moses, and, by implication, the word of God as it was incorporated
in Christ. It is Christ in whom the creatures live, move, and have
being, and thus the beavers are alive in him, and may be regarded as
especially appropriate in this verse, rather than inappropriate as non-
biblical, because they represent diligence, and are 'of y^c brook', which
is perhaps an allusion to the 'water of life'. In *Jubilate Agno*, then, as in
the Bible, the 'type' becomes identified with that which it figures forth;
and it is also apparent that in the poem the poet attempts to 'translate'
the Bible into a 'NEW SONG . . . to the glory of God'; and it is in this
sense that he is the 'scribe-evangelist' (B2. 327).[18]

This concern with reinterpretation, or translation, illuminates both
the form and the content of *Jubilate Agno*, but for the moment a brief
summary of some of its implications will suffice. Smart refers to his
poem as a magnificat, suggesting that it describes a reciprocal relation
with God. As the men, women, beasts, and inanimate objects
enumerated in the 'Let' verses of the poem are presented as engaged
in offering praise or thanksgiving to God, in magnifying God, they
become involved in a reciprocal relation with God, which magnifies
them. Through their mention in the poem they are interpreted or
translated, for they become subsumed in God in whom they rejoice,
and a part of that eternal attribute of goodness which simultaneously
bestows and receives all blessing and praise.[19]

The contents of the 'Let' verses are further purified and interpreted,

---

[18] Rev. 22: 1. Beavers may also be appropriate since they build lodges or 'arks'.

[19] On the reciprocal relation described by prayer, see Samuel Boyse, *Deity* (1741),
ll. 1043–56.

as the 'Let' lines represent an attempt to write, not only a magnificat, but a version of the divine poetry of the Bible. The structure of the 'Let' lines is strongly influenced by the biblical paradigm, and the faithfulness of 'imitation' this implies may imbue the 'Let' lines with some of the sublimity of their model. Lowth's enthusiasm for the power of the poetry of the Hebrews in his *Lectures* is so great that he suggests that the very representation or expression of an object or sentiment in this sublime style makes that object or sentiment itself potent and sublime. This implication is clearest in those lectures dealing specifically with the sublime style of the Hebrews, and in Lecture 6, on 'Poetic Imagery From Objects of Nature', and Lecture 7, on the use of 'Poetic Imagery From Common Life'. In these last two lectures Lowth discusses the frequent references to mundane objects in the Bible, and argues that these objects become sublime through their context, and through the sublime style in which they are discussed. He writes:

Indeed, to have made use of the boldest imagery with the most perfect perspicuity, and the most common and familiar with the greatest dignity, is a commendation almost peculiar to the sacred poets. I shall not hesitate to produce an example of this kind, in which the meanness of the image is fully equalled by the plainness and inelegance of the expression; and yet such is its consistency, such the propriety of its application, that I do not scruple to pronounce it sublime. The Almighty threatens the ultimate destruction of Jerusalem in these terms:

> 'And I will wipe Jerusalem,
> As a man wipeth a dish:
> He wipeth it, and turneth it upside down'.

He finds that the 'degree of sublimity the mere form and disposition of a Lyric Poem can impart to a subject not itself sublime' is a unique characteristic of Hebrew poetry.[20]

[20] Lowth, *Lectures*, vol. i, lect. vii, pp. 151–5; vol. ii, lect. xxvii, p. 253. Wordsworth expresses a similar apprehension of the potential sublimity of everyday objects in his description of clouds, where:

> . . . fixed resemblances were seen
> To implements of ordinary use,
> But vast in size, in substance glorified;
> Such as by Hebrew Prophets were beheld
> In vision—forms uncouth of mightiest power
> For admiration, and mysterious awe.

(*The Excursion*, bk. II, ll. 864–9, in *The Poetical Works of William Wordsworth: The Excursion; The Recluse*, pt. I, bk, 1, ed. E. de Selincourt and Helen Darbishire (Oxford, 1949).) For a discussion of why Lowth saw this characteristic as unique to Hebrew poetry, see pp. 173–4 below.

I see the rigorous structure of the 'Let' verses as an attempt to write 'pure' and 'sublime' poetry, which would similarly have the power to interpret its subject-matter, to express its spiritual significance, and thus to show the immanence of the divine revealed in it. This argument for the power of the form and content of the 'Let' verses is further reinforced by the attempt to express the synchronic unity of the biblical paradigm that they represent, for if the verses represent such an attempt, every man, beast, or object mentioned becomes identified with the saints and patriarchs, and, finally, with the 'Nations, and languages, and every Creature, in which is the breath of Life' (A. 2). In invoking that innate 'breath of Life' Smart is, of course, invoking the presence of the Deity, of the Word, in creation.

How then are the 'For' verses related to the potentially sublime magnificat of the 'Let' verses? The first few verses in which they are introduced, at the opening of Fragment B1, provide us with a clue. If we look through the 113 verses of Fragment A we do not find a single direct reference to Smart, or a single use of the personal pronoun, but when we turn to Fragment B1, although there is no direct reference to the poet, or use of the personal pronoun 'I' for the first 82 'Let' lines, we are immediately struck by the personal nature of the 'For' verses, and their continual use of the first person singular. The first two 'For' verses read:

For I am not without authority in my jeopardy, which I derive inevitably from the glory of the name of the Lord.
For I bless God whose name is Jealous—and there is a zeal to deliver us from everlasting burnings.

(B1. 1–2)

This personal tone, and continued use of the personal pronoun, persists throughout the first 156 'For' verses of Fragment B1, after which it gives way to an account of Smart's cosmological theories. If the antiphonal structure of *Jubilate Agno* rests on the parallelism of the 'Let' and 'For' verses, the hypothetical choir engaged for the performance of the work would presumably have been singing the 'Let' verses, and Smart's voice alone would have sung the 'responsive' 'For' verses.

The rationale behind this apparent imbalance can be found in Smart's claim: 'For I preach the very GOSPEL of CHRIST without comment & with this weapon shall I slay envy' (B1. 9): Smart's 'preaching' refers to the 'Let' verses, in which he reinterprets the Bible in his capacity as 'scribe-evangelist', in an attempt to make it compatible with 'the very GOSPEL of CHRIST'; and referring to this aim he writes: 'I have translated in the charity, which makes things better . . .' (B1. 11). The main interest of verse B1. 9, however, lies in the apparent contradiction it contains, for the verse is in itself a 'comment' on the 'Let' line it is paired with by Bond: 'Let Chesed rejoice with Strepsiceros, whose weapons are the ornaments of his peace' (B1. 9). The concept of the gospel of peace and love becoming a weapon is clearly developed from the strepsiceros, a sort of ibex, whose horns are a means of defence, but are also, according to Pliny, naturally shaped like lyres, and could be used as such when strung. But this apparent contradiction only appears if we read the 'For' verses as a public response, correlative to the 'Let' verses. If we read the 'For' verses as a private and personal commentary on the 'public' 'Let' verses, the paradox disappears.[21]

I argue that it can be fruitful to see the 'Let' verses as dependent solely upon one another, forming a sublime mode of poetry through the inter-connections created by their external exhibition of structural parallelism (each 'Let' verse parallels every other 'Let' verse), and the reflection of this in their internal, antiphonal parallelism. As Job's first speech illustrates, rigid repetition of rhythmic structure co-ordinates each sentence with the next in a relation that is strengthened, rather than swayed or weakened, by occasional deviation. Ideally, the form exalts its contents through rhythmic stress, and through their place in the structure of the whole, just as the participants named are magnified through their act of magnifying their creator. I also argue that the 'For' verses form a private response or commentary in relation to the 'Let' verses. The importance of the 'For' verses forming a *private* commentary is that as such they do not intrude upon, or change the nature of, the 'Let' verses; they exist in a dependent relation to the 'Let' verses, which they react to, comment on, or to some extent explain or make explicit, but the 'Let' verses have no correspondingly dependent relation with them, and are not in any way responsive to them, as they might be in an antiphonal 'dialogue'. Also, as a 'private' and separate set of responses, the 'For' verses are not bound to, or contained by, the

---

[21] Bond mentions the difficulty of imagining the performance, but does not seem to see it as posing any problem for his reading of the poem; see *JA*, 'Introduction', p. 20. 'Chesed' means 'mercy', or 'benevolence exercised without respect of merit': see *Christian's Magazine*, 2 (1761), 560, 678. Pliny, *Natural History*, trans. H. Rackham, 10 vols. (London and Cambridge, Mass., 1940), iii. 510–11 (XI. xlv).

rigid structure of the 'Let' verses, though their relation to this structure is significant.

In Fragment B1 the relation of the 'For' verses to the 'Let' verses is essentially one of contrast. Rather than being contained within the syntactical structure of the 'magnificat' itself, and creating an internal 'dialogue' within it, the 'For' verses take an external, dialectically opposed position. They are thus contained within a larger whole, but this does not form a unity in which the distinct natures of the two forms are lost. The role of the 'For' verses is at once to oppose an apparent syntactical freedom and flexibility to an apparent imposition of syntactical constraint; and to oppose a distinctly personal and individual voice to the ideally universal, super-personal language of the magnificat. The effect of this twofold opposition is complex, and its dual aspects must first, I think, be considered separately in so far as this is possible.

One implication of the nature of the opposition between the 'Let' and the 'For' verses is revealed by the freedom with which the commentary offered in the 'For' verses relates to the 'Let' verses. Each of the 'Let' verses forms a complete observation, a complete statement, confined within the compact unity of the verse, but the 'For' verses may contain a discussion of a subject raised in a 'Let' verse, and continue that discussion over as many as thirty lines. Bond concedes, at the beginning of one such particularly lengthy discussion, that 'From this point on, the relationship between *Let* and *For* verses rapidly deteriorates. Each section tends to go its own way, with only occasional and rather tenuous correspondence'; but Bond sees this 'deterioration' as symptomatic of 'the disintegration of Smart's original plan', rather than as indicative of the general function of the 'For' verses in relation to the 'Let' verses.[22]

I suggest (as I suggested in my discussion of the opening verses of the Book of Wisdom) that the 'For' verses also form a body of poetry which does not have to be understood through its relation to the body of poetry formed by the 'Let' verses, for a line-for-line correspondence between the two forms is not always apparent, and, though the 'For' verses may elucidate and make explicit the content of the 'Let' verses (though not necessarily of the 'Let' verses with which, in Bond's

---

[22] For example, Smart begins a discussion of his theocentric natural philosophy in 'For' verse B1, 157 which continues almost uninterrupted throughout the following 70 'For' verses, and perhaps at greater length, depending upon the interpretation of the subsequent verses. *JA*, p. 67 n. 2; 'Introduction', p. 22.

edition, they physically correspond), they still form a coherent unity where they do not do this. I argue for a far more fluid relation between the 'Let' and 'For' verses than that posited by Bond. I see the 'For' verses as a more general and flexible form of commentary than would be possible if the two verse forms were related through a line-by-line correspondence: they form an independent body of 'private' meditation, which may reflect on the more 'public', or less personal, 'Let' verses, but which may also possess an internal poetic integrity, as Fragment B2, which contains no 'Let' verses, shows.

Though the structure of *Jubilate Agno* is complex and unusual, the use of two distinct but complementary forms of devotional expression is in some respects comparable with the method of private or solitary prayer advocated by William Law in *A Serious Call to a Devout and Holy Life* (1728), a comparability that may reflect on the perception of tensions between private conscience and common faith, which is frequently expressed in the eighteenth century and is of particular concern in the sermons of the second half of the century. Law writes that the singing of a psalm should always accompany private devotion, allowing the Christian to exercise their imagination in order to achieve a suitably exalted state of mind:

. . . sometimes imagine to yourself that you saw holy David with his hands upon his harp, and his eyes fixed upon heaven, calling in transport upon all the creation, sun and moon, light and darkness, day and night, men and angels, to join with his rapturous soul in praising the Lord of Heaven.

Dwell upon this imagination till you think you are singing with this Divine musician; and let such a companion teach you to exalt your heart unto God.

Law argues that regular private prayer is essential to the Christian life, and while he distrusts forms of prayer which may permit an empty and superficial devotion, he proposes his 'method' of procedure to 'assist and direct' the less 'proficient', advocating a methodical combination of regular given form and spontaneous utterance. The 'true liberty of private devotion', he writes, is that 'it should be under the direction of some form' but able to employ 'new expressions' where these are 'more affecting'.[23]

These recommendations extend to subject-matter, as well as to

---

[23] See e.g. Beilby Porteus, *Sermons on Several Subjects*, 2 vols. (London, 1794), vol. ii, sermon xvi; George Carr, *Sermons*, 3 vols. (Edinburgh, 1777), vol. iii, sermon i; Thomas Pyle, *Sixty Sermons on Plain and Practical Subjects*, 2 vols. (Norwich, 1773), vol. ii, sermon vii; William Law, *A Serious Call to a Devout and Holy Life*, introd. Norman Sykes (1728; this edn. London, 1906, 1967), 204, 171.

form and expression, for Law suggests the combination of 'some fixed subject' with 'something at liberty', and advises that the fixed 'proper forms' should be petitions developed from any passage in scripture or pious literature that 'more than ordinarily affects your mind'. He concludes:

> Let, therefore, praise and thanksgiving, and oblation of yourself unto God, be always the fixed and certain object of your first prayers . . . and then take the liberty of adding such other devotions, as the accidental difference of your state, or the accidental difference of your heart, shall then make most needful and expedient for you.
>
> For one of the greatest benefits of private devotion consists in rightly adapting our prayers to these two conditions—the difference of our state, and the difference of our hearts.

It is not perhaps entirely adventitious, in the light of Law's style and subject, that these two sentences, the first containing an exhortation to praise, and the second a commentary upon that exhortation, begin with the words 'Let' and 'For', but that is not my point in quoting them, which is that Law represents these two parts of prayer as complementary. The first constant and chief part, which may be taken or adapted from the writings of others, prepares the worshipper's mind for the expression of particular prayers in the second, and his method involves a division into the general and fixed, and particular and free which lends support to an understanding of the 'halves' of *Jubilate Agno* in similar terms.[24]

Jubilate Agno, however, is not an exclusively private form of prayer, but a form which, I have suggested, juxtaposes private and personal devotion with a comprehensive, potentially universal, exhortation to praise. We can perhaps arrive at a clearer idea of how this divided structure works if we consider one further aspect of the performance of private and liturgical devotions. The 'fixed' part of *Jubilate Agno*, the liturgical invocations of humans and creatures, call on a congregation which includes the living and the dead, the animate and mute creation, to perform a service of praise and thanksgiving, whereas the 'free' 'For' verses express the particular meditations of the individual. The first fragment of the poem, where only 'Let' verses survive, is suitable to liturgical performance, but as soon as we attempt to read the 'Let' verses in relation to the 'For' verses, in Fragment B1, the poem demands to be read in silence. Religious poetry which addresses the

---

[24] Law, *Serious Call*, pp. 176, 175, 176. See Cumming, *Liturgy*, pp. 135–6.

individual as a private person, rather than as a member of a congregation, is usually, in the eighteenth century, intended for meditation, for careful reading, rather than for performance, and in *Jubilate Agno* the structure of the poem depends, I suggest, upon this distinction between the kind of language appropriate to public worship, and the silence appropriate to private devotion. Elizabeth Rowe's *Exercises*, for example, are adapted to private devotion, and while the terms in which Watts discusses them seem to encourage the reader to attempt to perform them, to speak their language, he also stresses the absolute privacy in which they should be read. He describes them as 'secret and intense Breathings' rather than articulate sounds, and he compares their transports with St Paul's vision, where the apostle heard unutterable things that he could not report to his followers. Watts's Preface to his *Hymns and Spiritual Songs*, similarly, distinguishes between the congregational singer and the retired reader of his 'pious Meditations': his *Hymns* perform different functions, and are read in different ways, depending on the circumstances of their audience. As part of the liturgy they are adapted to performance, but for the 'devout and retired Soul' they are suitable to meditative reading. The reactions of Fanny Burney and Mr Fairly to Young's *Night-Thoughts*, which I discussed in my first chapter, involve a similar distinction between reflective reading in solitude, and congregational performance: Young's private, meditative poetry is not to be 'read on regularly', but to be dipped into with an irregularity, a disregard for the poem's continuity, that is suitable only to private reading. *Jubilate Agno* demonstrates in its structure the distinction between private reading and congregational performance: the 'Let' verses express its liturgical character, but the flexibility of structure that is introduced by the 'For' verses, the disregard for regular sequential organization that their relation to the 'Let' verses involves, is suited only to private meditation.[25]

V

In the juxtaposition of the opposed syntactical structures of the 'Let' and 'For' verses, it might be supposed that the greater flexibility and

---

[25] *Exercises*, Preface, p. x. Watts, *Hymns*, (1707; this edn. London, 1781), Preface, p. xiii. *Diaries and Letters of Madame D'Arblay*, ed. Charlotte Barrett, 7 vols. (1842–6; this edn. 4 vols., London, 1891), iii. 165.

freedom of the latter form would emphasize the restrictive and fixed nature of the former. This is not, however, the case. The 'For' verse, expressing an apparently unambiguous and individual opinion often developed from some part of the 'Let' verse, reveals that the restrictive structure of the 'Let' verse creates a far less determinable meaning within the verse. In the 'For' verse the reader does not have to call into question the referential status of the language, unless the complexities of the 'Let' verse reflect back again on to it. In the 'For' verse words are placed in a 'natural' context which makes them readily acceptable as language 'counters' whose value is agreed. As Smart expresses it in a remark about language, among other things: '. . . a CHARACTER is the votes of the Worldlings . . .' (B2. 363). The range of reference and meaning available to the words within their given context is part of a social contract: it is something agreed upon by 'votes', by the predominant usage, and as such is as subject to time and change as are the opinions of the 'voters', and the 'voters' or 'Worldlings' themselves.[26]

In the 'Let' verses, however, the status of individual words is made ambiguous. Their context does not inform them for us, and denote their terms of reference, because their context is 'unnatural'. The context, the syntactical structure, 'fixes' the words, and renders them no longer language 'counters' whose value is established within an agreed referential framework. It extracts the words from the social language and places them in another structure—an almost ideographic structure; and if we attempt to see them as anything but parts of that larger framework they appear meaningless—a 'mad language', as Moira Dearnley has said. This is perhaps what Smart is telling the reader in the line: 'For a CHARACTER is the votes of the Worldlings, but the seal is of Almighty GOD alone' (B2. 363): and may be one reason why he informs us that his 'magnificat' is not verse: 'For I pray the Lord Jesus to translate my MAGNIFICAT into verse and represent it' (B1. 43). Verse, he explains (except as it might be purified by faith), does violence to language, perhaps because of the constraints attached to its conventional genres, or 'modes', and because of the contradictions or clashes that arise between these: 'For Clapper-claw is in the

---

[26] I do not wish to suggest, in the terms in which I describe the relation between the 'Let' and 'For' sections of the poem, that the 'For' verses are written in a language seen as of human invention, whereas the 'Let' verses employ a God-given language. The contrast I describe is rather between the terms in which the different 'sections' are accessible and interpretable, and might resemble the distinction suggested in John Cleland's discussion of language, quoted on p. 175 below. I shall discuss the issue of theories of the origin of language in my next chapter.

grappling of the words upon one another in all the modes of versification' (B2. 632).[27]

The notion that Smart's 'magnificat' is not 'verse' may be echoed in his confession that 'in my nature I quested for beauty, but God, God hath sent me to sea for pearls' (B1. 30). Blair explains:

The antient Arabs . . . valued themselves much on their metrical Compositions, which were of two sorts; the one they compared to loose pearls, and the other to pearls strung. In the former, the sentences or verses were without connection; and their beauty arose from the elegance of the expression, and the acuteness of the sentiment. The moral doctrines of the Persians were generally comprehended in such independent proverbial apothegms, formed into verse. In this respect they bear a considerable resemblance to the Proverbs of Solomon; a great part of which book consists of unconnected Poetry, like the loose pearls of the Arabians. The same form of Composition appears also in the Book of Job. The Greeks seem to have been the first who introduced a more regular structure, and closer connection of parts, into their Poetical Writings.

Smart's 'loose pearls' resemble the style of the Book of Job, and might perhaps have lost some of their 'elegance' and 'acuteness', their ability to make an impression upon 'docile minds', if they had been clapperclawed into verse; but they are not 'loose pearls' in the sense that this might imply that they are randomly scattered. The 'Let' verses represent a unified attempt to use a 'pure' language, inherently significant as a result of its God-given status—a language not dependent for the terms of its significance on arbitrary human contract (the 'votes of the Worldlings')—but dependent solely upon its relation to the divine seal of authentication. Smart's attempts to achieve this

---

[27] Dearnley, *Christopher Smart*, p. 166. 'Clapperclaw' means 'to claw or scratch', or 'to revile, abuse' (*OED*, 'Clapperclaw', *v. arch.* or *dial.* 1. *trans.*; 2. *fig.*); and Smart's noun therefore seems to describe a violent interlocking principle. See its use in his fable 'Madam and the Magpie' (1767), l. 44, in *Smart IV*. The implication that Smart's poetry is not verse may allude to Horace's *De Arte Poetica*, ll. 333–46 (see B2. 363). In Smart's prose translation the passage reads: 'The poets intend either to profit or to delight; or to deliver at once both the pleasures and the necessaries of life. Whatever precepts you give, be concise: that docile minds may soon comprehend what is said, and faithfully retain it. . . . The tribes of the seniors rail against every thing that is void of edification: the exalted knights disregard poems that are *dry and* austere. He who joins instruction with the agreeable, carries the votes of all *mankind*, by delighting, and at the same time admonishing the reader. This book gains money for the Sosii, this crosses the sea, and continues to its celebrated author a lasting duration' (Smart (trans.), *The Works of Horace, Translated Literally into English Prose; For the Use of those who are desirous of acquiring or recovering a competent Knowledge of the Latin Language*, 2 vols., (London, 1756), ii. 411; translator's italics). The Sosii were booksellers.

linguistic purity by, to extend his own metaphor, melting down the words employed in prosaic language, or currency, and re-casting them, giving them a pure 'image' or 'impression . . . by punching'.[28]

This attempt to use a language which has been 'translated' into purity emerges as one of the dominant themes of the poem, for, as I have said, Smart attempts to translate, or reinterpret as pure, all the objects enumerated in the 'Let' lines. The crocodile provides a pertinent example of this:

> Let Joseph, who from the abundance of his blessing may spare to him that lacketh, praise with the Crocodile, which is pleasant and pure, when he is interpreted, tho' his look is of terror and offence.

> (A. 46)

In this line Smart makes explicit the interpretative process that renders 'pure' both the language and the content of the 'Let' verses, and which is implicit in the description of the poem as a magnificat, for 'the praise of the Lord gives propriety to all things' (A. 79). The 'Let' verses are 'translated' in that they reveal the immanence of God in language, and express creation as involved in a universal magnificat; and it is this sense of a translation of the physical and accidental into the spiritual and ideal that I see as informing references to migration, travel and translation in the poem:

> Let Libni rejoice with the Redshank, who migrates not but is translated to the upper regions.

> For I have translated in the charity, which makes things better & I shall be translated myself at the last.

> Let Zohar rejoice with Cychramus who cometh with the quails on a particular affair.

> For there is a traveling for the glory of God without going to Italy or France.

> (B1. 11, 35)[29]

---

[28] Blair, *Lectures*, iii. 89–90. On the resemblance of the style of Ecclesiasticus and the Wisdom of Solomon to that of Proverbs, see the Introduction to these books in D'Oyly and Mant, and Lowth, *Lectures*, ii. 176–9. I refer to B2. 404: 'For my talent is to give an impression upon words by punching, that when the reader casts his eye upon 'em, he takes up the image from the mould which I have made.' The poet's interest in this analogy may be indicated by the number of terms here related to coinage, e.g. talent, casts, and punching.

[29] Both 'Libni' and 'Zohar' mean 'white' (Cruden). In the Bible whiteness signifies spiritual purity resulting from 'translation' or purification (except where it is associated with leprosy); see e.g. Isa. 1: 18; Dan. 12: 10; Rev. 7: 14. Stead notes that the cychramus 'migrates with snails', and that Smart's ideas on migration are not unusual (Stead, pp. 192, 191); see also Richard B. Schwartz, *Samuel Johnson and the New Science* (Madison, Wis., 1971), 43.

This process of translating or interpreting has significant implications for the poem's content, but it also indicates how the poem should be read, for our reading must be an interpretative act. As may have been apparent from my reading of the lines of the poem that I have quoted, I do not understand the poem as offering rules or guidelines determining or prescribing its interpretability. Smart describes himself as having 'a greater compass both of mirth and melancholy than another' (B1. 132), but the poem affords us no opportunity for distinguishing the poet's mirth from his melancholy, or for determining where our search for the 'proper' or appropriate significance of its contents should end, though Smart tells us that this search must be directed by an attention to 'the WORD' of the Bible. Thus in reading the following 'pair' of lines—

Let Bukki rejoice with the Buzzard, who is clever, with the reputation of a silly fellow.

For Silly fellow! Silly fellow! is against me and belongeth neither to me nor my family.

(B1. 60)

—we do not know whether the lines express mirth or melancholy, and we also do not know at what stage of analysis we may be overburdening the lines with significance, or 'reading too much into them'. Bond sees these lines as indicative of the bitterness Smart felt towards his family, and of his fears that he had been cuckolded by his wife, but the lines might just as well be read as expressing Smart's mirth, and even a confidence in the qualities he knows himself to possess, though others fail to recognize them. This reading would depend upon a pun involving the name 'Bukki', and reflected in the contradictory associations of the buzzard. For as the buzzard is at once a 'silly old buzzard' and a powerful bird of prey with keen eyesight, so 'Bukki' means 'wasting', and might thus apply to a 'Silly fellow', but is pronounced 'book-y' which may be appropriate to Smart as, according to his own description, 'a man who has made poetry, perhaps, too much the business of his life'. This kind of ambiguity of interpretation may reflect the poem's lack of an audience—it was not apparently, ultimately at least, intended for publication—but its presence in other parallel aspects of the poem suggests a further and more positive significance.[30]

[30] *JA*, p. 48 n. 2. Smart, *Horace*, 'Preface', vol. i, p. iii. This translation of 'Bukki' is given in *Helps to the Study of the Bible* (Oxford, n.d.), but the name is translated 'mouth of Jah' in Robert Young, *Analytical Concordance to the Holy Bible* (1879; this 8th edn.

Many of the animals mentioned in the poem reveal similarly ambiguous qualities: they are praiseworthy initially because they are God's creatures, and are involved in Smart's magnificat, but, at a less abstract level, Smart praises a number of them because they are guileful: their appearance is deceptive, and they can therefore survive in a hostile environment, and defeat their enemies.

> Let Ethan praise with the Flea, his coat of mail, his piercer, and his vigour, which wisdom and providence have contrived to attract observation and to escape it.
>
> Let Heman bless with the Spider, his warp and his woof, his subtlety and industry, which are good.
>
> Let Chalcol praise with the Beetle, whose life is precious in the sight of God, tho' his appearance is against him.
>
> (A. 36–8)

Each of these creatures is linked with a proverbially wise man— Solomon's wisdom is established in the passage from the Bible in which these men are named through the assertion that he is wiser than any of them—and the creatures seem to represent aspects of wisdom; but that wisdom is not only praiseworthy because 'wisdom and providence have contrived' it; it is also good because through it they escape observation, they elude being 'fixed' and analysed, or, in a limited sense, 'interpreted'.[31]

Some earlier lines describing similar qualities in animals may help to show how their description is related to the problems of interpretation raised by the poem:

> Let Jehoiada bless God with an Hare, whose mazes are determined for the health of the body and to parry the adversary.
>
> Let Ahitub humble himself with an Ape before Almighty God, who is the maker of variety and pleasantry.
>
> Let Abiathar with a Fox praise the name of the Lord, who ballances craft against strength and skill against number.
>
> (A. 22–4)

Here, again, the animals are praised for possessing qualities which might seem surprising in the moral and ethical context of a religious

Guildford, 1977; hereafter Young); Cruden does not list it. The name 'Bukki' may also refer to Smart's concern with issues of inheritance—whether of private land, or of the 'seed' of David and stewardship of Christendom—as the name occurs in a list of those appointed 'to measure out the quantity of land for each family', in order to avoid 'broils or jealousies'. See the note from Stackhouse to Num. 34: 17 in D'Oyly and Mant.

[31] See 1 Kgs. 4: 31.

poem: the hare makes mazes, the ape, pleasantry, and the fox is praised for his skill. Animals were frequently praised for their passive obedience in doing what God intended or created them to do, but here their actions have a further significance. For the actions of the animals are comparable with parables, designed 'to attract observation and to escape it'; Smart uses 'mazes', humour, craft and skill, to 'parry the adversary', and the 'subtlety and industry' which are apparent in the poem are 'contrived to attract observation' from those who are prepared to interpret the poem in terms of its complex relation to its biblical model, and 'to escape' the observation of those who do not perceive that mazes, pleasantry, and skill, are also attributes and creations of God. Thus the actions of the animals alert the reader to the notion that only he 'Who hath ears to hear, let him hear'.[32]

VI

Within these parabolic terms the 'Let' verses of the poem represent both an 'open' form, affording a variety of diverse interpretations, and a 'closed', recalcitrant form, eluding determinate analysis: they are not so fully explicit as to exclude apparently contradictory interpretations, or to express a single and determinate significance, but they nevertheless exclude the possibility of communicating impropriety or impurity. They interpret or translate their content 'in the charity' (B1. 11), into a congregation rejoicing in the lamb, and it is this 'charitable' understanding of the elements of creation and of the poem as engaged in thanksgiving that describes the scope, the range, of interpretations afforded by the 'Let' verses. This act of understanding produces the community of possible meanings made available by the connections and 'relations' expressed in the 'Let' verses.

[32] On the behaviour of animals see e.g. Law, *Serious Call*, p. 53; Joseph Butler, *The Analogy of Religion Natural and Revealed to the Constitution and Course of Nature. To which are added: Two brief Dissertations: On Personal Identity and on the Nature of Virtue; and Fifteen Sermons* (*Fifteen Sermons* preached at the Rolls Chapel, 1726; this edn. London, 1898 'Preface to the Sermons': 'Brutes, in acting according to . . . their bodily constitution and circumstances, act suitably to their whole nature' (p. 376); see also Smart, *Omniscience*, ll. 31–53, 160–5. For a debate on the moral qualities and instructive power of apparently undesirable creatures see *Christian's Magazine*, 1 (1760), 114–15, 256; 2 (1761), 630–1. Matt. 13: 9; Jesus ends the parable of the sower with these words, but the whole passage, Matt. 13: 10–15, illuminates the comparability of Smart's technique with the biblical function of parables. See also William Dodd, *Discourses on the Miracles and Parables of our Blessed Lord and Saviour Jesus Christ* (1757), vol. i, Preface.

The structure and language of the poem continually display or create the possibility of significance in unexpected, and unexplained, connections and pairings between words. As the poet states in the cryptic lines frequently taken to apply to the poem itself:

> For the relations of words are in pairs first.
> For the relations of words are sometimes in oppositions.
> For the relations of words are according to their distances from the pair.
>
> (B2. 600–2)

The lines offer a tantalizing possibility of access to the terms in which the poem means, the terms of the act of interpretation it involves and demands of its readers, but they also withhold that access through the abstract nature of the relations they describe. The lines seem to refer the reader to some further source of coherence and significance, the nature of which is not made explicit within the poem, and it is in this respect that the language of *Jubilate Agno* appears most closely to resemble—in its aspiration if not therefore in its achievement—that of the Bible as it is described by Lowth.

Lowth describes Hebrew poetry as able to employ a strikingly allusive language, a figurative language of analogy whose 'relations' and sudden transitions rely for their elucidation on the reader's knowledge of the customary, of a body of knowledge and belief shared by the members of a society, and which is one of the factors which constitute them as a society as distinct from other societies. By calling upon those interconnections which are second nature, shared and immediate, to its readers, Hebrew poetry, Lowth claims, is able both to express a determinate and forceful meaning and to exclude unwanted connotations and associations. Smart's *Jubilate Agno* employs a language of sudden transitions and apparently surprising connections which I have described as not offering explicit guidelines determining its interpretation. Clearly, it does not, cannot, rely on a notion of the common and the customary comparable with that created by the closed and simple society, undivided by occupations, diversity of labour, and specialist knowledge, that Lowth attributes to the Hebrews, but it may call upon the scriptures and Christian teaching as providing a generally accessible source of allusion and significance, determining and informing the transitions it describes. Lowth argues that for the Hebrew almost everything in nature had a religious significance, immediately and 'naturally' apparent, for their religion described the interrelations, the harmony of creation: *Jubilate Agno* refers, similarly, to a common or shared body of religious knowledge, accessible to all, and directly present to the devout Christian.[33]

I can best suggest how Smart might have believed that such a shared body of knowledge could determine or interpret the meanings generated by the highly allusive language of *Jubilate Agno* by placing Lowth's views alongside those of William Law, whose writings I have already suggested may have influenced, like Lowth's, the structure of the poem. According to Lowth, Hebrew poetry makes demands of its readers which do not require the operation of memory (or the sort of conscious effort referred to in Wordsworth's 'Essay Supplementary'), but require reference to a common body of assumptions, of experience shared by the members of an undivided society. Law writes of the Christian partaking of a common life, an everyday life informed by shared belief, and argues that in modern societies the Christian religion provides a common body of knowledge and belief, which unites believers whose experiences and occupations otherwise divide and differentiate them.

All men, therefore, as men, have one and the same important business, to act up to the excellence of their rational nature, and to make reason and order the law of all their designs and actions. All Christians, as Christians, have one and the same calling, to live according to the excellency of the Christian spirit, and to make the sublime precepts of the Gospel the rule and measure of all their tempers in common life. The one thing needful to one, is the one thing needful to all.

For Law, religion is common to all businesses and callings, 'all orders and conditions, either of men or women', and the duty of all Christians, in living according to this 'one common holiness', is to identify Christianity, their 'reason and order', as their customary law and rule.

Similarly, the allusive language of *Jubilate Agno* refers us to a common Christian life and body of belief which both Smart and Law (like many of their contemporaries) assume is accessible to their readership. Thus, the poem expects an understanding of the significance of particular instances of creation which for Smart might

---

[33] See Lowth's discussion of the figurative language of the Hebrews in *Lectures*, vol. i, lects. v–ix, and in particular lect. v, pp. 111–16, on the customary; lect. vii, pp. 144–6, on early Hebrew society; and lect. viii, pp. 168–71, on religious significance. Lowth is, of course, describing a society within which there is a sexual division of labour, and within which prophets or poets form a distinct group, 'removed altogether from an intercourse with the world' (vol. ii, lect. xviii, p. 12; see also lect. xxii, p. 127).

have appeared as second nature, immediately accessible to the Christian reader. This determines the terms in which *Jubilate Agno* is imagined to be interpretable, accessible: the terms in which its allusive and figurative language is neither cryptic nor 'open' and unlimited in significance.[34]

Such a theory of how poetry means will probably seem, to a modern reader, a good deal more mystical and vague than it appeared to writers for whom the idea of a Christian community, united by a shared spiritual and practical faith, was not dismissable as a utopian vision. It seems to me unlikely, however, that *Jubilate Agno* refers to a body of knowledge in its particular instances which would have been immediately and fully apparent to the eighteenth-century reader; but it does refer to a *way* of understanding those particulars, a framework for their very existence, which *was* available as the Christian common life. Lowth's *Lectures*, in their description of the Hebrew poetry, provide a model for a kind of allusive poetry which emerges from and reinforces a shared order of interpretation. Smart, in imitating the Hebrew poetry, imitates the terms of its allusiveness as that reinforces and demands a common method of interpretation, an accessible perspective. And where the assumption of this common order is fulfilled, the allusive poetry of its expression will effect the forcible impression, unmediated by memory, which Smart describes as essential to his poetry, and which reflects no longer a shared direct experience, a common salvific activity, but a shared faith, and a common *way* of apprehending, in Law's terms, the diverse experience of the members of modern societies.

Thus one interpretation of the 'relations of words' referred to in the lines I quoted above would be that in any given 'Let' line, the significance of the pairing of human and animate or inanimate creature is expressed in and formed by their relation, their joining together in

---

[34] The idea of the common religious life was, or course, far more prevalent than my description of it here in terms of Lowth and Law may suggest. See e.g. my discussion of it in relation to the poetry of Edward Young in ch. 1 above, and James Barry's discussion of it in *An Inquiry into the Real and Imaginary Obstructions to the Acquisition of the Arts in England* (London, 1775), 204–6. See Wordsworth, 'Essay Supplementary to the Preface' (1815), in *William Wordsworth*, ed. Stephen Gill (Oxford, 1984), 658–60. Law, *Serious Call*, pp. 109, 11. See also Thomas R. Preston, 'Biblical Criticism, Literature, and the Eighteenth-Century Reader', in *Books and their Readers in Eighteenth-Century England*, ed. Isabel Rivers (Leicester, 1982); Barbara Taylor, *Eve and the New Jerusalem: Socialism and Feminism in the Nineteenth Century* (London, 1983), p. 8. Lowth was, of course, no political radical or utopian visionary—the community he describes is alien, historically, geographically, and culturally remote, and the subject is of exclusively scholarly and antiquarian interest.

rejoicing in the lamb, rather than in their distinct natures, as it is through this combination that they express the significance of religion as a translation into common harmony. It is the perception of Christian charity as that which distinguishes the various relations and interpretations afforded by the poem which both describes what is common to them, and delimits the range, the diversity, available to them. So for example in the line, 'Let Azor rejoice with the Flounder, who is both of the sea and of the river' (B1. 146), there are various possible implications in the name Azor, as referring to an ancestor of Joseph, and in the various other Old Testament versions of the name. Cruden translates one of these as meaning 'he that assists, or he that is assisted', an interpretation that might relate to his pairing with the flounder, as might the wordplay suggested by the sounds of the name (As-or). It is also possible that the letters of his name may have some significance, and a fuller exploration of the name would no doubt reveal further possibilities. The various implications I have so far listed, however, should not, I argue, be seen as mutually exclusive, the grounds of their validity being rather their compatibility with the role of Azor in rejoicing. Thus the different kinds of knowledge and experience that might be brought to bear on the interpretation of this line will contribute to and culminate in its fullest significance as an expression of thanksgiving and celebration.[35]

VII

The structure I have described in *Jubilate Agno* is highly ambitious. The form places in opposition a distinct, individual voice, and an ideally super-personal language; and it is possible that this opposition may undermine the potentially harmonious dialectic of the whole. In one sense, it contributes to the unity of the whole, as the 'For' lines are prevented from effectively contradicting the 'Let' verses: their disparate discourses cannot interact in the sense that the content of the 'For' verse cannot displace the content of the inexorably structured 'Let' verse. If in a 'For' verse Smart describes the adverse qualities of some animal mentioned in the 'Let' verse, the description is made

---

[35] See Matt. 1: 13–14; Jer. 28: 1; Ezek. 11: 1; Neh. 10: 17; Cruden, 'Proper Names', 'Azur'. The name of the flounder suggests clumsiness, and perhaps a need for assistance; and the wordplay suggested by the biblical name—As-or—might allude to the flounder's liking for both salt and fresh water.

invalid and impotent by the fact that the animal has found a place in his magnificat, and only serves to emphasize its all-embracing scope. The 'For' lines are also sometimes auxiliary to the 'Let' lines: that which is implicit in the structure of the magnificat is made explicit in the 'For' lines. For example, though Smart calls on stones, plants, animals, and dumb fish to rejoice and praise the Lord in the 'Let' verses, it is in the 'For' verses that his belief that 'MATTER is the dust of the Earth, every atom of which is the life' (B1. 160) is expressed; as is the related assertion: 'For EARTH which is an intelligence hath a voice and a propensity to speak in all her parts' (B1. 234).

It is in the personal and individual 'voice' of the 'For' lines that Smart can express the train of thought behind the cryptic lines of the magnificat, and it is by following the linear development of this train of thought that we come to understand the synchronic, biblical form the 'Let' verses aspire to. This synchronic form then becomes apparent: there is no development in the 'Let' lines after the opening four lines—all the following lines are a restatement, an expansion, and an assertion of the validity of those lines:

Rejoice in God, O ye Tongues; give the glory to the Lord, and the Lamb,
Nations, and languages, and every Creature, in which is the breath of Life.
Let man and beast appear before him, and magnify his name together.
Let Noah and his company approach the throne of Grace, and do homage to
  the Ark of their Salvation.
                                                            (A. 1–4)

Within these terms, however, the 'Let' verses do change considerably, each surviving fragment displaying different characteristics. The 'Let' verses of Fragment A are the most elaborate, and the most fully explicit, for though the 'Let' verses of Fragment B1 continue the exploration of the potential of this apparently simply syntactical form, the verses here tend to be shorter and yet more cryptic. There are no 'Let' lines in Fragment B2, and in Fragment C, following the 'long hiatus' Bond describes as following B2, the 'Let' lines are reduced to a minimum. Their simple sentences enjoin a man and a plant to rejoice, but there is no antiphonal development from this. The 'For' verses of Fragment C are at first similar to those of B2 in content, and in them no evidence of a radical alteration of direction, or a 'long hiatus' is apparent. The reappearance of more complex 'Let' verses in Fragment D is therefore intriguing, and I think that these suggest a possible explanation of the earlier reduction of the form to its barest elements.[36]

[36] *JA*, p. 121.

The 'Let' verses of Fragment D are unlike those found in any other part of the poem in their continuous use of non-biblical figures, and in their use of a yet more emphatically repetitive and rigorous form. The lines do contain more informal comments or interjections, which might be described as 'personal' as they may refer to the poet's circumstances, or may express his personal and individual opinion, but these interjections hardly qualify the overall impersonality of tone that characterizes the Fragment. They seem to belong to so disparate a discourse that the sense in which they are 'personal' serves rather to emphasize the impersonal formality of the Fragment as a whole. In, for example, the line: 'Let Baimbridge, house of Baimbridge rejoice with Hippophaestum of the same kind. Horses shou'd be clock'd in winter.—Bambridge praise the name of the Lord' (D. 158), the comment about horses barely disturbs the formality of the verse, and seems to be an almost parenthetical interjection or observation, relevant only to the repetition of 'hippo' in the plants named in this and the preceding verse.[37]

The impersonal formality of this Fragment may exploit or reflect the potential dangers or difficulties of this unfamiliar poetic form, as a form which aspires to express infinite significance may, conversely, express nothing: the dividing line between an incomprehensible language, and a language which approximates to infinite significance is virtually indefinable. This form may have the potential power to imbue its contents with a significance which they could not possess in any other context, and this potential power lies in the repetitive and rigorous syntactical structure of the form; but it is this very power which may also render the form totally devoid of meaning. It can translate the words it contains into a private, mystical language, of no comprehensible significance even to the poet himself. In this Fragment the poem seems to encounter, and even to explore this possibility; the poem seems to hover on the dividing line, and the structure is in danger of negating itself, and rendering itself incomprehensible. Like a word repeated too often in one's own mind, it can become almost meaningless, and cut off from any informing referential context.

The use of non-biblical names, of names which do not draw any significance from an external context, serves to emphasize this lack of 'public' meaning. Although we can see traces of Smart's lively wit in

[37] In D. 158 *Smart I* reads 'dock'd', where *JA*, reads 'clock'd'. A further possible reading of the MS is 'cloak'd'.

some of the combinations of names, the Fragment, arguably, lacks the spirit that animated earlier parts of the poem.

Let Mount, house of Mount rejoice with Anthera a flowering herb. The Lord lift me up.

Let Wilmot, house of Wilmot rejoice with Epipetros an herb coming up spontaneous (of the seed of the earth) but never flowers.

(D. 85, 103)

Wilmot, like several of the names mentioned in this Fragment, does have a limited public accessibility as the family name of the Earls of Rochester, and we could read a wry comment on the deathbed penitence of the poet of that name in the pairing with the epipetros, which suggests the seed that fell upon rocky ground and failed to flower in the parable of the sower, representing faith that lacks sufficient will to support the word in adverse or inhospitable conditions. Or the line might suggest a contrast between Wilmot, a name or word of willed significance, and the spontaneous or unwilled herb that fails to blossom: an opposition which might have more positive implications for the willed act of interpretation or translation the poem involves.

The poet's hopes for this sublime form of praise may be expressed in these lines:

For Cipher is a note of augmentation very good.
For innumerable ciphers will amount to something.
For the mind of man cannot bear a tedious accumulation of nothings without effect.
For infinite upon infinite they make a chain.
For the last link is from man very nothing ascending to the first Christ the Lord of All.

(C. 34–8)

This sequence of verses on the cipher follows a discussion on the mystical significance of the numbers from one to nine, and, at the outset, these lines therefore appear to refer to the significance of nought (0), as the next unit in the series. This nought can be a 'note of augmentation very good', for it can multiply by ten the value of any number it is placed after; but if it is not placed after a figure or series it is of no independent value, it is void of significance. It is, therefore, comparable both with man and with the 'Let' verses of Smart's poem, for both are of no significance if they do not exist in relation to Christ. The nought or cipher is also related to the concept of infinity, for like infinity the cipher is either infinitely significant or infinitely void of significance, and the mathematical sign of infinity is made up of a 'chain' of ciphers: ∞. Smart's notion that 'the mind of man cannot bear a tedious accumulation of nothings without effect', and will therefore *decipher* those nothings or ciphers into the infinite chain connecting man and Christ, and thus into 'a note of augmentation very good', may therefore express the hope that the 'symbolic character' or 'secret and disguised manner of writing' of his 'Let' verses will be similarly deciphered or 'interpreted' as significant, and as infinitely full of meaning through the immanence of eternity expressed in its form, and through the immanence of the infinite represented in its content— through the harmonious relations of universal charity that it represents.[38]

This problem of the virtual interchangeability of the ultimately meaningful and the ultimately meaningless or incomprehensible, and the paradox this interchangeability creates, is suggested by a further interpretation of the symbol of the seal of God in the line: 'For a CHARACTER is the votes of the Worldlings, but the seal is of Almighty GOD alone' (B2. 363). For this seal represents the entirety of eternity and infinity, and all the elements of creation, and must, therefore, like the 'undecypher'd characters' in which 'INCOMPREHENSIBLE is wrote' (*Eternity*, ll. 5–6), express (or impress) everything and nothing. This paradox may be implicit in the line:

For my talent is to give an impression upon words by punching, that when the reader casts his eye upon 'em, he takes up the image from the mould wch I have made.

(B2. 404)

As I have argued, Smart may be describing here the process by which he 'purifies' language, but this interpretation contains its own paradox; for Smart cannot know whether the 'impression' he makes upon words (or coins) is in fact 'pure', and can reinstate language as a non-contractual entity, with an internal and fixed, self-generated or God-given significance. For this process may, inversely, deprive language of its universal significance, impressing upon its terms a purely private and personal significance, which might indeed make of it a 'mad language'. Smart's hope that he is purifying and objectifying rather than merely internalizing language is, of course, a hope based upon faith,

---

[38] See Stead, p. 253. *OED*, 'Cipher', †4. *gen.*; 5.

but the character of Fragment D may be the result of a fear that this attempt to 'transform' language has rendered it private, and devoid of significance, rather than sublime, and implicitly imbued with spiritual numinous meaning.

VIII

I am not arguing that the language of Fragment D can only be read as so private as to be totally inaccessible, but that the sublime form to which Smart aspires must involve the related possibilities of infinite significance and uninterpretably cryptic utterance, and that it is in Fragment D that we appreciate most fully the extent to which these two possibilities may become virtually interchangeable. Each line of Fragment D calls on a particular name and its 'house' to rejoice with an animal, plant or stone, and the poem's editors have identified a good many of the 'houses' named. But I suggest that whatever value these identifications may have as sources of biographical information, they add surprisingly little to our understanding of the Fragment, perhaps because the names are placed in a context in which their identification—their limited and direct reference to a specific person —no longer provides the clue to their significance:

Let Fisher, house of Fisher rejoice with Sandastros kind of burning stone with gold drops in the body of it. God be gracious to Fisher of Cambridge & to all of his name & kindred.

(D. 12)

Karina Williamson and Professor Sherbo both identify 'Fisher of Cambridge' with either William Fisher of Clare Hall, Cambridge, or a musician of the same surname who performed in a concert organized by Charles Burney in 1752; and Professor Sherbo adds that various other people of the same name identified in his research may also be included in the reference as a result of the phrase 'all of his name & kindred'. But one could surely extend this argument further, and include in Smart's exhortation and benediction *all* people bearing the name of Fisher, and all people who are in any way 'kindred' or similar to Fisher—for example, all fishermen and fishers of men, and their 'kindred'. The final prayer for 'Fisher of Cambridge' may do no more than single out a specific Fisher from his more comprehensive 'house', all of whom are invited to rejoice. A similar interpretation can be placed with equal propriety on any 'name' or 'house' mentioned in the Fragment, and seems particularly appropriate to, for example, the lines:

> Let Poor, house of Poor rejoice with Jasione a kind of Withwind—Lord have mercy on the poor this hard weather. Jan: 10th 1763.

> Let Pass, house of Pass rejoice with Salt—The Lord pass the last year's accounts in my conscience thro' the merits of Jesus Christ. New Year by Old Stile 1763.

(D. 216, 219)

The 'houses' are placed in a context which calls into question their status as names: the 'names' of the houses cannot simply be delimited to reference to a specific person—to, for example, a specific Mr or Mrs Poor of Smart's acquaintance—and 'Pass', in conjunction with 'Salt', cannot even be identified as a noun with any confidence. They seem to refer to a more comprehensive category, which might approximately be described as a 'tribe' in the biblical tradition.[39]

Smart writes that 'England is the head of Europe in the Spirit!' (C. 102), and that 'the ENGLISH are the seed of Abraham and work up to him by Joab, David, and Naphtali' (B2. 433), and his complex genealogies, and patriotic statements, indicate that he sees the English as the natural descendants of the true Israel, and as the chosen people. This belief is perhaps more clearly stated in his hymn for 'Whitsunday':

> Yea, the God of truth and pow'r
> Blesses Englishmen this hour;
> That their language may suffice
> To make their nations good and wise—
> Wherefore then no more success—
> That so much is much to bless—
> Revelation is our own,
> Secret things are God's alone.

---

[39] Arthur Sherbo, *Christopher Smart: Scholar of the University* (East Lansing, Mich., 1967), 145. See Aaron Hill, Letter to Mr Thompson, 17 Jan. 1734: 'I found myself a-ground, or led astray, by a confusion of nouns with verbs *of the same house* . . .' (my italics), *Works of the late Aaron Hill, Esq; In Four Volumes* (London, 1753), i. 214. See also E. Chambers, 'Surname': 'Du Tillett maintains, that all *surnames* were originally given by way of sobriquets, or nick-names; and adds, that they are all significant and intelligible to those who understand the antient dialects of the several countries' (*Cyclopaedia: or, an Universal Dictionary of Arts and Sciences*, 2 vols. (this 7th edn. London, 1751)).

His patriotic hymn on 'The King's Restoration' reiterates the theme:

> We give the glory for thy word,
>   That it so well becomes our tongue;
> And that thy spirit is transferr'd
>   Upon the strains of old in Hebrew sung.
> And for the services dispers'd abroad,
> —The church her seemly course of practic pray'r and laud.[40]

If the English are, then, the chosen people, with the language most appropriate to effective prayer and conversion, the enumeration of their 'tribes' is comparable with the enumeration of biblical figures found in other fragments of the poem; and the charity of the poem also becomes more comprehensive and all-inclusive through the expansion of the significance of the various names. Earlier in the poem Smart writes:

> For I have a providential acquaintance with men who bear the names of animals.
> For I bless God to Mr Lion Mr Cock Mr Cat Mr Talbot Mr Hart Mrs Fysh Mr Grub, and Miss Lamb.
>
> (B1. 113–14)

And in line B1. 116 he writes: 'I bless God for the immortal soul of Mr Pigg of DOWNHAM in NORFOLK'. Bond notes of these lines that 'These are the names of well-known families in the eastern counties', and though Williamson, in her edition, cautions that 'the names cannot be identified with any confidence', she tentatively identifies Mr Lion, Mrs Fysh, and Miss Lamb, and states positively that Mr Pigg is 'Andrew Pigge, a tanner of Downham Market, died 1751/2'.[41]

I do not wish to question these identifications, or to suggest that the research that has gone into their discovery is not valuable and

---

[40] Smart, 'Hymn XV', ll. 25–32; 'Hymn XVIII', ll. 73–8 in *Hymns and Spiritual Songs for the Fasts and Festivals of the Church of England* (1765); I quote from *Smart II* throughout. The identification of England with Israel was not unusual in the 18th c.; see *Hymns and Spiritual Songs*, Introduction, 'Theological and Religious Themes', pp. 22–3, in *Smart II*; M. F. Marshall and J. T. Todd, *English Congregational Hymns in the Eighteenth Century* (Lexington, Ky., 1982), 114 and n.; D. Davie, 'Lecture 2: Old Dissent, 1700–1740', in *A Gathered Church: The Literature of the English Dissenting Interest, 1700–1930* (London, 1978). See also A. J. Kuhn, 'Christopher Smart: The Poet as Patriot of the Lord', *ELH* 30 (1963), 121–36. A. D. Hope, 'The Apocalypse of Christopher Smart', in *Studies in the Eighteenth Century: Papers presented at the David Nichol Smith Memorial Seminar*, ed. R. F. Brissenden (Canberra, 1968), 269–84.

[41] *Smart I*, B. 116 n. Lion, Fysh, and Lamb are identified as subscribers to Smart's *Psalms*.

informative, but my main interest is in the poet's use of the names, rather than in their identification. As the case of Mr Pigg most clearly indicates, the names are not fabrications, but in line B1. 114 (if not in B1. 116) they are apparently introduced primarily for their implications as *words*, rather than for the purpose of identifying specific people. The names do, no doubt, identify in this way, but they are introduced as instances of a 'providential' dispensation; and we can find some indication of the nature of that dispensation by comparing this use of these names with that implied by the line in Fragment D in which Mrs Fysh is again cited: 'Let Pleasant, house of Pleasant rejoice with The Carrier Fish—God be gracious to Dame Fysh' (D. 65). Dame Fysh's name may be introduced here, playfully, as an example of a 'Pleasant'—pleasing and humorous—and decorative name. The sigificance, however, of the poet's providence in being acquainted 'with men who bear the names of animals' is not simply that they provide an occasion for pleasantry, as line D. 65 might suggest, but that their names indicate the harmony of nature. Their names are not an abuse of language, an instance of misinformation, but indicate that the significance of a word, and more particularly a name, is not delimited by reference to, or identification of, a single object or person, a single meaning; and through the broader range of meanings which inform the significance of a particular word or name, that word or name gestures towards the harmony which '*Mr.* R.B.——'s Dog, COLEBROOK' described in *The Student*:

As there is a sympathy in harmony, so there is in nature; and indeed, I have sagacity enough to conceive that all nature is no more than universal harmony . . .[42]

The names, like the lists of the earlier Seatonian poems, thus create an inclusive rather than exclusive catalogue, which describes the universality of the relations of analogy available in the Word of faith, hope, and charity.

Fragment D, then, gains a wider potential significance through its use of English as opposed to biblical names. In the earlier fragments of the poem, the people named are to some extent fixed and made specific in their significance through their mention in the Bible,

---

[42] The carrier-fish or carrier-trochus is appropriate to its context here as these molluscs 'decorate' their shells with small stones and pieces of coral, and are therefore perhaps decorative and pleasant, as is the name 'Fysh'. *The Student, Or, The Oxford, and Cambridge Monthly Miscellany*, 2 vols. (London 1750–1), ii/6, p. 217.

though the Bible may represent a context which renders those names spiritually, and perhaps eternally, significant. Many of the names in Fragment D, as Professor Sherbo has argued, may be selected, apparently arbitrarily, from the obituary lists in current periodicals, but their significance within the potentially sublime form of the poem is not arbitrary, and is not necessarily determined by their reference to a specific person, dead or alive. The extent to which the names are rendered significant in gesturing towards, and in being a part of, a greater harmony is indicated in the first five lines of the Fragment, where the 'names' exhorted to rejoice are, in sequence, Dew, Round, New, Hook, and Crook; for the Fragment, and indeed the poem, represents a 'new' kind of poetry, fresh as the dew, in which the poet praises the Lord 'by hook' (D. 4) and 'by crook' (D. 5), by every available means.[43]

To give only one further example, Smart writes:

> Let Moyle, house of Moyle rejoice with Phlox a flame-colour'd flower without smell. tentanda via est. Via, veritas, vita sunt Christus.

> (D. 84)

Here Smart quotes from Virgil's proposal to try 'new ways' of writing, and the new way, as the succeeding quotation emphasizes, is the way of Christ. This path, however, both traditionally and in Smart's later religious poetry, is described as narrow, steep, and rocky, and the best way to approach it is perhaps upon a 'Moyle' or mule, for not only are these animals sure-footed and strong, but one was ridden by Solomon to his coronation. The 'name' Moyle also suggests the troubles with which the 'new way' is attended, as it suggests 'moil' or trouble and toil. The new ways of writing Smart alludes to may not be as specific as Karina Williamson's note to this line suggests, but might be taken to refer to his enterprise as a religious poet; certainly the 'new way' represented by *Jubilate Agno*, and by this Fragment, is not always easy to follow.[44]

Fragment D, then, can be read as a yet more ambitious exploration of the potentially sublime form of *Jubilate Agno*, and as such it is, as I have argued, comparable with the cipher. To extend briefly my

[43] A. Sherbo, 'Christopher Smart, Reader of Obituaries', *MLN* 71 (1956), 177–82. I do not, of course, intend to suggest that this poetry is 'new' at the point at which this fragment now appears to begin, but that it represents an unprecedented *kind* of poetry.

[44] See *Smart I*, D. 84 n.: 'Smart is probably alluding to his hymns . . .'. The 'Moyle' referred to might be tentatively identified as Walter Moyle, d. 1721, or his offering; see *Dictionary of National Biography* (*DNB*), 'Walter Moyle'.

discussion of that passage, the cypher as nought—'0'—is both an empty nothing and the symbol of eternity, the all-inclusive circle with no beginning or ending. The circle is also the symbol of the 'pearl of great price', for which God sent Smart to sea (B1. 30), and which represents wisdom and faith in Christ. The dual significance of the circle as eternity and as the pearl, or again as potentially meaningless and infinitely meaningful, makes it an apt image of this last Fragment, and its appropriateness is reflected in the implications of those first three 'names' enumerated in the Fragment. 'Dew', 'Round', and 'New' as a sequence, I have suggested, describe a circular progression, as they suggest the cyclical renewal of the day, and as 'Round' directly describes the circle. This circle is also, of course, of religious significance, not only in relation to the symbolic meaning of the circle discussed above, but as dew in the Bible signifies the blessing of God descending upon the earth, and the physically and spiritually refreshing and regenerative powers of the Word of Christ. The Word of Christ, the pearl which is symbolized by the 'Round' circle, descends as the Dew, and in it all things are made New. Smart writes of the pearl in his version of the parable of 'The Kingdom of Heaven compared unto a Merchantman seeking goodly Pearls':

> All parts must centre in the whole.
> This pearl's salvation of the soul,
> And he that stedfastly denies
> To deal in pomp and vanities,
> Shall gain by tenure not to cease,
> His Saviour and eternal peace.

And the significance and interpretability of this Fragment, and of those preceding it, must, as the first line of this quotation emphasizes, be evaluated in relation to 'the whole' which is salvation.[45]

---

[45] See Cruden, 'Dew', 'Pearl'; John Brown, *A Dictionary of the Holy Bible* (1778), 'Pearl'; *A Compendious Dictionary of the Holy Bible* (rev. edn. London, 1800), 'Dew', 'Pearl'. Smart, 'Parable VI', ll. 7–12, *The Parables of our Lord and Saviour Jesus Christ done into familiar verse, with occasional applications, for the Use and Improvement of Younger Minds* (1768), in *Smart II*.

3 'All good words are from GOD'

The Language of *Jubilate Agno*

I

MUCH of *Jubilate Agno* is devoted to a discussion of language and its alphabetical particles, and it becomes clear, in the course of reading the poem, that the nature of Smart's attitude to language has considerable implications, not only for the way in which his ideas are expressed, but for the nature of those ideas, and in particular for his natural-philosophical theories. Smart writes of Newton that he is 'ignorant for if a man consult not the WORD how should he understand the WORK?' (B1. 220), and though I have argued that the Word here describes the context of revelation that informs his poetry, the quotation might also apply to his own work, and to the religious theory of language we should 'consult' in order to understand it.

Smart's most emphatic statement on the subject of language, confirming many that occur in *Jubilate Agno*, is to be found in his verse translation of Horace. In *Satire* i. 3, Horace describes the development and civilization of man from 'A race but just remov'd from brutes', and in the course of this description refers to the 'discovery' of language:

> . . . at last with arms they fought,
> Which long experience forg'd and taught,
> Till words at length, and names they found,
> To ascertain their thoughts by sound.
> Hence they began from wars to pause,
> To wall in towns and 'stablish laws.

Smart's footnotes to his translation are on the whole restrained and factual, so that his outburst at this passage is all the more striking:

The understanding of Horace was so benighted, that he supposed language to be gradual, and of human invention—nevertheless the Lord is the WORD, and all good words proceed from him, as sure as nonsense and cant are derivable from the Adversary.

Smart's belief in the divine origin of language might seem unusual in an age when it was, apparently, generally accepted that language was 'gradual, and of human invention', as was the related theory that words were merely the arbitrary signs of ideas, possessing no inherent significance, or necessary relation to the object signified, other than that assigned to them by contract. The age is usually described as having seen language as part of the larger social and secular whole: not as an entity significant in itself, but as an element of the social contract, brought into being by the (presumably tacit) 'votes of the Worldlings'. This notion is expressed most clearly by Locke, who argued that language was 'the great Instrument' and 'common Tye of Society', and was created 'by a voluntary Imposition, whereby such a Word is made arbitrarily the Mark of such an Idea'.[1]

Smart's belief was not, however, either as uncommon or as illogical and idiosyncratic as modern retrospective reinterpretations may lead us to believe. Contemporary language theorists such as Rowland Jones, L. D. Nelme, and John Cleland also believed that language was of divine origin, and thus that the common characteristics of different languages might enable us to recover the universal language shattered in the fall of the tower of Babel. Their attempts to recreate or to rediscover this universal language are an early form of the study of comparative linguistics, for they involved an analysis of the ways in which 'languages work into one another by their bearings' (B2. 62). Their belief in the divine origin of language derives from a tradition of linguistics whose most famous exponent in England was the seventeenth-century grammarian John Wallis; but it cannot be dismissed as merely a hangover from the seventeenth century. As James Knowlson warns:

We should . . . bear in mind that the belief that there had once been a common *lingua humana*, from which all other languages had descended, and that this common language had once provided an insight into supernatural truths, was

---

[1] Smart (trans.), *The Works of Horace, Translated into Verse. With a Prose Interpretation, for the Help of Students. And Occasional Notes*, 4 vols. (London, 1767), iii. 39 and n. For a discussion of Smart's translations, see the Introd. to *Christopher Smart's Verse Translation of Horace's Odes: Text and Introduction*, ed. Arthur Sherbo (Victoria, BC, 1979), and Arthur Sherbo, 'Christopher Smart's Three Translations of Horace', *Journal of English and Germanic Philology*, 66 (1967), 347–58. Similar statements on language occur in *JA*, B1. 231, B1. 85. For a fuller discussion of 18th-c. language theories see J. Knowlson, *Universal Language Schemes in England and France 1600–1800* (Toronto, 1975); Stephen K. Land, *From Signs to Propositions: The Concept of Form in Eighteenth-Century Semantic Theory* (London, 1974); M. Cohen, *Sensible Words: Linguistic Practice in England 1640–1785* (Baltimore, and London, 1977); James H. Stam, *Inquiries into the Origin of Language: The Fate of a Question* (New York, 1976). John Locke, *An Essay Concerning Human Understanding*, ed. P. H. Nidditch (1st pub. 1690; this edn. Oxford, 1975), bk. iii, ch. 1, sect. 1; ch. 2, sect. 1.

both long-standing and persistent, continuing to influence ideas on language very late in the eighteenth century.

Jones, Nelme, Cleland, and, one might add, Smart represent a dissenting 'school' of theorists and etymologists not yet fully assimilated into our picture of the eighteenth century.[2]

Belief in the divine origin of language has a logical basis as a solution to the 'chicken-and-egg' problem involved in the human invention of language, most clearly described in Blair's *Lectures*:

... either how Society could form itself, previously to Language; or how words could rise into a Language, previously to Society formed, seem to be points attended with equal difficulty. And when we consider farther, that curious analogy which prevails in the construction of almost all Languages, and that deep and subtile logic on which they are founded, difficulties increase so much upon us, on all hands, that there seems to be no small reason for referring the first origin of all Language to divine teaching or inspiration.

Blair argues that society could not have been formed prior to the invention of a common means of communication between people, but that there could have been no occasion for the invention of such a means previous to the formation of society; and he goes on to propose that God had given the bare rudiments of language, which men had added to as necessity dictated.[3]

Smart's use of language is dominated by his belief in its divine origin, for this belief recognizes a divine revelation in language, which becomes not only a means of communicating our ideas through a pre-given, arbitrary, and contractually agreed set of signs, but a system which, in reflecting the divine creative language which was instantaneously manifested in the created world, reflects the order and significance of nature. Language becomes nature translated and interpreted, and as the system of nature can be understood as a mediated revelation of the immanence of the deity, so language too can be understood as a potential source of revelation. Language describes a system made up of all the elements of creation—'For all the stars have satellites, which are terms under their respective words' (B2. 402). Creation is the language of God, for 'Action & Speaking are one according to God and the Ancients' (B2. 562), and the stars are thus synonymous with God's expression of their existence. This sense is perhaps more

[2] Knowlson, *Schemes*, p. 13.
[3] Hugh Blair, *Lectures on Rhetoric and Belles Lettres* (1783; this edn. Edinburgh, 1813), i. 115.

directly expressed in the line: 'For flowers have their angels even the words of God's Creation' (B2. 500). In the Old Testament the angel of the Lord is a manifestation, or reflection, of God, and in this verse Smart describes the process by which 'the spiritual herbs and flowers' (B2. 376) are made manifest in their angels, or their expression in 'the words of God's Creation'. This understanding of creation as the language of God is also implicit in Smart's description of the sun and moon as angels (B2. 317–18), and in his insistence that, as a result of the divine *fiat*, 'LIGHT is propagated at all distances in an instant because it is actuated by the divine conception' (B1. 284).

The genuine, God-given language describes or expresses a system of creation: it reflects the pre-given order and system of values that creation represents; and if these are seen as the values informing the genuine language, then it may bear some relation to that divine creative language which is made manifest in nature, for the divine language informs and forms nature, which may in turn inform genuine language. Man was made in God's image, and his language may therefore also be an 'image' of God's—a connection or parallel that Smart emphasizes in hailing God as the 'GREAT POET OF THE UNIVERSE' (*Eternity*, l. 21). Rowland Jones describes a similar idea in his discussion of the origin of language:

it has been the opinion of the wisest part of mankind, that Adam was furnished with a scheme of language by God himself; that this seems to be implyed by that passage of scripture, wherein God is said to have brought the beasts and birds before Adam, to see, or perhaps to oversee what he would call them, and by Adam's giving names to the several parts of nature agreeable to the property and qualities thereof, and as the deity appears to have made use of a form of speech, previous to the formation of Adam, in giving names to the several parts of the creation, which indeed seem to comprehend the genera of human speech, and as man is said to have been made after God's own image and in his own likeness, I think that language ought not to be considered as mere arbitrary sounds, or any thing less than a part, at least, of that living soul, which God is said to have breathed into man.

Jones argues that language not only ought to be, but *is* 'agreeable to the order of nature'; in words and phrases, and in the construction of individual letters; and this attitude is closely related to that implied in *Jubilate Agno*.[4]

---

[4] Rowland Jones, *The Origin of Language and Nations, Hieroglyfically, Etymologically, and Topographically Defined and Fixed, After the method of an English, Celtic, Greek and Latin English Lexicon* (London, 1764), Preface, 'Of the Origin of Speech'.

L. D. Nelme, whose argument is similar to Jones's, takes this idea rather further, and argues that the two forms basic to written language, the line and the circle, are also fundamental to all creation:

The Most High . . . is uniform in all HIS works: all HIS creation, and every minutest part thereof, participates of the most simple, most perfect, and most essential forms; the line | the symbol of altitude, and the circle ○ the symbol of the horizon.

These symbols contain in them the first elements, the forms of all created nature. There doth not exist in the whole creation any BEING, or THING, that doth not partake of these first principles; nor can the human mind conceive of any existence, without *ideas* that include these first elements; which are not only forms *essential* to all matter, but also to every *idea* of matter that arises in the human mind: they contain in them the elements of every art, and of every science, known to man.

These 'essential forms', he writes, are the

form of *forms*; the lines of beauty, and of deformity too: They are *bea-ti-ful* in themselves; by a just proportion and commixture of their parts, Hogarth formed his l-in-e of *bea-ty*; but a disproportion of their parts produces deformity.

This idea is strikingly similar to that implied in Smart's discussion of the Hebrew letter ל (lamed):

For the letter ל which signifies GOD by himself is on the fibre of some leaf in every Tree.
For ל is the grain of the human heart & on the network of the skin.
For ל is in the veins of all stones both precious and common.
For ל is upon every hair both of man and beast.
For ל is in the grain of wood.
For ל is in the ore of all metals.
For ל is on the scales of all fish.
For ל is on the petals of all flowers.
For ל is upon all shells.
For ל is in the constituent particles of air.
For ל is on the mite of the earth.
For ל is in the water yea in every drop.
For ל is in the incomprehensible ingredients of fire.
For ל is in the stars the sun and in the Moon.
For ל is upon the Sapphire Vault.

For L is light, and ל is the line of beauty.

(B2. 477–91, 548)

This letter, whose form is Hogarth's line of beauty, is to be found throughout creation as a visible form of God's seal, but like the 'great Name' described in the opening verses of *On the Eternity*, it is at the most negatively descriptive of that seal. The letter 'signifies God' and, by implication, light, but its very universality, and the comprehensiveness of its significance, render it incomprehensible: it apparently combines the essential forms of all significant and non-significant or non-interpretable forms, but the fact that it is essential and visible makes it invisible and uninterpretable. Smart implies this in declaring its presence in the 'incomprehensible ingredients' of fire: the significant letter is there, and manifests or represents the presence of God, but it does not make the ingredients comprehensible, any more than it reveals its own significance.[5]

The various alphabetical exercises in *Jubilate Agno* reflect this problem, for, as ל describes the essential form of all forms, so the letters of the alphabet are the essential forms or ingredients of all words: they are 'the atoms of language', and if they are significant or powerful in themselves the implications of their almost infinite interrelations and permutations in the words of language become potentially too complex to be grasped. The possibility threatens the coherence of both Nelme's and Jones's arguments, which attempt to bring out and emphasize the potential richness of a language in which every letter and syllable is potentially significant: a fully expressive language which is the creation of an infinite deity may be infinite itself, and infinitely too complex to be grasped by mere mortals.[6]

This aspect of the view of language as a divine institution persuaded James Harris, the philosopher of language most highly esteemed by Robert Lowth and Rowland Jones, that language must be an arbitrary construction, for if it were not, we would have to ask:

---

[5] L. D. Nelme, *An Essay Towards An Investigation Of the Origin and Elements of Language and Letters; That is, Sounds and Symbols* (London, 1772), 16–17, 68. For a comment on the spelling and presentation of words in Nelme, see below, p. 177. On the line of beauty see William Hogarth, *The Analysis of Beauty* (London, 1753). The play involved in the equation of 'l', lamed, and *el* (God) may derive from John Wallis, who stated that the letter had the same sound in all countries; see *Tractatus de Loquela* (1653; this 6th edn. London, 1765), 28. See also Charles Parish, 'Christopher Smart's Knowledge of Hebrew', *Studies in Philology*, 58 (1961), 516–32; A. J. Kuhn, 'Glory or Gravity: Hutchinson vs. Newton', *Journal of the History of Ideas*, 22 (1961), 303–22.

[6] John Cleland, *The Way to Things by Words, and to Words by Things* (London, 1766), 71; this phrase probably derives from Johnson's description of words as 'these fundamental atoms of our speech', in *The Plan of a Dictionary* (London, 1747), 18.

Have these Parts [words] again other Parts, which are in like manner significant, and so may the progress be pursued to infinite? Can we suppose all Meaning, like Body, to be divisible, and to include within itself other Meanings without end?

Harris is appalled by the prospect of infinite significance, and it certainly created problems for Nelme and Jones: Nelme becomes obliged, as his argument proceeds, to break up almost every word he uses with hyphens and oblique strokes, so that the radicals he has argued to be significant will emerge; though were the reader to attempt to assimilate their significance at the same time as trying to follow the argument itself, they would undoubtedly lose track of both. But I would argue that this is not necessarily a problem in *Jubilate Agno*: to take up Harris's simile of Body, while Body may be infinitely divisible, we do not necessarily have always to divide it; for if language was given by God for the use of finite man, he must have framed it in such a way that it is possible for men to delimit that infinite potential so that simple ideas can be expressed.[7]

The body of language *Jubilate Agno* represents may be infinitely interpretable, and its significance could perhaps be 'pursued to infinite'; in this respect its language may be comparable with that of the Bible, and Robert Lowth's discussion of the biblical use of metaphor provides an illuminating comparison with the problem of interpretation the poem presents. Lowth argues that, for the Hebrew,

The whole course of nature, this immense universe of things, offers itself to human contemplation, and affords an infinite variety, a confused assemblage, a wilderness, as it were, of images, which being collected as the materials of poetry, are selected and produced as occasion dictates.

Perhaps the most characteristic branch of metaphor selected by the Hebrews from the 'wilderness' was that described by Lowth as 'Mystical Allegory'. This is not simply the description of one thing in terms of another, but occurs when 'the same production, according as it is differently interpreted, relates to different events, distant in time, and distinct in their nature'. A single expression will then have a 'plain, proper, historical, and commonly-received sense', and a 'sacred, interior and prophetic sense', though both of these senses may not be equally or simultaneously apparent; for

---

[7] James Harris, *Hermes: or a Philosophical Inquiry Concerning Universal Grammar* (1751; this 4th rev. edn. London, 1786), 20.

there is a vast variety in the use and conduct of the mystical allegory; in the modes in which the corresponding images are arranged, and in which they are obscured or eclipsed by one another . . . Sometimes the principal or figurative idea is exhibited to the attentive eye with a constant and equal light, and sometimes it unexpectedly glances upon us, and breaks forth with sudden and astonishing corruscations, like a flash of lightning bursting from the clouds.

In the most effective variety, 'the two images equally conspicuous run, as it were, parallel through the whole poem, mutually illustrating and corresponding to each other'.[8]

In Lowth's discussion the use of mystical allegory is either restricted to particular important historical and sacred events, such as the crowning of David, and to traditionally established 'key' names and interpretations, such as David, Moab, Babylon, Jerusalem, and Israel, in which case the allegory is almost always prophetic, or its use can be extended to all the 'imagery of nature' which, he writes, is almost always open to interpretation as expressing both spiritual and human ideas. This second, less specific kind of mystical allegory, is that which I see as comparable with Smart's use of language, for Lowth argues that each strain of mystical allegory is valid in its own right, and without reference to the other. If we wish to read a given psalm as an historical account, we may, as we may equally read it as purely allegorical; and our choice does it no violence, does not threaten the validity of the chosen interpretation.[9]

In the use of 'key' names and events, this freedom of interpretation is restricted by the historical custom that has established those names and events as allegorically significant, but the 'imagery of nature', which is not restricted in this way, offers an interesting model for the language of *Jubilate Agno*. For Smart exposes a richness in language that may be 'pursued to infinite', but which, though it should not be ignored, may occasionally be 'obscured or eclipsed'. In *Jubilate Agno* the very number and variety of alphabetical exercises, playing on many different aspects of the letters—their sound, their shape, their 'powers', and so on—serve to indicate that the combination of letters that the poem represents is at once of indeterminable and of potentially infinite significance, and yet capable of being limited, by a concentration on a particular aspect of the letters' potential significance, to a determinable, if not fully comprehensive and satisfactory, interpretative

[8] Robert Lowth, *Lectures on the Sacred Poetry of the Hebrews*, trans. G. Gregory, 2 vols. (1787; repr. Hildesheim, 1969), vol. i, lect. v, pp. 116–17; lect. xi, pp. 235–6, 241–2.
[9] See ibid., vol. i, lect. xi, pp. 245–6.

significance. Every letter, finally, is a letter in the alphabet, in the given set of components of comprehensible language, but it is also expressive of the infinite and incomprehensible, 'For Christ being *A* and *Ω* is all the intermediate letters without doubt' (C. 18).

II

Both L. D. Nelme and John Cleland defend their analyses of language on the grounds that a proper understanding of its elements will reinvigorate and render more effective its use: Cleland writes that

The words we at present make use of, and understand only by common agreement, assume a new air and life in the understanding, when you trace them to their radicals, where you find every word strongly stamped with nature; full of energy, meaning, character, painting, and Poetry.

He argues that words, when properly understood, are 'big with meaning', and, like Nelme, he points out a contrast between this use of language and the 'futile, languid, unanimated method of expression' which results from an ignorance of the nature and power of words. Smart seems to make a similar contrast, by means of the traditional metaphor of language and money, between a debased and a freshly impressed coinage in language.[10]

Among the means by which Smart attempts to release the power of words, to re-mint them, to re-impress them with meaning, is the use of puns and word-play, which has frequently been noticed as one of the poem's most striking characteristics; but it remains to be explained *why* Smart should have been so preoccupied with a linguistic activity dismissed by Addison as 'false wit'. It seems to me that this use of language represents an attempt to explore its implications as a God-given significatory system, and tries to reveal or make explicit aspects of that numinous significance. Smart's word-play can be understood, not as false wit, but as an attempt to rediscover the system described by language which may ultimately also be the system, the significant structure, informing creation. It reanimates the figurative elements of speech which are the distinctive mark of the community of customary meanings language offers, and may thus reanimate the sense of community that might originally have informed its figurative nature. But Smart's explorations of the potential significance of language are

[10] Cleland, *Things*, pp. 23, 24. Nelme, *Investigation*, p. 6.

not limited simply to a single aspect of it, and in giving some examples of his 'explorations' I shall try to illustrate the extent to which his use of language exploits a wide range of the available avenues of potential discovery.[11]

Smart examines, for example, the potential of multilingual punning, simultaneously drawing on the biblical or historical meaning of the characters he names:

Let Lapidoth with Percnos the Lord is the builder of the wall of CHINA —REJOICE.

For I rejoice that I attribute to God, what others vainly ascribe to feeble man.

(B1. 97)

Lapidoth was the husband of Deborah, but it is perhaps the similarity of his name to the Latin *lapidosus*, meaning 'stony', that primarily occasions his mention here, for if the Lord has built the wall, using 'MATTER', which is 'the dust of the Earth, every atom of which is the life' (B1. 160), then it is a living wall of stone, as Lapidoth was a living man, made, by implication, of stone. The pairing of Lapidoth and the percnos can also be seen as illustrating the contrast between Smart and those 'others' mentioned in the 'For' verse, for the Hebrew meaning of Lapidoth is 'lamps' or 'lightnings', whereas the percnos, which is a kind of eagle, takes its name from the Greek word περκνός, 'dusky', and this light/dark contrast implies (as it does so often in the poem) the opposition of the light of revelation and faith illuminating Smart, and the darkness of superstition and atheism which blinds the 'others'. Lapidoth, meaning 'lightnings', may also be related to the theme of Smart's spiritual illumination, through association with the belief that 'LIGHTNING is a glance of the glory of God' (B2. 272); for Smart, through his illumination or 'lightning', has been able to attribute the wall to the glory of God. In this 'pair' of verses, then, Smart is playing on the multilingual significance of words in order to emphasize the religious nature of his beliefs, in contrast with those of less devout men.[12]

---

[11] Joseph Addison, *Spectator*, 61 (10 May 1711); (11 May 1711). See also Edward Young, *Conjectures on Original Composition* (London, 1759): 'It is with Thoughts, as it is with Words; and with both, as with Men; they may grow old, and die. Words tarnished, by passing thro' the mouths of the Vulgar, are laid aside as inelegant, and obsolete. So Thoughts, when become too common, should lose their Currency; and we should send new Metal to the Mint, that is, new meaning to the Press' (pp. 13–14).

[12] See Young, 'Lapidoth'; and Cruden, 'Proper Names', 'Lapidoth'; Judg. 4: 4. The 'Let' verse may allude to the saying of Lycurgus, that the walls of Sparta were made not of stone but of armed citizens; see Plutarch, *Lycurgus*, 19, and *Apophthegmata Laconica*, 29.

The discovery, in this line, of these multilingual levels of significance indicates, I think, the kind of interpretative effort that the poem works to foster: it asks us to question conventional and contractual meanings, to unearth in its language the talents obscured in customary usage. The example of figurative richness I detect here depends on the metaphorical and natural opposition of light and dark that Lowth describes as a distinctive characteristic of Hebrew poetry. He argues that the Hebrews are able to employ this kind of imagery with a boldness that is 'perspicuous, clear, and truly magnificent', because it is 'approved by constant and unvarying custom', but is not, in their poetry, obscured by familiarity, or deadened by the kind of staleness that Nelme and Cleland wish to cleanse their language of. Custom, in his argument, legitimates, and is itself reanimated by, daring and therefore the recognition that 'the Hebrews employ those Metaphors more frequently . . . than other people; indeed they seldom refrain from them whenever the subject requires, or will even admit of their introduction' produces peculiarly sublime and powerful beauties in their poetry, which encourage his admiring examination. His translator points out that all languages have this hidden wealth, but he notes that:

It is very observable in our own as well as other languages, how much Metaphors lose of the figurative sense by repetition; and it is curious to remark how Metaphors are in this manner derived from one another. From the resemblance of a narrow bed of metal running in the earth to the situation of a vein in the human body, it has taken that name; and hence I apprehend are derived the expressions, a *vein of poetry*, a *vein of humour*, &c.

It is exactly these kinds of figures of speech that Lowth argues made the poetry of the Hebrews so 'clear and luminous' that translation could not obscure its power, and which, I argue, Smart's poetry works to reanimate with figurative sense. Thus to detect an opposition of the kind that I have been discussing in this line from *Jubilate Agno* involves the recognition of the way in which the syntactical repetition of Smart's poem works to push this kind of figurative sense into unusual prominence, into daring animation.[13]

Smart also plays upon the divergent (rather than alternate) meanings of English words, for example in the line: 'For the propagation of light is quick as the divine Conception' (B2. 325). Here, through his use of the words 'propagation', 'quick', and 'Conception', rather than, for example, 'diffusion', 'instantaneous', and 'thought', Smart emphasizes

[13] Lowth, *Lectures*, vol. i, lect. vi, pp. 131, 128, 127, 125 n., 125, see 129.

the extent to which, for him, the instantaneous propagation of light is a physical reality revealing God's active presence in the world, rather than merely a theoretical article of faith, for the identity of the divine idea and act is described in physically immediate terms. This word-play does not, however, always depend upon exploiting a potential ambiguity or duality of meaning in the sense of a word, as can be seen in this line on witchcraft: 'For to use pollution, exact and cross things and at the same time to think against a man is the crime direct' (B2. 303). Here 'exact' may be used in the sense of 'afflict' or 'attack' (as Williamson suggests), but, by a play on its sound, may also suggest the action of crossing things, or X-acting.[14]

In a number of verses, Smart divides the syllables of words in order to play upon the potential meanings produced in this way, for example in the play upon 'deserted' and 'desert-ed' (meaning 'having desert' or 'deserving') in the lines:

For Adversity above all other is to be deserted of the grace of God.

For by the grace of God I am the Reviver of ADORATION amongst ENGLISH-MEN.

For being desert-ed is to have desert in the sight of God and intitles one to the Lord's merit.

(B2. 328, 332–3)

This play enables Smart to distinguish between the adversity that accompanies the 'adversary' himself, whose hell is 'without eternity from the presence of Almighty God' (B2. 322), and his own adverse situation, which he suggests is a kind of martyrdom which makes him more deserving of divine grace. A comparable use of word-play can be seen in the line: 'For envious men have exceeding subtlety quippe qui in-videant' (B2. 335); but here the contrast is between root and derivation, rather than, as in the case of 'desert', between two words of different derivations, and serves to emphasize that the 'subtlety', the sagacious penetration, of envious men ('in-videant'—'they see into things') cannot be a fruitful wisdom and insight as it is merely the product of their dominant characteristic ('invideant'—'they envy').[15]

[14] See *Smart I*, B. 303–4 n.
[15] See Murray Roston, *Prophet and Poet: The Bible and the Growth of Romanticism* (Evanston, Ill., 1965), 150. B2. 333 reads 'beeing' in the MS. These verses also imply that, though the two sorts of adversity are different, even hell may be 'without eternity'— without perpetual duration—as a result of God's presence ('from' here is ambiguous); and this implication is made explicit in B2. 330. For the bases of this belief, see the *Christian's Magazine*, 2 (1761), 666–8.

The use of word-play attracts attention to the sound of words, in counterpoint to their contractually agreed significance, and a concern with pronunciation is also evident in two of Smart's 'exercises' on the letters of the alphabet which are based on the way letters are sounded. In the first of these the phonetic development from letter to intelligible sound is initially straightforward:

For B is a creature busy and bustling.
For C is a sense quick and penetrating.

(B2. 514–15)

But it becomes more complex as the significance of the letters develops to include 'the power of the English letters taken singly' (B2. 517). The notion that a given letter is somehow particularly appropriate to the expression of a certain set of ideas or emotions, and has some inherent connection with them, does not necessarily need to be understood as related to cabbalistic or Freemasonic systems of occult significance, as some critics have suggested, for it was fairly commonly discussed and entertained by seventeenth- and eighteenth-century grammarians and writers on the origin of language. It proceeds logically from the belief that 'there is not probably a single word in any language on the globe, that is purely arbitrary; no, nor so much as a single letter, or form of a letter'. In Smart's alphabetical exercises this notion legitimizes the connection he describes between, for example, the letter 'e' and eternity (B2. 517), for the word 'eternity' is, in a sense, the extension or expression of a potential otherwise dormant in the initial letter 'e', and thus falls under its 'power'.[16]

This 'power' in letters may be corrupted or obscured by the mispronunciation of words, as Smart seems to suggest in a comment which appears immediately between two of his exercises on the sounds and 'powers' of the alphabet:

For in the education of children it is necessary to watch the words, which they pronounce with difficulty, for such are against them in their consequences.

(B2. 537)

W. H. Bond takes this as a reference to the Gileadites' use of the word 'shibboleth' as a password and test of nationality—the hostile

---

[16] See e.g. A. Sherbo, 'Christopher Smart, Free and Accepted Mason', *The Journal of English and Germanic Philology*, 54 (1955), 664–9; *Smart I*, B. 513 n.; Stead, pp. 232–3; *JA*, p. 106 n. 2. Cleland, *Things*, p. 87. On the origin of letters see the *Christian's Magazine*, 1 (1760), 29, 124–7.

Ephraimites pronounced the word differently, and would therefore be recognized and slain when they spoke it; but while this use of pronunciation as a test may well be relevant, the line may also say that in mispronouncing words children may distort or fail to appreciate their full significance. If language is regarded as significant in itself, rather than as an arbitrary system of signs, then it becomes a repository of potential meaning, and a distortion of language is a distortion of the truth it contains; but play, whether on the sound or the sense of a word, exploits a reservoir of potential meaning inherent in language.[17]

There is a further allusion to this concept of language as a system of potential revelation in Smart's discussion of the language of flowers:

For there is a language of flowers.
For there is a sound reasoning upon all flowers.
For elegant phrases are nothing but flowers.
For flowers are peculiarly the poetry of Christ.

(B2. 503–6)

A plausible, but by no means exhaustive, explanation of this passage could be based on an extension of the traditional image of elegant phrases as flowers: here that analogy describes the meaning of flowers in the divine language of creation. Flowers for Smart are also an expression of the harmony of creation: they combine in that harmony the respective harmonies of vision and sound, which ideally compose both written and spoken language, for 'flowers are musical in ocular harmony' (B2. 508). Harmony is that which joins elements together in 'agreement' or 'concord', and, as it joins them together in a consistent whole, they stand in no need of a means of communication, but only of a language of expression; for the harmony of flowers seems so complete that the single 'message' of their undivided unity can only be one of praise and glorification of Christ, which may be why they are 'peculiarly the poetry of Christ'. Williamson points out that Smart's concept of ocular harmony here may be related to Newton's tentative 'theory of a "harmony" of colour and sound', but where Newton

---

[17] *JA*, p. 107. n. 5. See Judg. 12: 5–6. It should be noted that pronunciation in the 18th-c. refers to general delivery—to, for example, intonation and gesture—as well as to the sound of particular words. See Blair, *Lectures*, i. 123–8; but see also George Campbell, *The Philosophy of Rhetoric* (London, 1776), i. 347–8: 'many words and idioms prevail among the populace, which, notwithstanding a use pretty uniform and extensive, are considered as corrupt, and like counterfeit money, though common, not valued. . . . Their currency . . . is without authority and weight. The tattle of children hath a currency, but, however universal their manner of corrupting words may be among themselves, it can never establish what is accounted use in language.'

argues that 'the *analogy* of nature is to be observed' between discrete phenomena, Smart recognizes, in analogy, the expression of phenomenal harmony.

If flowers, then, have a 'language' expressive of the harmony of creation, that 'language' is perhaps comparable with language itself as a potential source of wisdom, and it is through 'a sound reasoning upon all flowers' (where 'sound' may be either adjective or noun) that the potential wisdom of flowers as language can be exploited or appreciated. The poet's 'reasoning upon . . . flowers' exemplifies the way the poem works to reanimate customary forms of speech or language, to find, in these expressions, the characteristic meanings of the community the poem calls into praise.[18]

III

I have argued that Smart's exploitation, in word-play, of the potential wealth and power of language should be understood in terms of a theory of language as a divine institution, and so as an entity significant in itself; for in his word-play meaning appears not to depend upon context or contract, though these factors may to some extent determine our awareness of it, but to be a 'power' inherent in language. This power has considerable implications for the referential status of language—for the relation it implies between words and the ideas or objects they signify. As we have seen, Smart rejects the notion that language is 'gradual, and of human invention', and this implies also a rejection of the nominalist conception of words as the arbitrary signs of ideas, though the possibility remains that words might still be somehow 'naturally' or intrinsically related to the created objects they signify, or to ideas of those objects.

[18] OED, 'Harmony', 1, 2. *Smart I*, B. 508 n. *Newton's Philosophy of Nature: Selections from his Writings*, ed. H. S. Thayer (London, 1953; hereafter Thayer), iv. 98, my italics. Robert Nelson suggests, in *The Practice of True Devotion, In Relation to the End, as well as the Means of Religion* (1698; this 5th edn. London, 1721), that his readers should memorize their favourite passages of scripture, as 'a spiritual Nosegay, always ready to refresh our Minds' (p. 196); but the use of the imagery of flowers that is most strikingly reminiscent of Smart occurs in *Christian's Magazine*: in the 'Meditation on the Bee', the writer's soul is urged to 'visit continually the assemblies of the faithful, those flowers whose unfading beauty graces the inheritance of the beloved, and whose sweetness diffuses around them a savour of life unto life. There feed among the lilies of paradise, which shine invested with the righteousness of saints, and towering above the earth, keep their garments unspotted from the dust of corruption' (*Christian's Magazine*, 2 (1761), 673).

This naturalist conception of language might appear to be the logical alternative to the nominalist position, and one which might appropriately be adopted by a poet of Smart's beliefs, in that it could be understood to be the conception proposed by the Bible itself. In the second account of creation in Genesis, God, having created all the animals, 'brought *them* unto Adam to see what he would call them: and whatsoever Adam called every living creature, that *was* the name thereof'. This passage was used in the late seventeenth and early eighteenth centuries, by nominalists and naturalists alike, to justify their different positions: it is used by Locke, for example, to argue that Adam had a complete 'Liberty . . . of affixing any new name to any *Idea*', but it was also commonly taken to imply that the Adamic language had an exact correspondence with the objects it signified, and that Adam's names were the complete and natural expression of what he perceived, in that the naming process was overseen by God. This Adamic language could be seen, then, as the pure language intended by God to be spoken by man, the ultimate paradigm to which all language aspires. But it could therefore also be taken, of course, as the paradigm by which all human language must be judged and inevitably be found wanting; for man's relation to nature, and so the relation of his language to nature, had been drastically altered by his fall and expulsion from Eden, and such elements of this pure language as might have survived had been further corrupted and dispersed in the confusion of Babel. Smart's use of word-play does not appear to involve an aspiration to exact correspondence with the objects signified, which is beyond the reach of fallen man, but seems rather to be an attempt to show that words are not dependent for their meaning on a relation with the objects of a fallen creation, and not subject to the vagaries of common usage. The language of the poem seems to map out a series of correspondences and connections validated by its own internal echoes and 'powers' rather than by a systematic correspondence with things; as if those internal echoes are vestiges of the original integrity of Adam's language, and clues to its original construction.[19]

The nature of this enterprise is illuminated by the passages in which Smart discusses the animals which he sees as, somehow, characterizing particular languages: he writes that 'the Mouse (Mus) prevails in the Latin. / For Edi-mus, bibi-mus, vivi-mus—ore-mus' (B2. 638–9). He tells us that the mouse is particularly characterized by the qualities of

---

[19] Gen. 2: 19. Locke, *Essay*, bk. iii, ch. 4, sect. 51. On writers who held a contrary opinion, see Stam, *Inquiries*, pp. 14, 47–8.

'bravery and hospitality', which 'were said & done by the Romans rather than others' (B2. 644), and the Latin language imitates or indicates this connection.[20] The English language has a similar connection with the dog and bull:

For two creatures the Bull & the Dog prevail in the English.
For all the words ending in ble are in the creature. Invisi-ble Incomprehensi-ble ineffa-ble, A-ble.
For can is (canis) is cause & effect a dog.
For the English is concise & strong. Dog & Bull again.

(B2. 645–6, 648–9)

The connection between the animals and languages in these passages indicates the poet's recognition of significance in the sound of language, as well as in its contextually established referential meaning, and this attitude represents an attempt either to widen, or to explore the full width of, the different kinds and modes of reference available to, and informing the significance of, language. Smart's language does not become totally devoid of a readily comprehensible referential significance—*canis* is still a dog—but that mode of significance does not delimit his language, and *canis* (can is) is thus also 'cause & effect', 'A-ble' and actual.

In one way, however, Smart does seem to conceive of language as a structure of words informed by their relation to objects in creation. He writes 'all the creatures mentioned by Pliny are somewhere or other

[20] Stead, *JA*, and *Smart I* agree in translating B2. 639 as 'For we eat, we drink, we live—let us pray'; but as a result of Smart's hyphenation of the Latin words the line could also be translated: 'For I, a mouse, ate, I, a mouse, drank, I, a mouse, lived' (where 'I' and 'a mouse' are understood as in apposition), and 'ore-mus' might be translated as 'let us pray' or 'mouth/face-mouse'—perhaps, 'in face a mouse'. This first translation suggests that B2. 639 may allude to the saying, 'Let us eat, drink, and be merry, for tomorrow we die', where Smart substitutes 'oremus' and emphasizes the hope of the NT rather than the fatalism of the OT (the saying derives from Eccl. 8: 15; see also B1. 287–8). The reading, 'I ate as a mouse . . .', however, would confirm the allusion, implicit throughout the passage, to Horace (*Satires*, ii. 6), where the fable of the town and the country mouse is narrated. The significance of the allusion lies in the generous hospitality each mouse offers the other, and the terms in which the town mouse tempts the country mouse to return with him to town. In Pope's imitation, the town mouse pleads: 'But come, for God's sake, live with Men: / Consider, Mice, like Men, must die, / Both small and great, both you and I: / Then spend your life in Joy and Sport . . .' (ll. 178–81). The country mouse, having experienced the luxuries and dangers of the town, decides that he prefers his peaceful country life, and leaves, saying: 'Give me again my hollow Tree! / A Crust of Bread, and Liberty' (ll. 222–3). The allusion emphasizes the contrast between the two parts of B2. 639, for 'ore-mus'—'let us pray'—might parallel the country mouse's recognition of his true values after his taste of the luxuries of eating, living, and drinking in town.

extant to the glory of God' (B2. 622). This notion is comparable with an a priori 'proof' of the existence of God: if we have an idea of God, then he must exist, for there is no other possible source for our idea. Smart's comment could be taken to imply that if a creature is 'mentioned' in language, then it must be 'extant', for its name could only have been formulated in relation or reference to some actual (though not necessarily material) object; and if this is the implication of the line, then it may also involve the suggestion that language cannot lie—any creature for which there is a name must be 'somewhere or other extant'. This implication produces a problem which was foreshadowed earlier in this chapter, in Smart's forthright statement that 'the Lord is the WORD, and all good words proceed from him, as sure as nonsense and cant are derivable from the Adversary'. Smart is not simply saying here that the origin of language is divine, but is distinguishing between 'good words' and those 'derivable from the Adversary', for evidently not all language can be considered as God-given; there is the possibility that it may be polluted by 'nonsense and cant', 'curses and evil language' (B1. 221), and 'whispers and unmusical sounds in general' (B1. 231). It must be necessary, if language is to be regarded as an inherently significant repository of truth, that we should be able to discriminate between the 'true', God-given language and its 'shadow'—the 'false and faint images of the works of Almighty God' (B2. 308) manufactured by the devil.[21]

This problem, however, is not as awkward as it might at first appear, for the aspects of language Smart condemns as satanic are very similar to those condemned by many of his contemporaries, and they are condemned in very much the same terms. Beattie, for example, in his *Theory of Language* (1783), relegates curses, as an illegitimate abuse of language, virtually to the status of non-language or nonsense, for he writes that 'common oaths and curses' are 'utterly unlawful'—they are outlawed from the 'legally' or legitimately defined 'body' of language. 'Cant', which Smart condemns most strongly, was almost universally reviled as it signified religious hypocrisy, and was associated with sectarianism; it might also be taken to mean a 'Barbarous jargon' and a 'corrupt dialect' which, according to Johnson, 'cannot be regarded as

---

[21] The belief Smart expresses in B2. 622 was, in some respects, not uncommon, for God was understood to exercise divine providence in the maintenance of species; see e.g. John Ray, *Works of Creation*, bk. I, 'Of bodies endued with a sensitive soul, or animals'. On 'Whisperings and evil-speakings', see Law's portrait of 'Sussurus' in *A Serious Call to a Devout and Holy Life*, introd. Norman Sykes (1728; this edn. London, 1906, 1967), 308–10.

any part of the durable materials of a language', and are therefore to be excluded from the legitimate vocabulary. Cant as religious hypocrisy—compliance with the outward forms of worship, without attending to their significance—might also be described as non-language, for the falsehood it involves is an abuse of language as a means of communication, and as a means of expression it becomes self-contradictory nonsense. That the satanic 'language' Smart alludes to is in fact non-language, or the abuse of language, is implied in his statement that 'every word has its marrow in the English tongue for order and for delight' (B2. 597), for here he describes 'every word'—all language—as part of a unified and wholesome body or skeletal structure, and what he excludes as 'derivable from the Adversary' he therefore also excludes from the body of language itself.[22]

IV

That body, however, is liable to ill-health and corruption, and Smart's use of language may also be understood as an attempt to assert and strengthen its purity. This concern is perhaps best described in Smart's use of money as a metaphor for language, for the coinage, like language, can be seen as having a 'true' value which is subject to debasement through devaluation, erosion, and 'clipping'. The use of coinage as an image for language is, of course, by no means unique to Smart: Zeno provides what is probably the earliest known example of the comparison, and it recurs fairly frequently in classical literature. It is alluded to in Horace's discussion of neologisms in the *Ars Poetica*, for example, and Juvenal refers to the poet as 'minter' in his seventh satire. Charles Dryden retains the image in his translation, for example in the following lines on the relation of patron to poet:

> The tricks of thy base patron now behold,
> To spare his purse, and save his darling gold;

---

[22] James Beattie, *The Theory of Language* (1783; this edn. London, 1788), 318. See Joseph Addison, *The Freeholder*, 37 (27 Apr. 1716); Samuel Johnson, *A Dictionary of the English Language* (London, 1755), Preface; ibid., 'Cant', *n. s.*, 4, 1. For a further discussion of the criteria by which various words were excluded in the 18th c. from the authorized vocabulary of 'common usage', see John Barrell, *English Literature in History, 1730–80: An Equal, Wide Survey* (London, 1983), 128, 134–5, 153–8. It is unlikely, however, that Smart would, like Johnson, have excluded regional dialects from the body of language, as his use of Yorkshire words and phrases indicates: see e.g. B2. 569; and, on this point, see also Walter Harte, *The Amaranth: or, Religious Poems* (London, 1767), Preface, pp. vii–viii; p. 6 and n.

> In his own coin the starving wit he treats;
> Himself makes verses, which himself repeats.

And here the extent to which money is appropriate as an image for language is indicated by the patron's exchange of the one for the other. Swift and Addison both deplore the 'clipping' of words in fashionable conversation, and Greenwood writes in *The Tatler* that he is

. . . grieved to see our sterling *English* language fallen into the hands of Clippers and Coiners. That mutilated epistle, consisting of *Hippo*, *Rep's*, and such like enormous curtailings, was a mortifying spectacle.

Blackmore, in his *Satyr against Wit* (1700), plays on almost every aspect of the image, and suggests that wit should be 'recoyn'd', reassayed, and 'new Mill'd'; and a contributor to *The World* writes of women's use of language that they

take a word and change it, like a guinea into shillings for pocket money, to be employed in the several occasional purposes of the day. For instance, the adjective VAST and its adverb VASTLY mean any thing.

The connection between money and language as media of exchange provides one of the most common images in eighteenth-century literature, but, in *Jubilate Agno*, the poet creates a context in which the 'figurative effect' of the image is emphasized, and not lost 'by repetition'.[23]

Perhaps the best-known example of this image in *Jubilate Agno* is in the line (quoted earlier) in which Smart describes his method of writing:

For my talent is to give an impression upon words by punching, that when the reader casts his eye upon 'em, he takes up the image from the mould wch I have made.

(B2. 404)

In this line, however, the use of the metaphor is significantly atypical and ambiguous. Apparently, the reader's eye is represented simply as

[23] Horace speaks of the issuing of 'current' words, in *De Arte Poetica*, l. 59, suggesting the comparison of language and money, which Smart emphasizes in his verse translation. C. Dryden (trans.), Juvenal, *Sat.* vii, in *The British Poets. Including Translations. In One Hundred Volumes*, xcvi (Chiswick, 1822), 218. *Tatler*, 234 (7 Oct. 1710). Blackmore, *Satyr against Wit* (London, 1700), 9–10. [Earl of Chesterfield?], *World*, 101 (5 Dec. 1754). See also Swift, *Tatler*, 230 (28 Sept. 1710); Johnson, *Dictionary*, 'To Clip', *v. a.*, 2, 4, 5, where the image also refers to the clipping of birds' wings; *N-T*, Night 2, p. 29. For a fuller discussion of the image see Marc Shell, *The Economy of Literature* (Baltimore, Md., 1978). I quote from Lowth, *Lectures*, vol. i, lect. vi, pp. 124–5, and translator's note.

taking up the image made by the mould of the poet's impression, but the line may also suggest that the reader 'casts his eye' *according to* the impression Smart has made, as a bas-relief may be cast in bronze according to the impression made in the sand mould; and so, more generally, that he 'casts his eye' according to the impression made upon the language of the poem as a whole, and must do so, if he is to take up the image the poet has formed. This reading would contribute to the sense in which the poem should be read as a parable, interpretable only through faith. In so far, however, as the metaphor of coining relates to the words of the poem, rather than to the image in the reader's eye, it can be understood as primarily a metaphor that can distinguish between a coinage which preserves its value and one which is debased: the poet does not bury his 'talent', but inscribes or impresses a fresh image upon the 'coin', which is punched to indicate that its value has not been eroded by clipping.[24]

The concern in these verses with true and debased coinage is one that recurs frequently with the use of the metaphor of language and money, for example, in the observations that 'the Romans clipped their words', but 'God has given us a language of monosyllables to prevent our clipping' (B2. 417, 519)—a remark which takes a contrary opinion to Swift's, that the monosyllabic character of English is a mark of barbarity, reinforced by a national habit of abbreviating words as far as possible. But Smart does not understand the process of 'clipping' as one which operates simply on the physical extremities of words, as do Swift and Greenwood; it has implications also for their meaning. In line B2. 404 (quoted above), for example, two words are abbreviated, but this does not appear to have resulted in the 'clipping' or falsification of their significance, but may rather suggest that compact expression will best convey the full energy of the impression, and the full value of words, not only as tokens of exchange, but as commodities and repositories of value and meaning in their own right.[25]

The true and the debased symbols of value are, of course, related to each other: language is a body liable to corruption through abuse, just as a fiduciary system of monetary value is liable to corruption if the trust or understanding on which it is based is abused. But the health, the true value, of either system is reclaimable if the abuse or debasement

[24] *OED*, 'Punchable', *a.*; 'Punch', *sb.*[1] 3.
[25] Jonathan Swift, *A Proposal for Correcting, Improving, and Ascertaining the English Tongue* (London, 1712), 21–7. The passage from the *World*, quoted above, seems closer to Smart's view, though it does not refer specifically to 'clipping'.

ceases, and the authenticity of the system is reinstated and recognized. This potential for the purification or curing of both language and money as systems of value can be seen as implied in Smart's discussion of the lupine, where he writes:

For I prophecy that men will be much stronger in the body.
For I prophecy that the gout and consumptions will be curable.
For I prophecy that man will be as good as a Lupine.
For the Lupine professes his Saviour in Grain.
For the very Hebrew letter is fairly graven upon his Seed.
For with the diligence the whole Hebrew Alphabet may be found in a parcel of his seed.
For this is a stupendous evidence of the communicating of God in externals.
For I prophecy that they will call the days by better names.

(C. 74–81)

Smart's use of the lupine here, rather than of any other seed, has puzzled critics of *Jubilate Agno*, but is in fact very apt both in its implications and its context. The passage occurs, with apparent irrelevance, in the midst of the long section of Fragment C devoted to Smart's prophecies of the future improvement of mankind—'For it is the business of a man gifted in the word to prophecy good' (C. 57)— and it forms the bridge, as it were, between a passage on the religious conduct of life and its implications for man's health, and a passage on the improvement of language and of government, and Smart clearly sees these apparently diverse concerns as closely interrelated. The discussion of the lupine is central to these concerns, as it may be understood as describing the worth, the genuine and authentic value, that religious insight is capable of perceiving in a debased or abused system.[26]

Lupine seeds were used by the Romans as counters in playing games, and as a substitute for real money in theatrical performances, and Horace, in *Epistle* I. vii, uses them to represent a worthless or counterfeit coinage in contrast to genuine money. He writes:

vir bonus et sapiens dignis ait esse paratus,
nec tamen ignorat quid distent aera lupinis.

[26] Both Stead and *Smart I* note that the source of Smart's idea is untraced. The lupine Smart refers to is a pulse, eaten or used as cattle fodder. The system of government Smart prophesies, in e.g. the lines: 'For I prophecy that the King will have grace to put the crown upon the altar. / For I prophecy that the name of king in England will be given to Christ alone' (C. 86–7), parallels and echoes that described in Moses Lowman, *A Dissertation on the Civil Government of the Hebrews* (London, 1740).

Creech's popular translation does not reproduce the allusion to money, though it is retained by Philip Francis. In Smart's earlier prose version 'lupinis' is translated directly as 'lupines', but in each of his later translations of this passage he emphasizes the monetary allusion. In his verse translation he writes:

> The wise and good themselves profess,
> Ready for merit in distress,
> But, know, not easy to be bit,
> The medal from the counterfeit.

Here the phrase 'not easy to be bit' qualifies both the 'good and wise', who are not to be 'bit', or taken in, by counterfeit, and the true 'medal' itself, which is proved true by the resistance it offers to the teeth. The ability of the good and wise to distinguish true from false is pointed out equally emphatically in the subjoined 'Prose Interpretation': 'A good and wise man asserts himself ready to do kindnesses to the meritorious; and yet is not ignorant how true coins differ from counters.' I am not, of course, suggesting that the use of the lupine as an image for spurious or counterfeit coinage was commonplace in English, but that Smart's lines exploit an allusion that would have been familiar to classical scholars of the eighteenth century. The greatest of these, Richard Bentley, refers to this use of the pulse in his controversial discussion of *Phalaris*: 'as the Actors in Comedies paid all their Debts upon the Stage with Lupins, so a Sophist pays all his with words'. Bentley, like Smart, employs the allusion in connection with notions of value, and he does so with a casualness that underlines its familiarity: for both authors, it is an image of counterfeit coinage, and, by analogy, of the counterfeit language of 'Worldlings'.[27]

Language as money is language as the site and term of value, and counterfeit language therefore describes a false system of values, as Smart implies in the lines:

For the coffin and the cradle and the purse are all against a man.

For the purse is for money and money is dead matter with the stamp of human vanity.

For the purse is for me because I have neither money nor human friends.

(B1. 276, 279, 283)

[27] See Philip Francis, *Horace*, 4 vols. (London, 1743–6); Thomas Creech, *The Odes, Satyrs, and Epistles of Horace. Done into English* (London, 1684). *Horace. Satires, Epistles and Ars Poetica*, text with trans. by H. R. Fairclough (Loeb Classical Library, London, 1929), *Epistle* I. vii. 22–3. Smart, *Horace* (1767), iv. 56–7. Richard Bentley, *A Dissertation upon the Epistles of Phalaris* (London, 1699), 530.

Counterfeit language, like this money, has no significance in itself, for it is 'dead matter', and the stamp or seal of authentication which gives it an apparent value and significance is empty and vain, and merely causes it to reflect the values of human vanity. The significance of 'counterfeit' language turns in on itself, finding its validation only in the system of values which it both represents and establishes. This process is intimated in the line: 'For a CHARACTER is the votes of the Worldlings, but the seal is of Almighty GOD alone' (B2. 363)—where the 'CHARACTER' is validated by the contractual consent of those concerned with material things, and they, as 'Worldlings', men 'set upon profit', ascribe to it an arbitrarily established value that reflects their own material, mortal, and transitory interests. The character depends for its significance upon its context, the votes that inform it and endow it with value, whereas the seal of genuine authentication and validation is impressed by 'Almighty GOD alone', and depends upon nothing else.[28]

In Smart's lines on the lupine, however, the plant is not used simply as an image of a debased or counterfeit coinage: it is also considered as a plant in its own right, with its own properties and virtues. The lupine was thought to have a medicinal value, and to purify the inventive faculty, and we could therefore understand the passage from *Jubilate Agno* as implying that the lupine, whether eaten or considered as an object of contemplation, will purify and moderate between the inflammation caused by gout and the wasting caused by consumption; and the two afflictions it was used to treat may be understood metaphorically as the extremes of inflation and devaluation. The 'prophetic' passages of Fragment C, where the lines on the lupine occur, describe Smart's ideal vision of society: they describe a time in which every man will act in accordance with Smart's religious vision, and they invite comparison with the exhortative tradition of many of the Old Testament prophets. Smart's 'prophecies' describe a time that might be achieved were all men to be converted to the Christian 'common life', rather as Jeremiah's prophecies describe a state of affairs that might arrive if men continue in a course of degeneracy rather than of purification: Smart's view, in keeping with his evangelical outlook, is optimistic rather than pessimistic. In the ideal society, he 'prophesies', 'there will be full churches and empty play-houses' (C. 68), and there will therefore be no occasion for the use of

---

[28] Johnson, *Dictionary*, 'Worldling', *n. s.*

the lupine seed as a counterfeit monetary symbol. Genuine values will be restored, and the distinction between coins and counters, described by Hobbes in the remark: 'words are wise mens counters, they do but reckon by them: but they are the mony of fooles, that value them', will no longer be valid, for men will recognize the truth inherent in language, which, like the lupine, 'professes his Saviour in Grain'.[29]

The lupine, in *Jubilate Agno*, is an image of the counterfeit reclaimed, for both language and money as the terms of value will, like the lupine, no longer be 'dead matter with the stamp of human vanity', but 'stupendous evidence of the communicating of God in externals'. The recognition of all of creation as God's communication—both as the expression of the divine language, and as perpetually involved in a litany of communion in praise of God—will, the poem implies, result in the regeneration of mankind physically, morally, and spiritually, and will eventually result in the second coming of Christ. The lupine becomes, in this passage, the true term of value, the pulse replacing the purse, and it also reveals the extent to which creation and language are interrelated, for 'the whole Hebrew Alphabet may be found in a parcel of his seed': it contains the essential elements of language, which, in Smart's analysis, are perhaps also the essential elements of creation. These elements can be recovered not only as the lupine cures us, but as we 'diligently' examine counterfeit words for their true original significance.

V

It is not only language, however, that Smart depicts in this metaphor of language and money. I have already quoted some of the lines describing the coffin, cradle, and purse as devilish omens found in the fire, and discussed their relation to the image of money as language, but there is also a sense in which the metaphor can be taken to refer to the poet himself. The 'Let' verses with which these lines are paired

---

[29] See ibid., 'Lupine', *n. s.*; and *OED*, 'Lupine, lupin', *sb*. Hobbes, *Leviathan* (London, 1651), pt. i, ch. 4, p. 15. On the nature of prophecy as a function of poetry, see Lowth, *Lectures*, vol. ii, lect. xviii; John Brown, *A Dictionary of the Holy Bible* (this edn. Berwick, 1819), 'Prophecy'; *A Dictionary of the Bible: Dealing with its Language, Literature and Contents*, ed. James Hastings, 5 vols. (Edinburgh, 1898–1904), vol. iv, 'Prophecy and Prophets'. The connection between counterfeit money and fiction that Smart's image of the lupine suggests is also described in Campbell, *Rhetoric*, i. 98; see also i. 389–90.

refer to fossils, and the clearest point of incidence between this theme and the 'For' verses occurs in the following pair of lines:

Let Epaphroditus rejoice with the Opthalmias—The Lord increase the Cambridge collection of Fossils.	For the purse is for money and money is dead matter with the stamp of human vanity.

(Bl. 279)

This pairing emphasizes the distinction between God's seal, here the 'natural' impressions found in fossils, and the human seal, and thus reflects the distinction between the humanly impressed and recognized 'CHARACTER' and the 'seal of the righteousness of the faith'. Smart identifies himself as bearing this 'living' seal in the lines:

	For I have adventured myself in the name of the Lord, and he hath mark'd me for his own.
Let Achsah rejoice with the Pigeon who is an antidote to malignity and will carry a letter.	For I bless God for the Postmaster general & all conveyancers of letters under his care especially Allen & Shelvock.

(Bl. 21–2)

though here the context may also be taken to suggest that Smart conveys the Lord's letter or message, and bears his postal frank, or mark. This implication is also present in the lines:

Let James rejoice with the Skuttle-Fish, who foils his foe by the effusion of his ink.	For the blessing of God hath been on my epistles, which I have written for the benefit of others.

(Bl. 125)

and it may also be echoed in the pairing of the fossils and coinage, as Epaphroditus acted as a messenger between Paul and the churches.[30]

[30] Rom. 4: 11. Smart's application of images of minting and assaying to man may allude to Wisd. 2: 16, where the wicked say of the good man 'We are esteemed of him as counterfeits' (or, in the rubric, 'false coin'). See also Wisd. 3: 5–6; and the *Christian's Magazine*, 2 (1761), 569. For a discussion of the relation between fossils and ancient coins as productions of 'the Workmanship of God' see John Woodward, *The Natural History of the Earth, Illustrated, Inlarged, and Defended*, trans. B. Holloway (London, 1726), 155 ff. Letters did not, of course, carry postage stamps at this date, but they were marked, to indicate whether payment had been made. On the 'Skuttle-fish' or cuttle-fish, see *Christian's Magazine*, 2 (1761), 612–13, where it is described as 'furnished with a liquid magazine of a colour and consistency like ink, which, when pursued by an enemy, the creature emits, and blackens the water by this artifice: the foe is bewildered in the chace; and while the one vainly gropes in the dark, the other seizes the opportunity and makes his escape'.

Smart perhaps bears the seal or mark of authenticity punningly described in the verse 'Let Paul rejoice with the Seale, who is pleasant & faithfull, like God's good ENGLISHMAN' (B1. 136), for it is Paul who describes God's promise to the faithful as the 'seal of the righteousness of the faith', and the pleasantness or good nature which accompanies the 'Seale' in Smart's verse is described in the Preface to his verse translation of Horace as 'the grace of God in grain, and . . . the characteristic of an *Englishman*'. The pun on the name of the animal serves to emphasize that this is a living seal, rather than 'dead matter with the stamp of human vanity'. Man, who may bear this seal, is, during his life, molten or soft, like impressible wax or metal during minting, 'For man is born to trouble in the body, as the sparks fly upwards in the spirit. / For man is between the pinchers while his soul is shaping and purifying' (B2. 431–2).[31]

The analogy between man and language implied in the metaphor of sealing or coining might therefore stem from their shared characteristic of mutability, for both are apparently in a malleable state open either to purification or corruption; and the analogy also indicates the extent to which man and language are interrelated. Man is himself, of course, a 'word' in the divine language of creation, and as he is an expression of God, and created in his image, he epitomizes the self-reflexive nature of language. Language distinguishes man from the rest of creation; the language in which he is created, and the language he speaks which expresses or verifies the nature of that creation, are 'a part, at least, of that living soul, which God is said to have breathed into man'. A man, therefore, 'speaks HIMSELF from the crown of his head to the sole of his feet' (B1. 228), for his speech or voice is both the expression or effect, and the definition, of his nature; his speech and action are one, and are 'HIMSELF', as they describe, or are the terms of, his existential essence.[32]

Smart writes that 'a LION roars HIMSELF compleat from head to tail' (B1. 229), perhaps as, according to Rowland Jones, '. . . all nature, according to the psalmist, declares this handy work of providence, even the dull sheep, though perhaps insensibly, calls out ba, which signifies

---

[31] *Horace* (1767), Preface, p. xxx. Bishop Newton argued that Paul, and possibly also Simon, preached in Britain: see *Dissertations on The Prophecies, which have remarkably been fulfilled and at This time are Fulfilling in the World* (1754–8; this 13th edn. London, 1823), 394. On the good nature of the English, see Thomas Sprat, *History of the Royal Society*, ed. Jackson I. Cope and H. W. Jones (1667; this edn. St Louis, Mo., 1958), 61.

[32] Jones, *Origin*, Preface: 'Of the Origin of Speech'. See B2. 562: 'For Action & Speaking are one according to God and the Ancients.'

an earthly animal'. But there is a significant distinction between the self-expression of men and animals, for though in both 'the VOICE of a figure' is 'compleat in all its parts' (B1. 227), and the voice thus perfectly expresses the 'figure' that expressed it, it is only man that is made in God's image, and whose language and breath are therefore the image of that living soul which is the breath of God. Man's language is 'from the body and the spirit—and is a body and a spirit' (B1. 239), and thus reflects or re-enacts the process of God's creative language. Man also epitomizes the self-reflexive nature of language in that it is his duty to praise and worship God: the ultimate aim of man as the manifestation of God's language is to return to God, a process achieved by acknowledging and praising him: the purest use of man's language lies in the contemplation of God's glory and works, and as that human language of praise gestures back to the God whose mediated expression it is, it is an image not only of all language, but of all creation.[33]

The attitude towards language expressed in *Jubilate Agno* thus has a twofold significance. In the first place, the poem attempts to reveal the primitive and forceful significance expressed in language, but deadened and obscured by its customary usage as a collection of contractual counters. It attempts to reanimate language as the expression of the soul of man, of a communal identity fractured and devalued by worldliness, and it traces that primitive vigour in phrases, in words, in

---

[33] Jones, *Origin*, Preface: 'Of the Origin of Speech'. The verb 'is' in B1. 227 is an editorial emendation and does not appear in the MS. The concept of language as fully expressive of man's nature, and the distinction implied between the expression of man and of animal and inanimate objects, is strikingly similar to that described in Gerard Manley Hopkins's 'Scotist' sonnet:

> As kingfishers catch fire, dragonflies draw flame;
>   As tumbled over rim in roundy wells
>   Stones ring; like each tucked string tells, each hung bell's
> Bow swung finds tongue to fling out broad its name;
> Each mortal thing does one thing and the same:
>   Deals out that being indoors each one dwells;
>   Selves—goes itself; *myself* it speaks and spells,
> Crying *What I do is me: for that I came.*
>
> I say more: the just man justices;
>   Keeps grace: that keeps all his goings graces;
> Acts in God's eye what in God's eye he is—
>   Christ—for Christ plays in ten thousand places,
> Lovely in limbs, and lovely in eyes not his
> To the Father through the features of man's faces.

(*The Poems of Gerard Manley Hopkins*, ed. W. H. Gardner and M. H. MacKenzie (Oxford, 1918; rev. edn. 1970), 90.)

letters, and in the lines that make them up. In this enterprise, we can see Smart as sharing the concerns of, on the one hand, the reforming spirit of Johnson's *Dictionary*, and on the other, the more evangelical zeal of Jones and Nelme. As I pointed out at the beginning of this chapter, the particular nature of Smart's endeavour is also closely related to the more archeological and anthropological researches of Bishop Lowth, for where Lowth attempts to reanimate the poetry of an ancient people through placing it in its historical social context, and through attempting to understand it as if the reader heard and saw with the ears and eyes of an ancient Hebrew, Smart attempts to unearth primitive or original meanings embedded in an historical or prophetic idea of social harmony, of a Christian common life. For Smart's theories of language, like those of Johnson, Jones and Nelme, are also theories about the kind of society that might use that language: they are, as I suggested in my discussion of the lupine, theories based for Smart in the rightness of the godly community as opposed to a counterfeit society of worldlings—an ideal which for Smart in *Jubilate Agno* is still accessible in history and in prophecy, and which the poetry of congregational thanksgiving makes imminent.

4 'For I am inquisitive in the Lord'

The Natural Philosophy of *Jubilate Agno*

I

IN this final chapter on *Jubilate Agno* I shall be looking at the content of the poem; but, as my discussion has already indicated, there are peculiar difficulties involved in the attempt to consider the content of Smart's poem in a degree of isolation from other aspects of it. We cannot trace within the surviving fragments of the poem a single theme or argument the development of which would provide a comprehensive or unifying account of its content, which is, on the contrary, extraordinary for its variety and diversity. I have therefore chosen to look at the particular issue of the attitude to natural philosophy expressed in the poem, for this describes, in itself, an attitude to the idea of 'content', and to the apprehension of the variety of creation; and the concern with natural-philosophical theories which the poem frequently expresses places much of its heterogeneous content in a relation—of opposition or of assent—to a recognizable body of knowledge and opinion. The systematic approach to experience which natural philosophy, in its broadest sense, involves might provide a structure in relation to which we can understand, or describe, much of the poem without compromising or delimiting its diversity.

There are two major points which need to be made here about the attitude to natural philosophy and to creation which the poem expresses. The first of these is that Smart's philosophy proceeds from an understanding of man as fallen, and imperfect, and this belief has significant implications for the confident and systematic perception of divine order expressed in creation. The second point is that natural philosophy is described in *Jubilate Agno* not simply as a means of understanding the physical world, but as a metaphor or analogy in terms of which spiritual experience may also be comprehended. I shall discuss this issue at greater length in the conclusion to this chapter, when some of its implications will already have been encountered, but it is important to indicate here that analogical argument, which Newton himself employed, was not universally regarded in the mid-eighteenth century as foreign to a scientific habit of mind. Thus, though natural philosophy in *Jubilate Agno* provides what I describe as metaphors and analogies for spiritual experience, we should not assume that the kind of knowledge it offers of the spiritual is therefore merely provisional, tentative, or decorative. On the contrary, the assumption or belief of the poem is that it is the concordance and congruence of the physical and spiritual worlds that enable the one to represent the other. For the poet of *Jubilate Agno*, the resemblances and relations revealed by natural philosophy, like those revealed by other areas of language, are revelations of the immanence of the divine in creation.[1]

The natural philosophy described in *Jubilate Agno*, these points already suggest, cannot be considered in isolation from the religious beliefs the poem expresses, and cannot be assessed as the produce of a pure, empirical perception of experience untainted by the imperfections and particular positions of the perceiver; and these qualifications might seem immediately to set Smart apart from the inductive Baconian tradition associated with seventeenth- and eighteenth-century science, and in particular with the Royal Society.

Even before its official institution, the Society had established that its 'business was, precluding affairs of state and questions of theology, to consider and discuss philosophical subjects, and whatever had any connection with, or relation to them'; the Society was committed to 'the promoting of experimental learning', learning based on empirical observation and experience. But clearly every experiment had to be evaluated, and its implications studied, by methods which were, if only implicitly, interpretative, and the attempt to mark off a field of pure scientific enquiry, separate from politics and theology, serves to emphasize rather than contradict this point. A similar argument can be

---

[1] On Newton's use of analogy see P. M. Harman, *Metaphysics and Natural Philosophy: The Problem of Substance in Classical Physics* (Brighton, Sussex, 1982), 18–22. The two most important discussions of Smart's attitudes to natural philosophy are: D. J. Greene, 'Smart, Berkeley, the Scientists and the Poets: A Note on Eighteenth-Century Anti-Newtonianism', *JHL* 14 (1953), 327–52; and Karina Williamson, 'Smart's *Principia*: Science and Anti-Science in *Jubilate Agno*', *RES* 30. (1979), 409–22. See also *Smart I*, Appendix: 'Smart and the Hutchinsonians', pp. 131–2. Some of the material I use in sects. I–IV of this chapter appeared in my article ' "A Posture of Adoration": Christopher Smart and the Natural Philosophers', *The Eighteenth Century: Theory and Interpretation*, 25/2 (Spring 1984). I would like to take this opportunity to dissociate myself from the views expressed in the article 'Marxism, Ideology, and Eighteenth-Century Scholarship', by G. S. Rousseau, the editor of that issue of the journal, and, in particular, from his opinions on the work of Donald Davie.

made about Newton's famous rejection of hypotheses, and indeed the distinction or disjunction between Smart's approach to natural philosophy and that of the more 'orthodox' virtuosi of the period can be understood as stemming from his rejection of one of the hypotheses or assumptions most basic to the seventeenth- and eighteenth-century practice of scientific inquiry. This is the assumption, which, explicitly or implicitly, characterizes the works of poets and philosophers who might broadly be labelled as 'pro-Newtonian', or Baconian, and which I have already mentioned in my discussion of Smart's Seatonian poems, that the 'truth' of a theory or hypothesis can be recognized as in direct proportion to its conformity to the principles of human reason. So, for example, John Ray can be taken as representative of the tradition when he states that 'by how much the *Hypotheses* of Astronomers are more simple and conformable to Reason, by so much do they give a better account of the Heavenly Motions'.[2]

Ray's remark illuminates Pope's description of the ideal philosopher, who 'looks thro' Nature, up to Nature's God'. The philosopher's act of perception not only reveals God as his immanent presence is manifested in nature, but reveals that, in so far as the philosopher's rules of reason correspond to the system of nature they construct, they are a revelation of divine order. Pope's line suggests that the rational process of systematization ratified by the perception of nature is recognizable as absolute and divine in itself. When Sir Richard Blackmore writes of the philosophical perception of nature in *Creation* that 'stampt on Nature we Perfection find, / Fair as th'Idea in th'Eternal Mind', he credits the philosopher with the capacity to entertain divine ideas, and suggests that he may recognize his own reason, which has enabled him to establish the divine system manifested in nature, as itself divine in its operations and ideas. The 'Christian' deist Thomas Morgan describes a more extreme version of this line of thought in his polemical attack on atheism:

---

[2] Thomas Birch, *The History of the Royal Society of London for Improving of Natural Knowledge, from its first Rise* (London, 1756), i. 2, 5. For discussion of the problems involved in recognizing a mainstream tradition see Simon Schaffer, 'Natural Philosophy', in G. S. Rousseau and Roy Porter (eds.), *The Ferment of Knowledge: Studies in the Historiography of Eighteenth-Century Science* (Cambridge, 1980); Michael Hunter, *Science and Society in Restoration England* (Cambridge, 1981), ch. 3. On the role of hypotheses in Newtonian philosophy, see A. Koyré, 'Concept and Experience in Newton's Scientific Thought', in *Newtonian Studies* (Chicago, Ill., 1965), and Richard B. Schwartz, *Samuel Johnson and the New Science* (Madison, Wis., 1971), 63–8. John Ray, *The Wisdom of God Manifested in the Works of Creation* (1691), 45.

The Contemplation . . . of this universal Truth, Reason, Order, mutual Dependency, and Unity of Design throughout all Nature, is the true Knowledge and Contemplation of the Deity . . . All Nature shines with Deity, and divine Truth and Perfection irresistibly makes its Way to every rational, attentive Mind; and consequently a speculative Atheist . . . is . . . a Contradiction in Nature . . .

Morgan argues that the distinction between God and Nature is largely artificial and superfluous, a conclusion he arrives at through an argument which closely resembles that of Pope's *Essay on Man.* Morgan's argument does not only imply that the order of nature is itself divine, but that a comprehensive and systematic understanding of nature—the 'true Knowledge' he advocates here—involves or is identified with a true and comprehensive knowledge of God himself. Philosophy, it is implied, makes man Godlike, and the extent to which his reason is able to account for the 'Heavenly Motions' also describes the extent to which it is divine.[3]

It is, of course, necessary to this belief in the potential divinity of reason for its exponents to avoid any direct reference to the fall of man, as well as to any resulting lack of perfection, or possible distortion in his perception of nature. The more prominent pro-Newtonian poets of the early eighteenth century therefore interpret human history according to classical, or economic, models of progress or decline, as opposed to the scriptural model described by Moses; or, if they do sometimes acknowledge a lapse from perfection in the history of mankind, they represent this, at worst, as *felix culpa.* Both the inductive, experimental methods that characterize the new science and the arguments (or eulogies) of the poets who promote and celebrate its achievements depend on the notion of a perfect creation, and of man's perfect ability to observe and understand it: only 'uncorrupted eyes', and the 'Godlike Minds' which 'Philosophy exalts', will look 'thro' Nature, up to Nature's God'; and, if this privilege is not available to all,

---

[3] Pope, *Essay on Man*, epistle IV, l. 332. Sir Richard Blackmore, *Creation. A Philosophical Poem. In Seven Books* (London, 1712), i. 32–3; cf. Henry Needler's lines: 'So, in the fair Creation's Glass, we find / A Faint Reflection of th'Eternal Mind', in *The Works of Mr. Henry Needler*, selected with introd. by Marcia Allentuck (1728; this edn. The Augustan Reprint Society, 90; Los Angeles, Calif., 1961), 65. Thomas Morgan, *Physico-Theology: Or, a Philosophico-Moral Disquisition concerning Human Nature, Free Agency, Moral Government, and Divine Providence* (London, 1741), 141. Morgan follows Pope's argument for the development from self-love to social affection closely: see *Physico-Theology*, p. 123, and *Essay*, epistle III, ll. 131–46.

this is the result of a wilful ignorance, rather than of any shortcomings in the powers of man's reason.[4]

Roger Cotes writes, in the Preface to the second edition of Newton's *Principia*:

He must be blind who from the most wise and excellent contrivances of things cannot see the infinite Wisdom and Goodness of their Almighty Creator, and he must be mad and senseless who refuses to acknowledge them.

Cotes's argument depends not simply on the persuasive power of natural religion, but on the explanatory power of a 'sound and true philosophy . . . founded on the appearances of things': Newton has 'clearly laid open and set before our eyes' the truths of nature, and no lack of perfection, no innate distortion, now affects man's reason, or the system of nature, in such a way as might distort the relation between the two: 'The gates are now set open, and by the passage he [Newton] has revealed we may freely enter into the knowledge of the hidden secrets and wonders of natural things'. Clearly, the notion of a creation which has not remained perfect, which is even perhaps a potentially misleading source of knowledge and revelation, and which is liable anyway to be mis-perceived and misinterpreted by fallen man, would call into question the most basic principles of post-Baconian philosophy.[5]

II

This is, however, one of the notions on which Smart's natural philosophy is based. In contrast to the earlier poets I have mentioned, Smart refers frequently to the Fall, and to the actively distorting role of the devil, of 'the Adversary'. He writes, for example, possibly referring to the eclipses of Jupiter's satellites:

For the SHADOW is of death, which is the Devil, who can make false and faint images of the works of Almighty God.

[4] Thomas Sprat, *History of the Royal Society*, ed. Jackson I. Cope and H. W. Jones (1667; this edn. St Louis, Mo., 1958), 72; see Hunter, *Science*, p. 30. James Thomson, *The Seasons*, 'Summer', ed. James Sambrook (Oxford, 1981), l. 1715.

[5] Sir Isaac Newton, *Mathematical Principles of Natural Philosophy*, trans. A. Motte (1729; this edn. rev. Florian Cajori, 2 vols., Berkeley, Calif., 1934; hereafter *Principia*); Roger Cotes, 'Preface to the second edition' (1713), vol. i, pp. xxxii–xxxiii. The image of the New Science as retrieving or reclaiming 'forbidden' knowledge is common: see Sprat, *Royal Society*, p. 72; Edmund Halley, 'Ode to Newton', trans. L. J. Richardson, in *Principia*, vol. i, pp. xiv–xv.

For every man beareth death about him ever since the transgression of Adam,
  but in perfect light there is no shadow.

(B2. 308–9)

For Smart, the eclipses, or shadows, do not testify to the successive,
rather than instantaneous, propagation of light, but to the malignant
powers of the devil, and 'the glory of Almighty God' (B1. 285). Smart's
cosmology is based upon a radically different perception of man's
relation to nature: a nature in which experience and observation may
not be the most reliable tools of understanding and perception, and in
which distortions and 'false and faint images' conspire to mislead the
empirical philosopher.[6]

Smart's understanding of nature should not, however, be dismissed
as '*fundamentally* unscientific' on the grounds of its incompatibility with
an empirical inductive methodology of science based on the 'appearances
of things'. The natural philosophy expounded in *Jubilate Agno* certainly
seems to derive many of its apparent idiosyncrasies from the religious
perspective that informs it, but this perspective is not incompatible
with a coherent system of natural philosophy, and was certainly not one
that seventeenth- and eighteenth-century virtuosi were anxious to
discard. Newton may have expressed a desire for religion and
philosophy to be 'preserved distinct', but this remark, made in an
unpublished and probably early manuscript, seems to refer to the
traditional distinction between the laws of God and man, or the
provinces of caesar and heaven, rather than to a more specific notion
of the relation of natural philosophy and religion. Cotes's Preface to
the second edition of the *Principia*, and Newton's additional General
Scholium to Proposition XLII, were partly designed to refute
theological criticisms of his work, which he clearly therefore did not
view as irrelevant—as Professor Cajori flatly states in his Appendix to
the *Principia*, 'Newton saw no conflict between religion and science'.
Newton positively encouraged and aided the early Boyle lecturers in
their attempts to show the essential compatibility, and interrelation, of
religion and the new science. The significant distinction between this
view of the compatibility of science and religion and that which
informs Smart's *Jubilate Agno* is rather one of method, for the method
apparent in Smart's 'system' of natural philosophy is not simply or
purely inductive.[7]

---

[6] The context of B2. 308–9 suggests that they refer to eclipses, but the evidence
supplied by context in *JA* is not always conclusive.
[7] Williamson, 'Smart's *Principia*', p. 411. Cotes, 'Preface', *Principia*, vol. i, p. xxxii.

Smart's natural philosophy addresses a problem which, in a Newtonian world-view, is acknowledged only as the result of the technological difficulties impeding the progress of observational science: the difficulty of measuring the velocity of light by the observation of the eclipses of Jupiter's satellites, for example, is understood largely in terms of the problems of designing and constructing a sufficiently sophisticated telescope, and of accumulating a sufficient number of reliable observations, not in terms of the possibility that the evidence they offer is misleading, or that the method of interpreting it may be fundamentally unreliable. But for Smart, observation is a problematic enterprise, particularly as it involves the interplay of light and shadow understood as divine or diabolical manifestations; and it is, above all, in questions related to light, colour, and fire that he represents man as liable to misapprehension. Fire can be divine, diabolical, or, to some extent, neutral; it transforms, purifies, and destroys, and its nature must be recognized before its effects can be understood.

For Fire is a mixed nature of body & spirit, & the body is fed by that which hath not life.
For Fire is exasperated by the Adversary, who is Death, unto the detriment of man.

For there is a Fire which is blandishing, and which is of God direct.
For Fire is a substance and distinct, and purifyeth evn in hell.
(B1. 171–2, 175–6)[8]

Simon Schaffer writes of the role of fire in eighteenth-century natural philosophy that

The status of fire as a privileged analyst was called into debate: fire itself, and its manifestations as electricity, light, and other forms of active matter, were

Cambridge, King's College Library, Keynes MS 6, fo. 1ʳ. The MS consists of an autograph draft of seven statements on religion, and the implications of this first statement are clarified by the second: '. . . Religion & polity or the laws of God & the laws of man are to be kept distinct. We are not to make the commandments of man a part of the laws of God.' But see Frank E. Manuel, *A Portrait of Isaac Newton* (London, 1980), 119–20. Cajori, 'Appendix', *Principia*, ii. 679. See also R. S. Westfall, *Science and Religion in Seventeenth-Century England* (New Haven, Conn., 1958), 47, 116–17; Margaret C. Jacob, *The Newtonians and the English Revolution, 1689–1720* (Hassocks, Sussex, 1976), 137; Newton to Bentley, 10 Dec. 1692, in Thayer, p. 46.

[8] On science and technology see A. Rupert Hall, *The Revolution in Science, 1500–1750* (1954; this edn. London, 1983), 138. The account of fire in *JA* suggests that Smart accepted the phlogiston theory of its nature; see J. M. Stillman, *The Story of Early Chemistry* (1924; this edn. New York, 1960), ch. 11.

not merely the conceptual tools of a philosophical discourse, they provided the base for a complete cosmology of nature and of practice. On the one hand, in matter-theory in the eighteenth century, fire carried problematic contradictions between the preservation of nature and the transformation of nature, since fire had this dramatic effect upon matter in experience. On the other hand, fire and its manifestations provided a vocabulary of analogy and metaphor for natural philosophers to use.

Smart's theories of natural philosophy in *Jubilate Agno* are, I think, most fruitfully understood not simply as 'matter-theory', but as also providing a framework of analogy and metaphor in terms of which a complete cosmology might be constructed. Smart's comments on fire and its manifestations, for example, cannot be satisfactorily understood if they are taken to refer only to a 'coherent system of natural philosophy' as we now understand that science, but should rather be approached as Smart approaches the problem of dreams:

For a DREAM is a good thing from GOD.
For there is a dream from the adversary which is terror.
For the phenomenon of dreaming is not of one solution, but many.
(B2. 369–71)

For Smart, dreams, and also nature, have a problematic status— dreams may be from God, or they may be devilish delusions; and, in both dreams and nature, it is important to recognize that such delusions or instances of misinformation exist, and also to learn to distinguish them from genuine and God-given truths. The problem of making this distinction, however, is acknowledged by Smart to be complex—not 'of one solution, but many'—and if the terms of some of the various 'solutions' he considers may now seem more theological than 'scientific', more metaphysical than empirical, it is not this that sets him apart from the eighteenth-century tradition in natural philosophy.[9]

[9] Schaffer, 'Natural Philosophy', p. 83. Williamson, 'Smart's *Principia*', p. 422; Williamson argues, in her illuminating article, that 'Whatever else Smart was trying to do in *Jubilate Agno*, he was certainly not attempting to answer the scientists on their own grounds by offering an alternative explanation of phenomena in physical terms' (p. 412). While I agree with much of her argument, it seems clear that 18th-c. scientists themselves did not attempt to account for phenomena in physical terms alone, and that the differences between Smart's philosophy and theirs are therefore less great than she suggests.

III

Smart was not, of course, unique, or remarkably eccentric, in acknowledging that an understanding of the natural world must involve an interpretative act, but in a Newtonian world-view, as we have seen, the nature of this act is disguised by the assumption of the purity and rightness of man's reasoning power, and by the partly rhetorical device of ostensibly rejecting hypotheses; whereas, in the works of anti-Newtonian philosophers, the extent to which nature must be interpreted, rather than simply observed, is often given especial emphasis. The 'Hutchinsonian' philosopher William Jones of Nayland, for example, writes that an 'experiment in nature, like a text in the Bible, is capable of different interpretations, according to the preconceptions of the interpreter'. Jones does not reject the evidence of empirical observation, and describes the many experiments that support his arguments with an enthusiastic wealth of detail, but his explicit and frequent references to the analogy between scriptural and natural revelation serve to highlight the extent to which he regards all philosophy as an interpretative exercise. He writes in the Introduction to his *Physiological Disquisitions*:

Many have been the commentators on philosophy, and none in the world so happy and successful in every part of it as those of our own country: . . . but still, NATURE is the text; and where there is difference of opinion, and authority seems to be against me, then I must plead that text, as a good protestant pleads his Bible.

For Jones, the philosopher's position is comparable to that of the biblical commentator: he does not enjoy a direct access that permits him to unlock the 'hidden treasuries of Truth', as does Newton in Halley's 'Ode', but he is the expositor or annotator of the text that describes those truths. Newton is described as 'spelling out the secrets of the earth', as recounting the truths Jones believes he can only offer a marginal comment on.[10]

The nature of the interpretative act Smart regards as proper to the philosopher is indicated in his criticisms of Newton. I have already

---

[10] William Jones, *Physiological Disquisitions; or Discourses on the Natural Philosophy of the Elements* (London, 1781), 148 and Introduction, p. x. Halley in *Principia*, vol. i, p. xv. On Jones's connections with the Hutchinsonians, see Robert E. Schofield, *Mechanism and Materialism: British Natural Philosophy in the Age of Reason* (Princeton, NJ, 1970), 125 ff. On the function of the commentator see Johnson, *Dictionary*, 'Commentator', *n. s.*

discussed the most direct of these, but it may be worth pointing out some of the further implications of the criticisms they offer:

Let Barsabas rejoice with Cammarus —Newton is ignorant for if a man consult not the WORD how should he understand the WORK?—	For there is infinite provision to keep up the life in all the parts of Creation.
	(Bl. 220)

It seems unlikely that it is the *quantity* of Newton's reading of the Bible (the 'WORD' of God) that Smart refers to, as Newton's devotion to its study was well known, and it therefore seems probable, as I have said, that Smart is here criticizing Newton for his failure, or rejection of the attempt, to understand the work of creation in terms of the word of the Bible; this suggestion is supported, and perhaps amplified, by some of the implications of the naming of Barsabas in this context. The name 'Barsabas', as translated by Cruden, can mean 'son of conversion', perhaps suggesting Newton's need either to be converted himself, or to convert his philosophy in accordance with biblical precepts—an implication also suggested in the translation of his name as 'son of swearing', for Newton's philosophy may represent an abuse of the word which would confirm a pious oath. The name also means 'son of rest', and this translation could apply to Newton's belief in dead matter and the void, as opposed to the animated plenum Smart refers to in the 'For' verse here.

The application of these various translations is supported by some of Smart's earlier criticisms of Newton's faith and philosophy:

Let Candace rejoice with the Crawfish—How hath the Christian minister renowned the Queen.	For CHASTITY is the key of knowledge as in Esdras, Sr Isaac Newton & now, God be praised, in me.
Let The Eunuch rejoice with the Thorn-Back—It is good to be discovered reading the BIBLE.	For Newton nevertheless is more of error than of the truth, but I am of the WORD of GOD.
	(Bl. 194–5)

The eunuch here is the 'Christian minister' of Queen Candace whose conversion is described in Acts 8: 26–39, and he acts as a contrast to Newton. The apostle Philip encountered this 'man of Ethiopia' reading aloud from the book of Isaiah—consulting the 'WORD'—and asked him: 'Understandeth thou what thou readest? And he said, How can I, except some man should guide me? and he desired Philip that he would come up and sit with him.' The Ethiopian's attitude is traditionally interpreted as providing a model for the faithful convert, for he is a powerful Gentile, 'an eunuch of great authority', who nevertheless shows a proper humility in recognizing his need for instruction: not only does he study the word, but he recognizes that in order to understand it fully he needs a mediator—a minister or a messiah—to intercede between him and it. Newton, however, does not recognize the need for interpretative intercession, but appears to believe that he can perceive the truth in nature directly, without the mediation of an informing context of hypothesis and belief, and without the guidance of the 'WORD'.[11]

Smart's attitude to the Newtonian system, then, was not one of acceptance and admiration; and he was not alone in expressing at least some reservations about the new science. Recent research in the history of science has increasingly acknowledged the prevalence and influence of anti-Newtonian views in the eighteenth century, which the enormous impact and continuing influence of Newton's achievement had previously obscured, or relegated to the status of eccentricity; and it is now recognized that Newtonian views (and, indeed, the views of Newton himself) did not immediately find general and unqualified acceptance.[12]

The Newtonian philosophy was open to criticism on a number of counts. The early Boyle lectures, which did much to promote understanding and acceptance of the philosophy both as a system of nature and as a bulwark of religion, achieved this aim partly through emphasizing the value of natural religion at the expense of scriptural revelation; but this approach was liable to represent revelation as almost superfluous; and, as the new science demystified the complexities of nature, the universe could come to appear so well-regulated a mechanical system that there was no need to bring in God to account for its workings, but only for its creation. Newtonian philosophy could therefore be criticized for encouraging deism, and anti-trinitarianism,

[11] Cruden, 'Proper Names', Barsabas. For examples of 18th-c. scholarly interest in the meanings of biblical proper names, see *Christian's Magazine*, 2 (1761), 569, 678; 3 (1762), 63, and 1 (1760), 406, where a correspondent comments that 'It is a thing well known, and taken for granted, that there is a mystical importance in some scripture names.' Acts 8: 30–1, 27. The name 'thornback' could be 'Opprobriously applies to a person', as in 18th-c. slang it referred to an 'old maid'; see Captain Grose, *A Dictionary of Buckish Slang, University Wit, and Pickpocket Eloquence* (London, 1811), 'Thornback'. Candace's name—which may be a dynastic title—means 'pure possession' (Cruden, 'Proper Names'), and may thus refer to spiritual purity.

[12] See e.g. Schaffer, 'Natural Philosophy'; Margaret C. Jacob, *The Radical Enlightenment: Pantheists, Freemasons and Republicans* (London, 1981); John Redwood, *Reason, Ridicule and Religion: The Age of Enlightenment in England, 1660–1750* (London, 1976).

with which one recent critic has described it as 'indissolubly connected'. Opponents of the new science did not stop at objections to its religious and moral implications; they also attempted to advance counter-theories on a number of the most important scientific issues of the period. By the mid-eighteenth century the philosophy was widely criticized for having reduced nature to a lump of inanimate matter which stupidly followed pre-ordained mathematical and physical laws, and many anti-Newtonian theories of the period are characterized by a belief in dynamic materialism. The concepts of dynamic materialism, and of animism, did not represent a naïve reaction to Newtonian philosophy, but addressed a problem raised by Newton's account of gravitational force as an active force somehow attributed to inactive matter. It is in the context of this 'anti-Newtonian' reaction to the new science that Smart's natural philosophy—the theory implied, for example, in the statement that 'MATTER is the dust of the Earth, every atom of which is the Life' (B1. 160)—can, I believe, most fruitfully be discussed.[13]

Much of the natural philosophy referred to in *Jubilate Agno* can be described as 'anti-Newtonian', but it is important to qualify and describe the specific implications of the application of this label. For the division or distinction between philosophers described as of the 'Newtonian' or 'anti-Newtonian' traditions is often quite vaguely defined: the deist Thomas Morgan, for example, is cited among the 'Newtonian Pagans and Heretics' discussed by Robert E. Schofield, and his philosophy certainly departs from the Newtonian model, but he cites Newton as 'the great Philosopher, whom I chuse to follow', and claims Locke as 'my Master, and the first Guide and Director of my Understanding'. John Woodward, the eminent geologist, on the other hand, can be loosely grouped with the 'Newtonian' camp, but, in his *Natural History of the Earth*, it is difficult to determine his attitude to the issues of hypotheses and empirical evidence—to discern whether he is concerned to argue that the Mosaic account of the deluge is supported by this theory, or that his theory is made more credible by the Mosaic account.[14]

[13] Redwood, *Ridicule*, p. 169. See Schofield, *Mechanism*, p. 115; Rom Harré, 'Knowledge', in Rousseau and Porter (eds.), *Ferment*.

[14] Schofield, *Mechanism*, p. 128; I quote from the title of ch. 6. Morgan, *Physico-Theology*, pp. 36, 74. See John Woodward, *The Natural History of the Earth, Illustrated, Inlarged and Defended*, trans. B. Holloway (London, 1726), Preface and pp. 1, 158–62; also Joseph M. Levine, *Dr. Woodward's Shield: History, Science, and Satire in Augustan England* (London, 1977).

The phrase 'anti-Newtonian' can also be misleading if it is taken to imply the existence of two opposed and disparate schools of thought, for the 'anti-Newtonians' could hardly be described as a 'school'. Their diverse views range from a complete rejection of the Newtonian hypothesis (in the case of John Hutchinson) to milder attempts to modify, humanize, and animate the Newtonian system. John Michell, for example, can be described as anti-Newtonian in so far as he argued for the 'life' of matter, but it was he who designed and completed an apparatus for determining the force of attraction between two artificial masses which, through its use in Cavendish's experiment, was to become a powerful confirmation of the 'truth' of Newton's law of gravitation. This diversity can also be seen as reflected in the varying extent to which anti-Newtonian theories were 'thought out', and made apparently scientifically plausible, as Rom Harré points out, for

though the field theories of Michell and Greene were perhaps exceptional in being very fully developed, many people of the period held to some sort of force theory of matter, often inconsistently coupled with a vaguely substantialist basis.

Smart could perhaps be described as belonging to this latter, 'vague' group, though it is not clear how seriously we can take the distinction between the 'developed' and the 'vague' in an age when the Lucasian Professor of Mathematics could expect to be awarded a prize for determining longitude at sea by measuring the interval of time between an explosion on the coast and its reception on board ship—a method, as Newton pointed out, that would only help to establish the ship's longitude if its position were already known.[15]

Smart was not ignorant of the new science, and his interest in it was probably prompted, at least in part, by his masonic connections, for 'Freemasons appear to have been particularly receptive to the new scientific learning', and nor was the dynamic and substantialist form taken by his natural philosophy, in opposition to Newtonianism, an isolated or idiosyncratic phenomenon. His opinions should be understood as reflecting a more general trend towards materialism, though any direct connections with such a disparate and scattered 'group' as the anti-Newtonians would be hard to establish. Smart

[15] See A. Geikie, *A Memoir of John Michell* (Edinburgh, 1918). Harré, 'Knowledge', p. 29. William Whiston and Humphrey Ditton, *A New Method for discovering the Longitude both at Sea and Land* (London, 1714); see Richard S. Westfall, *Never at Rest: A Biography of Isaac Newton* (Cambridge, 1980), 834–5.

describes a universe of animated matter, filled with material and immaterial beings, in terms that are significant both as a means of explaining natural phenomena and as religious and theological concepts. His rejection of Newtonian science has a double thrust: on the one hand, he criticizes the religious bases and implications of the new science, and on the other he attacks its scientific or philosophical principles, for the main body of his cosmological theories rests upon the recognition of an apparently fundamental incoherence in the Newtonian system.[16]

IV

This incoherence, or paradox, emerges in the description of the principles of gravity and the *vis inertiae*, and it may have become apparent partly as a result of the difficulty of describing these principles with sufficient precision in non-mathematical language; though it can also be seen as inherent in the principles themselves, for both Newton and his more modern editors are obliged to devote considerable space and energy to explaining away the apparent contradiction. The concept of the *vis inertiae* is paradoxical in itself, but it becomes yet more problematic, and open to criticism, when Newton describes it as the 'inherent, innate, and essential force' of a material body otherwise represented as inanimate and stupid. This paradox becomes yet more complex when it is associated with the problematic concept of gravitational force. Newton took great care to emphasize that gravity was not a property inherent to matter: he wrote to Richard Bentley, the first of the Boyle lecturers, 'You sometimes speak of gravity as essential and inherent to matter. Pray do not ascribe that notion to me, for the cause of gravity is what I do not pretend to know . . .'—but his very care, and the fact that philosophers as distinguished as Bentley and Huygens had misunderstood him, indicate the extent to which the *Principia* had suggested that gravitational force was an essential property of matter. This was partly a problem of expression: Roger Cotes, who had probably not

---

[16] Jacob, *Radical Enlightenment*, p. 245. In the Appendix to *Smart I* Williamson suggests that Smart may have been influenced by the Hutchinsonian philosophers, but though aspects of their philosophy are similar, I see no direct connection, and no evidence that these similarities are any more conclusive than those between Smart and other, non-Hutchinsonian, anti-Newtonian philosophers.

misunderstood the status of gravity, nevertheless described it as 'the *attribute* of gravity . . . found in all bodies'; but this was perhaps also a result of the lack of a satisfactory explanation of the phenomenon, whose cause Newton did 'not pretend to know', and whose 'occult' status was vigorously defended by Cotes. If gravity were understood as an essential attribute or quality of matter, then matter would have to be understood as both passive and active; as lifeless and inert, but capable of exercising force not only in maintaining that inertia but in influencing and attracting other bodies at a distance.[17]

The 'occult' force of gravity was at once the key 'discovery' and potentially the weakest point of the Newtonian system. For Thomas Morgan, the paradoxical concept of *vis inertiae* provided the occasion for his departure from strict adherence to the Newtonian system; and Robert Greene, who disseminated anti-Newtonian views from Clare Hall, Cambridge, for more than twenty-five years in the early eighteenth century, made the corresponding weakness in the concept of gravity the starting-point for his attacks on the 'new science':

If we compare the original hypothesis of this philosophy with the Conclusions of it, the one seems to be little less than a confutation of the other. Matter is supposed to be entirely passive. The sum of all the mathematical reasoning upon that hypothesis is, that it has in every part of it a Force of Gravitation, that is, that it is entirely Active, and if such a conclusion is not a contradiction to such a Hypothesis, I cannot tell what is.

Greene's criticism is not necessarily based on a misunderstanding. For Newton's uncertainty about the cause of gravity had allowed him to speak of 'the attraction of every particle', as though matter had 'in every part of it a Force of Gravitation' or attraction. This problem of the representation of passive matter as the apparent source of an active attraction provided an opening not only for Greene and Morgan but for other philosophers concerned to establish the 'life' of matter, and Smart's natural philosophy addresses the same paradox.[18]

Smart writes that 'I have shown the Vis Inertiae to be false, and such is all nonsense', and the comment is often taken to refer to his tripos

[17] Newton to Bentley, 25 Feb. 1692/3, Thayer, p. 54; Newton is himself pointing out the 'absurdity' of this idea here. Newton to Bentley, 17 Jan. 1692/3, Thayer, p. 53. Cotes, Preface, *Principia*, vol. i, p. xxi, my italics; see also Cajori's discussion of this problem, in Appendix, *Principia*, ii. 632–5, and Koyre, 'Concept and Experience', pp. 56–8.

[18] Morgan, *Physico-Theology*, pp. 2–4. R. Greene, *The Principles of the Philosophy of Expansive and Contractive Forces* (Cambridge, 1727), 39; see Harré, 'Knowledge', p. 27. *Principia*, i. 197 (bk. I, prop. lxxv).

poem 'Materies gaudet vi inertiae' (1742), though, as Karina Williamson points out, these verses do not explicitly refute the concept. The notion is, however, implicitly 'shown . . . to be false' in the principles of natural philosophy described in earlier parts of *Jubilate Agno*:

Let Theophilus rejoice with the Folio, who hath teeth, like the teeth of a saw.	For MATTER is the dust of the Earth, every atom of which is the life.
Let Bartimaeus rejoice with the Quaviver—God be gracious to the eyes of him, who prayeth for the blind.	For MOTION is as the quantity of life direct, & that which hath not motion, is resistance.
Let CHRISTOPHER, who is Simon of Cyrene, rejoice with the Rough—God be gracious to the CAM & to DAVID CAM & his seed for ever.	For Resistance is not of GOD, but he—hath built his works upon it.
Let Timaeus rejoice with the Ling—God keep the English Sailors clear of French bribery.	For the Centripetal and Centrifugal forces are GOD SUSTAINING and DIRECTING.

(B1. 160–3)

Williamson notes here that matter, motion, resistance, and centripetal and centrifugal forces are the 'first five principles of Newton's *Principia*', but while Smart's five 'principles' certainly suggest a parallel with the opening 'Definitions' of the *Principia*, they diverge significantly from that model. Newton's first two definitions deal with the '*quantity of matter*' and the '*quantity of motion*', but his third and fourth definitions describe the *vis inertiae*, and refer to resistance only in passing; and Smart's concentration on resistance, rather than on the 'force of inactivity', appears to result from the incompatibility of the concept of *vis inertiae* with his account of matter and motion, and thus implies that he regards it as 'all nonsense'.[19]

We can approach an understanding of the ground of that rejection if we examine the relation of the 'Let' and 'For' verses quoted above. The 'Let' verse immediately preceding them enjoins Joses, the brother of Jesus, to rejoice with the sturgeon, and comments that he 'saw his maker in the body and obtained grace' (B1. 159); and this reference introduces a series of reflections on the nature of sight. Joses's perception of Jesus was immediate: he saw him in the flesh; but Theophilus 'saw' Jesus less directly. Theophilus here is probably the

[19] *Smart I*, p. 38 n. 'Definitions', *Principia* i. 1, 2.

patron to whom the Acts and the Gospel of St Luke were dedicated and addressed, and who was frequently confused with Theophilus of Antioch, the second-century theologian who developed the doctrine of the trinity and the creative Word; and St Luke's address to him lays particular emphasis on the value of an eyewitness account for establishing 'the certainty of those things, wherein thou hast been instructed'. Theophilus is to believe Luke's account not through 'blind faith', but as the direct evidence of 'eye witnesses, and ministers of the word', and the certainty this will create in him will be similar to that of the apostles themselves, 'To whom also he [Jesus] *shewed* himself alive after his passion by many *infallible proofs*, being *seen* of them forty days'.[20]

Bartimeus, however, believed in Jesus in spite of his blindness, and was cured or saved as a result of that faith. Luke writes that 'Jesus said unto him, Receive thy sight: thy faith hath saved thee. And immediately he received his sight, and followed him, glorifying God: and all the people, when they saw *it*, gave praise unto God.' Bartimeus is thus a type of the latter-day Christian, who is saved and will see God as a result of his blind faith, though 'all the people' who lack faith will praise God only when they have seen a miracle.[21]

The biblical figures named in these 'Let' verses suggest, by their association with modes of vision, that the key to Smart's natural philosophy lies in the method of perceiving nature and assessing visual evidence. Robert Greene, in common with many critics of the Newtonian philosophy and of natural religion, takes up St Paul's argument that the distinction between faith and reason is that faith is 'the *Evidence of things not seen*', whereas reason is 'the *Evidence of things which are seen*'; but our senses may be deceived. Reason, and especially inductive and mathematical reason, is fallible and potentially misleading,

[20] Luke 1, and 4: 2; Acts 1: 3 (my italics). Theophilus may have been a specific convert, or, as his name means 'lover of God', he may be a more general 'type' for all converts. The name may also refer to Theophilus the Monk, the alchemist or early chemist praised by Cornelius Agrippa in *The Vanity of the Arts and Sciences* (1530), or to Theophilus the early Greek chemist (see Stillman, *Early Chemistry*, pp. 220–1; Agrippa and Agricola, referred to in B1. 137, were both prominent alchemists). The folio with which Theophilus rejoices may suggest aspects of the relation between the 'Let' and 'For' verses of *JA*, as it is a fish with sharp teeth, as well as a sheet of paper or large book, whose 'bite' is in its sayings, or, in a further play on 'saw', in the insight it gives. In bookkeeping the word 'folio' refers to the two opposite pages in a ledger, or to a single page which shows both sides of an account. The MS of *JA* is made up of what were folio sheets. See *Smart I*, p. 38 n.
[21] Luke 18: 42–3; Mark 10: 46–52 specifies the name 'Bartimeus', but places less emphasis on the significance of sight in the incident.

and 'it is . . . we affirm, the most difficult thing in the World to arrive at the knowledge of what is real Truth in our conclusions from Reason', whereas faith can claim the support of the testimony of reliable witnesses (in the Scriptures), and is confirmed by the strong impression made by the evidence of natural revelation:

Nature it self, which is another kind of Revelation of the *Deity* . . . is an Argument, that what proceeds from GOD, may in general be thought to strike us with greater force and energy, than any thing our Reason can dictate to us . . .

Greene is concerned to attack the dictatorship of the 'weak and glimmering Light of *Reason*', rather than to defend the reasonableness of Christianity, for, as he points out, this defence would show Christianity to be a 'Rational System', but not necessarily a true one. Greene emphasizes the fallibility of reason largely by directing our attention to the extent to which reason is interpretative, and governed by preconceptions and implicit assumptions. Of those philosophers who argue for a void he writes:

not withstanding this firm and invincible persuasion which they have, there is nothing more demonstrable than that all their Arguments for it, are only so many Affirmations of what was intended to be prov'd . . .

He relegates their arguments to the status of opinion, and recognizes the importance of rhetoric in establishing that opinion as more convincing than another: 'the greatest part of that [*Mathematick*] Knowledge', he writes, 'rests as much on Authority, as perhaps it do's on Reason'.[22]

Greene and Smart both see nature, when viewed in the context of faith, as demonstrating the existence of the deity, but clearly for both that context actually changes the nature of vision. Greene rejects the '*Evidence* of things which *are seen*', but is prepared to accept the visual evidence of nature and the evidence seen by those reliable 'eye witnesses' of the scriptures, both of which must therefore involve a different kind of sight. Smart writes:

[22] R. Green[e], *A Demonstration of the Truth and Divinity of the Christian Religion* (Cambridge, 1711), 193–4 (see Heb. 11: 1–3), 203, 124, 198, 198–9, 200. Greene's attitude to reason should probably be understood as a reaction to the deistic, free-thinking arguments which promoted its role in religion at the expense of that of revelation; see Jacob, *Newtonians*, pp. 214–16. Though Morgan does not accept the doctrine of the fall, he also connects it with defective sight; see *Physico-Theology*, pp. 328, 332. See also Thomas Sherlock, *Several Discourses Preached at the Temple Church*, 4 vols. (1754; this 3rd edn. London, 1755), vol. iv, discourse XI.

For the Argument A PRIORI is GOD in every man's CONSCIENCE.
For the Argument A POSTERIORI is God before every man's eyes.

(B2. 359–60)

And though in its context the second of these lines may suggest that it is after the Second Coming that man shall see God face to face, it also appears to be a direct statement of the argument for natural religion.

But the natural religion Greene and Smart refer to is not the same as that described by Roger Cotes:

We may now more nearly behold the beauties of Nature, and entertain ourselves with the delightful contemplation; and, which is the best and most valuable fruit of philosophy, be thence incited the more profoundly to reverence and adore the great Maker and Lord of all.

The lines naming Joses, Theophilus, and Bartimeus indicate the nature of that difference. The three figures refer to three, or perhaps four, kinds of visual evidence for faith: Joses saw his brother in the flesh, and believed; Theophilus 'saw' Christ through the evidence of the reliable eye witnesses of the gospels and Acts; Bartimeus 'saw' Christ through faith, and the sight of his miraculous cure also enabled others to believe. But in each example what is seen and believed is Christ. Christ is not here seen and believed through an inference from the 'excellent contrivances' of gravity and the *vis inertiae*, but is directly the object of perception. The potential ambiguity of Smart's argument 'A POSTERIORI' may be a result of the transparency or immediacy of the natural revelation he describes, for in the creation that he sees, God is, it seems, directly 'before every man's eyes'.[23]

This kind of natural revelation can have disturbing philosophical implications. Newton himself considered the possibility that matter might be active and alive, but rejected the possibility partly because of its hylozoistic implications: if matter is active, it may become indistinguishable from its cause, and indeed from God himself. Smart, however, circumvents this problem by positing the existence of a sort of 'anti-matter':

For MOTION is as the quantity of life direct, & that which hath not motion, is resistance.

For Resistance is not of GOD, but he hath built his works upon it.

(B1. 161–2)

[23] Cotes, Preface, *Principia*, vol. i, p. xxxii. See Westfall, *Religion*, p. 24. See also Jonathan Richardson (the Elder), *Two Discourses*, (London, 1719) pp. 98–101. For discussions of the significance of sight and blindness see e.g. John Trapp, *A Commentary on the Old and New Testaments* (1646–56), on Matt. 20; Matthew Henry, *An Exposition of All the Books of the Old and New Testaments* (1708–14), on Luke 1: 1–4; 18: 35–43.

That these lines imply Smart's rejection of *vis inertiae* as 'all nonsense' becomes apparent through comparison with Newton's description of that force:

A body, from the inert nature of matter, is not without difficulty put out of its state of rest or motion. Upon which account, this *vis insita* may, by a most significant name, be called inertia (*vis inertiae*) or force of inactivity. But a body only exerts this force when another force, impressed upon it, endeavours to change its condition; and the exercise of this force may be considered as both resistance and impulse; it is resistance so far as the body, for maintaining its present state, opposes the force impressed; it is impulse so far as the body, by not easily giving way to the impressed force of another, endeavours to change the state of that other. Resistance is usually ascribed to bodies at rest, and impulse to those in motion; but motion and rest, as commonly conceived, are only relatively distinguished; nor are those bodies always truly at rest, which commonly are taken to be so.

Smart rejects the *vis inertiae* by representing the force and the inactivity, the 'motion' and the resistance, as distinct and not relative states, and his natural philosophy is thus integrated with his theological views.[24]

Smart writes:

For the grosser the particles the nearer to the sink, & the nearer to purity, the quicker the gravitation.

For the Centripetal and Centrifugal forces are GOD SUSTAINING AND DIRECTING.

For Elasticity is the temper of matter to recover its place with vehemence.

For Attraction is the earning of parts, which have a similitude in the life.

For the Life of God is in the Loadstone, and there is a magnet, which pointeth due EAST.

(Bl. 159, 163–6)

These lines act as a 'counterpart', or commentary on, Newton's Definition V on centripetal force, which begins with these words:

Of this sort of gravity, by which bodies tend to the centre of the earth; magnetism, by which iron tends to the loadstone; and that force, whatever it is, by which the planets are continually drawn aside from the rectilinear motions, which otherwise they would pursue, and made to revolve in curvilinear orbits.

The first of Smart's lines alludes to a theological as well as a natural philosophical system. Smart's theology involves an almost dualistic

[24] Jacob, *Newtonians*, pp. 243–4. Newton, 'Definition III', *Principia*, i. 2. Morgan also either rejects or misunderstands the *vis inertiae*, in so far as he understands motion and rest as opposed, rather than relative, states; *Physico-Theology*, pp. 2–4.

understanding of the polarity of good and evil, though evil exists only as the adverse, dependent upon its opposition to good; and that notion of polarity informs this line. Here the 'grosser . . . particles'—those that are heaviest and least pure—tend towards their 'similitude', the sink, which is perhaps hell as the centre of corruption; whereas those that are 'nearer to purity' are quicker, have more life, as they gravitate or are attracted towards life. And taken together the lines make it clear that God is in some way directly present in the universe: the centripetal and centrifugal forces are not, for Smart, manifestations of gravity, but are the work of God, as 'there is infinite provision to keep up the life in all the parts of Creation' (B1. 200); and similarly, elasticity, attraction, and magnetism are evidence of the life and power of God 'SUSTAINING and DIRECTING' the operations of lively matter, not through 'excellent contrivances', but directly.[25]

This theory of direct divine activity in Smart's religious and philosophical interpretation of nature is also implicit in his discussion of 'centres'. The concept of centres of gravity is necessary to Newton's account of *vis inertiae*, and of gravity itself, but it was also essential to Newton's system that these 'centres' should be understood as abstract mathematical points, rather than as tangible or 'real' centres; for if they were to be understood as 'really' existing—as having a definable spatial and/or temporal existence—they might also be seen as active focuses, exercising a gravitational force of attraction upon other active focal centres. Newton cautions:

I likewise call attractions and impulses, in the same sense, accelerative, and motive; and and use the words attraction, impulse, or propensity of any sort towards a centre, promiscuously, and indifferently, one for another; considering those forces not physically, but mathematically: wherefore the reader is not to imagine that by those words I anywhere take upon me to define the kind, or the manner of any action, the causes of the physical reason thereof, or that I attribute forces, in a true and physical sense, to certain centres (which are only mathematical points); when at any time I happen to speak of centres as attracting, or as endued with attractive powers.

This warning to his readers, like the disclaimer attached to the description of gravity, was insufficient as a counterbalance to the use of

---

[25] Newton, *Principia* i. 2. Smart's lines might also be seen as a 'commentary' on Morgan, *Physico-Theology*, ch. 1, sects. 4, 5, 6, 7, pp. 12–14, where Morgan discusses in sequence: gravity in relation to centripetal and centrifugal forces, the power by which fluids retain their equilibrium, elasticity, and attraction. 'Sink' might also be understood here as a kind of verbal noun. On the eternity of hell in *JA* see B1. 176, 291–3, and ch. 3 n. 15 above.

words 'promiscuously, and indifferently', but it indicates the importance Newton attached to the understanding of centres both as abstract points and as *not* endowed with 'forces, in a true and physical sense'.[26]

In Smart's 'system' of natural philosophy the centre is described as both physically 'real', and active or forceful:

Let Cosam rejoice with the Perch, who is a little tyrant, because he is not liable to that, which he inflicts.	For the Centre is not known but by the application of the members to matter.
Let Levi rejoice with the Pike—God be merciful to all dumb creatures in respect of pain.	For I have shown the Vis Inertiae to be false, and such is all nonsense.
Let Melchi rejoice with the Char, who cheweth the cud.	For the Centre is the hold of the Spirit upon the matter in hand.

(B1. 182–4)

The 'Let' verses here may describe some of the implications of the *vis inertiae*, which would render the centre not 'liable', or accountable for, that which it inflicts through attraction or impulse, and would imply an understanding of inanimate matter as incapable of any sensitivity or 'pain'; for if created matter is inactive and inanimate, then its reception of, or liability to, the forces of attraction and gravity remains as mysterious as its power to exert those forces. But though that interpretation is not conclusive, it is clear that in the 'For' verses Smart suggests that the centre is mysterious ('not known'), but that it can be discovered. The 'members' which would facilitate its discovery might refer either to the several parts (or members) of the body, which would reveal the centres as they must all tend towards it, or to the 'tools' described in the preceding verse: 'For the Skrew, Axle & Wheel, Pulleys, the Lever & inclined Plane are known in the Schools' (B1. 181). Smart may be suggesting that this mechanical equipment could be applied to discover the true centre of a body.

Smart suggests in this verse that a 'true and physical' centre is discoverable, and it follows that this centre might be found to exercise force and attraction, and to be active; for the active centre would be that part of the body most fully endowed with life, and that life or motion indicates the power of God in creation. It is, Smart writes, 'the hold of the Spirit upon the matter in hand'; the hold by which a body is

---

[26] Newton, 'Definition VIII', *Principia*, i. 5–6. See A. I. Sabra, *Theories of Light from Descartes to Newton* (1967; rev. edn. Cambridge, 1981), ch. 6 and pp. 160–1.

preserved in unity is the grip of the divine spirit who holds or maintains all of creation in his hand. This divine spirit sustains all matter, and it is in, or through, him that all things live, move, and have being. Smart goes on, in the following verse, to assert that the universe is a plenum, as opposed to a Newtonian void—an appropriate conclusion to be drawn from the 'SUSTAINING and DIRECTING' presence of a universal spirit which finds expression in the life of its works, rather than in their absence or inanimateness:

Let Joanna rejoice with the Anchovy—   For FRICTION is inevitable because
    I beheld and lo! a great multitude!   the Universe is FULL of God's
                                                                    works.   (B1. 185)

Smart's account of the 'Centre', and the plenum, emphasizes the active power of God in the universe, and the fullness of the universe suggests an explanation of the existence of evil, for friction is a tendency towards 'Resistance', or inactivity, on which God 'hath built his works' (B1. 162), but which, Smart implies, is 'of the Adversary'.[27]

Smart's world is maintained by the balanced opposition of good and evil, of the animate and inanimate; and this balance is epitomized, in *Jubilate Agno*, in the flower, which 'glorifies God and the root parries the adversary' (B2. 499): it is suspended between God and the Adversary, praising the one and parrying the other. Similarly the echo, which is 'the soul' of 'a good voice', cannot 'act but when she can parry the adversary' (B1. 235, 238, 236); the echo is a force for good in itself, for 'she can assist in prayer' (B1. 237), but she becomes effective or active only when she meets with resistance; then she must duel with evil, warding off its thrusts. Smart himself is also engaged in this duel or struggle, for his poem glorifies the word of God, which is 'a sword on my side' (B1. 20), designed to 'parry the adversary'.[28]

---

[27] The balance or dualism I describe is implicit in Smart's persistent naming of the Devil as the adversary; see J. F. Kermode, *The Genesis of Secrecy: On the Interpretation of Narrative* (Cambridge, Mass., 1979), 84–5; and John Cleland's etymological derivation of 'devil' in *The Way to Things by Words, and to Words by Things* (London, 1766), pp. 16–17; and Ecclus. 42: 23–5: 'All these things live and remain for ever for all uses, and they are all obedient. All things are double one against another: and he hath made nothing imperfect. One thing establisheth the good of another: and who shall be filled with beholding his glory?' On the plenum, see *Christian's Magazine*, 2 (1761), 611–12.

[28] See Edward Young, *N-T*, Night 4, pp. 74–5, where he describes reason and faith as the root and flower.

V

The natural philosophy of *Jubilate Agno* needs to be considered in the context of the contemporary debate about the relation between philosophy and religion. I have suggested that, in the mid century, the Church became increasingly concerned to distance itself from arguments from natural religion, not only in the works of deists like John Toland, but in the less explicitly controversial productions of recently eminent churchmen. The weaknesses which became a matter of concern, and undermined the support the Church had been able to gain from the arguments of natural religion, were paralleled, or repeated, in the criticisms that came to be levelled at the natural philosophy of the early century. The private comment Coleridge made on Newton's *Opticks*, in a letter to Thomas Poole in 1801, illuminates the common ground of these changing perceptions of both natural religion and philosophy:

I am exceedingly delighted with the beauty and neatness of his experiments, and with the accuracy of his *immediate* deductions from them; but the opinions founded on these deductions, and indeed his whole theory is, I am persuaded, so exceedingly superficial as without impropriety to be deemed false. Newton was a mere materialist. *Mind*, in his system, is always *passive*,—a lazy *Looker-on* on an external world. If the mind be not *passive*, if it be indeed made in God's Image, and that, too, in the sublimest sense, the *Image of the Creator*, there is ground for suspicion that any system built on the passiveness of mind must be false, as a system.

Coleridge's objection to the implied passivity of both man and God in Newton's philosophy, his rejection of a philosophy of mind that verges on deism, was, I have suggested, expressed in a number of areas of mid-eighteenth-century thought. Active engagement, an agency capable of actively intervening in and reanimating existing customary institutions, was seen as necessary by linguistic philosophers, opposed to the dead hand of contractual theory, by churchmen, concerned to address issues of faith and morality, and by natural philosophers, who addressed themselves to the problems of the nature of air and electricity, and questioned the role of dynamic forces in the Newtonian system.[29]

Natural religion had, in the early decades of the century, provided a

---

[29] *The Letters of Samuel Taylor Coleridge*, ed. Kathleen Raine (London, 1950), 108.

means of describing the compatibility of philosophy and religion: the uncorrupted eye of the disinterested philosopher had looked through a legible creation to perceive at once a demonstration of divine omnipotence, and of the system of nature, expressed in the immutable laws governing creation. But the mid century called into question all the values involved in this recognition of a Newtonian theodicy, in terms that placed the moral worth of philosophical enquiry in doubt as an occupation for the leisure hours of the faithful, if not as a pursuit in its own right. When Hervey contrasts his analogical meditations on nature with the investigations of Newton, he draws attention to the opposition between his retired leisure and Newton's professional interest, but he is more concerned to establish that his '*moral Picture*' displays a religious wisdom absent from Newton's abstruse researches. Hervey value the wisdom of interpretation over that of impartial observation, and though he concedes that the 'Eye of *Reason*' looks 'through the magnificent scene' to discover 'an Infinitude of Worlds', he cultivates instead the 'Eye . . . of *Devotion*' which meets 'the Deity in every View', and aspires to become 'if not wise as the Astronomical Adept, yet WISE UNTO SALVATION'.[30]

By 1774, when Oliver Goldsmith's popular and influential *History of the Earth, and Animated Nature* was first published, the appeal of natural philosophy to the polite reader has come to be identified firmly with its exclusion from the moral sphere. Goldsmith describes philosophy as an 'innocent amusement' for the 'idle and speculative' reader, suitable for whiling away the hours of 'those who have nothing else to employ them, or who require a relaxation from labour'. He distinguishes between the more 'difficult' tasks which achieve the primary object of philosophy, and which involve 'discovering, ascertaining and naming all the various productions of nature', and the second object of the science, which considers the 'properties, manners and relations' which those productions 'bear to us, and to each other', but neither of these objects is for him the moral activity that it had been for William Derham or Thomas Sprat. It is the second kind of philosophy that he makes available to his public, not because it affords the cope for interpretation or analogical understanding that the eye of devotion requires, but because it is 'more amusing' and 'exhibits new pictures to our imagination and improves our relish for existence, by widening the prospect of nature around us'. For Goldsmith, then, the philosophical

[30] James Hervey, *Meditations and Contemplations*, 2 vols (this 13th edn. London, 1757), vol. ii, Dedication, p. x; p. 251; see pp. 230–1 n.

detachment and disinterest that the primary object of science demands seems to translate directly into the moral passivity and detachment that the idle reader, the 'lazy *Looker-on*', is encouraged to entertain for its second object. Hervey's description of the religious apprehension of nature, on the other hand, had exploited the possibility that 'the Reader may learn his Duty, from his very Pleasures'. Whereas Goldsmith suggested that natural philosophy could be treated as an idle amusement without significant further implications, Hervey ran the risk of identifying the religious habit of mind with the pleasures of retired fancy, and thus of excluding religious morality from the public world. For he implies that devout retirement affords an understanding of creation in terms of pious but playful analogy, marginal to the serious concerns of the world. The distinction he makes between religion and empirical philosophy may imply that philosophical rationality and devout morality are incompatible, and while in Goldsmith's account the nature of that distinction has changed, the pleasures of philosophy nevertheless exclude considerations of religious as well as public morality, and philosophy is represented as a frivolous leisure pursuit.[31]

In the 1760s, however, the spheres of private morality on the one hand and pleasurable philosophy on the other are by no means clearly distinguished. In that decade, the move away from natural religion was not predicated on a divorce of religion and philosophy, but involved, rather, a reassessment of the relation between revelation and philosophical inquiry. In philosophy this could produce, as we have seen, a readiness to acknowledge the importance of hypotheses, exemplified in the recognition that the text of creation, like the text of the Bible, might involve difficulties, obscurities, and might similarly produce a plurality of interpretations. In religion—in so far as we can treat it as a distinct or unified area of concern—it involved the study of the book of nature that had been advocated earlier in the century, but with the important qualification that it no longer privileged systematic and analytic experiment over the experience of nature as a sublime and moral text. Religious writers attempted to reconcile, rather than to distinguish, the experiences of Thomson's vulgar herd and privileged few. Their writing on natural philosophy in this period is marked by a concern to emphasize that the truths revealed by faith are the

[31] Oliver Goldsmith, *History of the Earth, and Animated Nature*, 6 vols. (this edn. London, 1805), vol. i, Preface, pp. xiv, xiii, xiv, v. Hervey, *Meditations*, vol. ii, Preface, p. xvi.

touchstone of scientific truth, and the guides to the kind of study that it is appropriate for the religious philosopher to pursue. This conception of natural philosophy is not anti-rationalist, nor necessarily alien to the experiential methodology of the new science, but proceeds from an understanding of the relation of faith and reason that closely parallels the arguments I discussed in Sherlock's *Discourses*. It refuses to acknowledge that religious morality can be excluded from the sphere of natural philosophy any more than from the spheres of business or society; for morality, understood as a matter of faith as well as of practice, underwrites and provides the basis of every sphere of thought and action.[32]

This is not to say, of course, that the decade did not produce different, and perhaps contradictory, arguments. The Seatonian poems of this period, for example, tend to be dominated by concern either for the practical morality of the individual or for a *Purity of Heart* which, in James Scott's treatment of the theme in 1761, is seen as a result of the ambition to 'leave the world behind / And till with care the garden of my mind'. These poets, however, may be more ready to imply the incompatibility of devout and commercial morality than to concede any incongruity between natural philosophy and piety. But the decade did also produce a religious philosophy which took advantage of the increased importance of faith to claim that the analogies of religion are the foundations of all knowledge, not because they prescribe the conduct of every individual as an individual, or because they appeal to every heart in isolated retirement, but because the revelation available to faith describes the harmony and thus the truth of all wisdom. So, for example, John Newton writes in the Letters of Omicron (1762), that 'The doctrines, histories, prophecies, promises, precepts, exhortations, examples, and warnings, contained in the Bible, form a perfect WHOLE, a complete summary of the will of God concerning us, in which nothing is wanting, nothing is superfluous.'[33]

Newton's letter, describing 'A Plan of a compendious Christian Library', illustrates the concept of the central role of scriptural revelation which, I have suggested, is an important development in the theory of religion in the 1760s. He describes the Bible as the text in

---

[32] On Thomson, see pp. 230–1 below. On revelation and scientific truth, see pp. 212–14 above.

[33] James Scott, in *Cambridge Prize Poems*, 2 vols. (Cambridge, 1817), i. 135. John Newton, *Forty-One Letters on Religious Subjects*, letter xv, in *The Works of The Rev. John Newton* (Edinburgh, 1834), 70.

relation to which the three volumes of creation, historical providence, and human nature (both our private experience and our perception of others) can be understood as commentaries or secondary sources, and his argument has a significant correspondence with the structure I have described in *Jubilate Agno*. For he argues that the three secondary volumes function as the exegetical apparatus by means of which the 'perfect WHOLE' of the Bible can be applied to and interpreted in the specific historical moment, and this structure of text and exposition parallels the relation I have described between the 'Let' and 'For' verses of *Jubilate Agno*. Newton writes of the Bible that:

The general history of all nations and ages, and the particular experience of each private believer, from the beginning to the end of time, are wonderfully comprised in this single volume; so that whoever reads and improves it aright, may discover his state, his progress, his temptations, his danger, and his duty, as distinctly and minutely marked out, as if the whole had been written for him alone.

Reading and improving the Bible 'aright' involves an exercise of faith which reveals the relation between 'general history' and 'particular experience'—an exercise comparable to the charitable translation described in *Jubilate Agno*.

The primary importance of faith in Newton's discussion does, of course, reflect his evangelical Calvinism, but it is important to remember that the particular orientation of Newton's beliefs—or, for that matter, of Hervey's, or the Wesleys'—did not at this time represent a sufficiently significant departure from those of Anglican orthodoxy to prevent them from fulfilling their ecclesiastical positions, and the aspect of Newton's arguments which I think has a most significant relation to *Jubilate Agno* was, as we shall see, echoed in the works of less controversial figures, in terms that confirm its importance to an understanding of the development of religion in this period, rather than indicating any significant divergence from that process. Newton's views are interesting, in the context of my discussion of *Jubilate Agno*, because they are I think representative of an area of religious thought, rather than because they are exceptional, and they again indicate that the polarization of orthodoxy and dissent may not be the most fruitful method of approaching the various debates about the role of religion that occur in the mid-eighteenth century.[34]

---

[34] Newton, letter xv, p. 70, and see p. 69, where he writes that God 'has comprised all

Newton argues in his 'Plan of a . . . Christian Library' that the book of creation can only be understood in the light of revelation:

The lines of this book, though very beautiful and expressive in themselves, are not immediately legible by fallen man. The works of creation may be compared to a fair character in cypher, of which the Bible is the key; and without this key they cannot be understood.

The philosophical study of nature, with the aid of this key, can be a source of pleasure and profitable instruction to those who have the 'leisure, capacity, or opportunity' to pursue it, but it does not afford them any privileged or superior access to the secrets of creation, which is a book 'designed for the instruction of all believers'. Newton represents the philosophical knowledge of those who 'study of the works of God, independent of his word' as of marginal importance, irrelevant to the pursuit of true Christian wisdom: 'many reputed wise, whose hearts are not subjected to the authority of the Bible', he writes, are engaged in 'elaborate trifling and waste of time', because they are ignorant of the 'wonderful analogy between the natural and spiritual world'. The Bible reveals the analogical context in which history and experience can be understood, and it describes the terms of the correpondence between the apparently discrete areas of abstruse research and immediate experience, philosophical overview and mundane variety.[35]

The two features of this concept of faith which Newton is particularly concerned to emphasize, and which I think characterize a significant aspect of the religion of the 1760s, are that the insight he describes is available to all, not just in the sense that Young described the night sky as a lesson legible to all, but in terms that ensure that the 'learned, with respect to their own personal interest, have no advantage above the ignorant'; and that, despite this assurance that faith does not speak a language that is lofty to the learned but low to the humble, Newton nevertheless regards natural philosophy and the study of history as worthwhile. In order to be a 'wise person' it is necessary to be well read in the four books of the Bible, creation, providence, and human nature, though not to have a scientific or scholarly understanding

the knowledge conducive to real happiness in four comprehensive volumes. The first [the Bible], which may be considered as the text, is cheap, portable, and compendious . . . and the other three, which are the best and fullest commentaries upon this, are always at hand for our perusal, and pressing upon our attention in every place and circumstance of our lives.'

[35] Letter xv, pp. 70–1.

of them; but Newton emphasizes that all four books must be studied, and he values the philosophical knowledge that those with the ability to cultivate it can achieve.[36]

In Newton's argument, the correspondence between these two features—a correspondence that had not been apparent to Thomson, Young, or Hervey—is guaranteed by the assurance that the end of philosophical wisdom is that, for those who fear God, 'almost every object they see' in nature is a confirmation of the truths of revelation, and 'either leads their thoughts to Jesus, or tends to illustrate some scriptural truth or promise'. The end of philosophy is not for Newton, as it had been for Blackmore, the demonstration of the immutability of natural law, in opposition to the atheistic principles of free will that 'subvert the Throne of Princes, and undermine the Foundations of Government and Society'. It is rather the discovery of the power of revelation to intervene in and moralize the progress of laws of cause and effect: a progress that is indifferent to the fate of individuals, and appears incomprehensible to them. 'The believer', Newton writes, 'receives hourly and indubitable proof that the Lord reigns . . . while others live at an uncertainty, exposed to the impressions of every new appearance, and, like a ship in a storm, without rudder or pilot, abandoned to the power of the winds and waves.' For Newton, the analogical reasoning that provides the basis of this assurance is not a matter of private fancy, opposed to the rational researches of philosophy, though it does involve a logic that is not that of cause and effect. Where Hervey's figurative meditations could appear to be marginal to the society they excluded, and to demand a degree of playful whimsicality to justify and to temper the seriousness of their opposition to philosophical reason, Newton represents the logic of science as praiseworthy but possibly frivolous in comparison to the spiritual morality of his beliefs.[37]

A similar emphasis on religion as the measure of the worth of philosophical inquiry is expressed in the series of articles on 'Physico-Theology' which appeared in *The Christian's Magazine*. This periodical was edited, and largely written, by William Dodd, and appeared in the years 1760 to 1767, and for a few months in 1768. The magazine

---

[36] Ibid. Newton argues that 'They who know God in his word, my find both pleasure and profit tracing his wisdom in his works', but he concludes that 'though a man should be master of the whole circle of classical, polite, and philosophical knowledge, if he has no taste for the Bible, and has no ability to apply it to the works of creation and providence, and his own experience, he knows nothing yet as he ought to know.'

[37] Ibid. p. 71. Blackmore, *Creation*, Preface, pp. 11–12. Letter xv, p. 71.

published a number of Smart's poems, and his proposals for publications, and it provided a forum for the discussion of issues that concerned clergymen and the devout laity: it included a translation of some of Lowth's *Lectures*, and selected articles important in the debate over the character of David, which I will be discussing in my last chapter. Correspondents debated, among a range of topics, the origin of letters, points of scriptural interpretation, the role of hymns in the liturgy, and the need for a new translation of the Psalms, and they frequently treat themes raised in *Jubilate Agno*, and in Smart's later poetry, in strikingly similar terms. The articles on 'Physico-Theology' which regularly appeared in the magazine seem to have been, on the whole, the work of Dodd himself, though he borrows extensively from *Chambers's Encyclopaedia*, and from Hans Sloane's account of the West Indies, and the importance he attached to them as a feature of the periodical indicates the continuing importance of the study of God's works; and, in the similarity of their approach to that of Smart, or of John Newton, the extent to which natural philosophies which might appear in retrospect to be eccentric or evangelical were representative of some degree of consensus about how that study should be carried out.

Dodd's articles, like so much of the religious literature of the period, justify their analogical method by reference to the paradigm of Christ's teaching, the 'Divine Pattern' from which we learn to 'read a lesson of wisdom from every object'. Christ's teaching authorizes the fundamental perception that 'nature abounds with sensible images of celestial things'; it guarantees the validity of analogical interpretation, first, as a method of understanding creation, and secondly, as an instructive practice that is, for Dodd as well as for Newton, 'always intelligible'. Dodd contrasts this profitable method of studying creation, where the 'serious and contemplative mind sees God in every thing', with the more entertaining but superficial approach of popular natural philosophy:

Merely to present us with the print of a beautiful *bird*, or well coloured *animal*; and thence to amuse our imagination; is playing about the surface, without entering into the substance. Our intentions are to profit as well as to please; and to lead from the admirable *works* to the more admirable and adorable *Work-master*.

Again, the contrast is between the substantial wisdom of religious philosophy and the accidental or superficial knowledge afforded by secular enquiry; but, as is the case for John Newton, and, I think,

Smart, this opposition does not indicate that Dodd's approach is fundamentally alien to that of the new science.[38]

Dodd rejects the natural philosophy of the entertaining survey, but the main thrust of his discussions is not to show that all philosophy is 'exceedingly superficial' but to demonstrate that a substantial natural philosophy can be gauged by its profitability to the 'mind that sees God in everything'. Thus he gives this definition of philosophical methodology:

The most cursory and general observation demonstrates a Deity.—But when we come to survey matters more minutely, and to examine the nice coherence of things; when we trace the manifold marks of design, and of exuberant goodness; when we behold the stupendous provision of Providence, for human wants, as well as for the wants of the inferior creation—In short when with *philosophical* attention, we read the great volume of *nature*, we must derive from every page in the sacred code, arguments of faith and dependence; of gratitude and love.

Dodd does not, on the whole, place quite the degree of emphasis on faith and revelation that, I think, Newton and Smart share, and the relation of his arguments to the natural religion of the first half of the century can be more readily detected: he is, for example, 'at a loss to account for' the inability of the ancient world to understand the creation as the manifestation of God, whereas for Newton this blindness is clearly the result of the absence of the 'key' of biblical revelation. But Dodd's emphasis on the need to read actively the lesson discernible in the 'glass' of 'animal creation', his sense that a serious philosophy must be concerned to decode the 'lively emblem' of creation, produces a physico-theology based in analogy which resembles Smart's in the scope of its application, and in its refusal to acknowledge any incongruity in employing the discourses of experimental philosophy, scriptural interpretation, and commerce, in the context of arguments designed as proofs of theodicy.[39]

[38] *Christian's Magazine*, 1 (1760), 166–7; 2 (1761), 163; 1 (1760), 22. Perhaps the most striking parallel between Smart's work and *Christian's Magazine* can be seen in the resemblance between his poem 'On a Bed of Guernsey Lilies' (1764) and the article 'Some Account of the Guernsey Lilly, with Animadversions thereon' (vol. 1 (1760), 393–5); see Moira Dearnley, *The Poetry of Christopher Smart* (London, 1969), 209–11.

[39] *Christian's Magazine*, 2 (1761), 163; 1 (1760), 21–2, 20–1; see J. Newton, letter xv, p. 70, and Sherlock, *Discourses*, vol. i, discourse I, pt. i. *Christian's Magazine*, 2 (1761), 372; 1 (1760), 394. Stephen Prickett suggests, in *Words and the Word: Language, Poetics, and Biblical Interpretation* (Cambridge, 1986), that Dodd's magazine was strongly opposed to Wesleyan or Methodist dissent, but although Dodd's sermon *Cautions against Methodism; or Unity recommended* (3rd edn. London, 1769) would seem to support this

Analogy provides a framework of correspondences within which the physico-theologian need acknowledge no discontinuity between what might seem to be very different kinds of argument. The physico-theologian appropriates, as grist to his mill, arguments based on the detailed investigation of the physical structure of the Jamaican Wild-Pine, but when he turns to the honeycomb, he describes it almost entirely in terms of its biblical and emblematic significance:

And as, when risen from the dead, he accepted, at the hands of his disciples, a *piece of an honey-comb*, so in the person of his members, risen from the death of sin through the power of his resurrection, he expects from his disciples, and more especially from his ministers, a portion of that word which is declared by the holy Psalmist to be *sweeter than honey and the honey-comb*. And in this respect he is graciously pleased to say, that he does himself feed upon it: for so it is written—*I am come into my garden, my sister, my spouse, I have eaten my honey-comb with my honey*.

And in his discussion of linen and cotton the terms of his argument are different again. Here he admires the display of divine 'wisdom not only in the original formation and design of such useful supplies of our wants; but in rendering the supply of those wants so advantageous to thousands, by means of the necessary *commerce*, and *industry*, which the materials exert'. The physico-theologian, in these articles, is concerned to praise the variety of creation, and the privileged concept of necessary gratitude allows him to employ a variety of kinds of argument in order to achieve this end: he acknowledges no discontinuity between the emblematic, the economic, and the empirical because for him these are aspects of the same substantial and 'pleasing speculation'. They are unified by their analogical representation of the '*Work-Master*', manifested in his works.[40]

The emphasis that Smart's natural philosophy places on the role of

argument, it is complicated by the frequent and admiring references to the works of James Hervey in the magazine. See e.g. vol. 2 (1761), 611–13. Dodd's interest in natural philosophy may, like Smart's, reflect his involvement in freemasonry as well as his commitment to the Anglican Church.

[40] See *Christian's Magazine*, 2 (1761), 33: 'How could any knowledge of the Deity and his actions be conveyed to us, otherwise, than by *words* taken from our own language, and accommodated to our own ideas? We can arrive at *spiritual* knowledge only by Analogy, for the plain reason, because we have no direct or immediate conception of any thing *merely spiritual*.' On the Wild-Pine, see vol. 1 (1760), 22–3. 'A Meditation on the Bee', vol. 2 (1761), 674; this essay is signed 'ACADEMICUS', but the physico-theology of the magazine is eclectic to an extent that makes questions of individual authorship secondary to the consideration of the natural philosophy propounded by this series of articles. 'Reflections on the Cotton Tree, &c', vol. 2 (1761), 167; vol. 1 (1760), 22.

the Word of revelation, and his treatment of systematic theory and experimental evidence as secondary to the substantial analogy of religion in his discussion of Newtonian science, express a correspondence between the understanding of creation and the interpretation of scripture which, in the 1760s, could appear to present a valid and persuasive alternative to the perception of natural philosophy and religious morality as mutually exclusive concerns. I have already remarked that in the physico-theological discussions of the early century, and most notably in the Boyle lectures, the close relation between philosophy and religion, as well as the difficulty of combining their disparate discourses, was expressed in the structure of the argument: the philosopher would, typically, offer an experimental account of the phenomenon under discussion, and follow this with a celebration of its theological significance; or he would offer one of these kinds of description in the main body of the text, and subjoin the other in lengthy footnotes. But the religious philosophers of the mid century saw analogical arguments based in faith as the means of accommodating these diverse discourses within a single structure that described the harmony of the physical and theological universe. The science Smart's account rejects as unphilosophical, like that opposed by Newton and Dodd, is the superficial science which, in its concentration on means at the expense of ends, implies the moral passivity of the philosopher, and is therefore ἄλογος, excluded from the philosophy of the word. In the context of the 1760s it seems fair to say that Smart's philosophy is no more fundamentally unscientific than it is fundamentally irreligious.

The idea of natural philosophy which, I think, Smart shares with the physico-theologian of *The Christian's Magazine* needs to be understood not in terms of its success or failure in measuring up to the yardstick of scientific 'accuracy', but in the context of a much wider debate which questioned the methodology of the new science, first in terms of its ability to achieve the sort of disinterested and uncorrupted view that it claimed as its necessary premiss, and secondly, in the terms in which that methodology was popularized, the terms in which the Newtonian philosophy was presented as the paradigmatic explanatory model for the known world. In the first place, the new science claimed for itself, as we have seen, a pure impartiality which gave it access to the hidden secrets of nature. But the purity of the gaze of the natural philosopher was almost immediately recognized, as Robert Greene makes clear, as the expression of privileged authority rather than of disinterest. The poem by John Theophilus Desaguliers, fellow of the Royal Society and prominent Freemason, which described 'The Newtonian System of the World' as 'the best Model of Government', made explicit the relation between the anti-trinitarian and hierarchical structure of Newton's system, and the structure of monarchical government that is alluded to in Newton's 'scientific' discourse on God as the 'Universal Ruler' whose 'dominion' has 'respect to servants'. The new science claimed for itself a particular kind of 'Godlike' authority which, as Thomson seems at least implicitly to recognize, served to confirm the absolute distinction between, on the one hand, the 'sage-instructed Eye' which perceives in the 'white mingling Maze' of the rainbow the 'various Twine of Light' and, on the other, the wondering view of the swain, who sees its 'falling Glory' as an 'amusive Arch', as a source of entertainment (and perhaps enchantment) rather than instruction. If the new science is only available to those who have uncorrupted eyes, then it is, as Thomson writes, the privilege of 'th'enlighten'd Few', for 'superstitious Horrors' still 'enslave / The fond sequacious Herd' in their state of corrupt imperfection. As a complement and support to the teachings of the Church, it does not describe a natural revelation of God 'before every man's eyes' (B2. 360), or in every man's conscience, but a God whose secrets are revealed to the initiate alone.[41]

Secondly, there is the issue of the presentation of the new natural philosophy as a system of comprehensive explanatory power, and again Thomson's praise of the system is also revealing about its shortcomings. For Thomson presents the philosophy as one of a number of models—classical, Christian, and economic—which go towards building up a comprehensive view, but which he seems unable to combine, rather than to place side by side, and which do not finally produce a position from which the poet is able to make explicit any unifying explanatory thesis. The new science, indeed, appears as a system which produces, not comprehensive explanation, but the need for the complementary

---

[41] See pp. 95–8 above. I quote from the title of Desaguliers's popularizing account, *The Newtonian System of the World, the best Model of Government: An Allegorical Poem. With a Plain and Intelligible Account of the System of the World, by Way of Annotations* (London, 1728). He argues that 'The *limited Monarchy*, whereby our Liberties, Rights, and Privileges are so well secured to us, as to make us happier than all the Nations round about us, seems to be a lively image of our [Newtonian] System; and the Happiness that we enjoy under *His* present Majesty's Government, makes us sensible, that ATTRACTION is now as universal in the Political, as the Philosophical World' (Dedication, p. v). See Jacob, *Newtonians*, pp. 219–20. *Principia*, vol. ii, General Scholium, p. 544. Thomson, *Seasons*, 'Summer', l. 1715; 'Spring', ll. 210, 212, 211, 215, 216; 'Summer', ll. 1714, 1712, 1712–13. See Sprat, *Royal Society*, p. 72.

description of nature as it is viewed by the uneducated vulgar, the swain, the herd. For while the presence of philosophers allows the poet to describe their analytic perceptions of nature, and their godlike understanding of its operations, nature's glory and horror, its sublime affective power over men's minds, can only apparently be described through the wondering views of more corrupt and less enlightened men. For the poet of *The Seasons*, there are available a number of discourses appropriate to the description of nature, but he can collect these together only to demonstrate variety, and not to exemplify any coherent thesis, nor to establish the supremacy of any one privileged discourse.

In *Jubilate Agno*, and I think in much eighteenth-century poetry, the ability or even the desirability of penetrating with authority the hidden secrets of nature is called into question, not because science is somehow fundamentally unpoetic (or vice versa), but because of the sense in which its explanatory power is ἄλογος—unphilosophical, or inadequate. It presents the relations which the productions of nature 'bear to us, and to each other' as either perceptible only to the privileged few or merely amusive—it makes the book of nature, unlike the Anglican Bible, either a cabbalistic mystery or an entertaining picture-book. The natural philosopher does not plead his text 'as a good protestant pleads his Bible', but speaks with an absolute and commanding authority. This is not, of course, an authority foreign to eighteenth-century poetry, but, as I argued in my Introduction, it is an authority which much of the poetry concerned with religion in the first sixty years of the century seems reluctant or unable to claim.[42]

What Smart and the physico-theologian of the *Christian's Magazine* attempt to do, I think, is to reform the theological and philosophical bases of the new science, in the attempt to increase the ability of natural philosophy to describe more than a partial and exclusive understanding of the system of nature—to enable it to accommodate moral and religious arguments, through a flexibility, a space for the liberty of conscience and of interpretation, that would generalize rather than specialize its instructive and explanatory power. They attempt to resolve the distinction between nature as entertainment and as the study of a difficult discipline by calling into play issues of moral and religious significance. And it is an attempt that we can also see as developing from the concern of exemplary religious poetry with the

---

[42] Goldsmith, *Animated Nature*, vol. i, Preface, p. v. Jones, *Physiological Disquisitions*, Introduction, p. x.

issues of authority and accessibility that I discussed in my Introduction. We can perhaps best describe this attempt as addressing not only the need to explain nature but the need to show how nature may resist explanation. Smart writes in *Jubilate Agno*:

For the ASCENT of VAPOURS is the return of thanksgiving from all humid bodies.

For the RAIN WATER kept in a reservoir at any altitude, suppose of a thousand feet will make a fountain from a spout of ten feet of the same height.

For it will ascend in a stream two thirds of the way and afterwards prank itself into ten thousand agreeable forms.

(Bl. 208–10)

In these lines he is not only giving a 'garbled paraphrase' of the theory of the artificial fountain. He is bringing together the different accounts of this phenomenon made available by natural philosophy, Christian thanksgiving, and affective natural description—discourses Thomson had juxtaposed, but rarely attempt to mingle—in a description which is entertaining, instructive, and morally edifying, but is not an authoritative or Godlike attempt to circumscribe or penetrate the liberty of nature to prank itself in agreeable but indescribable forms.[43]

VI

Smart's rejection of the 'vain deceit' of science, and his belief in the need for a positive interpretation of nature in the context of belief, are exemplified in many aspects of *Jubilate Agno*, but I shall focus on only one of these: his discussion of methods of determining longitude. The importance of the problem of determining longitude at sea had been recognized ever since the early voyages of Sebastian Cabot and Christopher Columbus, but it acquired a renewed urgency in England early in the eighteenth century as a result of the wreck of Vice-Admiral Sir Cloudesley Shovell's fleet off the Isles of Scilly in 1707. Though in fact this disaster may have had little to do with the problem of longitude, it nevertheless focused public attention on the dangers and uncertainties to which mariners were exposed, and eventually resulted in a bill 'for providing a publick reward for such person or persons as shall discover the longitude at sea'. The act offered rewards of various sizes, depending on the accuracy with which a method might succeed

[43] *Smart I*, B. 209 n.

in determining longitude, and the value of the largest reward, £20,000, gives some idea of the importance of the problem. The act established a Board of Longitude to assess the various methods proposed, and attracted a flood of proposals of varying degrees of practicality. The general interest in the problem that the act excited is reflected in the fact that by 1828 the Board had paid out more than £100,000 in assistance and rewards to inventors.[44]

Smart's own interest in longitude would have been stimulated by the popular account of George Anson's circumnavigation in *A Voyage round the World* (1748), which he had read, and which illustrated dramatically, in its description of the difficulties of rounding the Horn, the need for the invention of a practical method of determining longitude at sea. Smart's interest also had religious implications, for he describes, in a number of poems, the life of the Christian as a voyage, and in this context the 'discovery of the longitude' becomes the discovery of a guide towards heaven.[45]

The image of life—and sometimes, more specifically, of the life of the poet, or the poem itself—as a voyage appears in *On the Eternity* and *A Hymn to the Supreme Being, on Recovery from a dangerous Fit of Illness* (1756) and it reappears on a number of occasions in *Jubilate Agno*, for example in the lines:

For in my nature I quested for beauty, but God, God hath sent me to sea for pearls.

For there is a traveling for the glory of God without going to Italy or France.

For I am making to the shore day by day, the Lord Jesus take me.

(B1. 30, 35, 142)

Elsewhere in the poem Smart claims to dwell 'within the sound of Success' (B2. 353), and I take 'sound' here to imply not simply 'noise' but also 'strait' or 'inlet', as if the 'sound of Success' had been named on the same principle as the Cape of Good Hope. But this is only one

[44] 12 Anne, c. xv (8 July 1714), quoted in E. G. Forbes, *The Birth of Navigational Science: The Solving in the Eighteenth Century of the Problem of Finding Longitude at Sea* (Maritime Monographs and Reports, 10) (1973; this edn. London, 1980), 1.

[45] The authorship of Anson's *Voyage* is disputed, but the principal contenders are Richard Walter and Benjamin Robins; Smart refers to it directly in D. 11, and some of his descriptions of plants and animals may derive from it. The phrase 'discovering the longitude' was commonly used in the eighteenth century to describe the process which might enable longitude to be determined. I retain it because it is symptomatic of approaches to the problem, both in Smart's work and in the theories of many of his contemporaries.

of many references in the poem to the sea and the creatures that inhabit it.

In *Jubilate Agno* the religious implications of the discovery of the longitude are inseparable from its nautical significance, for Smart's natural philosophy is also a philosophy of natural revelation. He writes:

Let Campanus rejoice with the Lobster—God be gracious to all the CAMPBELLS especially John.

For the life of God is in the Loadstone, and there is a magnet, which pointeth due EAST.

Let Martha rejoice with the Skallop —the Lord revive the exercise and excellence of the Needle.

For the Glory of God is always in the East, but cannot be seen for the cloud of the crucifixion.

Let Mary rejoice with the Carp—the ponds of Fairlawn and the garden bless for the master.

For due East is the way to Paradise, which man knoweth not by reason of his fall.

Let Zebedee rejoice with the Tench —God accept the good son for his parents also.

For the Longitude is (nevertheless) attainable by steering angularly notwithstanding.   (B1. 166–9)

These lines suggest that the discovery of the longitude is a step towards the discovery of the 'true' or spiritual east, where man will rediscover the Garden of Eden as it was before the fall, by which Christ had been (effectively) hanged or crucified on the tree of life and death, good and evil. The discovery of the longitude might offer some practical help in the recovery of paradise, as it would facilitate voyages which extended the area of Christendom and encourage the universality of faith, and the lines indicate and refer to various methods of discovering it.[46]

The first method Smart alludes to is that of the dipping needle, which would indicate longitude by the angle of its inclination towards the magnetic centre. This method was advocated by, among others, William Whiston, and may be referred to in Smart's prayer for the revival of the 'exercise and excellence of the Needle', which might tend towards the loadstone as the pilgrim with his scallop-shell tends towards his shrine; this interpretation would not of course exclude Williamson's suggestion that the needle exemplifies Martha's housewifely skills, as the scallop might suggest 'trimming on clothes'. The second

[46] The scallop (B1. 167) as the emblem of the pilgrim indicates that the Christian voyage is a pilgrimage towards perfection—towards the pure life of the eastern loadstone, with which the Christian's soul as 'a similitude in the life' (B1. 165). See *Christian's Magazine*, 3 (1762), 'An Enquiry, whether the LOADSTONE be mentioned in Scripture', pp. 360–2, which argues that the word for pearl is also used to describe loadstones or magnets.

method Smart suggests is 'steering angularly notwithstanding', and this method reveals the compatibility of Smart's religious beliefs with his more 'scientific' opinions. It describes, as I have suggested, a method of maintaining rather than establishing a course, and is similar, as Williamson notes, to 'Robert Hooke's proposal, based on the angle of a ship's rhumb-line in relation to the meridional circles'. Smart suggests, I think, that longitude can be determined by reference to fixed points, 'notwithstanding' their distance, but he also implies that the Christian will find his way to paradise by holding fast to his beliefs 'notwithstanding'.[47]

The problem of longitude, then, is immediately placed in a religious as well as philosophical context: its implications for 'travel in the spirit' are as great as those for nautical travel. Smart does not specifically advocate a method of determining longitude at this point; but twenty or so lines later, he writes:

Let Anna rejoice with the Porpus, who is a joyous fish and of good omen.

Let Jonas rejoice with the Sea-Devil, who hath a good name from his Maker.

Let Alexander rejoice with the Tunny —the worse the time the better the eternity.

Let Rufus rejoice with the Needle-fish, who is very good in his element.

Let Matthat rejoice with the Trumpet-fish—God revive the blowing of the TRUMPETS.

Let Mary, the mother of James, rejoice with the Sea-Mouse it is good to be at peace.

For I bless GOD in the discovery of the LONGITUDE direct by the means of GLADWICK.

For GLADWICK is a substance growing on hills in the East, candied by the sun, and of diverse colours.

For it is neither stone nor metal but a new creature, soft to the ax, but hard to the hammer.

For it answers sundry uses, but particularly it supplies the place of Glass.

For it giveth a benign light without the fragility, malignity or mischief of Glass.

For it attracteth all the colours of the GREAT BOW which is fixed in the EAST.

(B1. 190, 199–203)

[47] *Smart I*, B1. 167 n., B1. 169 n. The Campbell referred to in B1. 166 might be Captain, later Vice-Admiral, John Campbell, who accompanied Anson on his circumnavigation, and who established, by 1760, that Hadley's reflecting octant could only reliably show the longitudinal difference between the local and prime meridians to within one degree. In 1761 Campbell was asked to test Harrison's marine chronometer on a voyage to Jamaica on HMS *Dorsetshire*, but he was unable to undertake the voyage. See Forbes, *Navigational Science* pp. 6, 12, 19 and n. See also 'Epitaph on the late Duke of Argyle' (1764), *Smart IV*, 362. W. Whiston, *The Longitude and Latitude found by the Inclination or Dipping Needle* (London, 1721).

The substance Smart describes has been recognized as mica, and its description closely resembles Newton's description of a particular kind of mica, 'island crystal' or 'isinglass'. Smart writes that gladwick 'is a substance growing on hills in the East', and it is indeed found in India and East Africa, as well as in more western parts of Europe. Gladwick is 'candied by the sun', and mica, which can have a pearly lustre, 'loses is natural polish' in water, though when dry it is 'clear as water or crystal of the Rock'; and both gladwick and mica are 'of diverse colours'. Isinglass is soft and easily scratched, but can be cleaved into thin planes, in which form it is commonly known as 'Muscovy glass', which 'supplies the place of Glass', and might be described as giving 'a benign light without the fragility, malignity or mischief of Glass' as it is 'more bright and pellucid than the finest glass'.

Most interestingly, isinglass gives an unusual refraction, having a prism angle of 60°, which intrigued Newton: he wrote that

since the Crystal by this Disposition or virtue [. . . lodged in some Sides of the Particles of the Crystal, and not in their other Sides, and which inclines and bends the Rays towards the Coast of unusual Refraction . . .] does not act upon the Rays, unless when one of their Sides of unusual Refraction looks towards that Coast, this argues a Virtue or Disposition in those Sides of the Rays, which answers to, and sympathizes with that Virtue or Disposition of the Crystal, as the Poles of two Magnets answer to one another.

Newton was careful to qualify the notion of a magnetic virtue, but nevertheless speculated that

since the Particles of Island-Crystal act all the same way upon the Rays of Light for causing the unusual Refraction, may it not be supposed that in the formation of this Crystal, the Particles not only ranged themselves in rank and file for concreting in regular Figures, but also by some kind of polar Virtue turned their homogeneal Sides the same way.[48]

---

[48] Mica went by a number of names in the 18th c., e.g. Muscovy-glass, marien glass, isinglass, Iceland glass. Smart's name, 'gladwick', may derive, as *Smart I* notes, from the description of it as giving a 'benign light', for, as Woodward remarked, ' 'Tis certainly the Business of a Naturalist, by fit and descriptive Names, to clear up Things not well known; but by no Means to render them more obscure, by a Cloud of Names, which neither any Way explain the Nature of the Things in Question, or any others, nor indeed convey any right Notion of them to the Reader' (*Earth*, p. 83). Isinglass, probably the commonest name, could be confusing as it also referred to an edible sweet. See also Maurice P. Crosland, *Historical Studies in the Language of Chemistry* (1962; rev. edn. New York, 1978), 178–9. Isaac Newton, *Opticks* (1704; this edn., based on the 4th edn. of 1730, New York, 1979), bk. III, pt. i, query 25, p. 354; see queries 25–9, pp. 354–74. In B1. 199, 'candied' appears to mean 'crystallized' as well as 'whitened'; see B2. 326. Johnson, *Dictionary*, 'Isinglass *Stone*', n. s. Newton, *Opticks*, bk. III, pt. i, query 29, p. 373.

Newton's description contains the discovery of what is now known as the polarization of light: the realization that rays are 'sided'; and he uses magnetism as an analogy for the 'Virtue' by which crystal acts on the ray. It is generally agreed that, in comparison with the *Principia*, the *Opticks* is a model of clarity and lucidity, but it nevertheless seems possible that Smart's belief, which has been found puzzling by editors of *Jubilate Agno*, that gladwick would be of use in determining longitude, is based either on a misunderstanding or on a reinterpretation of Newton's remarks. Smart's account suggests that he imagined that the crystal exercised a magnetic attraction on light, and in his 'system' the crystal therefore 'attracteth all the colours of the GREAT BOW which is fixed in the EAST', visible in its prismatic reflections, which thus indicate the 'true' East, and provide a method of establishing longitude at sea.[49]

Smart's description of gladwick provides a further example of the extent to which his faith informs his interpretative approach to natural philosophy, for the substance he describes is significant both in terms of its physical properties and as an instance of the spiritual guidance offered by nature. The 'GREAT BOW' that its prism reproduces is a confirmation of the covenant between God and man signified in the rainbow that appeared to Noah, and the 'magnet, which pointeth due EAST' provides a natural 'lively emblem' for the attraction of the Christian soul towards paradise. Gladwick therefore provides both material assistance to terrestrial voyagers, and guidance for those that 'travel in the spirit' towards the true east.

Smart's final proposal of a method for establishing longitude is more straightforwardly related to recognized contemporary theory:

For the LONGITUDE may be discovered by attending the motions of the Sun. Way 2ᵈ.

For you must consider the Sun as dodging, which he does to parry observation.

---

[49] *Opticks*, bk. III, pt. i, qu. 31, p. 388. See Sabra, *Light*, pp. 221–9. If Smart's claims or gladwick rest on a reinterpretation of Newton's account of isinglass, this suggests that he was more familiar with Newton's work than has previously been claimed, for though the double refraction produced by the crystal had been studied by other philosophers, such as Huygens, it did not appear in the accounts of Newton's philosophy largely responsible for its popularization in the 18th c.: see Colin Maclaurin, *An Account of Sir Isaac Newton's Philosophical discoveries, in four books* (London, 1748); Henry Pemberton, *A View of Sir Isaac Newton's Philosophy* (London, 1728); Whiston, *Sir Isaac Newton's Mathematical Philosophy More Easily Demonstrated* (London, 1716).

For he must be taken with an Astrolabe, & considerd respecting the point he
    left.
For you must do this upon your knees and that will secure your point.

(B2. 349–52)

This method, which was often based on the motions of the moon,
involves comparing the apparent angle of elevation of the celestial body
with those of the fixed stars, and with the estimated course of the sun
(or moon), and then comparing this calculation with that resulting
from previous observations. As John Campbell showed in his
experiments with Hadley's octant, these calculations were liable to
inaccuracy, particularly when the difficulties of making an accurate
observation on board ship in rough weather were taken into account,
and Smart displays his awareness of some of the major problems
involved in this method. 'You must', he writes, 'consider the Sun as
dodging'; the sun actively attempts to 'parry observation', to elude,
perhaps, systematization as a material rather than spiritual force, and
its success may be described in terms of the distortion of its apparent
position by the atmosphere. This difficulty is overcome, in Smart's
proposal, by a remedy that is both practically and spiritually
efficacious, as kneeling will steady the observer, and ensure that he
displays a proper reverence, similar to that which Smart demonstrates
in his hymn for 'Epiphany':

> Lo! I travel in the spirit,
>   On my knees my course I steer
> To the house of might and merit
>   With humility and fear.[50]

VII

Smart's final proposal, then, once again combines elements of
contemporary natural philosophy with a belief in the transforming
powers of faith: again it is the subjective attitude of the observer, the
faith which inspires and informs his vision, that illuminates rather than
colours his perception. These proposals for discovering the longitude
are typical of the natural philosophy of *Jubilate Agno* in that they are
capable of bearing both a literal and a figurative significance. Like the
poetic language of the Old Testament, as it is described in Lowth's

<hr>

[50] 'Hymn III', ll. 9–12, *Smart II*, p. 37.

Lectures, the language of *Jubilate Agno* reveals the accidental forms of nature as elements or emblems of a spiritual as well as material order.

This revelation, in *Jubilate Agno*, can be traced to the central role of fire in the dynamics of nature, in both a natural-philosophical and religious perception. Fire, Smart writes, is 'a mixed nature of body & spirit' (B1. 171): it describes or reveals the congruence of the spiritual and the material. It therefore provides the basis not only for a matter theory, an empirical natural philosophy, but for an understanding of the operations of the divine spirit in creation. Its central role is described in the assertion that 'all spirits are of fire and the air is a very benign one' (B1. 263), and the poem clearly implies that a natural philosophy which fails to take account of the presence of the spirit, of the mixed nature, in the elements of creation, can only describe an 'αλογος unphilosophical' (B2. 650) materialism. The poem itself, in contrast, describes the agreement between physical and spiritual nature: as the utterance of a good and praiseful voice it both 'is from the body and the spirit—and is a body and a spirit' (B1. 239): the voice of the poet, in the act of reiterating the jubilation of creation, expresses the harmony of the physical or literal and the spiritual or prophetic and figurative.

The contrast between the mechanical materialism of the new science and Smart's apprehension of the harmony of spirit and matter is not, however, reducible to a contrast between the perceptions appropriate to science and to poetry, for it is precisely this opposition that *Jubilate Agno* attempts to invalidate. The poet subjects the 'truths' of natural philosophy to a rigorous standard, in which the relative position of the philosopher, the perspective that allows him to view the system of nature, must be taken into account. I have already referred to Smart's criticism of Newton's *Opticks* as 'unphilosophical' (B2. 650), and in the 'order' of colours Smart proposes, the role of the observer in assessing and evaluating the evidence of nature is emphasized. In Smart's discussion, brown, for example, is described as 'of ten thousand acceptable shades' (B2. 661), and it is its acceptability, as well as its relation to the adjacent colours of purple and pale, that determines its place in his 'spectrum'. His description reveals that he has accepted the relation of colour to light—he discusses colours as 'shades' and writes that 'ten thousand distinct' shades of green are 'visible to a nice observer as they light upon the surface of the earth' (B2. 656, 670)—but that he regards it as necessary to the full appreciation of colour that it is perceived as 'the blessing of God unto perfection' (B2. 671). His song of praise attempts to iterate the full and spiritual as well as physical significance of colour, for 'nothing is so real as that which is spiritual' (B2. 258). The use of colour in painting, he suggests, divorces it from the 'real' and employs it in 'dead work'—painting cannot represent the spiritual significance of its subjects, but the voice iterates creation fully, and is 'compleat in all its parts' (B1. 227), and it thus achieves 'the first entrance into Heaven . . . by complement' (B2. 567), by completeness. The poem's theories of natural philosophy can therefore be understood as engaged in a debate about the nature of the 'real', of the subject-matter of empirical and philosophical survey, and as questioning the ability of different modes of description or explanation to represent the full significance of the creation that forms their content.

In *Jubilate Agno* Smart 'DARED' a celebratory and prophetic poetry of extraordinarily comprehensive scope. I have suggested that the language of the poem reveals the divine harmony of creation, both as a product of language, as a God-given system of significance, and in the integrity of matter and spirit that it describes. But the iteration of the poem, on which finally the fulfilment of its complementary potential depends, demands an understanding of the role of the poet as the prophet and scribe evangelist of Christian society, which the fragmentary state of the poem makes it difficult for us to recognize or assess. It is this issue of the relation of the poet to the society he addresses that I shall examine in Smart's later published poetry.

5 'I speak for all'

The *Song to David* and *Hymns and Spiritual Songs*

I

J UBILATE A GNO and Smart's Seatonian poems address and explore
the nature and function of the religious poet, but in *Jubilate Agno* the
nature of the audience the poet is supposed to address becomes an
issue no less important. This is not simply a matter of the fact that
Jubilate Agno did not find, until the discovery of the manuscript by
Stead, any identifiable readership; for the chief problem the poem
raises, as my discussion of Lowth's account of the customary
community of the Hebrews may have suggested, is that it appears to
presuppose and address an impossible audience, or no imaginable
audience at all. If this is the case, it is not this that sets the poem apart
as unique: a large body of the poetry of the mid-eighteenth century, of
which Gray's 'Elegy', and Chatterton's and Macpherson's medieval or
Ossianic forgeries are among the most striking examples, seems in
different ways to imply that there cannot be—or is no longer—any 'fit
audience' for poetry to address, however 'few'. On the one hand, the
poem seems to have meaning only in terms which resemble those in
which the ancient poetry of the Hebrews had meaning; it seems to
presuppose the kind of harmonious and enclosed society Lowth had
described, whose simple structures, and undiversified occupations,
create and are expressed in a shared and customary body of meaning
and analogy—a society which seemed the antithesis of eighteenth-
century England. To this extent, it participates in the problems of
address of Gray, Chatterton, Macpherson, Collins, Goldsmith, or any
other of the poets of the mid century who at one time or another write
as if there can be no common ground of understanding in a modern,
commercial, and highly ramified society. But Smart is not content simply
to lament the disappearance of a community of understanding; for, on
the other hand, *Jubilate Agno* seems to offer itself as a Christian liturgy,
addressing and exhorting a congregation able to perceive in it 'an
account of the world, in this one single view, as God's world'.

The poem presupposes and, through the act of its communal

iteration, reconfirms its participating audience as a community, for it gives a congregational or single form to their solitary perceptions of history and prophecy; but that community of readers or actors is, in the first place, a biblical, historically *past* community, who can be exhorted to participate in the synchronic 'Let' verses of the poem, but whose inability to perform the 'For' verses of the poem indicates its absence from the diverse forms of the present; and, secondly, it is a community whose presence is a function of the prophetic power of the poem itself—a community or congregation that is conjured or exhorted into immanent being in the prophetic future the poem gestures towards. It is the absence of that congregation from the present the poem addresses that enforces its silence, and that reveals the polarized form of the poem itself as able to be *read*, but as an unimaginable performance.[1]

We might expect this function of poetry as prophecy—and 'the Poetical and the Prophetical character of style and composition . . . are really one and the same'—to be most fully expressed, and to become particularly salient, in Smart's *Hymns and Spiritual Songs*, and in the *Song to David*. For of all the genres of verse, the hymn seems to require and to solicit a congregation of readers or performers which is able to understand what it is singing or reading, and which is confirmed in that congregational, as opposed to various and several, identity by that act of understanding. It is this expectation, and its justification, that I shall explore, but I want first to approach the problem of the supposed identity of the audience of the hymns and the *Song*, by looking again at *Jubilate Agno*, and at the question of the identity, the nature, of the creatures and people it exhorts to participate in thanksgiving.[2]

I have described *Jubilate Agno* as made up of two distinct but complementary bodies of verse: the formal and liturgical 'Let' verses place a public and sublime language in opposition to the more 'familiar' language of the 'For' verses. The 'Let' verses, I have argued,

---

[1] On the lack of common meaning in a diverse society, see Joseph Butler, 'Dissertation II: Of the Nature of Virtue': 'For it is impossible not to forsee, that the words and actions of men, in different ranks and employments, and of different educations, will perpetually be mistaken by each other: and it cannot but be so, whilst they will judge with the utmost carelessness, as they daily do, of what they are not, perhaps, enough informed to be competent judges of, even though they considered it with great attention' (*The Analogy of Religion, Natural and Revealed, to the Constitution and Course of Nature* (1736; this edn. Edinburgh, 1813), 343). I also quote from p. 294, where Butler discusses the Bible and such books 'as are copied from it'.

[2] R. Lowth, *Isaiah. A New Translation; with a Preliminary Dissertation, and Notes* (London, 1778), Preliminary Dissertation, iii.

are not contained by or limited to a local or occasional significance. For example, in the main clause of the line: 'Let Anna bless God with the Cat, who is worthy to be presented before the throne of grace, when he has trampled upon the idol in his prank' (A. 57), Anna and the cat are not presented as characterized by any idiosyncratic or accidental traits: they are not responsive to any occasion, but are engaged in the act of worship expressive of their substantial natures as created beings. The simplicity of their presentation, and of the act in which they are engaged, involves the exclusion of those particular characteristics that might delimit them and qualify their identification with the 'Tongues' of the opening line of the poem. The context, the series in which the verse occurs, emphasizes this identity further:

Let Zadok worship with the Mole—before honour is humility, and he that
  looketh low shall learn.
Let Gad with the Adder bless in the simplicity of the preacher and the wisdom
  of the creature.
Let Tobias bless Charity with his Dog, who is faithful, vigilant, and a friend in
  poverty.
Let Anna bless God with the Cat, who is worthy to be presented before the
  throne of grace, when he has trampled upon the idol in his prank.
Let Benaiah praise with the Asp—to conquer malice is nobler, than to slay the
  lion.

(A. 54–8)

In each of these lines, the construction and relation of the subjects to the succeeding clauses is different: a main 'Let' clause is followed, either by one or more subordinate clauses, or by a dash, and one or more main clauses which are 'subordinate' to the first in meaning, if not in construction; but this variety is counterbalanced by the overall similarity of one 'Let' verse to another. The structural resemblance of one 'Let' clause to another, and the presence of a parallel succeeding clause, outweighs the diversity of the particular nature of the verses, and works to confirm their uniformity rather than their difference.

The clauses that follow each 'Let' clause may attribute apparently particular qualities or activities to the creatures, but these do not appear to particularize their substantial natures. The qualities and activities of the animals are understood as ordained by God, and as implicitly worshipful, and they are therefore expressive of the animal's essential nature and function. This is most apparent in these lines where the attributes of the animals derive largely from the descriptions of them offered in the Bible: the activities of the cat, for example, derive from the Epistle of Jeremy in the apocryphal book of Baruch, where 'bats, swallows, and birds, and the cats also' sit on Babylonian idols, and through this disrespect reveal their impotence; an act which may illustrate or confirm the essential nature of cats, both in itself and as it is supported by the authority of Jeremiah. The description of the cat also reveals that the significance of the name 'Anna' here is not restricted by contextual proximity to the mother of Tobias alone, as the subordinate clauses allude to the presentation in the temple, when Anna the prophetess is described by Luke as able to discern the true God.[3]

The 'substance', the substantial nature of the creatures named in the 'Let' verses, is indicated by the apparently random and indiscriminate presence and omission of definite and indefinite articles; and even the exceptional use of the possessive pronoun, applied to the dog here as the property of either Charity or Tobias, may indicate the domesticated and faithful nature of the animal, which symbolizes the qualities enjoined on Tobias by his father Tobit, and by the poem, rather than characterizing it as a particular and identifiable dog. The substantial, as opposed to the accidental, status of these creatures is clearly exemplified by the contrast between this reference to the cat and Smart's celebration of his cat Jeoffry, in a long series of 'For' verses (B2. 697–770); for though some of the appeal of that passage results from its applicability to all cats, it is the poet's expression of the intimate and occasional pleasure of the close and affectionate observation of one particular animal that is delightful. In short, the expression of interest in the activities of a particular animal would seem inappropriate to the language of the 'Let' verses, which expresses a creation of forms which approach as nearly towards the substantial as their post-lapsarian state allows, whereas the 'For' verses are concerned rather with an accidental and familiar world.

The relation between the accidental and substantial qualities of created things in the two 'parts' of *Jubilate Agno* is mirrored in the relation of any 'Let' verse to the body of verse to which it belongs, for though any single 'Let' verse may indicate the substantial quality of the pair exhorted to rejoice, their accidental nature, contingent on time and place, is revealed, as is that of the verse itself, when its relation to other verses is acknowledged. That relation reinforces the formal and structural properties of the verse, and thus confirms its potential as the

---

[3] Baruch 6: 22. See Luke 2: 36–8.

comprehensive utterance of the thanksgiving of creation, even as it
frustrates it in revealing its relative and accidental nature as part of a
continuous series. The poem describes the gathering of a congregation,
and construction of a temple, expressive of all creation: in its opening
lines, the various priests and patriarchs named are permitted,
exhorted, or perhaps assumed to enter the temple which becomes
apparent—we could almost say, which is 'constructed'—through their
actions, and their reference to it. Aaron, the Levites, Eleazar, and
Ithamar, sanctify, perform their priestly functions, serve and minister,
and thus indicate and make substantial the temple of the poem, as they
'appear before' God, and are themselves called into being (A. 15–18, 3).
Kohath, whose name means 'congregation', serves 'with the Sable',
and thus reveals the 'ornaments of the Temple' in which he worships,
which was covered with the best skins (A. 21); but the poem's
movement towards synchronism, towards the expression of the full
presence of the congregation in the completed temple, is at odds with
its cumulative, diachronic development of history, which represents
that congregation as made up of an occasional collection of individuals,
rather than as an ideal form giving simultaneous presence and
expression to creation as a whole. It is these problems, of the relation
of substantial and accidental, of the congregation and the individual,
and of the 'grand Chorus' and the 'youthful, uninspired Bard', that I
wish to discuss in Smart's later religious poetry.[4]

II

Much of the poetry Smart published in the years immediately
following his confinement belongs as much within the Davidic tradi-
tion of psalmody as do the Seatonian poems—a tradition directly
concerned with the relation of poet and congregation; and it is in this
context that I shall discuss, in the remainder of this chapter, two of the
major projects of those years, the *Hymns and Spiritual Songs for the Fasts
and Festivals of the Church of England* (1765), and *A Song to David*. The
Song was first published in 1763, the year Smart regained his freedom
and also published his *Poems* and *Poems on Several Occasions*; and he
republished it in 1765 with some minor corrections, in the handsome
volume which contained his *Psalms* and *Hymns*. This second publication,

---

[4] Cruden, 'Proper Names', Kohath.

I think, has significant implications for the interpretation of the *Song*, for its first appearance, in a separate volume, had presented the song as a heroic high ode, comparable, in its treatment of the King of Israel, to the heroic treatment of the Earl of Northumberland, or Admiral Sir George Pocock, to whom Smart also composed odes of praise. But in the context of the *Hymns* and *Psalms*, the *Song* provides, as it were, a bridge between the sacred poetry of 'human composure' on the one hand and the paraphrase of the inspired poetry of the Bible on the other. The *Song* takes for its epigraph some of the last words of David: 'DAVID the Son of Jesse said, and the MAN who was RAISED UP ON HIGH, the ANOINTED OF THE GOD OF JACOB, and the SWEET PSALMIST OF ISRAEL, said, The SPIRIT OF THE LORD spake by ME, and HIS WORD was in my TONGUE.' This passage from the second book of Samuel had been described by Bishop Chandler as the key to the Psalms, and in the context of the edition of 1765, it may indicate that the *Song* has itself become the key to the *Hymns* and *Psalms* it appears with.[5]

The *Song*, of course, has attracted a fair measure of critical attention, and formed the basis of Smart's reputation in the last century, but the achievement of Smart's *Hymns* has only come to be acknowledged in more recent years. Critics have emphasized the highly unusual nature of Smart's project, in composing a complete cycle of hymns for the major occasions in the calendar of the Anglican Church, for almost all the hymns for which the period is famous were the work of dissenters, evangelicals, and Methodists. Smart alone produced, out of the conviction of the need for liturgical reform that he expresses in *Jubilate Agno*, a complete version of the Psalms, and a set of hymns, explicitly intended for the Church, and, presumably, envisaged as a part of the programme of reform he and many others wished to see. We can indeed see Smart's project as a response to a generally recognized need, rather than as the product of an eccentric ambition, for perhaps the most influential work on liturgical reform in the mid century, J. Jones's *Free and Candid Disquisitions relating to the Church of England* (1749), had argued for the introduction of hymns into the service. The need for new translations of the Psalms had been

---

[5] 2 Sam. 23: 1–3. *Christian's Magazine* remarked, on the separate publication of the *Song to David*, that 'This is proposed as a recommendation of Mr. Smart's intended translation of the Psalms' (vol. 4 (1764), 479), emphasizing its connection with the later volume. Edward Chandler, *Defence of Christianity*, ch. 3, sect. 3, pp. 193–8, quoted in George Fenwick, *The Psalter in its Original Form: or The Book of Psalms Reduced to Lines* (London, 1759), 355.

recognized throughout the century: it was frequently discussed, with considerable strength of feeling, in numerous periodicals, and prompted the versions of, amongst others, Isaac Watts, Anna Steele, James Merrick, and George Fenwick. Like Smart, they produced versions of the Psalms thought to be more in keeping with the spirit of the New Testament, and, usually, better adapted for musical performance than the standard Old Version of Sternhold and Hopkins.[6]

The great hymn-writers of the century—the Independent dissenter Isaac Watts, the Methodist Wesleys, and the evangelical Calvinist John Newton—had each prefaced their collections of hymns with explanations of their functions in worship, and discussions of their relation to poetry as the object of criticism: they all argued that the writing of hymns for congregations of mixed capacities demanded clarity rather than poetic elegance, and that, if they succeeded in pleasing the critics of poetry, this was no more than a lucky side-effect of their primarily didactic intentions. Smart did not produce a preface of this kind, and it is difficult to apply the precepts of other hymn-writers to his uniquely Anglican work, but the internal evidence of the *Hymns* and the *Song* allows us to draw some conclusions about the nature of his project, and to make some tentative comparisons with other hymnists. One of my aims in this chapter, as I have already suggested, is to explore the concept of the Anglican congregation which the *Hymns* imply—which they address, or speak for. Watts, the Wesleys, and Newton each use their hymns to confirm and consolidate the congregation they are

---

[6] The *Song* has received more critical attention than any of the rest of Smart's work. Some of the most important contributions, to which my own discussion is indebted, are: Laurence Binyon, *The Case of Christopher Smart* (The English Association, Pamphlet 90; Dec. 1934); Sophia B. Blaydes, *Christopher Smart as a Poet of his Time: A Re-Appraisal*, (The Hague and Paris, 1966), ch. 6; *A Song to David with other poems*, ed. Edmund Blunden (London, 1924); *Poems by Christopher Smart*, ed. Robert Brittain (Princeton, NJ, 1950, 292–310); *A Song to David*, ed. J. B. Broadbent (London, 1960); Moira Dearnley, *The Poetry of Christopher Smart* (London, 1969), ch. 7; Christopher M. Dennis, 'A Structural Conceit in Smart's *Song to David*', *RES* NS 29 (1978), 257–66; Christopher Devlin, *Poor Kit Smart* (London, 1961). ch. 11; R. D. Havens, 'The Structure of Smart's *Song to David*', *RES* 14 (1938), 178–82; K. M. Rogers, 'The Pillars of the Lord: Some Sources for *A Song to David*', *PQ* 40 (1961), 525–34; P. M. Spacks, *The Poetry of Vision* (Cambridge, Mass., 1967), 119–39; and the invaluable critical apparatus provided by Marcus Walsh in *Smart II*. On the *Hymns*, see Donald Davie, *A Gathered Church: The Literature of the English Dissenting Interest, 1700–1930* (London, 1978), lecture 2: 'Enlightenment and Dissent', and his Introduction to his anthology, *Augustan Lyric* (London, 1974); Marcus Walsh, '*Hymns and Spiritual Songs*: Introduction', in *Smart II*; Karina Williamson, 'Christopher Smart's *Hymns and Spiritual Songs*', *PQ* 38 (1959). None of the versions of the Psalms that I mention was, of course, as successful as the New Version of Nahum Tate and Nicholas Brady (1696).

offered to in the manner of David's Psalms, which had, in the words of Patrick Delany, expressed a religious gratitude that

when it is poured out for public blessings, in which all partake, naturally mixes with every social affection, and blends them, as it were, into its own being; and by this means, becomes the very best bond of society.

The Methodists were notorious for their distinctive attachment to hymn-singing: the Cornish Methodists, for example, were known as the 'Canorum', a word derived from the Cornish *canor*, 'singer'. The Wesleys' collections of hymns offered a complete body of practical and theoretical divinity, as did the Psalms, and John Wesley described the *Select Hymns* of 1761 as the means of effecting his wish for 'the people called Methodists to sing true the tunes which are in *common use* among them': the consolidation of the Methodists as a distinct 'religious community' within the Anglican Church is, in part at least, a product of this common practice.[7]

John Newton, in the Preface to his and Cowper's *Olney Hymns* (1779), writes that he hopes his hymns will be acceptable to the beliefs of 'real Christians of all denominations'. He describes them as the expression of a sincere faith, which is intended to be free from all controversial content, and as free from any debatable context 'as . . . if I had composed hymns in some of the newly-discovered islands in the South Sea, where no person had any knowledge of the name of Jesus but myself'. But while his hymns may set an example for other congregations, their title, and the contents in particular of the second of their three books, 'On Occasional Subjects', clearly confirm both his commitment and that of his congregation to their identity as a parish. In a striking example, they sing 'On the Fire at Olney. Sept. 22, 1777':

> Oh, may that night be ne'er forgot!
> Lord, still increase thy praying few!
> Were Olney left without a Lot,
> Ruin like Sodom's would ensue.

Newton's South Sea island is specifically placed in his Buckinghamshire village, and despite his appeal to all denominations, he vigorously defends his right to express his Calvinism in his Preface, and bases the

---

[7] Patrick Delany, *An Historical Account of the Life and Reign of David King of Israel*, 3 vols. (London, 1740, 1742), iii. 235. *The Works of John Wesley*, vii. *A Collection of Hymns for the Use of the People Called Methodists*, ed. Franz Hildebrandt and Oliver A. Beckerlegge, with the assistance of James Dale (Oxford, 1984), Introduction, pp. 62–3. See Rupert E. Davies, *Methodism* (London, 1963), 95.

first hymn in the collection on its tenets. He describes Adam, the representative man, fallen and unrepentant:

> But grace, unask'd, his heart subdued,
> And all his guilt forgave;
> By faith the promised Seed he view'd,
> And felt his power to save.

He introduces immediately the primary importance of grace and faith—rather than works or even repentance—which is the foundation of his beliefs.[8]

It is, not surprisingly, more difficult to argue that Watts's hymns work to confirm congregational identity in the way that the Wesleys' and Newton's do, for the nature of his Independent dissent promotes, precisely, independence from the sort of paternal authority John Wesley exerted over his followers. Watts argues in the Preface to his *Hymns and Spiritual Songs* of 1719—rather more emphatically than Newton was to do seventy years later—that he has not only not intended to include, but has positively excluded, all possible sources of controversy: 'The Contentions and distinguishing Words of Sects and Parties are secluded, that whole Assemblies might assist at the Harmony, and different Churches join in the same Worship without Offence'; though nevertheless it is difficult to imagine many Anglicans singing of themselves, with sincere understanding of the kind Watts advocates, the lines:

> Our Characters were then decreed,
> 'Blameless in Love, a holy Seed.'
>
> Predestinated to be Sons,
> Born by Degrees, but chose at once;
> A new regenerated Race,
> To praise the Glory of his Grace.

The use of the terms of predestination, regeneration, and grace, in a hymn titled 'Electing Love', seems hardly to avoid contentious 'distinguishing Words', however willing the audience may be to read with the charitable latitude the Preface recommends. Only the whole assembly who shared Watts's particular beliefs could, I think,

---

[8] I quote from *The Works of the Rev. John Newton* (Edinburgh, 1834), 523, 524; hymn lxix, p. 594; hymn i, p. 525. Wesley also described his hymns as available to all churches, in his Preface of 1761, but that offer too was perhaps more generous than acceptable.

participate in claiming the redeemed and and elected 'Characters' the singers describe in these lines.[9]

Watts's official intention, to write for 'different Churches', may, in hymns such as this, be subverted by the nature of the dissenting audiences he was accustomed to address. He spent most of his life in the family of Sir Thomas Abney, an alderman of London, and addressed almost exclusively audiences drawn from the City of London. As Madeleine Forell Marshall and Janet Todd point out, in their discussion of *English Congregational Hymns*, 'The Mark Lane setting of prosperous, educated London Independency suited Watts's talent and distinguishes his hymns from those of many of his successors. He wrote for a relatively sophisticated, homogeneous group that could be trusted to understand and to respond appropriately to his verses.' Many of Watts's hymns are characterized by a use of the first person that might seem strongly individualistic for the period in which he wrote, but which may equally reflect his confidence in the unanimity, the univocal faith, of the congregation he addresses. His hymns, like those of Wesley and Newton, but perhaps with rather different implications, frequently express a sense of community isolated from and opposed to the world beyond the congregation, for example in his hymn on 'God the Glory and the Defence of Sion':

> Happy the Church, thou sacred Place,
> The Seat of thy Creator's Grace;
> Thy holy Courts are his Abode:
> Thou earthly Palace of our GOD.
>
> Thy Walls are Strength, and at thy Gates
> A Guard of heav'nly Warriors waits;
> Nor shall thy deep Foundations move,
> Fix'd on his Counsels and his Love.
>
> Thy Foes in vain Designs engage,
> Against his Throne in vain they rage;
> Like rising Waves with angry Rore,
> That dash and die upon the Shore.
>
> Then let our Souls in Zion dwell;
> Nor fear the Wrath of Rome and Hell;
> His Arms embrace this Happy Ground,
> Like brazen Bulwarks built around.

[9] Isaac Watts, *Hymns and Spiritual Songs* (1719; this edn. 1781), Preface, p. ix; bk. I, hymn liv, p. 39.

Where for the Wesleys the worst foes are always 'The enemy within', and for Cowper and Newton they threaten the seclusion of retirement, or of the parish church, for Watts the protected ground of Sion is perhaps the educated and tolerant milieu of the City of London, where his life could be, as Johnson puts it, 'no otherwise diversified than by successive publications'.[10]

These three major hymn-writers, then, all write to some extent to reinforce the identities imposed on their congregations through their opposition or dissent: they make the alienation their nonconformity brings the basis of their distinctive and strong sense of community; but the Church of England, and in particular the broad church of the latitudinarian Anglicans, provides no such oppositional focus of congregational identity for the hymnist to exploit. In the 1750s and 1760s, I have suggested, the Church is involved in an unstable dialectic between, primarily, the discourses of rational natural religion and revelation, that makes univocal congregational expression seem a remote possibility, unless it is engaged in the kind of attack on Roman Catholicism and rebellion that became especially popular after the uprising of 1745. Thus, though Smart's *Hymns* do, I think, promote a form of ideal congregational expression, which I will need to discuss later in this chapter, the nature of that congregation, and the poetry appropriate to its offer of worship, can best be approached indirectly, as it were, through the treatment the hymns offer of some of the issues concerning the Church at this period. I shall therefore look now at three related areas, in the *Hymns* and *Song*, which will reveal both the comparability of Smart's project with those of Watts, the Wesleys, and Newton, and the terms in which his *Hymns* are distinctively Anglican: first, the treatment of scriptural interpretation and figurative language; secondly, the attitude this poetry describes towards one of the key areas of religious debate—the use of riches; and thirdly, the relation of this religious poetry to dissent and Anglicanism.

---

[10] Madeleine Forell Marshall and Janet Todd, *English Congregational Hymns in the Eighteenth Century* (Lexington, Ky., 1982), 56. Watts, *Hymns*, bk. II, hymn lxiv, pp. 187–8. Wesley, *Collection*, pt. IV, sect iv, hymn 301, p. 456; see *Olney Hymns*, bk. I, hymn xcvi, which opens with the lines: 'Thy mansion is the christian's heart, / O Lord, thy dwelling-place secure! / Bid the unruly throng depart, / And leave the consecrated door', in *The Poems of William Cowper*, i. *1748–1782*, ed. John D. Baird and Charles Ryskamp (Oxford, 1980); Samuel Johnson, 'Watts', in *Lives of the English Poets* (1779, 1781; this edn. 2 vols., Oxford, 1906), ii. 381–2.

III

It has often been pointed out that Smart's religious poetry expresses a delight in creation that is largely absent from the work of other hymn-writers of the century, unless they are paraphrasing the words of David. Newton and Cowper, it is true, describe nature as a source of joy and instruction, but the Wesleys seem, often, too preoccupied with the beauty of death to value that of life, and Watts, in his warnings against love for the material and physical world, seems to see love of the natural world as a sign of moral weakness and unworthiness. This characterization of Watts and the Wesleys is perhaps not entirely justified in its severity, but it is nevertheless difficult to imagine them singing with Smart as he celebrates Christ's nativity:

> Spinks and ouzles sing sublimely,
> 'We too have a Saviour born;'
> Whiter blossoms burst untimely
> On the blest Mosaic thorn.

The striking contrast Smart's work presents to that of earlier hymn-writers is, I think, a result of the different understanding of the relation between the accidental and the substantial that we saw in *Jubilate Agno*, and which, in Smart's later poetry, also involves a particular understanding of the relation between type and antetype, revelation and history.[11]

I can best explain the connection I am describing here by discussing the controversy about the character of David, outlined in Marcus Walsh's Introduction to the *Song to David* in the Oxford edition, for this debate, which provided a focus for many of the issues which concerned the Church at this period, turns in part upon the issue of the interpretation of the scriptures. The debate was sparked off by a sermon given by Bishop Samuel Chandler on the death of George II, in which Chandler compared the characters of George and David in eulogistic terms. Almost immediately, an anonymous reply appeared, called *The Life of David: or, The History of the Man after God's Own Heart* (1761), in which it was argued, with an irony that seemed to reflect almost as much on the King as on David, that Chandler's comparison

---

[11] See e.g. Wesley, *Collection*, pt I sect. ii. 3, hymn 47, p. 38; Watts, *Hymns*, bk. II, hymn xlviii, p. 171. Smart, 'Hymn XXXII. the Nativity of our Lord and Saviour Jesus Christ', ll. 29–32.

had been insulting to the memory of the dead king, because David, far from being 'a Great and Good King', had been a romantic and opportunistic 'young Adventurer' who behaved like an actor in a tragi-comedy. This attack in turn provoked a series of responses in defence of David, many of which were printed in Dodd's *Christian's Magazine*. These responses took their lead from a sermon by Bishop Porteus on *The Character of David*, which argued that David was admirable and heroic in his public and regal character, rather than in either his private failings or those characteristics which should be understood as the product of the manners and morals of the age in which he lived. The controversy turns on the extent to which the Bible can be read in the terms applicable to 'common history', as Chandler argued in the *Critical History* of David he went on to produce.[12]

The treatment of the Bible as common history, in the anonymous attack, could be seen as the result of the kind of biblical criticism advocated by the rather unlikely alliance of Locke, Joseph Trapp, Robert Lowth, and John Wilkes. Locke, in his posthumously published *Essay for the Understanding of St. Paul's Epistles*, had argued that sectarian strife had arisen from 'some distorted text of Paul' (in Smart's phrase), because his letters were treated as collections of aphorisms, rather than as continuous arguments. This point was adopted by most churchmen in the eighteenth century, who wished to see a revised translation of the Bible, divided into less misleading chapters and verses. Locke had added that Paul's letters could only be understood in the context of 'the particularities of the history' of the time at which they were written: he argues, in effect, that national histories and customs must be the subject of scholarly study in order for ancient texts to be understood clearly. We can trace the development of this argument in Trapp's insistence that the unlettered cannot interpret the Bible for themselves, but must submit to the authority of 'Persons skill'd in Languages, History, and Antiquity, and

---

[12] I quote from the title of Chandler's sermon on George II and David, *The Character of a Great and Good King full of Days, Riches, and Honour* (1760). [?Peter Annet], *Life of David* (1761; this edn. London, 1772), 62. See *Smart II*, p. 105. Beilby Porteus, *The Character of David King of Israel. Impartially stated: in a Discourse Preached before the University of Cambridge, November 29. 1761* (Cambridge, 1761). I quote from Patrick Delany's argument that biblical events should be described in the terms appropriate to 'a noble pourtrait', because 'Minute description would bring them too near the level of common history; and, on occasions so very extraordinary, would, with all the strictness of truth, debase them even to an air of romance' (*Historical Account*, i. 47, 46–7). See the similar terms of Chandler's discussion in *A Critical History of the Life of David* (1766; this edn. Oxford, 1953), 239–40.

254 'I SPEAK FOR ALL'

such as have made Learning their Study, and Profession'; and we can
see its fruition in Lowth's *Lectures*, which tie the poetry of the Hebrews
firmly to their historical and religious customs, but nevertheless
describe the scholarly interpreter as able to break through the barriers
of custom, and to grasp the true meaning of the Old Testament.[13]

Eleven years after the first publication of Lowth's *Lectures* (in 1753),
however, the barriers of national custom had come to present a more
formidable obstacle. Lowth had argued that, despite the intimate
relation between the Hebrews' poetry and circumstances, the sublime
Mystical Allegories of scripture were clearly visible through the mists of
custom, and were, in their prophetic nature, more clearly understood
by the modern interpreter than by the Hebrews themselves; but for
John Wilkes, reviewing a new edition of the *Lectures* for the *Supplément
à la Gazette littéraire* in 1764, this aspect of Lowth's argument seemed
hardly comprehensible—'Nous sommes fâchés de trouver plusieurs
pages inutiles dans l'Ouvrage de M. Lowth: c'est un Chapitre sur
l'Allégorie Mystique que nous n'entendons guère.' Lowth himself
bowed to the change in the perception of historical and cultural
boundaries, of which Wilkes's angry incomprehension is symptomatic:
his translation of *Isaiah* (1778) eschews allegorical interpretation in
favour of the attempt to make the text accessible to scholars through
research we might describe as archaeological and anthropological.
Perhaps more significantly, for the purposes of my argument, Lowth
feels obliged to defend himself for having occasionally offered
conjectural translations, rather than leaving blank spaces in the text:
'But I desire to be understood as offering this apology in behalf only of
Translations designed for the private use of the reader; not as
extended . . . to those that are made for the public service of the
Church.' By this date the text appropriate to the scholar is different
from that made available to Trapp's *'unletter'd Laics'*, and there is thus
little possibility of any challenge to the authority of the interpretations
advanced by scholarly researchers.[14]

[13] 'Hymn V. King Charles the Martyr', l. 8. See John Locke, *Essay for the
Understanding of St. Paul's Epistles*, in *The Works of John Locke. A New Edition, Corrected, In
Ten Volumes* (London, 1823), viii 7, 13–14; I quote from the argument that 'the
particulars of the history, in which these speeches are inserted, show St. Paul's end in
speaking; which being seen, casts a light on the whole, and shows the pertinency of all
that he says' (p. 16). Joseph Trapp, *The Nature, Folly, Sin, and Danger of being Righteous
over-much* (1739; this 4th edn. London, 1739), 12. Robert Lowth's discussion of the
sublime in *Lectures on the Sacred Poetry of the Hebrews*, trans. G. Gregory (1787; repr.
Hildesheim, 1969), esp. vol. i, lect. xvii, pp. 365–7. See also pp. 95–8, 152–5 above.

[14] See Lowth, *Lectures*, vol. i, lect. xi, pp. 246–8. *Gazette littéraire de l'Europe*, iii/37 (30

The point of this brief excursion into the history of biblical criticism is to establish that, by the time Smart's *Song to David* appears, the treatment of Old Testament figures as the exemplary and heroic subjects of poetry has come to involve a range of issues, about the accessibility of the Old Testament, and the extent to which anybody in it can be represented as exemplary, that poetry must attempt to engage with. Bishop Porteus's apology for the character of David, in the emphasis it places on the barbarism of the Hebrews, the sheer foreignness of David's behaviour, is in a sense closer to the anonymous attack on him than to Chandler's comparison of him with the King. The anonymous controversialist, as I have said, is accused of describing David as though he were a merely historical figure: the language in which he discusses David has none of the reverence of Delany's or Chandler's lives:

As he has now a quiet residence, those who entertain an opinion of David's sanctity, would be apt to suppose he would here confine himself to agriculture, to composing psalms, and to singing them to his harp; but David found employment more suited to his genius. It is not intended here to be insinuated, that he might not sing psalms at leisure times; but his more important business was to lead his men out to plunder the adjacent country.

Were it not for the persistent tone of ironic mockery in this account, it would, I think, seem no more remote from the praise of Smart's *Song* than does Porteus's suggestion that we can best understand David's cruelty by comparing it with the barbarity of the early Saxon kings of England.[15]

There is, however, a further important distinction to be made between those who defended David and his attacker: for his defenders rest much of the weight of their case on the inaccessibility of ancient history to the non-specialist reader. Porteus, in suggesting that David's manners are those of his times, is also implying that they can only be understood by those who have 'made Learning their Study, and Profession'. His defence can be seen as a part of a process by which the attention of lay readers was confined to the New Testament, and they were invited only to glance at selected and well-annotated parts of the Old. The controversialist, on the other hand, bases his case on the grounds that

Sept. 1764), 77. Lowth, *Isaiah*, Preliminary Dissertation, p. lxxiii. Trapp, *Righteous over-much*, p. 10.

[15] See Porteus, *Character of David*, p. 28. [?Annet], *Life of David*, p. 69.

If the Reformed religion means any thing, it must mean a religion founded by the authority, not of councils and synods, but of conviction, the result of private judgement.

This emphasis on private judgement implies that the private reader is able to interpret the Old Testament with as much authority as the professional: a position which churchmen of the second half of the century rarely contradict as flatly as had Trapp, but which their emphasis on the need for scholarship at least implicitly denies. Smart, however, echoes this assertion of the accessibility of the Old as well as the New Testament in several of his later poems, for example in his hymn on 'Trinity Sunday':

> Ye poets, seers and priests,
> Whose lore the spirit feasts,
> And keep the banquet on,
> From Moses ev'n to John;
>> On your truth I will regale,
>> 'Which is great and must prevail.'

> The Trinity is plain,
> So David's psalms maintain,
> —Who made not God his boast
> But by the HOLY GHOST;
>> Thence prophetick to record
>> All the suff'rings of the Lord.

In these stanzas, Smart is not just arguing for the sufficiency of scripture as the source of doctrine—an argument fundamental to the Protestant Churches, but one they were not always anxious to stress— but is asserting that the Old Testament plainly supports the doctrine of the trinity, and that the Bible offers a feast to the worshipper 'From Moses ev'n to John'.[16]

Now clearly the kind of interpretation of scripture that allows Smart to praise David as 'Great, valiant, pious, *good, and clean*, / Sublime, contemplative, serene, / Strong, constant, pleasant, wise!' (my italics), and to claim that the Psalms support the plain doctrine of the trinity, does not involve the reduction of the Bible to 'the level of common history', and, though Smart's poetry is sometimes difficult, it does not present Old Testament figures as more properly the objects of archaeological research. It has more in common with the attitude to

---

[16] Trapp, *Righteous over-much*, p. 12. [?Annet], *Life of David*, Preface, p. xii. 'Hymn XVI. Trinity Sunday', ll. 43–54.

the Bible described in the Preface to George Fenwick's translation of
1759:

Many of them [the Psalms] are now used, it is to be feared, even in our solemn
Offices, with little or no Benefit, because they are considered only as the
Words of *David*, dictated on some particular Occasions relating only to
Himself, or the People of *Israel*, in Circumstances which have often little or no
Resemblance to our own. But if we were to enlarge our View, and would
regard *the Mind of The Spirit*, as they were designed for the Church of *Christ*,
or rather for the whole Race of Men; every Soul, in every State and Condition
of Life, might find his Devotion raised, and be enabled to join feelingly in the
Use of Words, which are pointing out to all Men the blessed Hope of
Immortality . . .

In Fenwick's Hutchinsonian rendition of *The Psalter in its Original
Form* the Book of Psalms is represented as an 'awful *Drama*', of which
Christ is 'the glorious Hero', and the apparent incoherence of 'this
divine Poem' is described as the result of the failure to apreciate that it
is spoken by a number of speakers, in dramatic form. I do not want to
suggest that Smart shared fully this elaborate and imaginative view of
the psalmic drama, or to overstate the comparibility of Smart's views and
those of Hutchinsonian thinkers—Smart's descriptions of cherubs, for
example, do not suggest that they were trinitarian symbols, as the
Hutchinsonians argued—but to point out that in the mid century this
kind of reading of the Old Testament, in terms primarily of Lowth's
early theory of Mystical Allegory, rather than of cultural relativity,
seemed a means of making the scriptures accessible to 'every Soul', in
contrast to the historicism advocated by Trapp, and increasingly by
Lowth.[17]

I argue, then, that in the 1760s the language of analogy and type that
Smart's *Hymns* proclaim almost immediately as their distinctive feature
could be seen as the guarantee of their comprehensible accessibility,
rather than as a sign of their obscurity, or of an anachronistic return to
the religious discourses of the seventeenth century. Smart writes, in
the hymn on the 'New Year' that begins his cycle, of the angelic spirits:

[17] *A Song to David*, st. iv, ll. 19–21 (all quotations from the *Song* are from *Smart II*).
Delany, *Historical Account*, i. 46. Fenwick, *Psalter*, Preface, pp. xxvii–xxviii, vii, xvi, xxviii.
On the tradition of interpreting the Psalms as a heroic drama, see George Horne, *A
Commentary on the Book of Psalms* (1771; this 4th edn. Oxford, 1790), Preface, pp. xx–
xxx.

Which, the type of vows completed,
Shall the wreathed garland send,
While new blessings are intreated,
And communicants attend.

Emblem of the hopes beginning,
Who the budding rods shall bind,
Way from guiltless natures winning,
In good-will to human kind.

The types and emblems of this poetry seem intimately related to the claim it makes to 'speak for' communicants, for 'human kind'. The *Hymns*, like the *Song*, employ a typological language of religious zeal which asserts the clarity, and direct exemplary force, of the Old and New Testaments in response both to the treatment of David as no more than an actor, and to the defence of him as historically remote, and inaccessible to emulation.[18]

The perception that the language of types provided a means of transcending the obstructions of custom, and of describing the Old Testament as accessible not only through scholarly research, was not limited to Hutchinsonian theologians; and indeed, by the 1770s and 1780s, Bishop Horne and William Jones of Nayland, both of whom admired and followed the example set by Hutchinson's work, saw the typological interpretation of scripture as itself a scholarly pursuit. Horne describes his influential *Commentary* (1771) on the evangelical significance of the Psalms as secondary or complementary to their historical interpretation along the lines exemplified by Lowth. Though later readers might explore the typological meanings of the Old Testament, they are usually cautioned, like Hester Chapone's niece, to do so under the guidance of notes describing its historical context. But in the 1760s, the perception that the historical continuity of event described in the Old Testament should not be a matter for private judgement—judgement of a kind that might lead readers like the anonymous controversialist to make comparisons with modern history which undermined the authority of both ancient and modern heroes—could lend encouragement to the reading of the Old Testament according to the principles of Mystical Allegory, of type and of emblem. For this kind of reading excluded the perception of it either as common history or as lost in the mists of antiquity. This method of interpretation was highly selective: it favoured the static emblem,

---

[18] 'Hymn I', ll. 9–16. 'Hymn VI', l. 41.

rather than the historical process that produced it, and it read the Old Testament, as it were, through the filter of the New. For Bishop Chandler, for example, as perhaps for Smart, it afforded an understanding of David as the type of Christ and thus filtered or blotted out the particular sins which belonged to his historical rather than typical character. But, as I have said, perhaps the most significant shared characteristic of writers who explored the typological interpretation of scripture in the late 1750s and 1760s was their belief that this method made the Old Testament accessible to all diligent Christians, and that it disclosed a transhistorical revelation of the salvation available through Christ. It described the accidental forms of history in terms of the substantial revelation of the Gospels.[19]

Thus John Newton argues that every object in creation offers instruction to the devout Christian, and that the prophecies, types, and ceremonies of the Old Testament foreshadow and confirm the promises of the Gospel. This predominantly optimistic message of the Old Testament is available, through analogical interpretation, to every devout reader:

A critical knowledge of the original languages, a skill in the customs and manners of the ancients, an acquaintance with the Greek and Roman classics, a perusal of councils, fathers, scholiasts, and commentators, a readiness in the subtleties of logical disputation; these, in their proper place and subserviency, may be of considerable use to clear, illustrate or enforce the doctrines of scripture: but unless they are governed by a temper of humility and prayer; unless the man that possesses them accounts them altogether as nothing, without that assistance of the Spirit and of God which is promised to guide believers into all truth; unless he seeks and prays for this guidance no less earnestly than those who understand nothing but their mother-tongue; I make no scruple to affirm, that all his apparatus of knowledge only tends to lead him so much the further astray; and that a plain honest ploughman, who reads no book but his Bible, and has no teacher but the God to whom he prays in secret, stands abundantly fairer for the attainment of true skill in divinity.

---

[19] See William Jones, *A Course of Lectures on the Figurative Language of the Holy Scripture* (1787), lect. i, Introduction. Horne, *Commentary*, Preface, pp. xxx–xxxi, iv–x, xlii–xliv. See Hester Chapone, *Letters on the Improvement of the Mind* (1773), letter ii, 'On the Study of the Holy Scripture', where she recommends Delany's *Historical Account* and Thomas Newton's *On the Prophecies*. I do not want to suggest that typological interpretation was an ahistorical method, but to emphasize that it privileged readings which did not depend upon abstruse scholarly or archaeological research—see e.g. Fenwick's acknowledgements of his debt to Lowth both in the notes to his psalms, and in the Preface to his *Psalter*.

In Smart's poetry the language of type and emblem may seem to demand a knowledge of scripture which requires an extraordinarily diligent attention on behalf of the Christian, but that language can also be seen as the key to an attempt to reclaim, for poetry and thus for the congregation, an access to the Bible, and in particular to the Old Testament, which was increasingly denied, or granted only to the scholar, as a result of the development of kinds of biblical criticism which did not remove the Bible from controversy because they clarified its obscurer passages, but because they appropriated them only to the enquiries of the learned.[20]

IV

Several of Smart's *Hymns* approach the issue of typological and emblematic language fairly directly, in terms that make clear its significance for his idea of congregational religious poetry. In his hymn on 'The Ascension of our Lord Jesus Christ', for example, he first asserts the sufficiency of the text of the Gospel, and then goes on, perhaps paradoxically, to amplify it:

> For not a particle of space
>   Where'er his glory beam'd,
> With all the modes of site and place,
> But were the better for his grace,
>   And up to higher lot redeem'd.

> For all the motley tribe that pair,
>   And to their cover skim,
> Became his more immediate care,
> The raven urgent in his pray'r,
>   And those that make the woodland hymn.

> For every creature left at will
>   The howling WASTE to roam,
> Which live upon the blood they spill,
> From his own hands receive their fill,
>   What time the desert was his home.

---

[20] John Newton, *Discourses, or Sermons, as Intended for the Pulpit* (1760), 'Sermon V. On Searching the Scriptures', in *Works*, p. 335.

> They knew him well, and could not err,
>   To him they all appeal'd;
> The beast of sleek or shaggy fur,
> And found their natures to recur
>   To what they were in Eden's field.

The ascension itself is not mentioned until the final lines of the hymn, and in these stanzas Christ is described as caring for a variety of creatures, probably drawn, according to Marcus Walsh's illuminating notes, from both the Old and New Testaments, and perhaps also from the apocryphal Gospel of Pseudo-Matthew. The tenses used in the description of Christ's care for the creatures are puzzling, in the juxtaposition of the habitual present and the past: does he refer to every creature which lives upon blood now, or only those present 'What time the desert' was Christ's home? Indeed, the specificity of that 'time', and of Christ's 'more immediate care' for the birds, seems incongruous, following the assertion that Christ's grace redeems the accidental 'modes of site and place' to a 'higher lot'. But it is exactly this movement which, I think, characterizes Smart's emblematic language. The creatures described in these lines 'recur' to their pre-lapsarian natures, natures which were substantial rather than accidental, and their 'ascension', their elevation to the 'higher' plane of the substantial, parallels that of Christ, which is the subject of the poem. But this ascension is achieved not through denying the accidental and particular nature of the beasts Christ feeds, but rather through the description of this as simultaneously substantial and pre-lapsarian. Throughout the hymn, Christ's ascension is described as a miraculous achievement that denies historical process, rather than as a specific historical event. It redeems through a translation in the charity of grace every 'particle of space', every accidental incident and place. To 'the working mind's review', to its perception of the analogical coherence of the Bible, there is no disjunction between the historically distinct events of Eden and Christ's life: Christ here feeds the animals of Isaiah's prophecy, for the logic of the hymn is typological rather than historical.[21]

Later in the same hymn Smart writes:

> For on some special good intent,
>   Advancement or relief,

---

[21] 'Hymn XIV', ll. 11–30. Smart writes, in the second stanza of this hymn: 'The text is full, and strong to do / The glorious subject right; / But on the working mind's review / The letter's like the spirit true, / And clear and evident as light' (ll. 6–10).

Or some great evil to prevent,
Or some perfection to augment,
    He held his life of tears and grief.

'Twas his the pow'rs of hell to curb,
    And men possess'd to free;
And all the blasting fiends disturb
From seed of bread, from flow'r and herb,
    From fragrant shrub and stately tree.[22]

In the first of these stanzas, Christ's mission is described with apparent specificity: Christ came 'on some special good intent', or with a particular aim, but in the second stanza the speciality, the potentially accidental and historically specific nature of that aim, is revealed to be universal and substantial: ''Twas his the pow'rs of hell to curb'. The language appropriate to Christ's mission, as the God of eternity manifested in time, must represent both substance and accident, both the historically specific and the typological revelation, and it does so, in these stanzas, through the elusive particular indicated by 'some special . . . intent', which, devoid of the context only interpretable by the historian, is revealed to be universal—to disturb 'all the blasting fiends'. Smart's poetry, in its adherence to the language of the Bible, within a syntax that is peculiarly eighteenth-century, reclaims the logic of prophecy for the Anglican congregation.

These typological relations may seem too complex to serve any congregational function, or to fulfil the idea of a biblical interpretation as accessible to the ploughman as to the scholar, and there is a sense in which the *Song to David* also involves a degree of obscurity, most notably in the image of the seven pillars, which seems at odds with the reasons for introducing hymns into the service, and for retranslating the Psalms, that I mentioned earlier. *The Christian's Magazine* commented, on the first publication of *A Song to David*, that 'This is proposed as a recommendation of Mr Smart's intended translation of the Psalms: but, we fear, it will have the contrary effect, as it is, in many places far beyond all comprehension', and there is clearly some justice in the complaint. I will return later in this chapter to the problem of difficulty in the *Song*, but here I want to point out that we should be careful to distinguish between a kind of poetry that presents problems both for modern critics and for the eighteenth-century reader, and poetry that might have been understood, in the eighteenth century, to follow

[22] 'Hymn XIV', ll. 46–55.

principles which, albeit for a brief period, were thought to make the language of revelation accessible to 'every Soul', whether or not, in fact, they did so. While there may clearly be dangers in attributing any remarkable degree of sophistication to the eighteenth-century reader confronted with Smart's poetry, we cannot treat the statements of eighteenth-century poets and divines about the incapacity of readers to understand religious texts as though they were simple statements of fact, for they were also contributions to a lively debate both within and without the Church. We are not in a position to assess whether or not a ploughman might have experienced difficulty with the length of John Newton's sentences, but we can distinguish between the ministerial attitude of a man like Trapp, who regards the laity as unqualified to read the scriptures, and those of the Wesleys, who were confident that their followers could extract 'all the most important truths of our most holy religion' from their hymn-book.[23]

The typological language and prophetic or parabolic logic of Smart's *Hymns*, I therefore suggest, do not provide, in the degree of difficulty they seem to involve, a means of assessing the suitability of the hymns for congregational performance. The hymns of the Wesleys, as has frequently been observed, also involve a considerable degree of sophistication, in their 'literary' qualities, in their treatment of complex theological issues, and in the music appropriate to their performance, but they nevertheless provided a powerful means of consolidating the people they were commonly used among. The use of hymns in the eighteenth century could take any one of a number of forms: Watts notes that he has divided his hymns into short units of sense, of a line or two, so that they can be performed in the same manner as the Psalms, where the clerk would read out a line or couplet to be repeated in song by the congregation, and it seems likely that the Methodists were also obliged to adopt a version of this practice, though their hymns seem also to have been performed by the congregation without this leadership. Both Watts and the Wesleys also describe their hymns as suitable for reading in private, as meditations or devout exercises. By the mid century, the practice of engaging special choirs to perform hymns, psalms, and anthems in four or five parts was popular, though there were also advocates for simpler harmonies like those of ballads.[24]

---

[23] *Christian's Magazine*, 4 (1764), 479. Fenwick, *Psalter*, Preface, p. xxviii. Wesley, *Collection*, Preface, pp. 73–4. See Marcus Walsh's Introduction to the *Hymns*, 'Style, Genre, and Structure', pp. 23–7, in *Smart II*.

[24] Watts, *Hymns*, Preface, pp. x, xiii–xiv. See Beckerlegge, 'The Hymn-book in

With this wealth of methods of performance to choose from, it certainly seems difficult to exclude the possibility that Smart's *Hymns* were designed to be sung as part of the service, and the absence of music composed for the purpose may have more to do with their disappointing reception than with their internal qualities. Smart's prayer in *Jubilate Agno*—'The Lord magnify the idea of Smart singing hymns on this day in the eyes of the whole University of Cambridge' (D. 148)—and perhaps his reference to his habit of singing at night 'a psalm of my own composing' indicate his wish, at that early date at least, that his hymns should be sung, as well, perhaps, as read, and that they should be publicly performed. Several of the hymns themselves also provide evidence that they may be appropriate both for the private prayers of the closet and for church worship, and the hymn for 'St. Peter', which contrasts the practice of the Anglican Church with that of Roman Catholicism, seems to confirm that Smart saw hymns as complementary to the liturgy, and to imply that the hymnist, like David, has the almost ministerial duty to supply the congregation with a common language of praise. The Anglican congregation, in the hymn, take occasion to celebrate their possession of the true legacy of Peter,

> Wherefore too this day we hold
> As of honourable note,
> We of Christ's peculiar fold,
> That protest against the goat.
>
> Wheresoe'er we are dispers'd,
> In the ocean, or ashore,
> Still the service is rehears'd,
> Still we worship and adore.
>
> Thanks to God we have a form
> Of sound words aboard the ship,
> In the calm, or on the storm,
> To exalt him heart and lip.

Methodist worship', in the Introduction to Wesley's *Collection*. See also Donald Davie, 'The Language of the Eighteenth-Century Hymn', in *Dissentient Voice: The Ward-Philips Lectures for 1980 with Some Related Pieces* (Notre Dame, Ind., 1982); Marshall and Todd, *Congregational Hymns*, chs. 2–3. See *Christian's Magazine*, 2 (1761), 121–3, 263–6; 3 (1762), 170–1, 595; Simon Browne, *Hymns and Spiritual Songs. In Three Books* (1720), Preface; William Tans'ur, *Sacred Mirth: or, The Pious Soul's Daily Delight* (1739), Preface.

There Jehovah's dove may perch
On the topmast as she swims—
Ev'ry vessel is a church
Meet for praise, for pray'r, and hymns.[25]

V

I have suggested, then, that the figurative language of Smart's later poetry can best be understood in the context of contemporary debates about the accessibility of biblical history and poetry, and I shall look now at *A Song to David* as 'a recommendation' and introduction to the idea of the religious poet, in relation to the interpretation of history, that informs Smart's more directly liturgical poetry. The *Song*, as I have said, employs a figurative language of emblem and typology which could be understood as guaranteeing the accessibility, the immediacy of the divine revelation which might otherwise appear historically, geographically, and culturally remote. Though that language might also be responsible, in some passages of the poem, for the obscurity noted by contemporary reviewers, it nevertheless represents, in the *Song* as well as in the hymn for 'St. Peter', the 'form / Of sound words' which underwrites the figurative unity of a Christian congregation dispersed through time as well as place.[26]

The distinctive character of the poetic language of the *Song* can perhaps most clearly be demonstrated through the contrast it presents to the treatment of David in other eighteenth-century hymns. The opening stanzas of the *Song* emphasize the primary importance of David's character as the king and high priest of Israel, whose responsibility it is 'To *keep* the days on Zion's mount, / And send the year to his account, / With dances and with songs'. As Walsh points

[25] *JA*, B1. 32. See e.g. 'Hymn XXIV. St. Michael and All Angels', 'Hymn I. New Year', 'Hymn IX. The Annunciation of the Blessed Virgin', 'Hymn XI. Easter Day'. 'Hymn XX. St. Peter', ll. 45–60; ll. 53–4 allude to 2 Tim. 1: 13: 'Hold fast the form of sound words, which thou hast heard of me, in faith and love which is in Christ Jesus.' This text was commonly applied to the liturgy, or to established doctrine: see e.g. John Gill, *The Form of Sound Words to be held fast: Being a Charge Delivered at the Ordination of the Rev. Mr. John Reynolds. To be the Pastor of a Church of Christ Meeting near Cripplegate* (1766). See also the nautical imagery employed in the discussion of this festival in Robert Nelson, *A Companion for the Festivals and Fasts of the Church of England* (1707; this edn. Dublin, 1817), 287.

[26] *Christian's Magazine*, 4 (1764), 479. For a fuller account of the discussion of the *Song* in contemporary reviews, see Marcus Walsh, '*A Song to David*: Introduction', in *Smart II*.

out, David's task is here both to observe the religious festivals, and to record the history of Israel: history, in the religion of the Hebrews, is constantly recapitulated or rehearsed in ceremony. David, as the 'minister of praise at large', is engaged in representing the process of history in the fixed forms of ritual, and the *Song* parallels or repeats this ministerial act in describing the events of David's life not as a continuous history, but as a sequence of fixed and emblematic incidents which exemplify his twelve typologically significant virtues. Smart introduces this achronological account of David's deeds in a stanza which emphasizes its emblematic as opposed to historical character:

> Great, valiant, pious, good, and clean,
> Sublime, contemplative, serene,
>   Strong, constant, pleasant, wise!
> Bright effluence of exceeding grace;
> Best man!—the swiftness and the race,
>   The peril, and the prize!

The echo, in the fourth of these lines, of Milton's invocation to light as the 'Bright effluence of bright essence increate' serves to underline the typological nature of David's virtues, and thus the sense in which the incidents 'from the history of his life' not only describe stages in that particular historical process but also exemplify the super-historical drama of redemption. They describe both the peril and the prize, both the accidental event and its substantial significance.[27]

Thus, for example, Smart writes of David's most famous battle:

> Valiant—the word and up he rose—
> The fight—he triumph'd o'er the foes,
>   Whom God's just laws abhor;
> And arm'd in gallant faith he took
> Against the boaster, from the brook,
>   The weapons of the war.

David's encounter with Goliath becomes the triumph of faith over the adversary, and the symbol of valiant Christianity. Charles Wesley sees a similar significance in the popular story in his hymn 'David and

---

[27] *Song*, st. ii, ll. 10–12. Walsh notes, on l. 10, that 'the italics emphasize the double sense, to celebrate or observe a festival, and to maintain a record' (*Smart II*, p. 430). *Song*, st. iii, l. 14. See stt. iv–xvi. St. iv, ll. 19–24. Milton, *Paradise Lost*, bk. III, l. 6. *Song*, Contents, p. 128.

Goliath': the Christian protagonist takes the part of David, and is victorious, as in Smart's hymn, through faith:

> In the strength of God I rise,
>   I run to meet the foe;
> Faith the Word of power applies,
>   And lays the giant low;
> Faith in Jesu's conqu'ring name
>   Slings the sin-destroying stone,
> Points the Word's unerring aim,
>   And brings the monster down.

But Wesley's treatment of the story involves a very different understanding of the relation between the Old Testament and the modern believer to that implied in Smart's *Song* and *Hymns*. In this hymn, as in the more famous 'Wrestling Jacob', or hymn 156 on Daniel in the lions' den, Wesley employs the dramatic first person, apparently to identify the singer with the Hebrew hero, but that identification appropriates the biblical narrative to the situation of the Methodist worshipper, and does not establish the kind of typological correspondence that characterizes Smart's poetry.[28]

In Wesley's hymn, the singer repeatedly questions the identity of Goliath, until he finally recognizes him at the end of the second stanza:

> Tallest of the earth-born race,
>   They tremble at his power,
> Fly before the monster's face,
>   And own him conqueror;
> Who this mighty champion is,
>   Nature answers from within:
> He is my own wickedness,
>   My own besetting sin.

The lyric narrative, like that of 'Wrestling Jacob', is more concerned to struggle with the terms on which the biblical story can be undertood to enact or to dramatize the Methodist's personal search for salvation, than to explore its historical or typological significance. This, of course, is the strength of Wesley's rare hymns on Old Testament subjects—it gives them a striking dramatic power, but it clearly involves a very different method of biblical interpretation to that implicit in Smart's hymns. For Wesley, the identity of Goliath, the

---

[28] St. vi, ll. 31–6. *Collection*, p. iv, sect. ii, hymn 269, st. 6. See pt. iii, sect. ii, hymn 136, 'Wrestling Jacob', and hymn 156.

meaning of the Old Testament narrative, is achieved when the singer recognizes in it an internal drama of conversion, when the giant has been fully appropriated to the context of Methodist faith, whereas in Smart's treatment of the incident, and of the character of David, analogy provides a method of interpretation which, like Lowth's Mystical Allegory, allows the several possible interpretations of the biblical narrative to coexist. Where, in Wesley, the framework of the biblical story provides a means of describing the process of the believer's struggle for salvation, in Smart, the history of David provides instances which are both the 'peril, and the prize'—which are the means of representing the historical event, its typological representation of the substantial Christian hero, and the exemplary qualities the religious poet and the devout worshipper emulate.[29]

Cowper's hymn 'Jehovah-Nissi, the Lord My Banner' provides a further contrast with the *Song*, which illuminates the nature of its typological language. Cowper praises the two Christian champions, David and Gideon, and contrasts their confident trust in God to the singer's own weakness. The singer knows that trust in God has given his soul the strength to quell 'a thousand foes', but he fears that his faith is not constantly deserving:

> But unbelief, self-will,
>   Self-righteousness and pride,
> How often do they steal,
>   My weapon from my side?
> Yet David's LORD, and Gideon's friend,
> Will help his servant to the end.

The Old Testament stories of David and Gideon are sources of encouragement to the worshipper, though they are not fully appropriated to his condition, and he is as concerned to emphasize the contrast between his faith and that of the Hebrew heroes as he is to draw comfort from the parallel they suggest.[30]

Cowper's use of the biblical stories, however, has more in common with John Newton's emblematic hymns than with Smart's *Song*. The authors of the *Olney Hymns* draw comparisons between the circumstances of the worshipper and the emblem or story which depend as much on the asymmetry between the two as on the correspondence they reveal.

---

[29] Hymn 269, st. 2. *Song*, st. iv, l. 24.
[30] *Olney Hymns*, bk. I, hymn 4, ll. 23, 25–30, in *The Poems of William Cowper*, ed. Baird and Ryskamp, vol. i.

For example, in his hymn on 'Lightning in the Night', Newton carefully establishes the particular details appropriate to the comparison he wishes to make:

> The lightning's flash did not create
> The op'ning prospect it reveal'd;
> But only shew'd the real state
> Of what the darkness had conceal'd.
>
> Just so, we by a glimpse discern
> The glorious things within the vail,—
> That, when in darkness, we may learn
> To live by faith, till light prevail.

He excludes all those features that do not further his lesson, and delimits the interpretative significance of the (in this instance) natural event. The terms of Smart's analogical interpretations, however, in their conciseness, and in their lack of explicit application, suggest a lesson that is both less specific and less determinately interpretable. Smart's poetry works continually to suggest the figurative richness of its subjects—even commonplace plants and animals seem charged with an implicit significance that application to the accidental circumstances of the worshipper would not exhaust; whereas for Cowper and Newton, the point of explicit correspondence and comparison—the recognition of the moral to be drawn from the lightning flash—seems to conclude its emblematic significance.[31]

Critics have often praised the *Song to David* for the conciseness of its imagery, reinforced by the exceptional skill with which Smart's poetry handles complex metrical rhythms. In his stanza on David and Goliath, these qualities produce a poetry capable of compressing, and yet clearly expressing, themes Charles Wesley explored over eight more protracted stanzas. This kind of concise, emphatic, and yet musical poetry is peculiarly hospitable to the syntactical sophistication Smart's use of analogy demands. Thus, for example, Smart writes of David's poetic treatment of 'the works of nature in all directions, either particularly or collectively considered':

> Of beasts—the beaver plods his task;
> While the sleek tygers roll and bask,
> Nor yet the shades arouse:

---

[31] Newton, *Olney Hymns*, bk.II, hymn lxxxiv, stt. 5–6, in *Works*. See Watts, *Hymns*, bk. I, hymn cxlvi; bk. II, hymn xiii.

> Her cave the mining coney scoops;
> Where o'er the mead the mountain stoops,
> The kids exult and brouse.

Here the relative times and spaces indicated by 'while' and 'yet' and 'where' seem to describe a syntactical continuity which establishes the specificity of the beaver and tiger, or coney and kid, but defines their temporal and spatial positions in relation to an evasive symbolic topography. The beasts are, as it were, caught in a moment of suspended animation, in which the very particularity of the verbs they govern seems to guarantee their timelessness. Thus, the beaver's intent, as he 'plods', seems to express an enduring and substantial characteristic, rather than, or as well as, a particular aim, just as the sense in which 'the mountain stoops' describes a permanent inclination, rather than a specific intent or finite task. This kind of slippage between the particular and the collective, the transitory and enduring act, is in part a function of the absence or elusiveness of the perceiving subject, or of the difficulty of determining, in these passages of the poem, whether we read David's poetry, or an account of it. In comparison to, say, the classical landscape of Pope's introduction to *Windsor-Forest*, where the repeated use of 'here' and 'there' establishes a topographical structure familiar from landscape painting, this poetry presents a series of emblematic pictures whose syntactical relations resemble rather the formal structures which lend an overall unity to the panels of a stained-glass window.[32]

In Smart's description of the beasts, the indeterminate and yet precise designation of their spatial relations informs them with emblematic significance, and his lines on the vegetable creation describe a similar doubling of apparently specific temporal relations:

> Trees, plants, and flow'rs—of virtuous root;
> Gem yielding blossom, yielding fruit,
>   Choice gums and precious balm;
> Bless ye the nosegay in the vale,
> And with the sweetners of the gale
>   Enrich the thankful psalm.

[32] On the musical qualities of Smart's poetry see Davie, *Augustan Lyric*, Introduction, p. 21. I quote from the Contents, *Song*, p. 128. St. xxv, ll. 145–50. I refer to the lines: 'Here waving Groves a checquer'd Scene display, / And part admit and part exclude the Day; / As some coy Nymph her Lover's warm Address / Nor quite indulges, nor can quite repress. / There, interspers'd in Lawns and opening Glades, / Thin Trees arise that shun each others Shades. / Here in full Light the russet Plains extend; / There wrapt in Clouds the blueish Hills ascend' (Alexander Pope, *Windsor-Forest*, ll. 17–24).

The play, in the second half of the stanza, on the relation between scent and language, smell and sound, is of course a favourite device of Smart's poetry, but here the lines that introduce this theme seem to pave the way for that more fully figurative idea. Smart introduces the three main categories of vegetable, and describes what might be either the process of growth, the organic progress from root to gem (or bud), to flower, fruit and balm, or a series of discrete and simultaneously present images, which yield or give way to one another in the sequence of the verse. The minimal syntactical relations decribed in the stanza and the stress the rhythm places on isolated phrases seem to emphasize the relevance of both possibilities to a poetry that describes nature 'in all directions'.[33]

The almost imagistic quality of Smart's poetry, and its ability to suggest a wealth of significance in the images it isolates, is perhaps most explicitly demonstrated in the passage on the adoration exemplified in and excited by the 'right use' of the seasons. Smart writes:

> With vinous syrup cedars sprout;
> From rocks pure honey gushing out,
>   For ADORATION springs:
> All scenes of painting croud the map
> Of nature; to the mermaid's pap
>   The scaled infant clings.

The stanza represents the scenes of creation as at once natural, prophetically imagistic, and pictorial: the first line describes the luxurious natural bounty of the cedars, the second describes the honey which fed Jacob, and which enlightened Jonathan to the oppressiveness of Saul's government, and the second half of the stanza describes the painterly or cartographic image of the mermaid as appropriate to 'the map / Of nature'. The contexts from which these images are drawn— the history and poetry of the Bible, the iconography of pictorial geography—are strikingly discrete, and yet they share a common language of adoration, and their emblematic significance is increased rather than diminished by the abruptness of the transitions between their juxtaposed descriptions. The stanza thus obeys the injunction with which this sequence on the seasons opens: 'Heap up the measure, load the scales, / And good to goodness add': it heaps these images together without reducing their almost ostentatiously displayed variety and incongruity to coherent uniformity.[34]

[33] St. xxii, ll. 127–32. Contents, p. 128.
[34] Contents, p. 128. St. liv, ll. 319–24. See 1 Sam. 14: 24–30. St. l, ll. 296–7.

The nature of the poetry these heaped and loaded images produce may be indicated by the reference to the honey gushing from the rock, which alludes to the prophetic ode Moses addressed to the 'congregation of Israel'. Moses reminds them of God's goodness to Jacob, the progenitor of their tribe:

So the LORD alone did lead him, and *there was* no strange god with him.

He made him ride on the high places of the earth, that he might eat the increase of the fields; and he made him to suck honey out of the rock, and oil out of the flinty rock;

Butter of kine, and milk of sheep, with fat of lambs, and rams of the breed of Bashan, and goats, with the fat of kidneys of wheat; and thou didst drink the pure blood of the grape.

Lowth argued, in his *Lectures*, that the ode combined the qualities of lyric and prophetic poetry, and that it

consists of sentences, pointed, energetic, concise, and splendid; that the sentiments are truly elevated and sublime, the language bright and animated, the expression and phraseology uncommon; while the mind of the poet never continues fixed to any single point, but glances continually from one object to another.

Smart's ode, I think, may be read as an attempt to imitate these qualities, in order to produce a poetry whose 'prophetic' power will, like the prophetic poetry of the Bible, transcend the continuity of history, and translate the 'modes of site and place' into the redemptive 'higher lot' of charitable adoration.[35]

The figure of David describes, in the *Song*, the ministerial mediation through which this translation is effected. David is represented, in the closing stages of the hymn, praying for the creation of which he is the pastoral leader:

> Beauteous, yea beauteous more than these,
> The shepherd king upon his knees,
>   For his momentous trust;
> With wish of infinite conceit,
> For man, beast, mute, the small and great,
>   And prostrate dust to dust.

The 'infinite conceit' of David's prayers may refer to their ability to praise nature both particularly and collectively, to express the private

---

[35] Deut. 31: 30; 32: 12–14. Lowth, *Lectures*, vol. ii, lect. xxviii, p. 257; vol. i., lect. xv, p. 325. 'Hymn XIV. The Ascension of Our Lord Jesus Christ', ll. 13, 15.

circumstances both of the life of David and of every worshipper, and to describe prophetically the progress of the Church and of Christ in the universal drama of salvation. The nature of that conceit, which gives it this figurative power, is perhaps indicated in the central stanzas of the poem, where David's science, exemplified in the cryptic figure of the seven pillars, is described:

> O DAVID, scholar of the Lord!
> Such is thy science, whence reward
>   And infinite degree;
> O strength, O sweetness, lasting ripe!
> God's harp thy symbol, and thy type
>   The lion and the bee!

David, the type of Christ, is himself the antetype of the lion and the bee, and the praise he offers, which expresses the thanksgiving of creation, employs the figurative language of inspiration. In these lines, God's harp is David's symbol, and David is thus the instrument on which, in *Jubilate Agno*, God played a tune which was 'a work of creation' (B1. 247).[36]

   This image is not, of course, the private property of Smart's poetry: an article in *The Christian's Magazine* on the 'inspiration of the Sacred Scriptures' employed a similar musical image (derived from Justin Martyr) to describe the sacred penmen, who

had not need of any art to compose their works; all that was required on their parts was, that they should have a *purified* mind, wherein to receive the operation of the Holy Ghost, who descending from heaven, as a *musical bow*, all divine, made use of upright men, as a musical instrument, to reveal to us the knowledge of divine things.

David acts as the medium through which 'the knowledge of divine things', expressed in the cryptic science of the seven pillars, is revealed, and his symbolic presence also provides the occasion for the expression of the praise and adoration of creation. The elements of creation, in the poem, become the emblematic expression of David's adoration, strength, sweetness—the heroic attributes that characterize him as the super-historical champion of the Christian cause. David represents or repeats the 'genuine word' of creation, which expresses its prophetic and figurative significance—the infinite conceit of his prayers manifest the glory and grace of creation in the redeemed

---

[36] St. lxxx, ll. 475–80. St. xxxviii, ll. 223–8. See Judg. 14, and Rev. 5: 5.

language of passion, as one of the concluding stanzas on the use of the senses suggests:

> For ADORATION, all the paths
> Of grace are open, all the baths
>   Of purity refresh;
> And all the rays of glory beam
> To deck the man of God's esteem,
>   Who triumphs o'er the flesh.[37]

VI

The symbolic and typological significance David takes on in the *Song* may represent, as I have suggested, a key to the liturgical poetry of Smart's *Hymns* and *Psalms*, for while the relation of the *Song* to the *Psalms* is clearly more direct, it also illuminates the ministerial function and analogical language of the *Hymns*. When, for example, Smart writes in his hymn on 'The Annunciation of the Blessed Virgin' that the 'new work' of the incarnation requires a new song, a new kind of poetry, the nature of the poetry he then goes on to offer depends upon a logic most fully explored in the *Song*. Smart writes, in the concluding stanzas of the hymn:

> Praise Hannah, of the three,
> That sang in Mary's key;
> With her that made her psalm
> Beneath the bow'ring palm;
>   With the dame—Bethulia's boast,
>   Honour'd o'er th'Assyrian host.
>
> Praise him faith, hope, and love
> That tend Jehovah's dove;
> By men from lust repriev'd
> As females best conceiv'd;
>   To remount the man and muse
>   Far above all earthly views.

[37] *Christian's Magazine*, 2 (1761), 3–4. St. xlix, l. 291. St. lxx, ll. 415–20; these stanzas on the senses do not, I think, involve the denial of the pleasures of the senses, in terms of a simple opposition between the body and the soul, but the translation of those pleasures into a 'higher lot', where all 'paths' are means of adoration. It is therefore interesting to note the correspondence between these stanzas and the five engravings after Francis Hayman depicting the senses; see Brian Allen, *Francis Hayman* (New Haven, Conn. and London, 1987), 142–4.

Here the transcendent achievement of 'man and muse' is to recognize the analogical relation between the women of the Old Testament— Hannah, Deborah, and Judith—and the personifications of faith, hope, and love: a feat which, as Marcus Walsh notes, shows the redeemed worshipper's freedom from lust, because it shows his ability to use the pure emblematic language of iconography, which, in its association with the Virgin Mary, so frequently denotes the corruption of the Catholic Church.[38]

The praiseworthy purity of the worshipper's conception of Judith as love is particularly striking. Judith dressed herself in 'all her woman's attire' in order to gain access to King Holofernes alone in retirement in his tent. When Holofernes, in delight, had drunk 'much more wine than he had drunk at any time in one day since he was born', Judith cut off his head. Biblical commentators experienced some difficulty in describing Judith's conduct as exemplary, but here the conception of it as an emblem of love exemplifies the nature of the new song appropriate to the miraculous occasion the hymn celebrates:

> Hail mystery! thou source
> Of nature's plainest course,
> How much his work transcends
> Thine usual means and ends—
> Wherefore call'd, we shall not spare
> Louder praise, and oft'ner pray'r.

The hymn celebrates a work which transcends 'means and ends', transcends the causal logic of nature and history, and the treatment of Judith, not as the object of Holofernes' lust, but as the pure emblem of love, involves a conception of history that shows the charity or candour of the believer, in his ability to abstract Christianized types of virtue from their context in Hebrew history and thus to reprieve them just as he is himself reprieved.[39]

The analogical language of the *Song to David* may also illuminate a feature of the *Hymns* which is perhaps more puzzling, and more

---

[38] 'Hymn IX', ll. 43–54. See *Smart II*, p. 384.

[39] Judith 12: 15, 20. See e.g. the Introduction to the book in D'Oyly and Mant, where Dr Robert Gray (Bishop of Bristol) comments that 'If the address, with which she accomplished her designs, should be thought to partake too much of an insidious character; we may be permitted at least to admire the heroick patriotism and piety which prompted her to undertake the exploit: the urgency and importance of the occasion will likewise excuse the indiscreet exposure of her person to intemperate passions; and in the general description of her character, she may be allowed to have presented an exemplary display of the virtues which become the widowed state.' 'Hymn IX', ll. 19–24.

significant. The *Hymns* frequently emphasize the salvific and effective importance of divine grace, and the correspondent duty of man to offer gratitude, and while the concepts of grace and gratitude form an important element of Anglican faith, the prominence they are given in Smart's liturgical poetry is surprising in this period. For the power of grace, as opposed to works, is a distinguishing feature of dissenting beliefs, and the increasing emphasis on practical piety which marks Anglican sermons of the second half of the century reflects the Church's concern to dissociate itself from those beliefs, as well as the development of the perception of the personal or individual, rather than the social, as the focus of moral concern that I discussed earlier in relation to the sermons of Bishop Sherlock. We might expect the determinedly Anglican nature of Smart's *Hymns* to be evidenced in the kind of emphasis on the personal religion of the heart, and the morality of intention, of sincerity, that the Seatonian poems of this period show, rather than in the concept of grace as the determinant of action that the opening stanzas of Smart's hymn on the 'Epiphany' describes:

> GRACE, thou source of each perfection,
>   Favour from the height thy ray;
> Thou the star of all direction
>   Child of endless truth and day.
>
> Thou that bidst my cares be calmer,
>   Lectur'd what to seek and shun,
> Come, and guide a western palmer
>   To the Virgin and her Son.[40]

The hymn for 'Epiphany' does also, of course, refer to virtuous actions or works—the worshipper has been 'Lectur'd what to seek or shun', and Smart's emphasis on grace may reflect the prayers for the festival, or other sources. But these qualifications do not pose a satisfactory answer to the questions raised by the frequency with which grace is mentioned in his hymns: religious debates, in this period, and in particular the controversies that distinguish Anglican orthodoxy from other Protestant movements, often turn on the consideration of relative emphases, rather than on more substantial contradictions; and in the context of such well-aired disputes, we cannot relegate the importance of grace in Smart's hymns to a question of the influence of sources without considering the implications of that influence. I do not, however, want to suggest that the role of grace in the hymns is

---

[40] See pp. 96–103 above. 'Hymn III', ll. 1–8.

˙inconsistent with their Anglican character and possible complementary
relation to the liturgy, but to suggest that, in the period at which Smart
is writing, the concepts of grace, perfection, works, and riches are the
'distinguishing Words of Sects and Parties', and they are therefore
used with a cautious precision which demands, and will repay, close
inspection. The particular nature of the beliefs Smart describes in his
hymns are, I want to show, intimately related to the issue of their
congregational and liturgical function: like the hymns of Watts,
Wesley, and Newton, Smart's hymns instruct the reader in divinity,
and thus confirm their congregational identity.[41]

The importance of grace, then, may provide a route to the
understanding of the kind of Anglicanism, the idea of the Church, that
Smart's hymns involve; but before I discuss the use of grace I want to
look briefly at the treatment of the related issue of works in the hymns,
for grace and works are so closely related that they can hardly be
considered in isolation. The works, or ethical precepts, to which Smart
gives primary importance, and with which he is most concerned,
involve the use of riches. Smart discusses this theme in many of his
hymns, but it is particularly important in Hymns XVIII to XXII. The
first of these celebrates the festival of St Barnabas, and is appropriate
to this subject because Barnabas was celebrated for having sold his
inheritance in order to support his fellow Christians. Smart takes
occasion from this to condemn worldly possessions. He writes:

> Hence instructed, let us learn
> Heav'n and heav'nly things to earn,
>   And with want by pray'r to cope;
> To the Lord your wealth resign,
> Destribution is divine,
>   Misers have no hope.

As Marcus Walsh notes, this unequivocal statement marks an unusual
position in the contemporary debate provoked by the commercialization
of eighteenth-century society. It departs decisively from the advice
given in Nelson's *Companion for the Festivals and Fasts of the Church of
England*, which Smart's hymns otherwise employ extensively. Nelson

---

[41] The fourth prayer Nelson recommends for this festival asks 'That thy holy Word
may govern all my Paths and direct all my Ways', but the emphasis of his account is on
the practical implications of the duties of charity, prayer, and mortification, and the
dependence of these on the exercise of the will, rather than on the governing power of
grace or the Word (*Companion*, p. 106, see also pp. 103–4). See Walsh's notes to 'Hymn
III', *Smart II*, p. 374. Watts, *Hymns*, Preface, p. ix.

observes that this festival teaches us 'To be ready to contribute to the Relief of our Fellow Christians; and when their Necessities are great and pressing, to abridge ourselves of some Conveniences, rather than suffer them to be oppressed with want.' Nelson's lesson, of course, where the Christian exchanges for present plenty an 'Interest in . . . Faith', presented a very much more attractive bargain than did Smart's, and it is difficult to find anybody else, in the 1760s, advocating as extreme a rejection of acquisitiveness as the hymn enjoins.[42]

This uncompromising rejection is interesting in relation to Smart's attitude to grace because it distinguishes his position if anything more sharply from that of Methodist and Evangelical dissent than from that of the Church of England. While the Church, to put it baldly, spent the first half of the century accommodating itself to commercial values, and in the third quarter of the century was primarily concerned with issues of conduct, of practical piety, and of missionary endeavour, John Wesley preached on the viciousness of undercutting your neighbour's prices, while Newton advocated fair dealing and the full payment of taxes. Edward Young devoted much of his *Night-Thoughts* to the immorality of commercial behaviour and the acquisition of wealth, but, like Nelson, he employs a discourse of spiritualized mercantile exchange to describe the square deal offered by faith, and he assumes that the believer who rejects commercial gain has a 'Competence . . . vital to Content' to fall back on. Smart's divine 'Destribution' (notably mitigated by his enthusiasm for imperial expansion) is paralleled most closely in the work of William Law, whose antipathy towards material possessions had come, by the mid century, to indicate mystical insanity rather than holiness. Law argued, in his *Practical Treatise upon Christian Perfection*, which was in other respects an important source of Wesley's beliefs, that Christ's injunctions against riches applied directly to the modern Christian. While he acknowledged that some aspects of Christ's teachings were peculiar to the age in which he lived, the duty of distribution appealed, he argued, to the transhistorical inward state of the believer:

Let us therefore not deceive ourselves, the Gospel preaches the *same* Doctrines to us, that our saviour taught his first Disciples, and though it may not call us to the same *external* State of the Church, yet it infallibly calls us to the same *inward* State of Holiness and Newness of Life.[43]

---

[42] See Acts 4: 36–7, and Nelson, *Companion*, ch. 25. 'Hymn XVIII. St. Barnabas', ll. 31–6. See *Smart II*, p. 406. Nelson, *Companion*, p. 263.

Law argues that the unity of identity, to which the Gospel directs its lessons, is dissipated by worldly and material interests, which make man 'every Minute different from himself', but is consolidated by the 'entire Change' that faith brings about, and which reveals

that Christianity is a Calling that puts an End to all other Callings; that we are no longer to consider it as our proper State or Employment to take care of Oxen, look after an Estate, or attend the most plausible Affairs of Life; but to reckon every Condition as equally trifling.

The change faith brings about, which unifies identity, and makes the teaching of Christ directly accessible, involves the rejection of material goods in favour of Christian perfection—the controversial conception which Wesley adopted, and progressively adapted, from Law's teaching. Smart's use of the term 'perfection' is ambiguous, but he takes from Law, I suggest, both his radical condemnation of riches and his conception of a Christian community at odds with the divisive commercialism of the age.[44]

The particular importance Smart attaches to grace, in his *Hymns*, can best be understood in the context of his idea of the congregation— an idea modelled on Law's concept of the community. Grace is the reward of prayer.

> O CHARITY! that couldst receive
>   The dying thief's repentant pray'r;
> And didst upon the cross relieve
>   Thy fellow-suff'rer there!
>
> Tho' he revil'd among the rest—
>   Before the point of utmost dread,
> Grace unto pray'r was first imprest,
>   And then forgiveness sped.

---

[43] Anglican teaching on conduct and practical piety involved, at this period, a clear distinction between the acquiescence and submissive conduct enjoined on the working poor, and the duties appropriate to the urban middle class in leisure time, in domestic situations, or in retirement. See Wesley, 'Sermon L. The Use of Money', *First Series*, in *The Works of John Wesley* (1872), vol. vi, and esp. p. 128, where Wesley argues that 'We cannot, consistent with brotherly love, sell our goods below the market price'. See Newton, *Forty-One Letters*, letter xl, 'A Word to Professors in Trade', in *Works*, pp. 122–3. *N-T*, Night 6, p. 262; and see Harriet Guest and John Barrell, 'On the Use of Contradiction: Economics and Morality in the Eighteenth-Century Long Poem', in *The New Eighteenth Century: Theory, Politics, English Literature*, ed. Felicity Nussbaum and Laura Brown (New York and London, 1987). William Law, *A Practical Treatise upon Christian Perfection* (London, 1726, this 5th edn., London 1759), p. 77.

[44] Law, *Christian Perfection*, pp. 237, 39, 67.

Grace is impressed into the service of the ship of prayer as a result
of Christ's charity, but it is also the offering the worshipper makes to
Christ: the prayers of the congregation 'Can avail' because in them
Christ sanctions the return of the gift he has given:

> Take ye therefore what ye give him,
>   Of his fulness grace for grace,
> Strive to think him, speak him, live him,
>   Till you find him face to face.

Through grace, and the correspondent expression of gratitude (which
both derive from the Latin *gratia*), the 'pray'r and praises' sung by the
devout establish their direct relation to Christ, and it is in terms of that
relation that the poet can claim to speak for the congregation.[45]

In his hymn on 'The Presentation of Christ in the Temple', Smart
argues that the 'highest GRACE' was absent from the first temple of
Solomon, but was made incarnate in Christ, in the 'fabrick of the
poor', and it is as a result of the incarnation that the poet is able to offer
his hymn:

> Present ye therefore, on your knees,
>   Hearts, hands resign'd and clean;
> Ye poor and mean of all degrees,
> If he will condescend and please
>   To take at least what orphans glean—
>
> I speak for all—for them that fly,
>   And for the race that swim;
> For all that dwell in moist and dry,
> Beasts, reptiles, flow'rs and gems to vie
>   When gratitude begins her hymn.

The poet speaks for the congregation of creation in the figure of
gratitude, in the emblematic personification that expresses the uniting
presence of grace in the congregation. The use of this personification
indicates that the poet and congregation are 'from lust repriev'd' in
their commitment to the belief that 'By Jesus Christ came truth and
grace, / But none indulgence, pension, place, / The slaves of SELF to
suit': the grace available through Christ expresses their transhistorical
and congregational nature, as opposed to the divided selves of those
who are slaves to their own acquisitive lusts and interests. This

---

[45] 'Hymn VII. Ash Wednesday. First Day of Lent', ll. 1–8. 'Hymn I. New Year',
ll. 31, 33–6, 31; in this hymn the prayers of the faithful 'Can avail' because they are 'By
the Lamb himself sublim'd' (l. 32).

conception of the congregation, unified in singing the hymn of gratitude and striving to become like Christ, indicates the achievement of praise in the language of analogy, which is 'To remount the man and muse / Far above all earthly views'. The poet and the congregation are reprieved and 'remounted' by their common commitment to an identity that transcends the 'usual means and ends' of history.[46]

Redemptive grace, then, forms the conception of the congregation united in gratitude and 'remounted' above historical accident, just as it had formed the early saints of the Church. Smart describes 'St. Stephen', for example, as the miraculous effect of grace intervening in history:

> His therefore is the champion's crown—
> And his the firstlings of renown—
> O GRACE, thou never rais'd a sweeter flow'r,
> Which sprang, and gemm'd, and blossom'd in an hour.

He describes Stephen's works only in terms of the race for the 'immortal prize' and stresses that his martyrdom is the 'Sublimest work of Christ'. Smart does not suggest that the works of gratitude— repentance, resignation of wealth, or patriotic service, for example— have nothing to do with salvation, but the 'work of grace' which makes these means of salvation available is performed through the intervention of Christ. The relation between grace and works that the *Hymns* describe and imply is, I think, paralleled in Law's assurance that 'CHRISTIANITY is not a *School*, for the teaching of moral Virtue, the polishing Manners, or forming us to live a Life of this World with Decency and Gentility', but is an '*entire Change* of Life' which implies a reformation of morals and manners. Grace raises 'in an hour' the flower of Christian virtue, which is then demonstrated in historical works of goodness.[47]

This conception of the relation between grace and works, in which grace produces a 'Temper of Mind' where virtue is continually 'resisting and opposing all the Temptations to the contrary Vice', is adopted in the earlier sermons of John Wesley, and influenced Bishop Sherlock's ideas of the roles of faith and reason. In the context of the Anglican Church of the 1760s, it did not necessarily describe a

---

[46] 'Hymn VI', ll. 25, 27, 36–45. 'Hymn IX. the Annunciation of the Blessed Virgin', l. 51. 'Hymn X. The Crucifixion of Our Blessed Lord', ll. 82–4. 'Hymn IX', ll. 53–4, 22.
[47] 'Hymn XXXIII. St. Stephen', ll. 21–4, 18, 14. 'Hymn XXXV. The Holy Innocents', l. 28. *Christian Perfection*, p. 39. 'Hymn XXXIII', l. 24.

sectarian belief, but a belief in grace as the means of transcending the obstacles of culture and history, and overcoming the divisions which increasingly presented enlightened rational belief as the prerogative of a small section of the congregation. In this context, it lends a particular force to Smart's insistence that the English are the chosen tribe of 'Christ's peculiar fold', because it replaces the apparent divisions within that fold with the concept of grace as the basis for a unity of identity that overcomes the accidental differences of history and circumstance. The logic of analogy, which informs Smart's *Hymns* and *Song*, is legitimated by the transhistorical power of grace, and by the perceived urgency of the need to consolidate the congregation in the face of the divisive worldliness of commercial society. But there is of course a case for saying that the very perception of that need, and legitimation of that logic, indicate that the salvation it offers has come too late to resuscitate the identity of a congregation that has already suffered diaspora, and experienced a division that confirms that the common voice of the 'cherub Gratitude' is 'more than voice can tell'.[48]

VII

It is this possibility which, I suggest, the difficulty of Smart's *Hymns*, and the obscurity of passages of the *Song to David*, reflect. In the *Song*, David's science is exemplified by the cryptic figure of the seven pillars, designated by seven letters of the Greek alphabet, which describe the wisdom of God manifested in creation:

> The pillars of the Lord are sev'n,
> Which stand from earth to topmost heav'n;
>   His wisdom drew the plan:
> His WORD accomplished the design,
> From brightest gem to deepest mine,
>   From CHRIST enthroned to man.

Since the publication of the *Song*, critics and reviewers have puzzled over the meaning of the letters ascribed to these pillars without discovering a satisfactory explanation, and their researches have made it evident that, even if the code that unlocked the cipher were to be

[48] Law, *Christian Perfection*, p. 125. See John Wesley, *The Doctrine of Absolute Predestination Stated and Asserted*, in *Works*, xiv. 196–7. 'Hymn XX. St. Peter', l. 47. *On the Goodness*, ll. 72, 77.

found, we would be left with the question of why Smart incorporated this strong-box of esoteric knowledge as the centrepiece of the *Song*. For David's virtue, as the exemplary priest and religious poet of Israel, is intimately bound up in the *Song* with his ability to provide a form of sound words, an infinite conceit, which expresses the praise and thanksgiving of creation, and yet we seem unable to decipher the praise which the *Song* at least implicitly exhorts us to offer. In the terms of the *Song*, David is praiseworthy because he fulfils 'God's holiest charge' in his capacity as 'The minister of praise at large', but the cryptic science of his ministry seems to resist rather than invite the participation of the congregation he speaks for.[49]

The 'word' of David's science, however, also expresses the design of the WORD: it expresses a kind of knowledge, of the analogical correspondence between the created and the divine, which by this date can no longer be satisfactorily described in terms of the chain of being alone, but which poetry has found no alternative means of expressing. The most cryptic passage of the *Song* purports to represent an idea that it was, arguably, no longer within the capacity of poetry to describe, but the mysterious terms in which it does this displace any failure of comprehension from the poetry of David, and onto the congregation he addresses. A knowledge of Freemasonry, or the cabbala, may not provide the solution to David's riddle, but it may nevertheless offer a means of understanding the *kind* of challenge the seven letters present, for the enigmatic 'word' formed by the pillars appears as a piece of esoteric science, and our failure to decode its inspired wisdom indicates our exclusion from the community of those privileged by the possession of the key to its secrets. The congregation for whom David is the minister are consolidated by their membership in a society based on secret knowledge, which describes the relation between the order of creation and the variety of nature.

There is no passage in the *Hymns* which involves either the kind or the degree of difficulty the seven pillars represent; but nevertheless the syntactical and analogical sophistication of their poetry might have presented problems for the worshipper who attempted, like St Paul, to pray and sing 'with the understanding'. I have already suggested that, in this respect, the hymns may not present greater difficulties than did those of the Wesleys, but, of course, there is a significant distinction to

---

[49] St. xxx, ll. 175–80. For an account of some of these researches, see Marcus Walsh's illuminating 'Appendix: The Seven Pillars of the Lord', *Smart II*, pp. 148–55. St. iii, ll. 13, 14.

be made between them. The Wesleys' hymns are intended for an audience who could, if in difficulty, turn to a range of other forms of instruction offered to the followers of Methodism. The library Wesley published for his followers was voluminous and comprehensive, and the Methodists could always discuss their difficulties with fellow-members of their group. Watts's independent congregation could also resolve any problems presented by his hymns by turning to his extensive prose works, which would tell them how to go about thinking and reading. But it is difficult to argue that Smart's hymns fulfil a comparable congregational function, though many of the difficulties they present could be clarified by reference to the Bible, the Book of Common Prayer, and Nelson's *Companion*. The *Hymns* speak for an audience united in gratitude, and by their opposition to worldly greed, but the common nature of that audience may be more a *product* of the poetry of the hymns than a pre-existent condition of their logic.[50]

In his hymn on 'The King's Restoration', Smart describes the history of England in terms that might suggest that the audience his hymns demand has existed at least since the Reformation. In the Reformation, and the ensuing translation of the Bible, he claims, the spirit which had inspired ancient Hebrew was transferred to the English tongue, and the Church established the 'seemly course of practic pray'r and laud' which confirmed it as the descendant of the primitive Church, and the inheritor of 'The simple truth of Christ, and praise of pristine times'. He praises the 'just and fair' independence of ancient Britain, over which God exercised a special care, and traces its glorious descent through the reigns of Henry V, Elizabeth, Anne, George, and, with some delicacy, Charles II. The final stanzas of the hymn, however, explain the terms on which this patriotic celebration of Church and State is possible. There, Smart endorses the remembrance of Charles's reign with reference to his various foundations, and to the traditional celebrations of Oak-Apple Day, which commemorated the restoration of the king, but in the final stanza he makes it clear that this history should not be confused with the less golden image customary history would perceive in the same events:

> Remember all ye may of good,
>   Select the nosegay from the sod;
> But leave the brambles in the wood—
>   Remember charity is God—

[50] 1 Cor. 14: 15.

    Which, scorning custom, her illib'ral crowds
    Brings virtue to the sun, while slips and crimes she clouds.

The history he offers is concerned less with recording the continuity of historical events than with the discovery, in history, of images which offer incentives to praise. Smart repeatedly conjures the worshipper to remember, but to remember an optimistic history, rather than an exact one. Similarly, the congregation he addresses is, I think, present rather to a liberal and poetic idea of the Church, than to the illiberal custom which crowds the idea from view: it is a congregation which the poetry of the *Hymns* exhorts into being.[51]

    The difficulty of the language of the *Hymns* reflects the ambivalent sense in which the congregation they speak for is both lost in a past accessible only to analogy and exhorted out of a prophetic future. The figurative language of David's seven pillars speaks, on the one hand, to an exclusive community like that of the ancient Hebrews, who shared an esoteric understanding of the divine language of nature, and, on the other, to the Christian common life which is the idea described by Law's arguments, and the prophetic vision of Fragment C of *Jubilate Agno*. With the *Hymns*, it conjures out of the future a Christian community united by their opposition to the acquisitiveness of commercial society, and their rejection of the divisions of self and society that commerce produces. The analogical language of the *Hymns* and *Song*, in its transcendence of historical continuity, affords both these possibilities of prophetic future and nostalgic past, as well as the hope of an intervention in the present which would similarly, and miraculously, remount the man and muse, the congregation and the hymn, above worldly views.

    Thus in the hymn on 'The Nativity of our Lord and Saviour', for example, the poet employs the images of a classical golden age of the past, and of a millennial age of the future, to describe the ideals made simultaneously possible by the miraculous birth of Christ:

        O the magnitude of meekness!
           Worth from worth immortal sprung;
        O the strength of infant weakness,
           If eternal is so young!
        If so young and thus eternal,
           Michael tune the sheperd's reed,
        Where the scenes are ever vernal,
           And the loves be love indeed!

[51] 'Hymn XVII. The King's Restoration', ll. 78, 72, 12, 115–20.

The incarnation of Christ is the conjunction of time and eternity, the miraculous event which makes possible the reconciliation of the shepherds of classical pastoral with the apocalyptic figure of Michael, the archangel warrior. The description of nature, transformed by the presence of Christ, is similarly atemporal, in its allusions both to the miracles that attended the birth of Christ—the silencing of the oracles—and to a prophetic present that evidences the intervention of divine grace in history:

> Nature's decorations glisten
> Far above their usual trim;
> Birds on box and laurels listen,
> As so near the cherubs hymn.
>
> Boreas now no longer winters
> On the desolated coast;
> Oaks no more are riv'n in splinters
> By the whirlwind and his host.
>
> Spinks and ouzles sing sublimely,
> 'We too have a Saviour born;'
> Whiter blossoms burst untimely
> On the blest Mosaic thorn.

The reference to the Glastonbury thorn, planted after the crucifixion, confirms that these events refer not to a specific historical event alone, but to a present which transcends the 'usual trim' of nature, the 'plainest course' of history. This miraculous present may be the achievement of the fully congregational performance of the hymn: were the ideal community of gratitude to rehearse these praises, the hymn implies, the miraculous redemption of nature which it describes would be effected.[52]

The poetry of Smart's *Hymns*, then, attempts to exhort into being the congregation capable of rehearsing its praises, and it is the task of criticism to understand the nature of that congregation despite its failure to appear in history. The exemplary didacticism of Smart's religious poetry reclaims for the poet the role of national psalmist and minister of praise described in the *Song to David*, but the national Church whose days he keeps seems to have shared, in the 1760s, the confidence Robert Lowth expresses in the progressive improvement of the future through the advance of commercial prosperity. For the

---

[52] 'Hymn XXXII', ll. 9–16, 21–32; for a contrasting reading of this hymn, see *Smart II*, pp. 424–7. 'Hymn IX. The Annunciation of the Blessed Virgin', l. 20.

Church, the role of the psalmist and hymn-writer, who provides a form of sound words which unite the congregation in a gratitude that made commercial acquisitiveness both redundant and corrupting, was marginal. In this context, the prophetic tradition of poetry, which described the analogical identity of a remote, pre-commercial, Hebrew community with the nation of Britain, might seem to the Anglican establishment to hold more of a threat than a promise.[53]

[53] See Robert Lowth, sermon II, in *Sermons, and Other Remains, of Robert Lowth, D.D. some time Lord Bishop of London; Now first collected and arranged, partly from Original manuscripts* (London, 1834).

Index